T0340356

# Feminist Political Ecology and the Economics of Care

This book envisages a different form of our economies where care work and care-full relationships are central to social and cultural life. It sets out a feminist vision of a caring economy and asks what needs to change economically and ecologically in our conceptual approaches and our daily lives as we learn to care for each other and non-human others.

Bringing together authors from 11 countries (also representing institutions from 8 countries), this edited collection sets out the challenges for gender aware economies based on an ethics of care for people and the environment in an original and engaging way. The book aims to break down the assumed inseparability of economic growth and social prosperity, and natural resource exploitation, while not romanticising social-material relations to nature. The authors explore diverse understandings of care through a range of analytical approaches, contexts and case studies and pays particular attention to the complicated nexus between re/productivity, nature, womanhood and care. It includes strong contributions on community economies, everyday practices of care, the politics of place and care of non-human others, as well as an engagement on concepts such as wealth, sustainability, food sovereignty, body politics, naturecultures and technoscience.

*Feminist Political Ecology and the Economics of Care* is aimed at all those interested in what feminist theory and practice brings to today's major political economic and environmental debates around sustainability, alternatives to economic development and gender power relations.

**Christine Bauhardt** is Professor at Humboldt-Universität zu Berlin, Germany, where she heads the division of Gender and Globalisation. The division focuses on the impacts of global political restructuring on economic and gender relations in different societies with respect to both urban and rural areas.

**Wendy Harcourt** is Professor of Gender, Diversity and Sustainable Development and Westerdijk Professor at the International Institute of Social Studies of Erasmus University Rotterdam, The Netherlands. She is also Coordinator of the EU H2020-MSCA-ITN-2017 Marie Sklodowska-Curie Innovative Training Networks (ITN) WEGO (Well-being, Ecology, Gender, and Community).

'This book aims to develop a feminist political ecology, which will enrich ecological economics and feminist economics, by integrating experience-based knowledge. With examples from struggles to cope with social and environmental degradation, it builds a bridge from human values, feminist values, care values, nature values, and solidarity values into economic thinking and policy, challenging the mainstream approach of expressing values in economic terms.'
  – *Iulie Aslaksen, ecological and feminist economist*

'This outstanding book traces the possibilities offered by linking feminist political ecology and feminist economics. It brings out an innovative analytical and normative framework, develops economic alternatives as transformative praxis and shows that care can contribute not only towards transforming economies but also society and politics to become intrinsically caring for humans and non-humans.'
  – *Daniela Gottschlich, Humboldt University Berlin, Germany*

# Routledge Studies in Ecological Economics

# Feminist Political Ecology and the Economics of Care

In Search of Economic Alternatives

**Edited by**
**Christine Bauhardt and**
**Wendy Harcourt**

Routledge
Taylor & Francis Group

LONDON AND NEW YORK

First published 2019
by Routledge
2 Park Square, Milton Park, Abingdon, Oxon OX14 4RN

and by Routledge
52 Vanderbilt Avenue, New York, NY 10017

First issued in paperback 2020

*Routledge is an imprint of the Taylor & Francis Group, an informa business*

*British Library Cataloguing-in-Publication Data*
A catalogue record for this book is available from the British Library

*Library of Congress Cataloging-in-Publication Data*
Names: Bauhardt, Christine, 1962- editor. | Harcourt, Wendy, 1959- editor.
Title: Feminist political ecology and the economics of care: in search of economic alternatives / edited by Christine Bauhardt and Wendy Harcourt.
Description: 1 Edition. | New York: Routledge, 2019. |
Series: Routledge studies in ecological economics | Includes bibliographical references and index.
Identifiers: LCCN 2018031925 (print) | LCCN 2018045224 (ebook) |
ISBN 9781315648743 (Ebook) | ISBN 9781138123663 (hardback: alk. paper) |
ISBN 9781315648743 (ebk)
Subjects: LCSH: Social service–Economic aspects. | Feminist theory. | Ecology.
Classification: LCC HV41 (ebook) | LCC HV41 .F455 2019 (print) |
DDC 331.4/81361–dc23
LC record available at https://lccn.loc.gov/2018031925

ISBN 13: 978-0-367-66389-6 (pbk)
ISBN 13: 978-1-138-12366-3 (hbk)

Typeset in Bembo
by Deanta Global Publishing Services, Chennai, India

# Contents

# Contributors

**Ana Agostino** is Defensoria de Vecinas y Vecinos Montevideo, Uruguay.

**Christine Bauhardt** is Professor at the Humboldt-Universitä t zu Berlin, Germany where she heads the division of Gender and Globalisation. The division focuses on the impacts of global political restructuring on economic and gender relations in different societies with respect to both urban and rural areas.

**Karijn van den Berg** is a PhD candidate, Aberystwyth University, United Kingdom.

**Meike Brückner** is a PhD candidate, Gender and Globalisation, Faculty of Life Sciences, Humboldt University, Germany.

**Kelly Dombroski** is a Senior lecturer, Department of Geography, University of Canterbury, New Zealand.

**Maria S. Floro** is Professor of Economics, College of Arts and Sciences, American University Washington, USA.

**Jacqueline Gaybor** is a PhD candidate, International Institute of Social Studies (ISS) of Erasmus University Rotterdam, The Netherlands.

**Azucena Gollaz Morán** is a PhD candidate, International Institute of Social Studies (ISS) of Erasmus University Rotterdam, The Netherlands.

**Wendy Harcourt** is Professor of Gender, Diversity and Sustainable Development and Westerdijk Professor at the International Institute of Social Studies of Erasmus University, The Netherlands. She is also Coordinator of the EU H2020-MSCA-ITN-2017 Marie Sklodowska-Curie Innovative Training Networks (ITN) WEGO (Well-being, Ecology, Gender, and Community).

**Stephen Healy** is a Senior research fellow, Institute of Cultural Studies University of Western Sydney, Australia.

**Katharine McKinnon** is a Senior lecturer, College of Arts, Social Sciences and Commerce Humanities and Social Sciences, La Trobe University, Australia.

**Mary Mellor** is Professor Emerita, Northumbria University, UK.

**Andrea J. Nightingale** is Chair of Rural Development in the Global South, Swedish University for Agricultural Sciences (SLU), Sweden, and Associate Professor, University of Oslo, Department of Geography.

**Georgia Poyatzis** is a PhD candidate, American University, College of Arts and Sciences, American University Washington, USA.

**Pamela Richardson-Ngwenya** is a Postdoctoral research fellow, German Institute for Tropical and Subtropical Agriculture (DITSL), Germany.

**Joyce-Ann Syhre** is a Graduate student, Gender and Globalisation, Faculty of Life Sciences, Humboldt University, Germany.

**Carla Wember** is a PhD candidate, Gender and Globalisation, Faculty of Life Sciences, Humboldt University, Germany.

**Christa Wichterich** is a Scholar activist, Germany.

# Acknowledgements

We would like to thank all the people who have been working and caring for us as we have been putting together the book, not only our colleagues, students, friends, as well as partners and families but also the often-invisible care workers that are so necessary for our modern lives to function. A special thank you to all the authors for their contributions and patience with the process. We would also like to thank the women who met with the editors and some of the authors for a 'slow workshop' funded by Erasmus University Rotterdam at the Convento, Punti Di Vista in Bolsena, Italy where the book was originally discussed: Sabrina Aguiari, Giovanna Di Chiro, Constance Dupuis, Loes Keysers, Simona Lanzoni, Barbara Muraca, Martina Padmanabhan, Angelica Pino and Giulia Simula. Thank you also to Carolyn Yu for all her careful work on completing the final manuscript.

Christine Bauhardt and Wendy Harcourt
18 June 2018

# 1 Introduction
## Conversations on care in Feminist Political Economy and Ecology

*Wendy Harcourt and Christine Bauhardt*

### Introduction: more questions than answers

The conversations leading to the making of the book have been held over the last five years as we walked the streets of Berlin and The Hague, visited each other's rural retreats and organised meetings that reached out to others engaged in feminist political economics and ecology, as well as our MA and PhD students. In this introduction, we look at the issues at the core of these conversations by reviewing some of the questions and concepts which form the genesis of the book in order to map out for readers what is to come in the following chapters.

This book emerges out of many layers of conversations since we first met in Berlin five years ago. Though coming from different intellectual backgrounds we found, as feminist theorists, that we shared common interests in queer ecology, ecofeminism and alternatives to mainstream economies such as degrowth and solidarity economies. We were both interested in the gender-economic-environmental nexus in addressing issues of deep social inequality. We were both wanting to explore further the important contributions of feminist analysis to critiques of capitalism and the debate about what constitutes a good life. In particular, we felt that the economic and social value of social reproductive work done by women, both in the paid care sector as well as in the private sphere of families and interpersonal relationships and what this meant in terms of the current crises, needed more attention beyond feminist circles. Moreover, we discovered that we had published on these topics almost simultaneously (Bauhardt 2014, Harcourt 2014).

Our conversations traversed discussions on the new green deal, solidarity economies, the degrowth movement, community economies, *buen vivir* (living well), queer ecologies and ecofeminism. As we discussed how to envisage a different kind of economy, one that questions the assumption that economic growth is the basis for individual and social well-being, we found ourselves asking more questions than finding answers. Questions like: What does such a project imply in feminist terms? If care work and care-full relationships are central aspects of the post-growth society, in the realms of paid as well as unpaid care work, how could we revalue traditionally female activities and jobs? How can we bring awareness about the gendered practices of healthcare and care for the elderly, as well as better education and childcare into ecological economics? How do we conceive an economy that exploits neither humans nor the environment? What could the feminist vision of a caring economy look like in practice when productivity is understood as inseparable from re/productivity in people's day-to-day activities? What possibilities do solidarity or community economies or post-capitalist politics offer in a feminist reassessment of the capitalist exploitation and hegemonic appropriation of the re/productivity of nature as well as of women and their work? What are viable solutions for the post-growth (post-capitalist) society, and how does the hierarchical gender order need to change in ways that respect both natural and social limits to growth? How do we understand care in economic and ecological terms with neither an assumed environmental resilience nor an assumed resilience of women's care work? How can we learn to care for each other and non-human others in increasingly unequal, politically toxic and deteriorating natural environments?

Wendy Harcourt has summarised such post-capitalist concerns in an earlier essay as,

> ways to live with and redefine capitalism aware of social and ecological limits and to see how to change our economic values to include care and respect for our families, communities, other knowledges and cultures. The concept of living economies proposes that we redesign our economies so that life is valued more than money and power resides in ordinary women and men who care for each other, their community and their natural environment. The challenge for the future is to build a broad platform for living economies or alternatives building up from community needs, which are inter-generational and gender aware, based on an ethics of care for the environment.
>
> (Harcourt 2014: 18–19)

Such questions have led us to look for alternative visions for different ways of organising the economy based on the values of ecological, gender and social justice. We looked for ideas on alternatives to mainstream economics built on the ethics of care, gender justice, the centrality of responsibility for oneself and for human and non-human others and community livelihoods. Our conversations also looked beyond Eurocentric understandings of care in the search for intercultural, pluriversal, political, ecological rethinking of the economy and ecology beyond capitalist principles.

Our political and scholarly discussions challenged how to break down the apparent inseparability of economic growth and social prosperity and the invisibility of natural resource exploitation, while not romanticising social-material relations to nature. Most of all, we wanted to deconstruct the age-old intertwining of nature and femininity discourses. This is a huge challenge given the centuries-old analogy between the life-creating potential of both nature and the female body.

These questions were informed by earlier feminist writings about the relationship between gender relations and social relations to nature (Merchant 1980, Plumwood 1993, Braidotti *et al.* 1994, Mellor 1997). We also discussed the critiques of feminist political economists, feminist political ecologists and environmental feminists who are resisting the trend of a feminisation of environmental responsibility (Bauhardt 2013).

What we understood was that at the hub of all of these discussions is our diverse understandings of care.

The book explores the various understandings of care through a range of analytical approaches, contexts and case studies. The chapters reflect the multilevel conversations among feminist ecologists and feminist economists. On the one hand, these conversations highlight the importance of caring for humans and the more-than-human world in ecological economics. On the other hand, they stress the necessity to think through the still awkward (even romantic and essentialising) connection between women and nature, a problematic that has been sidelined during the last two decades in feminist theory. We have welcomed how feminist environmentalism has again become a vivid field of research, inspired by New Materialism (Alaimo and Hekmann 2008, Coole and Frost 2010), the work of J.K. Gibson-Graham (1996, 2006) and the new Feminist Political Ecology (FPE) (Harcourt and Nelson 2015).

In the following we introduce the readers to the book's discussions in four sections. The first section discusses the diverse meanings of care in the feminist economic and feminist ecological political debates, paying particular attention to the complicated nexus between re/productivity, nature, womanhood and care. We then look in section two at the discussions that use care as a conceptual tool to imagine how to go beyond capitalism with a focus on the contributions of community economies, everyday practices of care, the politics of place and care of non-human others. In a third section we discuss three concepts that weave throughout the book – the concept of naturecultures, the debates around gender and sustainability, alternatives to development and body politics. The last section looks at the shared visions that underpin the book.

## Diverse meanings of care

The jumping off point for our discussion on care in the book is that care is about how communities organise their community and their livelihoods. Care is about looking after and providing for the needs of human and non-human others; it is about the provision of what is necessary for the health, welfare, maintenance and protection of humans and the more-than-human world (Tronto 1993). Care is also assumed to be linked to the sense of feeling affection or liking or love. In interpersonal relationships, care often means to give or provide for the well-being of those who cannot take care of themselves because of age or disability. This work is characterised by its time intensity, the continual requirements of the dependents and the inability of the carer to postpone the care needs. Care work can be performed as unpaid work in households and communities or as work for wages in childcare facilities, in hospitals or in nursing homes for the elderly. Empirically, and globally, this work is mostly done by women and it is socially considered to be 'women's work' (Budlender 2010). The symbolic gender order of masculinity and femininity naturalises this understanding of women's work in the care sector. It is hardly valued in capitalist and patriarchal societies which take care work for granted (Waring 1988, Benerìa 2003).

Related to understandings of care for feminist political economists is the concept of social reproduction which builds on the Marxist concept of individual and collective reproduction of the workforce. Whereas in the field of political economy the working subject is a person with a contract, income and social recognition, Feminist Political Economy emphasises the prerequisites for the wage relationship: The next generation of workers has to be born, brought up and educated, and this work is done by female members of the family and community. Family income is designed to enable the male worker to reproduce his workforce in the home. The heterosexual family structure ensures that women are available for this essential work which is performed outside the wage contract and delegated to the sexual contract (Pateman 1988). Despite its indispensability, this work is unpaid and receives little social recognition. Feminist Political Economy thus sees a parallel between the exploitation of industrial work in the capitalist production mode by capitalists and the exploitation of housework in the reproductive sphere by each 'head of household' and 'breadwinner.'

Silvia Federici adds to this classic picture that women need to disentangle their social reproduction from the world market and in solidarity amongst North and South. She advocates for a 'communalisation/collectivisation of housework,' reversing the capitalist privatisation of reproductive work. She argues that 'women must build the new commons, so that they do not remain transient spaces, temporary autonomous zones, but become the foundation of new forms of social reproduction' (Federici 2011). Christine Bauhardt in her chapter provides a more in-depth view to these debates among feminist political economists.

Another set of authors look at care in relation to what Tronto speaks about as repairing our world that 'includes our bodies, our selves, and our environment, all of which we seek to interweave in a complex, life-sustaining web' (Tronto 2017: 31). Harcourt looks at how care in terms of self, community and others is inspired by different feminist theorists, in particular Val Plumwood. Harcourt revisits history and interspecies care as she asks us to reimagine ourselves ecologically as we link environmentalism and social justice, understanding our connection with the world of animals, plants and minerals – what Plumwood poetically calls Earthothers (Plumwood 1993: 137). Harcourt looks at care as not only about acts of love and friendship but also about appropriate reciprocity among the human and non-human natural world through practices that respectfully acknowledge the agency of all beings in the world. Her message is that such acts of care require acts of imagination to reappropriate, reconstruct and reinvent our personal and political lifeworlds (Escobar and Harcourt 2005).

Jacqueline Gaybor takes up Tronto's understanding of care in her discussion of menstrual activism in Argentina to look at how care goes beyond 'the narrow confines of the private sphere' (Tronto 1993: 7). Gaybor argues that caring for the body by menstrual activists can be seen as part of a broader relationship of caring for the environment and caring for the community and future generations.

Tronto's idea of a life-sustaining web inspires Kelly Dombroski, Stephen Healy and Katharine McKinnon in their discussion of Care-full Community Economies highlighting the centrality of care work – women's care work in particular – in the intellectual and empirical heritage of Community Economies Collective (CEC). They follow the work of J.K. Gibson-Graham on how to transform our economies in order to allow human and more-than-human communities to 'survive well together' and place care for planetary companions at the heart of our endeavours (Gibson-Graham *et al.* 2013). Their chapter looks at the ethical negotiations around everyday care practices and care concerns that community economies of care emerge.

Pamela Richardson-Ngwenya and Andrea J. Nightingale also explore embodied, more-than-human relations and the need to see how ethics of diverse community economies emerge through a poststructuralist, feminist lens. Ana Agostino takes up the ethics of care in her discussion of care and human rights, arguing that just being human is about caring (for ourselves, for others, for nature). For her the practice of human rights is about the mutual responsibility towards one another and the general well-being. She argues that care is central to being human – refuting the stereotypical presentation of care as a female trait – calling for society to 'recognise for both sexes the central importance in adult life of the connection between self and other, the universality of the need for compassion and care' (Gilligan 1985: 28).

### Re/productivity, nature, motherhood and care

Several of the chapters tackle the tension and unease around the identification of women as 'closer to nature'. This equation has its historical roots in the European Enlightenment and has been used to justify the exclusion of women from politics and economics. Because of their potential ability to give birth, women are assumed to be closer to nature and vital processes. This results in several dilemmas from a feminist environmental perspective. One of the central questions is how the material re/productivity of the female body and potential motherhood can be recognised without repeatedly assuming women's proximity to nature. The hierarchisation of culture and nature, mind and body, masculinity and femininity points to another dilemma. Can a positive relationship to nature be conceived without romanticising and recourse to regressive notions of femininity and maternity? These questions have important implications in relation to the organisation of the economy and to assumptions about women's normative responsibility for care due to the re/productivity of the female body. Bauhardt looks at how to resolve these dilemmas in her contribution with recourse to queer ecologies.

Karijn van den Berg in her contribution also investigates the woman–nature nexus in relationship to subjectivity and intersectionality. She turns to feminist new materialism and posthumanism which help to blur the boundaries between human and more-than-human worlds. By combining these approaches, FPE has the potential to overcome the anthropocentrism in environmentalist research and politics.

## Going beyond capitalism

### A search for alternatives

The book as a whole is responding to economic and environmental challenges in a search for alternative ways of conceptualising and organising economic activities in order to transcend/transform the global capitalist economic systems. As Bauhardt has earlier explained:

> individual and social well-being depends heavily on care work [...] the crisis of capitalism should be analysed as the finiteness of natural resources, as well as the finiteness of women's caring labor. [...] Economic change needs to respect both natural and social limits to growth. [...] Sustainable economic change would then imply a fundamental transformation of male-biased economic concepts, of gendered modes of knowledge production, and thus of gendered power relations.
>
> (2014: 66)

The book takes up the search for economic alternatives via several entry points analytically arguing why it is important to go beyond capitalism as the all-encompassing economic imaginary and system to looking at actual alternatives to capitalist practices in community economies.

Mary Mellor in her chapter looks at care as wellth, arguing for a rethinking of the money system in order to recognise unpaid care activities and uncosted environmental damage and misuse. She suggests that reorientating the money system would mean that care and other externalised 'women's work' would then become the major focus of wealth/well-being. Scarcity/austerity economics would be replaced by sufficiency provisioning on the bases of social justice and ecological sustainability. Such an approach to care practices is echoed in Azucena Gollaz Morán's analysis of the politics of care in relation to economically marginalised Mexican women brickmakers' care for their community, and their place.

The work of J.K. Gibson-Graham which informs several of the chapters in the book, offers a sense of possibility and hope about economic and ecological values in ways that decentre capitalism as the only economic framework. Gibson-Graham argue that there are other forms of economies that exist alongside capitalism which offer alternatives to capitalism and open up possibilities for alternatives. Their framing of the economy allows us to study non-capitalist practices from a gendered cultural and ecological perspective (Gibson-Graham *et al.* 2013). Gibson-Graham's feminist critique of political economy (1996, 2006) does not aim to count in what had been invisible care work into traditional economic models, but redefines the economy itself to include a diversity of care labour, care transactions and care enterprises. As Dombroski, Healy and McKinnon explain in their chapter, scholarship on community economies, care and gender has focused on care for the more-than-human and the environment, caregiving and ethical negotiations, care for households and social reproduction, care for distant others, care for infants and children, and care for maternal and birthing bodies.

Richardson-Ngwenya and Nightingale also look at community economies and at how people's sense of self and community are relationally produced in everyday, affective socio-natural practices. They argue for the need to take account of not only alternative understandings of economy, but for a more profound rethinking of how everyday practices produce political economies. They ask readers to take seriously multiple ways of imagining society-environment boundaries and the economic consequences of such boundary making and un-making.

## Everyday practices of care

Meike Brückner and Joyce-Ann Syhre also examine everyday practices in their discussion of urban agriculture in Nairobi. They show how women use urban land for the cultivation of indigenous vegetables to improve the diet of families and communities as well as the urban environment. Urban farmers contribute to food sovereignty in Kenya with their day-to-day activities of caring for fresh and healthy produce and of caring for tasty meals. Yet, the women farmers care much less about money; contrary to prevalent assumptions in agricultural economics, they are not concerned about income generation. They are more interested in improving their lives and those of their children – and they enjoy the economic independence and the personal freedom that urban farming allows them. Brückner and Syhre suggest that urban farming in Nairobi allows the women farmers to actively engage in food provisioning, collective organisation and developing knowledge about biodiversity. Women's agency here starts from day-to-day activities and expands to active citizenship. These activities are about being attentive to embodied interactions and labours as well as emotional and affective relations with our environments and natures where we live (Harcourt and Nelson 2015: 13). They argue for an understanding of farming in the city that shifts from a strategy of survival towards economic and political practices that allow developing a good life, personal and communal well-being and ecological commitment.

Wember in her chapter turns to the everyday practices of care in the Global North when she scrutinises the embodiment and embeddedness of gender and economic practices through the field of food. Her field research in Toronto, Canada shows how economic actors are not only producers or consumers but instead practitioners of citizenship through their contributions to socio-technical projects such as food networks. She asks for change in food politics that go beyond the 'eat for change' mantra which she critically examines as part of the feminisation of environmental responsibility. In her critique of the social construction of motherhood as 'naturally' providing care in relation to food she analyses the embedded, lived and shared experiences of food practices using the insights of FPE on citizenship as an expression of ecological social justice.

Gollaz illustrates in her case study of everyday livelihood practices among a community of brickmakers how care for people, land and home is essential for survival, for connections and relations among humans and the environment. She demonstrates how women play a major role in the reconstruction process of a community that was once an abandoned land, to a place that could offer them the possibility to realise their aspirations.

## Politics of place

The concept of the politics of place takes this analysis of everyday practices of care further. Gollaz uses a politics of place perspective inspired by the work of Doreen Massey (2002, 2005) and Arturo Escobar (2008) and in the edited collection on women and the politics of place by Harcourt and Escobar (2005). Hers and other chapters reflect on the politics of place as an answer to capitalocentrism, looking at places as sites of negotiation and continuous transformation, arguing that alternatives to capitalism must take into account place-based models of nature, culture and politics.

Key to these proposals is a transformative politics of place. Such place-based politics can be about resistance but it is also about reappropriation, reconstruction, reinvention of places and place-based practices, and the creation of new possibilities of being-in-place and being-in-networks with other human and non-human living beings (Harcourt 2016). In this understanding, places become the locus of possibility, the material manifestations of worldviews, knowledges, virtual and physical transactions, and the relational performance of subjectivities. For example, *Buen Vivir*, a concept that has now travelled widely around the world as an alternative 'horizon' to capitalism, comes from the Andean peoples' engagement with their history and culture in place which is inspiring new forms of economies in communities around the world.

Conceptualising place in this manner opens up the possibilities for a trans-formative politics of place. As Harcourt (2014) has highlighted, place-based politics may be about resistance but they are also about the reinvention of practices and possibilities: 'even in a globalised world, place is still the way people know and experience life' (Harcourt and Escobar 2002: 8). It is where resistances and realities unfold, where events take place, where we are able to see (and to not see), understand and propose ways for transformation. As several chapters mentioned, in Harcourt and Escobar's analysis of the politics of place they talk of a global sense of place that includes the body, the home, the environment and the social public space.

Politics based around these four areas question the presumption that knowledge is only 'important' if it is detached, objective and rational, and instead points to the importance of material, subjective and personal vantage points. Women's place-based politics is embedded in, rather than removed from, the material lives they are trying to change.

(Harcourt and Escobar 2002: 11)

### Care for the more-than-human

The search for alternative economies is deeply intertwined with different strands in FPE which has its roots in ecofeminism and in political ecology as well as in feminist movements for environmental, economic and social justice. The chapters push this debate forward in a number of ways.

Adding to the debate begun in Bauhardt's discussion of Feminist Political Economy, ecofeminism and queer ecologies, Karijn van den Berg reviews ecofeminism, new materialism and posthumanism in relation to FPE. She looks at key writers in the field suggesting how these different strands of feminist thought are building new approaches for thinking about the relationship among human and more-than-human, environmentalism and feminism. Van den Berg argues that FPE works from an intersectional approach that avoids essentialism, challenges power relations, and explores agency among different actors, taking into account differences of gender, race, class, sexuality, age and ability. FPE goes beyond dualisms in order to challenge and disrupt dominant hierarchies between humans/nature, men/women, North/South and focus on the relation between the exploitation of both nature and women through critiques of (patriarchal) capitalism (albeit in different ways) as well as heteronormativity.

Van den Berg adds to the debate the contribution of feminist new materialism and posthumanism which displaces humanity from its pedestal and corrects that idea that the environment and other species are mere resources, restraints or context to humanity. Such approaches need to be scrutinised 'at a time when the interactions between human, viral, animal and technological bodies are becoming more and more intense' (Bennett 2009: 108).

These writers invite us 'to understand the materialising effects of particular ways of drawing boundaries between 'humans' and 'non-humans' (Barad 2012: 31), by looking at how 'human life is embedded in material and discursive processes – without putting the potential (re)productivity of the female body on the ideological pedestal of heterosexual maternity' (Bauhardt 2013: 371).

## Gender, sustainability and post-development

### Naturecultures

One of the key concepts that helps to break down anthropocentrism for several authors in the book is naturecultures. As Donna Haraway proposes in her book *When Species Meet* (2008) nature and culture are intertwined and intra-actively co-producing each other. Haraway's concept of naturecultures helps us to transgress the idea of a binary opposition and hierarchy of nature and culture. It allows us to understand how humanity is part of nature, and therefore if we exploit nature we are directly exploiting ourselves, our health, our well-being and our future.

A major set of concerns for FPE is how to bring together the human and non-human, the biological with the technological and the material with the virtual. In seeking to think how to go beyond such dualisms, it is crucial to open up questions around the scientific truth of nature, knowing that 'nature and culture are tightly knotted in bodies, ecologies, technologies and times' (Haraway 2016: 107). In asking what sort of connections we can form with Earthothers we are able to decentre not only economics but also humanity.

Given the current crises, the concern to understand naturecultures carries with it a sense of urgency. As Haraway states, we need to 'attune rapidly evolving ecological naturalcultural communities, including people, through the dangerous centuries of irreversible climate change and continuing high rates of extinction and other troubles' (2016: 11).

The current multiple crises are entangled in a mutual reinforcement of the ecological and the care crisis. Climate change in peripheral regions for example aggravates the scarcity of vital resources such as land and water leading to food insecurity and overburdening of women's care work for human and non-human others. Accordingly, the objective of an economic transformation would be to secure the availability of natural resources as well as to recognise and support women's care work that are essential for survival, allowing them greater use over their time.

Maria S. Floro and Georgia Poyatzi in their chapter look at environmental degradation, emphasising its impact on the care economy. They look at who benefits and who shoulders the costs; and who has the means to mitigate and manage risks. They are concerned about the rising conflicts among communities, ethnic groups, regions and countries over water and the growing scarcity of this precious natural resource and the increased time in unpaid work to collect water as well as adverse impact of water scarcity on the livelihoods of the poor, for example, fishing and subsistence production, as well as overall market production. The chapter points to the tensions between conventional economic growth that relies upon market expansion by demonstrating how natural resource management based on (monetary) economic cost-benefit analysis can give priority to the use of scarce natural resources e.g. water and arable land, towards production for the market rather than their use for household production maintenance.

### Gender and sustainability in alternatives to development

One of the backdrops to the book is the response of feminists to mainstream development thinking about environment and sustainability. Agostino from a post-development and gender perspective, argues that women's views on sustainable livelihoods need to be taken into account in the UN and governmental calls for resilient, environmentally friendly, inclusive and sustainable growth. Her chapter looking for a new urban agenda based on her engagement at UN, women's movements and recently local government in the *Defensoria in Montevideo*, deconstructs the concept of development as a sphere of intervention of power and forms of subjectivity which moulds individuals and societies (Escobar 1987: 13–14) in an effort to Westernise the world. She posits that FPE needs to unpack how such cultural and economic power relations impact on the use, access and control of nature. She argues for a new agenda that is based on human rights and a gender perspective which challenges the continuity of the dominant views, associated with production and growth. As argued by Christa Wichterich:

> Ecology and sustainability are not gender neutral; the analysis of gender relations is vital for understanding the relationships between nature and society and for overcoming the environmental crisis; without gender justice there will be no environmental justice, no sustainability nor a good life for all.
>
> (Wichterich 2015: 94)

Agostino argues that FPE places gender 'as a crucial variable – in relation to class, race and other relevant dimensions of political life – in shaping environmental relations' (Harcourt and Nelson 2015, Sundberg 2015). She focusses on the importance of bringing a gender analysis into the relationship, management and use of nature and to the decision-making processes and socio-political forces that influence development and environmental policies.

While Agostino and other authors in the book emphasise gender in relation to the sustainability debate, other authors argue that FPE does not necessarily have 'a fixed approach to a single focus on women and gender' (Rocheleau 2015: 57). Feminism in this strand of thinking in the book is not just about women but about all kinds of 'Others' – sexual, cultural, class, ethnic, indigenous – whose perspectives are essential to a process of engaging with diverse ontologies and decolonising knowledge. In this sense going beyond gender requires a recognition of diversity as a starting point for a hopeful politics of transformation, something which Harcourt explores in her discussion of 'differential belonging.'

### Body politics

The concept of body politics informs the book in diverse ways. Body politics from a feminist ecological perspective is an essential part of environmental concerns as the body is our first environment (Harcourt 2009). Bodies are considered 'nature' in the body-mind split; bodies are indicators for environmental degradation as well as vital assemblages of diverse matters; therefore, we consider bodies are naturecultures *per se*.

Mellor argues that thinking about an ecologically sustainable economy starts from 'the embodiment and embeddedness of human lives, from the life of the body and the ecosystem' (Mellor 2005: 145). Mellor in her chapter and the studies by Carla Wember and Joyce-Ann Syhre and Meike Brückner on urban agriculture and food politics explore the connections between gendered agency and the economy, the ways of rethinking and re-doing economic and ecological practices based on embodied acts of care.

Others look at the body as a material site of knowing one of Jacqueline Gaybor's interviewees states:

> The body is a territory of a great memory – memory of the places where I have been, of my relations with others and of my entire lineage. In my body is the violence and love that I have felt. Everything is there, I see it without denial, receive it; but I also have the ability to transform it. We all do.
>
> (Verona 2016 cited in Gaybor)

Gollaz looks at the visible marks of the injuries and scars of women bricklayers arguing that these bodies contain painful and happy memories of situations and people they have encountered. Christa Wichterich focusses on body politics through the changing practices of biological reproduction as a socially, politically and economically constructed form of societal nature relations and of embodied naturecultures and technoscience, looking at the fragmentation and extraction of body parts and biological material through a Taylorised division of labour involved in reproduction. In these explorations bodies are not just inert and passive matter onto which biological and social categories are inscribed. Rather, the body and the processes around it are sites of knowledge, resistance and empowerment, where traditional or modern practices and narratives can be challenged.

Gaybor's discussion of menstrual activism and Wichterich's analysis of the ongoing transformation of bodily naturecultures examine the reconfiguration of reproduction and the complex interweaving of body politics at an individual and social level as patriarchal, class, racial and imperial/colonial power relations co-construct the new forms of (re-)production and of control over women's bodies.

These chapters focus in on women's practices of difference, bodies and places, in transformation processes where the practices of care are integral to their gendered social and cultural being. They question patriarchal and economic development regime over women's bodies looking at how body politics can be seen as 'contests over meaning: the interplay between culture and power' in ways that can 'open spaces for the creation of different and "potentially transformative solutions"' (Harcourt and Escobar 2002: 11–12).

## A shared vision?

As stated at the beginning the book comes from diverse conversations that are based on imagining possibilities of economic and ecologically just futures, informed from our own individual privilege as those being able to take time to think and reflect and share together. The book is informed actively by the differences amongst us, our partiality, contradictoriness and becoming-ness of the research process that does not progress towards an ultimate goal but 'stays with the trouble'. This, as Haraway points out, helps us to 'generate richer, more complex theories and understandings beyond a simplistic and hierarchical God's-eye view and "ground-up" view. The question of disclosing/sharing/representing what is "known" is complex' (Haraway 2016: 15).

Undoubtedly we are all searching for an imaginary of the economy and environment where everyone can engage in its making. To create such a global imaginary, local and place-based initiatives are needed to get people involved in their everyday life, their situated knowledge as well as their situated experience. Thinking together about care has been part of this process.

In response to Haraway, yes, these conversations are undoubtedly complex. The chapters link economics with ecological, social and political spheres, connected through not only in academic writings but also learning from social movements, virtual debates and kitchen table conversations. These feminist visions of how to transform capitalism, how to think and be ecologically, demand an analytical and political project that connects particular sites of practice and resistance that acknowledges care work, community livelihoods, body politics and engagement in alternatives to hegemonic development processes.

The book argues in its partiality for attention to care, community and personal and interspecies relations in economic and ecological analysis in ways that link ethics, nature and culture. Whether the language used is about climate crisis, solidarity economies, care economy, social reproduction, place-based feminist alternatives, the chapters build on the search for a new ethics and for the need to change current ways of living by adopting lifestyles that respect ecological limits.

The line-up of the book is as follows. The chapters by Bauhardt, Harcourt and van den Berg introduce readers to the debates around ecofeminism and care from the different approaches to care in feminist ecological and economic writings. These three chapters are followed by explorations of community economies and debates about care in economic writing on climate, social reproductive work and money with contributions by Floro and Poyatzis, the Community Economies Collective and Mellor. The three case studies which follow – from Zimbabwe by Richardson-Ngwenya and Nightingale, Toronto food networks by Wember and urban gardens in Nairobi by Syhre and Brückner – look at the everyday practices of women in the specific contexts and politics of place. These chapters are followed by three further case studies which offer close examinations of the body as a site of political contestations. Wichterich looks at bioeconomics and surrogacy in India, Gaybor presents menstrual activism in Argentina and Gollaz analyses the care work of brickmakers in Mexico. The final chapter on Agostino's work in Uruguay explores the possibilities for a new urban agenda taking forward the ideas and visions underlying her engagement in FPE research on care.

With such a rich and diverse collection of analysis and experience around care, we hope the book will contribute to new understandings of economy, gender relations and ecology for alternatives to capitalism, building up from community needs, in ways that are inter-generational, interspecies and intersectional, based on an ethics of care for human and non-human others.

## References

Alaimo, S. and S. Hekman, eds., 2008. *Material Feminisms*. Bloomington: Indiana University Press.

Bauhardt, C., 2013. Rethinking gender and nature from a material(ist) perspective: Feminist economics, queer ecologies and resource politics. *European Journal of Women's Studies*, 20 (4), 361–75.

Bauhardt, C., 2014. Solutions to the crisis? The Green New Deal, degrowth, and the solidarity economy: Alternatives to the capitalist growth economy from an ecofeminist economics perspective. *Ecological Economics*, 102, 60–8.

Benería, L., 2003. *Gender, Development, and Globalisation: Economics as if All People Mattered*. London: Routledge.

Bennett, J., 2009. *Vibrant Matter: A Political Ecology of Things*. Durham, NC: Duke University Press.

Braidotti, R., Charkiewicz, E., Häusler, S. and Wieringa, S., 1994. *Women, the Environment and Sustainable Development. Towards a Theoretical Synthesis*. London: Zed Books

Budlender, D., ed., 2010. *Time Use Studies and Unpaid Care Work*. London: Routledge.

Coole, D. and Frost, S., eds., 2010. *New Materialisms: Ontology, Agency, and Politics*. Durham, NC: Duke University Press.

Escobar, A., 1987. *Power and Visibility: The Invention and Management of Development in the Third World*. Berkeley: University of California.

Escobar, A., 2008. *Territories of Difference. Place, Movements, Life, Redes*. Durham, NC: Duke University Press.

Escobar, A. and Harcourt, W., 2005. Practices of difference: introducing 'women and the politics of place'. *In*: W. Harcourt and A. Escobar, eds, *Women and the Politics of Place*. Bloomfield, CT: Kumarian Press, 1–19.

Federici, S., 2011. Feminism and the politics of the common in an era of primitive accumulation. *Commoner* [online]. Available from: http://www.commoner.org.uk [Accessed 14 June 2018].

Gibson-Graham, J.K., 1996. *The End of Capitalism (As We Know It): A Feminist Critique of Political Economy*. Oxford: Blackwell.

Gibson-Graham, J.K., 2006. *A Postcapitalist Politics*. Minneapolis: University of Minnesota Press.

Gibson-Graham, J.K., Cameron, J. and Healy, S., 2013. *Take Back the Economy: An Ethical Guide for Transforming Our Communities*. Minneapolis: University of Minnesota Press.

Gilligan, C., 1985. In a different voice: women's conceptions of self and of morality. *In*: H. Eisenstein and A. Jardine, eds, *The Future of Difference* [online]. New Brunswick, NJ: Rutgers University Press. Available from: http://sfonline.barnard.edu/sfxxx/documents/gilligan.pdf [Accessed 5 February 2013).

Haraway, D.J., 2008. *When Species Meet*. Minneapolis: University of Minnesota Press.

Haraway, D.J., 2016. *Staying with the Trouble: Making Kin in the Chthulucene*. Durham, NC: Duke University Press.

Harcourt, W., 2009. *Body Politics in Development: Critical Debates on Gender and Development.* London: Zed Books.

Harcourt, W., 2014. The future of capitalism: a consideration of alternatives. *Cambridge Journal of Economics*, 38 (6), 1307–28.

Harcourt, W., 2016. Gender and sustainable livelihoods: linking gendered experiences of environment, community and self. *Agricultural Journal of Human Values*, 33 (4), 1007–19.

Harcourt, W. and Escobar, A., 2002. Women and the politics of place. *Development*, 45 (1), 7–14.

Harcourt, W. and Nelson, I.L., eds, 2015. *Practising Feminist Political Ecologies: Moving Beyond the 'Green Economy'*. London: Zed Books.

Massey, D., 2002. Globalisation: What does it mean for geography? *Geography*, 87 (4), 293–6.

Massey, D., 2005. *For Space*. London: Sage.

Mellor, M., 1997. *Feminism & Ecology*. Oxford: Blackwell.

Mellor, M., 2005. Ecofeminist political economy: integrating feminist economics and ecological economics. *Feminist Economics*, 11 (3), 120–6.

Merchant, C., 1980. *The Death of Nature: Women, Ecology and the Scientific Revolution*. San Francisco: Harper and Row.

Pateman, C., 1988. *The Sexual Contract*. Stanford: Stanford University Press.

Plumwood, V., 1993. *Feminism and the Mastery of Nature*. London: Routledge.

Rocheleau, D., 2015. A situated view of feminist political ecology from my networks, roots and territories. *In*: W. Harcourt and I.L. Nelson, eds, *Practicing Feminist Political Ecology: Moving Beyond the 'Green Economy'*. London: Zed Books.

Sundberg, J., 2015. *Feminist Political Ecology* [online]. Available from: http://www.acad emia.edu/14495915/Feminist_Political_Ecology [Accessed 19 June 2017].

Tronto, J.C., 1993. *Moral Boundaries: A Political Argument for an Ethic of Care*. London: Psychology Press.

Tronto, J.C., 2017. There is an alternative: homines curans and the limits of neoliberalism. *International Journal of Care and Caring*, 1, 27–43.

Waring, M., 1988. *If Women Counted: A New Feminist Economics*. London: Macmillan.

Wichterich, C., 2015. Contesting green growth, connecting care, commons and enough. *In*: W. Harcourt and I.L. Nelson, eds, *Practising Feminist Political Ecologies: Moving Beyond the 'Green Economy'*. London: Zed Books, 67–100.

# 2 Nature, care and gender

## Feminist dilemmas

*Christine Bauhardt*

Like many other feminists, ecofeminism was like a red rag to me for a long time. It seemed old-fashioned and retrograde, celebrating women's otherness to rationality and intellectuality, a weird mixture of naive adoration of nature and veneration of regressive womanhood. It took me some time and effort to approach what this strand of feminist thinking was saying with less animosity. In contrast, I was always inspired by Feminist Political Economy and its radical critique of capitalism in the search for alternatives to the capitalist economy. At the outbreak of the latest economic crisis in 2008, I was curious to know how alternative thinking about the economy understood the organisation of the economy and of society as a whole beyond the capitalist principles of competition, exploitation and greed (Folbre 2009, Wright 2010). I was surprised to find out that the core concept of Feminist Political Economy, the care for and about the well-being of others and of oneself, did not appear in most of the alternative economic conceptions by critical male thinkers (Speth 2008, Jackson 2009). This finding triggered my curiosity to find out more about feminist utopias and how to imagine the economy beyond capitalism (Bauhardt 2014). It was in this search that I came across Feminist Political Ecology (FPE), which helped me to reconcile some of my earlier concerns about ecofeminism. I found in FPE a useful way to engage in radical thinking about the economic and the societal organisation of the relationship between humans and nature. Gender relations are focal because of the potential of the female body to procreate but there is no plain congruence – nature, bodies, gender, the reproduction of economy and society are tied together in a complex structural and cultural entanglement. In particular, ecological issues, the ways the environment is used and misused for economic objectives, are central for feminist ecological enquiry (Harcourt 1994, Rocheleau *et al.* 1996, Harcourt 2014, Harcourt and Nelson 2015, Alaimo 2016, MacGregor 2017).

These concerns tap into the huge debate around the uncomfortable nexus between nature, care for others and about the environment, and the sex/gender relation. Poststructural analysis produced unease in feminist debates around questions of nature, the nature of sex and any analogy between the re/productivity of nature and the re/productivity of the female body (Soper 1995, Ferguson 2005, Chambers 2007). The theoretical stance of Queer Ecologies has allowed for a new appraisal of nature, social reproduction and care. I am particularly interested in how the radical critique of capitalism in ecofeminism and the deconstruction of heterosexuality and social reproduction within queer ecologies can be successfully combined in FPE. The aim of my chapter is to develop this line of thought more fully.

First, I retrace the arguments of Feminist Political Economy. I look at the central categories of a feminist analysis of capitalism: work, social reproduction and care. Feminist economists criticise an understanding of economics that focuses one-sidedly on market processes, the monetised economy and profit maximisation. The key criticism here is the concept of work. From a feminist economics perspective, only a comprehensive view of work that includes both paid work for wages and unpaid work in private households can capture the entire volume of work performed in society. The time spent on paid work and unpaid work in households and communities is deemed the instrument to measure this volume. This also leads to an expanded understanding of individual and social prosperity: not only the availability of money but also the availability of time count as indicators for the distribution of resources and power in a society. The focus of feminist economic analysis is the social reproduction of the society. This does not mean, as in classical economic theory, only individual reproduction of labour power, namely the maintenance and regeneration of the capacity to work, but also generative reproduction, safeguarding the next generations.

In the second part of this chapter, I will discuss ecofeminism and queer ecologies in relation to FPE, looking at the analytical debates around capitalism and re/productivity. At the heart of ecofeminist analysis is the idea that in capitalism, the re/productivity of the female body and the labour of women in social reproduction is exploited and appropriated by society as though they were themselves natural resources (Floro 2012, Rai *et al.* 2013). The exploitation of nature and of the labour of people is foundational to capitalism. The analogy between women's work and nature in ecofeminist analysis serves to emphasise the material prerequisites for capitalist production. As is the case with natural resources such as mineral resources, water, soil and air, capitalism deals with the work of women in social reproduction. Capitalism assumes that these resources are infinite and are available to capitalist exploitation virtually for nothing. In ecofeminist analysis, both nature and women's work count as material prerequisites for the capitalist process of exploitation and appropriation. This is what the term re/productivity means: nature is productive, not the capitalist production process, which is essentially analysed as destructive for the environment and the relationships between humans.

Queer Ecologies unravel the knot of desire, heterosexual reproduction and the symbolic order of the gender binary. The re/productivity of women's bodies and the social and cultural construction of gender allot responsibility for care work to women. Due to potential motherhood, symbolic maternity is socially addressed as a normative expectation to all women. Queer Ecologies deconstruct this connection of symbolic order, material and cultural aspects of sexuality and desire as well as social reproduction.

In the concluding section of this chapter, I will sketch my thoughts on how to bring together the insights of these lines of thought as a way forward for FPE when thinking about care.

## Central concepts of Feminist Political Economy: Social reproduction and the care economy

Different concepts are used in Feminist Political Economy depending on the theoretical reference and focus of the analysis. The concept of 'social reproduction' follows from the Marxist discussion about the value of labour and the structural organisation of society through work. With the concept of the 'care economy,' subjective needs, motivations and the creation of meaning shift to the centre of the analysis, which express people's emotional and psychosocial needs in care relationships.

### Social reproduction: Work and its value

The core of the feminist debate about the concept of work is the question of what value work creates. The Marxist concept of work considers work as manufacturing wage labour that produces goods to be exchanged for money.

The exploitation of labour power by capital is the fact that the wage being paid is systematically lower than the value of the commodity produced: the value of the labour power is determined by the hours of work that are necessary for the production of the corresponding commodity. This value is determined not only by the time spent by the labourer for the production of commodities in the work process and for the reproduction of his own labour power, but in addition by the time that is necessary to prepare the next generation of labourers for the capitalist production process. The family wage is thus designed so that generative reproduction is ensured in the family (and thus by women).

In feminist understanding, labour is not restricted to commodity production that is geared towards *exchange value*, nor is labour reproduced solely by wages. Feminist analysis considers labour as creating *material and immaterial use values* and thus creating 'value.' From this perspective, women's unpaid work is the basis for capitalist reproduction by continuously renewing the commodity of labour power, both in individual reproduction in everyday life and through generative reproduction. At both levels, the vital work performed by women renews and maintains the life of people (Hennessy and Ingraham 1997, Folbre 2001, 2010). The individual capacity to work is reproduced by eating, sleeping and training; the reproduction of the society comprises bearing and bringing up children, and socialising and educating them, which ensures the continuity of the economic system.

In contrast to and complementing Marxist analysis, in feminist understanding the exploitation of labour does not take place solely in paid employment, namely on the labour market. In addition, the exploitation and appropriation of the work of others take place in the household and the family. The sexual contract of heterosexual marriage and family structures ensures the patriarchal gender order of social reproduction (Pateman 1988). While the wage relationship is characterised by the hierarchy between capital and labour, the power imbalance between men and women becomes manifest in gender relations. Both attempts to define relationships – wage relationships and gender relations – are expressions of domination: while the structural dominance of the capital side is continuously renewing itself by appropriating surplus value, the structural dominance of men over women renews itself through the unpaid appropriation of female work in the household. Both power relationships are secured by the symbolic order of the binary gender system and through material power asymmetries (ownership, heritage, income); they reproduce a social order structured along the categories of class and gender. A third key category of inequality in feminist theory – 'race' – is particularly significant in the feminist economic analysis of global care chains (Parrenas 2001, Ehrenreich and Hochschild 2004), in which the work of social reproduction is delegated to women who are in socially and ethnically subordinate positions.

### Care economy: Work and needs

From a feminist perspective, this structural analysis of the macro-organisation of economy and society is complemented by a subjective view of the needs that are satisfied in care work. Particular attention is paid to endowing this work aimed at interpersonal relations and communication with meaning both for those giving and for those receiving care. In this perspective, one speaks more of care work or the care economy to specify the core of what this work is about, namely caring for and caring about lives (Tronto 1993, 2013). The concept of the care economy comprises the work that is necessary to take care of people who are not yet or no longer able to look after themselves. This work can take place on an unpaid or a paid basis in private households or in public institutions of education, training, healthcare or in care for the elderly. In contrast to the analytical concept of social reproduction, which is primarily focused on the commodity of labour power, its provision and maintenance, the concept of the care economy describes the forms, contents and objectives of work in care. To understand why these activities are feminised, recourse to the naturalisation of female work and the associated symbolic gender order is helpful (see middle section of this chapter).

What the two approaches referred to have in common is that they assume the work defined as female is indispensable for the economy. Both stress its relevance for understanding capitalist societies. The feminist Marxist perspective on social reproduction tends to advocate for a rationalisation of housework and the socialisation of care work, while the care approach tends to refer to the limits of rationalisation for care work oriented towards human needs and instead argues for better working conditions and greater time sovereignty in this spectrum of activities and professions.

## The economic value of unpaid work: Time as an indicator

Women's work in care work is looked on as work that is taken for granted, carried out in the privacy of one's own four walls and thus not seen as economically relevant – it is considered 'work for love' (Folbre and Nelson 2000). Time-use surveys, which exist for the OECD countries as well as for countries of the Global South, indicate the time scope of paid and unpaid work that is necessary for society (Budlender 2010). For Germany, the current time-use survey has been demonstrating again that women and men work approximately the same amount of time, but that considerably less of the work carried out by women is compensated monetarily (Statistisches Bundesamt 2017).

From an economic perspective, monetisation can show the value of housework by internalising the costs. Thereby, a quantifiable value expresses the scope and significance of unpaid work. If the time spent on housework and care work is calculated in monetary values based on the so-called third-party criterion, this then yields the economic significance of household production for the economy. In Germany, even with a rather cautious monetisation of unpaid work, the gross value added of household production in 2013 – 987 billion Euros – was significantly above the gross value added in the manufacturing industry (769 billion Euros) (Schwarz and Schwahn 2016).

In the feminist debate about wages for housework (Dalla Costa and James 1975), a possibility was seen by paying housework to release wives from their dependency on family income and thus on the male breadwinner, enabling women an independent financial livelihood. The counterargument maintains that housework and care work are a qualitatively different form of work, based not on alienation as in the capitalist production mode but on interpersonal attention, the quality of which would be jeopardised through economisation and monetisation. In order to challenge the idea that care work is 'only' reproductive whereas capitalist production is considered productive, Ann Ferguson and Nancy Folbre (1981) thus speak of 'sex-affective production' to highlight the productivity of female work and in particular the aspect of emotional care, in this way also differentiating conceptually from the Marxist reproduction concept.

In order to overcome the conceptual distinction between the so-called productive sphere (the market economy) and the so-called reproductive sphere (private households) the term re/productivity has been coined (Biesecker and Hofmeister 2010, Bauhardt 2013). The concept brings together the two artificially separated spheres to stress their mutual interdependence. The term is especially useful for FPE: it shows how the so-called reproductive spheres of nature and female work are in fact the ground for the so-called productive sphere. In fact, why should the construction and trade of weapons be considered more productive for the economy than the bearing and rising of children?

## Gender analysis in macroeconomics

The gender perspective in macroeconomics examines, among other things, the gender-based segregation of the employment market and associated differences in income between the sexes. The vertical segregation of the employment market positions men and women in hierarchical relationships: men still mostly fill management and decision-making functions, whereas the majority of women work in assisting positions. The horizontal segregation of the employment market indicates that activities and competencies continue to be gendered. Here, subjective preferences play a role in choosing a profession, as do stereotyped hiring practices. The two phenomena explain the differences in income between men and women: both professions identified as 'male' and 'female' and higher-status positions privilege male workers and their earnings opportunities. Hardly anything has changed about this finding in Germany from 1990 to 2014 (Hausmann and Kleinert 2014).

From a feminist perspective, it becomes clear that the organisation of the labour market alone does not explain the gender hierarchy of professions and income. Only by intertwining paid work and care work and their respective time patterns can the access to the employment market and the income opportunities of men and women be analysed. For women, the normative responsibility for social reproduction proves to be an access barrier to the labour market. Their time availability for paid work is constrained by taking on the work of social reproduction, while for men, due to their assumed ongoing availability to the employment market, the work for social reproduction constitutes additional and voluntary efforts. The institutions of the heterosexual family and the gendered labour market are mutually dependent: the organisation of social reproduction that is enclosed in the private realm of the heterosexual family, institutionalised by law, restricts women's participation in the labour market; this family organisation enables men, in contrast, full integration into and unrivalled availability for the paid labour market. Accordingly, gender is a structural category for the economic analysis of society: only the gender perspective explains the hierarchical organisation of socially necessary work and the related power relations not only in the economy, but also within society (Hennessy and Ingraham 1997).

The female worker proves to be a buffer at various levels for the functioning of the capitalist economy. She represents on the one hand the resource for socially necessary work, the time scope of which is tremendous and which is provided extremely cost-effectively for capitalism based on the family organisation, as a look at the time-budget studies shows. On the other hand, in times of economic expansion she can be mobilised for the labour market so long as the state supply of social infrastructure services compensates for the private support and care for dependent persons, as is the case in welfare states and in regions oriented towards economic growth. If the state withdraws from the collective organisation of education, care and nursing in order to reduce public spending, female workers are either forced out of the employment market due to the privatisation of social reproduction, or solutions are found at the household level to shift the housework and care work of women in employment to women of lower social and ethnic status.

In this way, the household itself becomes the paid workplace of usually migrant women with limited opportunities on the formal labour market

(Anderson 2000, Parrenas 2001). Gender-specific migration patterns here meet the demand for female workers for social reproduction. This so-called global care chain indicates first that an equitable distribution of unpaid and societally lower-value housework and care work has not taken place between men and women in the industrialised nations of the Global North. Second, by shifting care work to unprotected and poorly paid employment relationships, the social and economic hierarchies between women are intensified. Third, the delegation of housework and care work to lower-status women maintains in the long run the symbolic order of the responsibility of women for social reproduction. The organisation of social reproduction in capitalism demonstrates the intersectional entanglement of gender with the categories class and 'race.'

Feminist Political Economy expands the understanding of what is considered the economy in the study of economics – the production of and trade with commodities to maximise income and capital. Feminist economists conceive of the economy starting from social reproduction, namely from the question of how a society ensures its livelihood. From this perspective, people's needs for care are at the centre; in both private households and public institutions, women primarily take these on as unpaid or underpaid work. If the state reduces the financing of public institutions, then work pressure increases both there and in private households. This crisis of social reproduction is compensated individually by extra work by women in the private realm or is absorbed by migrant household and care workers. Therefore, work in capitalism is organised hierarchically according to gender and ethnicity, and this structures society's power relations beyond class relations. Social reproduction is considered symbolically to be female and is empirically performed by women. This is an entry point for FPE.

## Ecofeminism and Queer Ecologies: Feminist analyses of socially constructed relations between society and nature

Social and political ecology links critiques of social hierarchies to an analysis of socially constructed relations between society and nature. Social hierarchies are rooted in economic, sexual and racist domination created by humans, and from which many humans suffer. Socially constructed relations between society and nature are the expression of how people engage with the more-than-human world, be it living creatures such as plants and animals, or abiotic substances such as air, soil, water, minerals, oil. From this perspective, in capitalism the two relationships are interconnected through the exploitation and hegemonic appropriation of the productivity of humans and nature (*cf.* Bookchin 1996, Foster *et al.* 2010).

FPE combines the analysis of the capitalist economy with the critique of patriarchal domination. Patriarchal domination is not only class domination but also the contempt of women's work and social values that goes beyond the capitalist rationale of Economic Man (Mellor 1997a, Nelson 1997, Ferber and Nelson 2003). Moreover, FPE looks at the embodied and performative agency of gendered subjectivities and identities (Elmhirst 2011).

FPE has been inspired by ecofeminism. Ecofeminism as a feminist social movement and as a theoretical stance focuses on the women–nature nexus. It is a way of thinking as well as a practice that integrates ecological, economic and feminist concerns. Ecofeminism sees a connection between the subordination of women and the inferiority of nature in Western capitalist societies. Women and the environment are both marginalised from what is acknowledged as important and relevant (Plumwood 1993, Mellor 1997b, 2005).

Historically, the nature–culture dichotomy and the hierarchy between them are closely related to the binary and hierarchical gender order: women, due to the female body's potential to bear children, i.e. the re/productivity of the female body, are seen as being closer to nature than are men. Since the European Enlightenment, men have been attributed greater distance to nature, and thus a greater proximity to culture. The symbolic order thereby constructed, the dichotomy of masculinity and femininity, culture and nature, transcendence and immanence, is deeply inscribed into Western traditions of thought. This legitimation of relations of domination is the basis for the development of capitalism in Europe as well as colonialism (Merchant 1980, Plumwood 1993, Holland-Cunz 2014). The ecofeminist perspective analyses capitalist, patriarchal and racist exploitation of humans and nature as hegemonic domination and appropriation of the re/productivity of life.

The term 'ecofeminism' comprises a number of currents of thought that consider the relationship between humans and nature from a feminist perspective. The focus, however, is on the analogy of women and nature, due to the female body's re/productivity. The more or less explicit analogy 'women-nature-mother' is the source of much unease in feminist environmental inquiry (*cf.* Alaimo 1994, Sandilands 1999, MacGregor 2006, Nightingale 2006, Leach 2007). Both the meanings ascribed to the female body's potential to procreate and thus to reproduce society, and the degree to which the symbolic order of femaleness and motherhood determines the socially constructed relations between society, gender and nature, are highly controversial. The question arising from a feminist perspective – that is to say, a perspective critical of patriarchal hegemony and domination – is whether a positive and emancipatory framing of nature is possible, a framing which does not reproduce the assumed inferiority of women and nature (Alaimo 2000). Can nature be so conceived that humans' existential dependence on the natural, material necessities of life – encompassing both the ecological environment and women's re/productive labour, including their potential to procreate – is neither dramatised nor idealised (*cf.* Bauhardt 2013)?

## Currents of thought in ecofeminism

In her seminal book *Ecofeminist Natures: Race, Gender, Feminist Theory and Political Action*, Noël Sturgeon (1997: 28–9) distinguishes five positions within ecofeminism in terms of how each analyses society's relations to nature. The shared starting point of these analyses is the relationship between the destruction of the environment and the exploitation of women's work and undervaluation of women in general under capitalism.

The first position starts with the understanding that environmental problems can only be appropriately analysed against the background of the oppression of women: wherever women are oppressed, nature is also dominated and exploited. When it is taken for granted that women's bodies and labour are endlessly available for ruthless economic use, then it is also assumed that nature is infinitely usable and exploitable.

The second position turns the argument around and says that the subordination of women in industrial capitalism can only be comprehended when the relationship between humans and nature in Western modernity is understood. Western modernity since the European enlightenment is characterised by the dichotomy of culture and nature, mind and body, reason and emotion, masculinity and femininity. The more highly valued pole is allocated to men and the subordinate one to women; women, accordingly, embody the inferiority of nature and of natural vital processes. To an economy that considers nature a resource to be exploited, a moral, ethical or emotional relationship to nature becomes suspect.

The third position is based on a historical and cross-cultural analysis of women's labour in social reproduction. Due to their responsibility for the subsistence economy in agrarian and household production on a global scale, women are more quickly, more directly, and more gravely affected by ecological issues and crises than are men. Women are not especially affected by ecological impacts on their bodily nature but on their workload and their responsibility for the health and the well-being of others.

The fourth position argues that women's potential to procreate, based on biological premises, means the female body is more closely tied to natural rhythms and life processes. Because of this greater closeness to the inherent logic of nature, this argument goes, women are capable of greater empathy with nature. This empathy for natural life processes benefits not only women, with their interest in a healthy environment, but the environment itself.

The fifth position draws on the spiritual resources of an ecological-feminist consciousness in which non-Western religious references such as witch ceremonies, goddess cults and ritual practices from non-Christian belief systems take on solidarity-building meaning. In many of these spiritual practices, embodiments of female strength become important; these images contradict dominant Western images of female dependency and subordination.

Noël Sturgeon (1997) notes that the various ecofeminist voices share many elements of these positions, though with differing emphases. As such, the positions cannot be easily attributed to individual authors. Only positions one and two would be irreconcilable with position four: while the first two positions locate the political potential of ecofeminism in the overcoming of patriarchal oppression of women and nature, position four would view the identification of women with nature as empowering and the creative potential of women's supposed proximity to nature as a reinforcement of ecofeminism. Position five also contains elements of a positive view on feminist self-empowerment; Sturgeon compares the reference to spiritually inspired rituals in ecofeminism with the solidarity-building singing and dancing of leftist movements like the civil rights and workers' movements. Position three connects to structural analyses of capitalism and links them to feminist economic critique.

With this overview, it becomes clear that debates conducted under the label 'ecofeminism' are often prematurely and unjustifiably blended into one mixture and falsely accused of essentialism – Noël Sturgeon speaks of a 'straw woman' (Sturgeon 1997: 38) which serves for distancing oneself and policing others. Indeed, it remains challenging, from a feminist perspective, to address the relationship between humans and nature, for the historical rucksack of the woman–nature nexus is always present (Mann 2010).

### Motherhood, female re/productivity and care responsibility

At its core, feminist environmental enquiry circles around the normative attribution of responsibility for life and life processes to women. Biological re/production and vital processes, the creativity of nature and of female bodies, are part of this. Because of women's potential to bear children, they are supposed to be more likely involved with the issues surrounding the creation and maintenance of life than are men. Since women are, normatively and empirically speaking, responsible for the care, hygiene and health of people who are not yet or are no longer able to care for themselves, they are also more personally affected by the consequences of environmental destruction than men are. Lack of water or poor water quality endangers health and hygiene, polluted air and food negatively affect developing children. Because of their responsibility for social reproduction, women are especially vulnerable when it comes to the management of the concrete consequences of ecological problems in daily life; this additional unpaid labour places an extra burden on their time and emotions.

At the same time, this labour of care responsibility also contributes to women's ecological expertise – or so goes the theory of feminists seeking a way out of ecological crises and hoping for better ways of approaching the natural environment. Accordingly, competence in caring for people widens out to an ethics of care for the environment. Critics of this reframing of female labour burdens as including expertise in ecological care thus speak of a privatisation and feminisation of responsibility for the environment (Wichterich 1992, MacGregor 2006). With this perspective, the actual causes of the exploitation and destruction of natural livelihoods – industrial capitalism and global male decision-making elites in politics and economics – fall from view.

The discourse on motherhood in some ecofeminist voices is highly controversial within feminist debates on the environment. This recalls the idea that the justification for women's closer relationship to nature lies in the female body's potential to bear children, in its re/productivity. As such, ecofeminist approaches are accused of constituting an essentialist conception of the analytical category of gender, which has led to a virtual blockade of any text with the term 'ecofeminism' in its title (Gaard 2011). However, upon a closer reading of these texts, this interpretation and its associated criticisms do not bear up.

Essentialism means the ascribing of unchangeable, intrinsic characteristics to a firmly defined group of people. The accusation is that through such ascription, static categories are defined that negate complexities and difference. But without a certain measure of abstraction, writes Anne Phillips (2010) in her essay 'What's wrong with essentialism?,' it would be impossible to construct any theoretical analysis at all. Normally, in the course of such processes of abstraction, a centre and a periphery are distinguished, as well as substantive and accidental qualities. In sociology, this led to the construction of ideal types, in philosophy it led to a distinction between essence and contingency: 'If we take essentialism to mean the process of differentiating something deemed essential from other things regarded as contingent, this can appear as a relatively uncontroversial description of the very process of thought' (Phillips 2010: 5). In her view, the construction of categorical groups only becomes problematic when it is accompanied by normative valuations and devaluations, and when it entails consequences of policing and punishment (Phillips 2010: 19–20).

In ecofeminist debates, the charge of essentialism is an obvious one, since essentialisation is very often identified with naturalisation. As such, the construction of analytical thought categories approaches ontological determinations. For an analysis of relations between nature and society, this becomes, from a feminist perspective, especially problematic. This questioning of the nature of human bodies slips easily into the suspicion of using the biological potential of the female body to procreate to construct an all-encompassing, naturalising category of the equation 'woman–nature–mother.' Yet, not all women bear and rear children, and men are not unable to care just because they cannot get pregnant. Nevertheless, the re/productivity of the female body and the social and political effects derived from it remain the pivotal element of ecofeminist analyses.

## Feminist analyses of the socially constructed relationship between society and nature

Contrary to prevalent interpretations, here I would like first to show that in ecofeminism the category 'woman' is understood not in a naturalising way, but as an analytical category of capitalist–patriarchal domination. Second, I will show how queer ecologies conceive the question of sexuality and social reproduction in relation to the human–nature nexus.

### Ecofeminism: motherhood, division of labour and class analysis

Ariel Salleh (1997) contrasts the middle-class, equality-based feminism of the Global North with its rhetoric of discrimination and emancipation with a global ecofeminism in which women from 'non-metropolitan cultures' take on a prominent role (Salleh 1997: 104) based on their concrete labour experiences as mothers. Unlike in middle-class feminism of the Global North, motherhood in the Global South is not judged as negative or as a disadvantage, but primarily describes a social position. In her critical take on Marxist analysis, Salleh designates mothers as a class (Salleh 1997, chap. 7). The practice of motherhood, she argues, allows women from the Global South to have a political consciousness and a political practice that also does not necessarily exclude men: '[A]n ecofeminist is anybody who carries out ecofeminist activities. That is, the term applies to a man or a woman whose political actions support the premise that the domination of nature and domination of women are interconnected' (Salleh 1997: 108). Ariel Salleh describes ecofeminism as a synthesis of socialism, feminism and ecology.

Arguing in a similar vein, Maria Mies and Vandana Shiva (1993) link a feminist class analysis to a (post-)colonial perspective. Their book, *Ecofeminism*, is currently enjoying renewed interest, as the 2014 reprint proves. This interest goes hand in hand with a renewed interest in feminist-materialist critiques of global capitalism (*cf.* Rai and Waylen 2014). Mies and Shiva emphatically criticise global hierarchies and domination based on the exploitation of women (and their labour), subsistence farmers and natural resources. They do not, however, consider the transformation of these poor conditions solely or even primarily as the task of women, acting as from ecological misery. The authors rather speak explicitly of the powerful potential of a transformed masculinity based on a 'new understanding of non-patriarchal sexuality' (Mies and Shiva 2014: 295), which:

> can develop only together with changes in the sexual division of labor, the economy and politics. Only when men begin seriously to share in caring for children, the old, the weak, and for nature, when they recognize that this life-preserving subsistence work is more important than work for cash, will they be able to develop a caring, responsible, erotic relationship to their partners, be they men or women.
>
> (Mies and Shiva 2014: 295)

Here we can see that two conventional interpretations of ecofeminism are not entirely accurate: first, the oft-assumed ascription of responsibility for the environment exclusively to women based on their potential to bear children, and second, the heteronormative foundation of the ecofeminist argument. At issue is the practice of care labour and not an essentialising of the female body; this practice can be experienced by men and women and in both hetero- and homosexual relationships.

### Queer Ecologies: Critique of the heteronormative nature–culture dichotomy

Discussions around Queer Ecologies negotiate questions of heteronormativity, queer desire and social reproduction. Considerations of how these epistemological approaches can be combined with Feminist Political Economy on a global scale are still in the early stages (*cf.* Bauhardt 2017).

The Queer Ecologies approach represents an explicitly critical take on the nature–culture hierarchy and its interdependence with heteronormative notions of masculinity and femininity (Bagemihl 1999, Mortimer-Sandilands and Erickson 2010, Harcourt *et al.* 2015). In her article 'Toward a Queer Ecofeminism,' Greta Gaard (1997) develops her argumentation as demarcated from the dominant perspective that views heterosexual sexuality as natural, since it is procreative, while non-procreative sex is devalued as 'unnatural' and 'perverse.' She names erotophobia – the anti-pleasure rationalism of Western culture – as the reason for both the rejection of queer sexual practices and a general disassociation from nature. She postulates: 'A queer ecofeminist perspective would argue that the reason/erotic and heterosexual/queer dualisms have now become part of the master identity and that dismantling these dualisms is integral to the project of ecofeminism' (Gaard 1997: 118–19).

This outspoken ecofeminist position takes a critical stance against the separation and hierarchy of culture and nature, mind and body, masculine and feminine, postulated since the European Enlightenment (*cf.* Merchant 1980, Plumwood 1993, Holland-Cunz 2014). It extends this dualism to the opposition between heterosexuality and queer desire, thus suspending the identification of sexuality, re/productivity and motherhood. From the perspective of Queer Ecologies, it is a matter of dissolving the coercive connection between the re/productivity of the female body and motherhood – Greta Gaard speaks of 'compulsory motherhood' (Gaard 1997: 120). In Greta Gaard's view, the erotophobia of Christianity and the history of colonialisation are closely connected. The Christian missionaries labelled any practices that were not the heterosexual ones of the European colonisers as 'wild' and 'uncivilized': 'Colonization can therefore be seen as a relationship of compulsory heterosexuality whereby the queer erotic of non-westernized peoples, their culture, and their land, is subdued into the missionary position – with the conqueror "on top"' (Gaard 1997: 131).

Catriona Sandilands (2001) also works with the concept of erotophobia when she argues for a sensual and erotic desire for nature beyond heteronormative ascriptions of nature and femininity. In her work, she posits an individual and social relationship to nature that is not based on the denigration and exploitation of nature as a resource. From a queer perspective, it becomes possible to approach nature with erotic desire – queer desire fosters a resistant potential in the encounter with nature:

> I would like to suggest that a queer erotogenic desire in and for nature underscores the richness of touch as a currently undervalued mode of worldly perception. [....] Touch is simultaneously impact and reception [....]; touch relies on proximity [....]; touch leaves an impression, and the eroticized transformation of the touched leaves desire for repetition.
> (Sandilands 2001: 185)

Sandilands sees in the sensual experience of lust and eroticism the potential to end ecologically and sexually destructive relationships and to develop an ethics of queer-ecological eroticism.

The deconstruction of heterosexual reproduction as 'natural' reproduction from a queer-ecological perspective creates non-heteronormative relations between society and nature. The feminist environmentalist Noël Sturgeon (2010) shows how the policies of reproduction – of people, of kinship relations, of economies, of the environment – are organised around gendered arrangements of work and sexuality and that these arrangements are heteronormative. They are based on a heteronormative organisation of work and love, which is stabilised by social and economic institutions:

> The politics of gender are often both the politics of reproduction and the politics of production – the intertwined ways that people produce more people, manage bringing up children, figure out how to do the work at home at the same time as the work that brings in a paycheck, decide how and where to buy food, clothing, shelter, and transportation, take care of elders, and create and maintain all of the social institutions that surround this work. And all of this is central to whether or not our ways of living cause environmental degradation.
>
> (Sturgeon 2010: 104)

The approach of Queer Ecologies makes it possible to look at the nature of generative reproduction without having to refer to an unquestioned 'naturalness' of heterosexual desire, heterosexual reproduction and correspondingly socially legitimised heteronormativity. The Queer Ecologies perspective allows understanding biological generativity as a web of biological, social and cultural dimensions. At the same time, this view deconstructs the alleged naturalness of heteronormative lifestyles and consumption patterns.

### Ecofeminism and spirituality

According to Noël Sturgeon (1997), one current of ecofeminism makes use of spiritual practices to create social bonds and to appeal for more than rational ways of communication and experience. This is another reason why ecofeminism is so highly controversial between feminists. Ecofeminist academic and activist Chaone Mallory in an insightful article of 2010 states: 'Nowhere is ecofeminism more fraught and fractured than over the question of spirituality' (50).

Some authors have been differentiating cultural and social(ist) ecofeminism (Buckingham-Hatfield 2000, Carlassare 2000). Cultural ecofeminism is rooted in a women-centred ground of experience and in a women-based worldview in opposition to the patriarchal devaluation of women and women's work, women's thinking and women's achievements. 'In response to this devaluing, cultural ecofeminists [...] celebrate and revalue qualities, such as intuition, care, nurture, emotions, and the body, for example, that have been associated culturally and historically with women' (Carlassare 2000: 93). Cultural ecofeminists therefore seek to rediscover women's history and women-based spiritualties and cultures as empowering women against the male representations of God-the-father-based monotheistic religions. Mother earth becomes the female counterpart of God the father.

> In contrast to religions that assume a transcendental god, the spirituality these cultural ecofeminists advocate is based on the divine as immanent in nature, including people. Ecofeminist spiritualists emphasize the values of interconnectedness and biological and cultural diversity. They conceive of the earth as a living organism and humans as one part of the community of life on earth.
>
> (Carlassare 2000: 94)

Cultural ecofeminists focus on language, symbols and values through which patriarchal power takes shape. Therefore, much emphasis is put on other forms of thinking and expression, e.g. poems, art, fiction or storytelling. These means of expression are supposed to speak differently about power by creating a counterhegemonic strategy. In a very lucid philosophical analysis Karen Warren (1990) concludes: 'Such activity helps counteract the sometimes immobilizing sense that, once one sees patriarchy for what it is, it seems too big, too old, and too powerful to do anything about' (Warren 1990: 131). Therefore, cultural or spiritual ecofeminism creates a space for women – and other Others of rationality – of self-empowerment.

Ecofeminism nowadays is imputed to be politically regressive because of a pre-social, pre-linguistic understanding of women: ecofeminists are blamed to see women on an ontological, epistemological and moral level as closer to nature. One reason for this accusation is the close link between ecofeminism and spirituality. Ecofeminist spirituality and its earth-based myths and rituals are said to embody the myth of women being closer to nature and therefore subject to male domination. Ecofeminism is considered to repeat eternally the dualisms of reason and emotion, science and ethics, spirit and matter, culture and nature, men and women.

In defence of ecofeminism, philosopher Karen Warren (1990) comes up with several arguments that underpin the importance and legitimacy of ecofeminist spiritualties: historically, they played a vital, grassroots role in the creation of ecofeminism as a social movement. Politically, ecofeminism unites women activists from all over the globe, from diverse ethnic backgrounds and from regions where spiritual practices have always been part of everyday culture. Ethically, ecofeminist spiritualties raise important issues of ethics and values that are underestimated in traditional patriarchal value systems. Epistemologically, practitioners of ecofeminist spiritualities bring about intuitive and affective ways of knowledge production, which certainly differ from scientific knowledge production but are nonetheless interesting ways of knowing. Conceptually, this leads to critically examining the notion of the self-reflexive subject and the role of reason and rationality which is crucial when it comes to issues of domination, exploitation and destruction of the environment that we live in and on which we are dependent. Theoretically, the question of spirituality raises issues about how we conceive theory-building in feminism. In other words: is the personal experience of spirituality a valuable source for thinking and analysing political problems?

Chaone Mallory's (2010) answer to this question is a clearly pronounced 'yes'; her article is called 'The Spiritual is Political.' She concludes this statement from an analysis of ecological activism that she conducted in 2008 and 2009 in the Pacific Northwest in the USA. In a wilderness area in Northern California and Southern Oregon where the defence of forests is an important social movement, she analysed the motivations and practices of women and transgender forest defence collectives. These people consider themselves as part of the global resistance movement against deforestation and they call their activities 'Womyn's and Trans Action Camps.' Mallory states:

> For some activists, protest and engaging in forest defence is a spiritual matter. It can be motivated by a deeply held belief in the sacredness of wild nature […]. For others, it is the work and play of activism on behalf of the environment that itself constitutes the spiritual practice. For most activists, who express a spiritual orientation, it is both – the spiritual is political.
>
> (55)

Mallory's work shows that spirituality is still a powerful resource for environmental activism, which is not restricted to 'women' according to the binary gender order but open to all queer bodies and genders.

## Feminist Political Ecology – a promising future for a strong feminist critique of capitalism and for creating economic alternatives

In my analysis of ecofeminist texts, I defend ecofeminist analysis of capitalism as a powerful critique of this form of economy. The exploitation of nature and the exploitation of women's work as if it were a natural resource are at the core of the analysis. The re/productivity of life and vital processes create the analogy of women and nature.

However, the charge of essentialism is a strong and powerful reproach. Of course, the idea that women are supposed to be closer to nature expresses the patriarchal assumption that women are less rational, too emotional and dangerously close to the caprices of nature. It has been the ultimate goal of feminism since its beginning with feminist activism in the eighteenth century to overthrow these assumptions that most obviously are linked to the re/productivity of the female body. Therefore, it is evident that any positive reference to women's presumed closer link to nature is considered regressive and anti-feminist. To see women as the embodiment of nature is harmful to women and is damaging to egalitarian gender relations.

Yet, the reproach of essentialism more often than not is unjustified. The issues around social reproduction and care can be discussed in analogy to Marxist analysis as a form of exploitation and appropriation of female productivity. If we take queer ecologies seriously, the entanglement of nature, heterosexuality, re/productivity and care are to be deconstructed. This approach in feminist environmentalism enables us to acknowledge social reproduction beyond the heteronormative construction of motherhood and family structures. Thinking with queer ecologies allows for an appreciation of care, emotionality and responsibility for the well-being of human and non-human others without binding these qualities to the female body. Social reproduction in both ecofeminism and queer ecologies is not an essential and 'natural' feature of women. It is at the same time a relationship of labour and exploitation and a source for creating bonds with the material foundations of life.

FPE has the potential to integrate several inspirations from ecofeminism and queer ecologies. The critique of capitalism as an intersectional structure of class, race and patriarchal domination and the exploitation of nature is an integral part of ecofeminist analysis. Queer ecologies enrich this structural approach with poststructuralist insights. The power of language in the social and cultural construction of reality is key for this way of thinking.

Donna Haraway also looks critically at the culture–nature dualism, especially in the correlation of culture with scientific and technological development. Incidentally, she would seem to have no reservations about the term 'ecofeminism,' since, in her essay 'Situated Knowledges' (Haraway 1988) she places the word prominently in the conclusion, speaking of hopes for a feminist perspective in technoscience: 'Perhaps our hopes for accountability, for politics, for ecofeminism, turn on revisioning the world as coding trickster with whom we must learn to converse' (Haraway 1988: 596). With her neologism 'naturecultures' (Haraway 2003), she aims to remove the dichotomy and hierarchy of culture and nature, and to bring their mutual interdependence into the term. Therefore, what is considered 'the environment' in fact is an entanglement of nature and culture, *naturecultures* of technological, scientific, emotional and spiritual approaches to the natural world around us.

Therefore, when we think about care in the context of FPE, it is essential to keep both perspectives, ecofeminism and queer ecologies, in mind. In capitalism, the work of responsibility and care attributed to women based on their re/productivity is considered a quasi-natural resource in the process of economic exploitation. From the point of view of the Queer Ecologies, this connection between social reproduction, the binary gender order and the responsibility to care for people and the more-than-human world is by no means compelling. Even if we must not lose sight of the exploitation of care work and the associated structures of power in socially constructed relations between society, gender and nature, the view of queer ecologies goes beyond this perspective. The uneasy connection between 'women–nature–mother' is thus dissolved and care responsibility can be a source of lust, joy and desire as well as of a positive, erotic relationship to the natural environment.

# References

Alaimo, S., 1994. Cyborg and ecofeminist interventions: challenges for an environmental feminism. *Feminist Studies*, 20 (1), 133–52.

Alaimo, S., 2000. *Undomesticated Ground. Recasting Nature as Feminist Space*. Ithaca, NY: Cornell University Press.

Alaimo, S., 2016. *Exposed: Environmental Politics and Pleasures in Posthuman Times*. Minneapolis, MN: University of Minnesota Press.

Anderson, B., 2000. *Doing the Dirty Work? The Global Politics of Domestic Labour*. London: Zed Books.

Bagemihl, B., 1999. *Biological Exuberance: Animal Homosexuality and Natural Diversity*. New York: St. Martin's Press.

Bauhardt, C., 2013. Rethinking gender and nature from a material(ist) perspective: feminist economics, queer ecologies, and resource politics. *European Journal of Women's Studies*, 20 (4), 361–75.

Bauhardt, C., 2014. Solutions to the crisis? The Green New Deal, degrowth, and the solidarity economy: alternatives to the capitalist growth economy from an ecofeminist economics perspective. *Ecological Economics*, 102, 60–8.

Bauhardt, C., 2017. Economics. *In*: S, Alaimo, ed., *Gender: Matter*. Farmington Hills, MI: Macmillan Reference USA, 223–36.

Biesecker, A. and Hofmeister, S., 2010. Focus: (re)productivity: sustainable relations both between society and nature and between the genders. *Ecological Economics*, 69 (8), 1703–11.

Bookchin, M., 1996. *Toward an Ecological Society*. Montréal: Black Rose Books.

Buckingham-Hatfield, S., 2000. *Gender and Environment*. London: Routledge.

Budlender, D.D., ed., 2010. *Time Use Studies and Unpaid Care Work*. New York: Routledge.

Carlassare, E., 2000. Socialist and cultural ecofeminism: allies in resistance. *Ethics and the Environment*, 5 (1), 89–106.

Chambers, S.A., 2007. 'Sex' and the problem of the body: reconstructing Judith Butler's theory of sex/gender. *Body & Society*, 13 (4), 47–75.

Dalla Costa, M. and James, S., 1975. *The Power of Women and the Subversion of the Community*. 3rd ed. Bristol: Falling Wall Press.

Ehrenreich, B. and Hochschild, A.R., eds, 2004. *Global Woman. Nannies, Maids, and Sex Workers in the New Economy*. New York: Metropolitan Books.

Elmhirst, R., 2011. Introducing new feminist political ecologies. *Geoforum*, 42, 129–32.

Ferber, M.A. and Nelson, J.A., eds, 2003. *Feminist Economics Today: Beyond Economic Man*. Chicago, IL: University of Chicago Press.

Ferguson, A., 2005. Butler, sex/gender and a postmodern gender theory. *In*: B.S. Andrew, J.C. Keller and L.H. Schwartzman, eds., *Feminist Interventions in Ethics and Politics: Feminist Ethics and Social Theory*. Lanham, MD: Rowman & Littlefield, 59–75.

Ferguson, A. and Folbre, N., 1981. The unhappy marriage of patriarchy and capitalism. *In*: L. Sargent, ed., *Women and Revolution: A Discussion of the Unhappy Marriage of Marxism and Feminism*. Cambridge, MA: South End Press, 313–38.

Floro, M.S., 2012. The crises of environment and social reproduction: understanding their linkages. *Journal of Gender Studies*, 15, 13–31.

Folbre, N., 2001. *The Invisible Heart. Economics and Family Values*. New York: The New Press.

Folbre, N., 2009. *Greed, Lust & Gender: A History of Economic Ideas*. Oxford: Oxford University Press.

Folbre, N., 2010. Holding hands at midnight: the paradox of caring labor. *Feminist Economics*, 1 (1), 73–92.

Folbre, N. and J.A., Nelson, 2000. For love or money – or both? *Journal of Economic Perspectives*, 14 (4), 123–40.

Foster, J.B., Clark, B. and York, R., 2010. *The Ecological Rift. Capitalism's War on the Earth.* New York: Monthly Review Press.

Gaard, G., 1997. Toward a queer ecofeminism. *Hypatia*, 12 (1), 114–37.

Gaard, G., 2011. Ecofeminism revisited: rejecting essentialism and re-placing species in a material feminist environmentalism. *Feminist Formations*, 23 (2), 26–53.

Haraway, D.J., 1988. Situated knowledges: the science question in feminism and the privilege of partial perspective. *Feminist Studies*, 14 (3), 575–99.

Haraway, D.J., 2003. *The Companion Species Manifesto: Dogs, People, and Significant Otherness.* Chicago, IL: Prickly Paradigm Press.

Harcourt, W., 1994. *Feminist Perspectives on Sustainable Development.* London: Zed Books.

Harcourt, W., 2014. *Women Reclaiming Sustainable Livelihoods: Spaces Lost, Spaces Gained.* Basingstoke: Palgrave Macmillan.

Harcourt, W. and Nelson, I.L., eds, 2015. *Practising Feminist Political Ecologies: Moving beyond the 'Green Economy'.* London: Zed Books.

Harcourt, W., Knox, S. and Tabassi, T., 2015. World-wise otherwise stories for our endtimes: conversations on Queer Ecologies. *In*: W. Harcourt and I.L. Nelson, eds., *Practising Feminist Political Ecologies: Moving beyond the 'Green Economy'.* London: Zed Books, 286–308.

Hausmann, A.C. and Kleinert, C., 2014. Berufliche Segregation auf dem Arbeitsmarkt: Männer- und Frauendomänen kaum verändert. *IAB Kurzbericht*, 9, 1–8.

Hennessy, R. and Ingraham, C., eds., 1997. *Materialist Feminism. A Reader in Class, Difference, and Women's Lives.* New York: Routledge.

Holland-Cunz, B., 2014. *Die Natur der Neuzeit: Eine feministische Einführung.* Opladen, Germany: Verlag Barbara Budrich.

Jackson, Tim, 2009. *Prosperity Without Growth. Economics for a Finite Planet.* London: Earthscan.

Leach, M., 2007. Earth mother myths and other ecofeminist fables: how a strategic notion rose and fell. *Development and Change*, 38 (1), 67–85.

MacGregor, S., 2006. *Beyond Mothering Earth: Ecological Citizenship and the Politics of Care.* Vancouver: University of British Columbia Press.

MacGregor, S., ed., 2017. *Routledge Handbook of Gender and Environment.* London: Routledge.

Mallory, C., 2010. The spiritual is political: gender, spirituality, and essentialism in radical forest defense. *Journal for the Study of Religion, Nature and Culture*, 4 (1), 48–71.

Mann, B., 2010. What should feminists do about nature? *Konturen*, 2 (1), 79–100.

Mellor, M., 1997a. Women, nature and the social construction of 'economic man'. *Ecological Economics*, 20 (2), 129–40.

Mellor, M., 1997b. *Feminism & Ecology.* Oxford: Blackwell.

Mellor, M., 2005. Ecofeminist political economy: integrating feminist economics and ecological economics. *Feminist Economics*, 11 (3), 120–6.

Merchant, C., 1980. *The Death of Nature: Women, Ecology, and the Scientific Revolution.* San Francisco: Harper & Row.

Mies, M. and Shiva, V., 1993. *Ecofeminism.* London: Zed Books.

Mortimer-Sandilands, C. and Erickson, B., eds, 2010. *Queer Ecologies: Sex, Nature, Politics, Desire.* Bloomington, IN: Indiana University Press.

Nelson, J.A., 1997. Feminism, ecology and the philosophy of economics. *Ecological Economics*, 20, 155–62.

Nightingale, A., 2006. The nature of gender: work, gender, environment. *Environment and Planning D: Society and Space*, 24 (2), 165–85.

Parrenas, R.S., 2001. *Servants of Globalization: Migration and Domestic Work*. Stanford, CA: Stanford University Press.

Pateman, C., 1988. *The Sexual Contract*. Cambridge: Polity Press.

Phillips, A., 2010. What's wrong with essentialism? *Distinktion: Scandinavian Journal of Social Theory*, 11 (1), 47–60.

Plumwood, V., 1993. *Feminism and the Mastery of Nature*. London: Routledge.

Rai, S., Hoskyns, C. and Thomas, D., 2013. Depletion: the cost of social reproduction. *International Feminist Journal of Politics*, 16 (1), 86–105.

Rai, S. and Waylen, G., eds, 2014. *New Frontiers in Feminist Political Economy*. London: Routledge.

Rocheleau, D.E., Slayter, T. and Wangari, E., eds, 1996. *Feminist Political Ecology. Global Issues and Local Experiences*. London: Routledge.

Salleh, A., 1997. *Ecofeminism as Politics: Nature, Marx and the Postmodern*. London: Zed Books.

Sandilands, C., 1999. *The Good-Natured Feminist. Ecofeminism and the Quest for Democracy*. Minneapolis, MN: University of Minnesota Press.

Sandilands, C., 2001. Desiring nature, queering ethics: adventures in erotogenic environments. *Environmental Ethics*, 23 (3), 169–88.

Schwarz, N. and Schwahn, F., 2016. Entwicklung der unbezahlten Arbeit privater Haushalte: Bewertung und Vergleich mit gesamtwirtschaftlichen Größen. *WISTA Wirtschaft und Statistik*, 2, 35–51.

Soper, K., 1995. *What is Nature? Culture, Politics, and the Non-Human*. Oxford: Blackwell Publishing.

Speth, J.G., 2008. *The Bridge at the Edge of the World: Capitalism, the Environment, and Crossing from Crisis to Sustainability*. New Haven, CT: Yale University Press.

Statistisches Bundesamt, 2017. Wie die Zeit vergeht. Analysen zur Zeitverwendung in Deutschland. Berlin: Statistisches Bundesamt.

Sturgeon, N., 1997. *Ecofeminist Natures. Race, Gender, Feminist Theory and Political Action*. London: Taylor and Francis.

Sturgeon, N., 2010. Penguin family values: the nature of planetary environmental reproductive justice. *In*: C. Mortimer-Sandilands and B. Erickson, eds., *Queer Ecologies: Sex, Nature, Politics, Desire*. Bloomington, IN: Indiana University Press, 102–33.

Tronto, J., 1993. *Moral Boundaries: A Political Argument for an Ethic of Care*. London: Routledge.

Tronto, J., 2013. *Caring Democracy: Markets, Equality, and Justice*. New York: New York University Press.

Warren, K., 1990. The power and the promise of ecological feminism. *Environmental Ethics*, 12 (2), 125–46.

Wichterich, C., 1992. Die Erde bemuttern. Frauen und Ökologie nach dem Erdgipfel in Rio. Köln: Heinrich-Böll-Stiftung.

Wright, E.O., 2010. *Envisioning Real Utopias*. London: Verso Books.

# 3 White settler colonial scientific fabulations on otherwise narratives of care

*Wendy Harcourt*

## Introduction

When we read every day stories about the climate crisis, dying lakes and seas, refugee crises, rampant consumerism and disappearing animal and plant life we often feel despair that we have not done enough nor can we ever do enough to addresses these issues, and, despite our caring, we often just want to turn away and disengage. My chapter stays with these troubled feelings[1] as I explore how to keep on engaging and caring, with a sense of humility and compassion, for others including non-human others, in order to learn to live with the mess we are undoubtedly in. As a feminist political ecologist, my chapter asks what stories about care can we tell so that those trained in different disciplines, living in other places and with other histories can respond. Like Donna Haraway I consider 'it matters which stories we tell as a practice of caring' (Haraway 2015: 160), so my aim is to create fabulations in order to unpack what we can learn from white settler histories of care.

My chapter is indebted to some very good storytellers. I am inspired by Anna Tsing's (2015) tale of mushrooms at the end of the world, that builds mesmerising stories of the matsutake mushroom in the age of economic decline and globalisation. I build on Donna Haraway's concept of naturecultures where she proposes that nature is not other to culture but rather the two concepts inform and co-create each other (Haraway 2016). I aim to evoke otherwise (Walsh 2016)[2] meanings of ecology and economics, responding to the call to reappropriate, reconstruct and reinvent our personal and political lifeworlds (Escobar and Harcourt 2005). And I explore the possibilities for more ethical economic and ecological relationships around care, taking my cue from the work of J.K. Gibson Graham (2008) on feminist imaginaries.

My chapter engages with post-development and post-capitalist readings of the economy and environment as part of the exploration of how to include 'Earthothers' in ecological theory and practice of care.[3] It is an experimental chapter in ideas that resonate with my life, practice and theorising as a feminist political ecologist as I open up questions that are important according to Haraway, not because we are 'in charge of the world,' but because 'we just live here and try to strike up non-innocent conversations' (Haraway 1991: 199).

I am particularly inspired to write in this experimental way after rereading Val Plumwood, an Australian ecofeminist and philosopher, not only because of her insights into care but also because of her art of telling stories from Australia, our shared birth place.[4] Her work helps me to think further about care and the conversations between Feminist Political Ecology (FPE) and feminist economists and others. I am writing aware of my heritage as a white middle class Australian who is learning to care otherwise, aware of how those histories and privilege allow me to boldly situate myself into the debate. But I try to do it a non-innocent way as I look at care and responsibility in the context of white settler Australia by tracing a trajectory of erasure, loss and care of natureculture across time and place.

Admittedly, this may seem an unimportant story in the bigger scheme of things, but I want to understand what my personal story could reveal about care and responsibility for white Australians. I am deeply aware that I am also indebted to silences that surround these stories of white settler life. I am still learning to listen more directly to voices and experiences of First Nations in Australia which push beyond token celebrations of voice. Trying to understand the institutions, practices and norms that condition who is heard, on whose terms and to what effect is also why I write in this experimental way. I write in order to unsettle and to acknowledge the uneven flows of power and privilege that are part of these issues. My writing is about trying to find ways to listen to difference in order to disrupt the stark racism in Australian natureculture (Bassel 2017). My story tries to open up to different historical layers of vulnerability. It is a beginning as I aim to open to a politics of listening as part of a political practice to find justice and a new ethics of relations with First Nations in Australia and their stories of ongoing injustice and inequalities. So I am experimenting as I stay with the trouble and discomfort about whether this is a history to be told or not. But I will deal with the contradictions and difficulties of telling this history as a practice of care, and in so doing, I can hope to contribute to finding ways to tackle environmental damage and white privilege in a post-capitalist Australia.

I am using the concept of care for Earthothers as a motif that allows me to look beyond the idea of care as the gendered work of social reproduction and to explore ecological/cross-species care which I suggest offers the potential to heal the historical and contemporary violence and fear towards human others.

## What we can learn from ecofeminism

Let's start with a confession. Ecofeminism is a term with which I have had a lasting love–hate relationship. As a young, white social feminist engaged in environmental issues in Australia I would fiercely argue against it. I did not want women to end up being responsible for the mess men have made for the world. But at the same time, I have been drawn by the ecofeminist appeal to other ways of seeing – of care and community and valuing the spiritual. Given the environmental, social and political mess we are in right now, I am looking again into the insights of ecofeminism. While I want to move beyond its biological determinism, I value how ecofeminism allows us to think about how to care differently and in more responsible ways for natureculture in our shifting, transitioning, scary lifeworlds. Reengaging with the work of Val Plumwood (1991a, 1991b) I am keen to be guided in how to live with Earthothers, and in greater awareness of the place of the non-human in nature, learning to navigate modernity and capitalism and its damaging ways of being.

Ecofeminism emerged in the 1970s and 1980s bringing together feminist and ecological critiques of capitalism, modernity and science. Writers such as Vandana Shiva (1988) saw the domination of women and the domination of nature as intimately and intricately connected and rooted in concrete historical socio-economic conditions as well as oppressive patriarchal cultures. Maria Mies (who wrote with Vandana Shiva the classic 1993 publication *Ecofeminism*), Karren Warren (1997), Ariel Salleh (1997) and Mary Mellor (1997) among others asked questions about how to counter the violence of extractive development and the links among biodiversity, indigenous knowledge and reproductive technology, intellectual property, development, war, responsibility and globalisation. They argued for limits to growth, reciprocity among peoples and a rejection of exploitation, the endless commoditisation of needs and violence (Mies and Shiva 1993).

Ecofeminism integrates discourses on science, the body, culture, nature and political economy. My inspiration for this article is Plumwood's ecofeminism which speaks in particular to diversity and difference among women, people of colour, human and non-humans. She speaks of all living beings as members of an ecological community and sees relations among them as central to the ecological discussion of self with others. Her writing calls for the transcendence of dualism and the need to integrate mind and body/nature and culture. She advocates for the recognition of care for others, love, friendship, diversity and appropriate reciprocity. She asks that we look at human interactions with the non-human natural world respectfully acknowledging the agency of all beings in the world.

Her analysis strongly criticises anthropocentrism as she links environmentalism with social justice. She decentres the human in order to understand our connection with Earthothers in stories about animality and humanity and how they fuse in embodiment and living. She helps us understand how human flesh is part of the food web, and how nature and animals are part of ethics and culture. Her writing enables us to think about humanity in ecological terms, and asks that we recognise non-human kin and sentient beings, returning the soul to animals and to nature.

She speaks to how our bodies do not belong to us but to the earth, and does so in relation to the particular place of Australia. She describes the disfiguring Australian colonial past which defies the complexities of natureculture which humans cannot know or control fully. She speaks out about the white Australian cultural cringe and its inability to see the environment as nature because the Australian natureculture was not part of the 'mother country' so far away in Europe. She describes this lack of understanding and being in place as a huge obstacle to a full understanding by white Australians of their (our) surroundings.

In her beautiful stories, including her tales of cross–species mothering of a wombat and her escape from death by a crocodile, her writing deals with the world of wounds (Plumwood 2012). She meditates on bloody and violent histories, and helps us imagine how to move away from the complicity of colonial life that was/is based on instrumentalising Earthothers. Her discussion of ecological animalism is built on the fundamental insight that human culture is embedded in ecological systems and dependent on nature and that humanity is part of that complex web of relations.

What I take from Plumwood is the importance of living in place and of everyday practice not only in terms of my individual activities in specific places but also in terms of how to think ecologically, in ways that require political, societal, cultural and historical awareness of lived relations with Earthothers.

I have earlier written about place in relation to women and the politics of place (Harcourt and Escobar 2005) where I looked at place in relation to bodies, home, community environment and public space. In that writing I focused on the political engagement of feminists in international development and social movement struggles to change gender power relations in different places, including the UN arena or global social movement gatherings. In such debates, I neatly sidestepped my original place of Australia. Plumwood's stories of Earthothers have inspired me to return imaginatively to my original place and to try to come to grips with white settler histories of colonial oppression and how to be cognisant of what those histories mean to my feminist political ecologist understanding of care.

## White settler narratives and erasures

Another confession: I have a PhD in the history of ideas – that looked at European medical practice and gender power relations in late nineteenth century Melbourne. But, like many others of my education, race and class, I did not know about or how to relate to indigenous cultures or peoples' history. In my PhD days such knowledge was called 'prehistory,' and I did not think those stories mattered to my own learning or living.

As a child, I was taught that my town, Adelaide, had been settled peace-fully and that where I lived the land was not used by indigenous people. I only found out much later that my house was built in 1910 on the traditional lands of the Kouwandilla band of the Kaurna people. I learnt the story of how the initial settlement of the Adelaide area took place without any conflict. It turns out this was partly because it happened in summer when the Kaurna people traditionally moved from the plains to the foothills. In the first two decades the records show that white settlers wanted to set up a colony where white and black lived alongside each other. Paintings depict settlers living near indigenous wurlies (stick and bark homes). There were attempts by Europeans to learn the language. But by 1854 the 1,000 Kaurna people that the first Europeans reported were living in the area was reduced to 180. They had been devastated by small pox and typhoid, brought by Europeans and their pollution of the River Torrens. The indigenous animals moved on and the peoples' annual move to the hills was blocked by settlers who wanted to prevent the Kaurna practice of fire-stick farming which damaged the colonists' newly established farmlands and grasslands. Indeed, by 1879 the Kaurna were declared 'extinct.' Indigenous people living in camps were finally cleared from the land only in 1912 and threatened with imprisonment if they returned.

The history of colonialism in Adelaide continues to be a long-lasting narrative of erasure that places Kaurna people as peripheral to the dominant narrative of settler colonialism and white Australia. Since the 1970s and 1980s, the histories of the Kaurna people have been reclaimed based on culture, place and language. 'Nunga' has emerged as a general term used by South Australian Aboriginal people and in the last two decades a group of Aboriginal people have re-emerged who speak for the Adelaide Plains and identify as Kaurna.

The Kaurna call the area around Adelaide city and parklands *Tarntanya* (red kangaroo place). Before 1836 it was an open grassy plain with patches of trees and shrubs, the result of skilful generations of land management. Kaurna people were cleared off the land to create the Botanical Garden and green parks. The River Torrens that runs through Adelaide was called *Karrawirra Pari* (red gum forest river) and provided water, fish and other foods. The knowledge of land is based also on spiritual understandings. There is now contemporary recognition of Kaurna dreaming, in the statues and plaques and walkways which honour the connectedness of people and culture with the worlds of plants, the animals and stars, and Dreaming ancestors of the Tjilbruke (Adelaidia n.d.; South Australian Museum 2013).

It is difficult to reconstruct histories of those early encounters in Australia because the records of the white settlers conflict with the oral history of the indigenous Australians. One narrative speaks of peaceful settlement in what were seen as largely unoccupied lands, the other of frontier conflict. These are the narrative battlegrounds between the documented and imagined history of white settlement and the Aboriginal oral history of the frontier that emerge in current land-right claims. They are also the stuff of public events held around Australia called 'sorry days' which began in 1998 and which are forms of public healing and processes of reconciliation for indigenous and non-indigenous Australian people. At official events, acknowledgements are verbally made to indigenous people as the traditional owners and custodians of Australian land. National reconciliation week recognises the contributions that indigenous Australians make to the community and country. Land claims though continue, as do incarcerations, poor health and poverty. The damage continues to be embodied in living memories.

My understanding of these conflicting stories fits what Patrick Wolfe (2006), an Australian settler scholar, describes as the logic of erasure that marks white settlers' relations with the indigenous people. There are different narratives of this erasure. The 'frontier homicide' marks the death of indigenous peoples during early settler colonialism due to conflict, disease and starvation. This is combined with the story of assimilation, re-socialising or 'integrating' them into settler society (Wolfe 2006: 388), undermining their claim to their land, their language, culture and livelihoods.

The violence of colonisation, the erasure of indigenous peoples' histories and lives, has been quietly understood as necessary by white Australians, for white people to colonise, settle, immigrate and own the land of others. The narrative further elaborates that these whites who settled in Australia were themselves marginalised as convicts or outcasts. They were poor people escaping economic hardship and political persecution, who were looking to work the land and find new means of livelihoods in the hopes of building a better life. These were, the narrative suggests, courageous civilisers, settlers far from home who pushed aside or did not understand indigenous law or knowledge as they struggled to learn to care for what was for them new and unknown land.

## Feminist political ecology in conversation with white settler narratives

In trying to engage with such white settler narratives I draw on the insights of Plumwood and other feminist writers to my attempt to understand 'otherwise' meanings for care. In this experimental engagement with the natureculture to which I was born, I have chosen to look at a puzzle that has intrigued me. Though there is now a rewriting of early settler histories and a stronger recognition of indigenous peoples' presence, there is a large majority of white Australians who do not care about indigenous peoples or their cultures and continue to want to replicate some part of the 'old country' natureculture. Thinking about how to include them in the seeing differently about our shared histories and the importance of recognising different cultures that share the land, I started to ask: so what do these people care about?

I asked this question of members of my own family, fifth and sixth generation white Australians living in rural Victoria. I realised they are among a considerable number of settled white Australians who have spent many happy years of their life caring for flowers, in my family's case the Begonia, 'a genus of perennial flowering plants with 1,795 different plant species native to moist subtropical and tropical climates' (Wikpedia 2018). For Australia it was an exotic breed of flowers. White Australians' habit of caring for the colourful garden flower, the Begonia, might seem an odd subject of interest for a feminist political ecologist. Most Begonia fanciers do not see themselves as involved in any feminist or political project; they enjoy privileged status and live comfortable lives. But it is precisely my concern how to include such people, literally my kin, by staying with the trouble of how to engage with people who are not interested in political or ecological change *per se*. So I search for possibilities for connecting with their very real care for flowers. In doing so I dig deeper into that natureculture that shapes my history and query traditional white settler narratives of conquest and erasure of the other. I would like to understand what are the possibilities in the act of care that generations of white Australians felt in the raising of the Begonia. Can this care and love for 'their' place and non-human others be extended to an inclusion of nurturing for others in those places be rekindled?

My story is about the possibilities for inclusive ecological justice that embraces Earthothers, as well as humans, as I probe for otherwise understanding of care within histories of violence and erasure.

## Caring for non-human others over generations

My sense of possibility for this form of care for Earthothers, is triggered by a tiny story of care captured in a short memo written for a local Australian orchid species society: a 2016 memo which was my uncle's memoriam for his mother, my maternal grandmother.

In the memo to the orchid society, my uncle speaks about the responsibility of care for begonia flowers through generations. My grandmother's grandmother came from Kilmarnock and the Isle of Skye, to the colony of Victoria in a scheme similar to that of Caroline Chisholm's project to settle poor Scottish immigrants by providing farming land to couples. Her family was given land around Ararat and Ballarat (Ilitis 1966, Harcourt 2018). My grandmother told me that story when she solemnly gave me a carved wooden plate that her grandmother had brought to Australia from Scotland. My grandmother lived all her life in the rural areas of the Western district of Victoria, though she always spoke of Scotland as home and would proudly use the odd Scottish word.

In his memo, my uncle speaks of the family's care for a fibrous Begonia Semperfloens with large pink double flowers originally grown by my great grandmother in Aarat, a rural town of the Western district of Victoria sometime in the 1890s. In the memo my uncle describes how he is now taking up his role as caretaker of the plant, recalling how my grandmother, who died in 1999, 'became responsible for it' in 1916. He goes on to note, that while his mother has died, the plant renews itself each year and lives with him still, in Melbourne (Bartrop 2000).

This story touched me because it was about cross-species caring for flowers by humans in communities through time, and it was happening in a very conservative part of my family. They would not consider themselves political but do belong to various local clubs and societies such as the Orchid Society or the Rotary Club. Why, I thought when reading it, was I touched by this memo? What did it say about the support and care shown in a rural community in Australia for the celebration and continuation of the life of a Begonia? What was this sense of responsibility for foreign flowers over generations, that intertwined with my uncle's care for my grandmother? The type of care and support shown, made me wonder – how does care for Earthothers by generations of white middle-class settlers sit alongside the violence of white settler Australia?

One story behind that memo is a story of privileged white middle class living with other species. My uncle, a retired engineer for many years, took care of flowers. He is considered eccentric, unmarried, with whole houses and sheds for his begonias and orchids. He also, as a single elderly man, took care of my grandmother in her last years as she became a child again. My childless uncle would feed his mother with custard tarts and tomato soup and buy her teddy bears. She was cared for, even as her eye sight faded, and her long grey hair, once so neat, became an unruly tangled nest. She was happy, cocooned in her son's house with its flowers and love. Leaving aside the story of love between elderly son and ageing mother, unusual in its own way, let me turn to look deeper into the culture of the begonia.

As it turns out, begonias have their own complex colonial history (Stevens, 2002, Tebbit 2005). Begonias were also settlers in Australia. Their original habitats vary from the hot and humid lowlands of Brazil to the mountains in Malaysia; dry areas of Mexico; as well as the river plains of southern Africa. Begonias were 'discovered' by Europeans in the seventeenth century in the Caribbean and named by a French King's botanist Charles Plumier. They play a modest role in the story of opening up of the 'new' world by colonialism, or the plundering of global natureculture by the Europeans. The Begoniaceae was officially recognised in 1700 by Joseph Pitton de Tournefort in his book *Institutiones Rei Herbariae Vol I*, and later by Carl Linnaeus in 1753 in his *Species Plantarum*. Begonias were transported to Britain in 1777 and then cultivated and bred. They became a popular export in the late 1800s to Australia as it was establishing itself as an outpost of civilisation, outgrowing its prisoner colony status. They became symbols of elegance, grown by families of means in rural towns and cities in the newly established suburban gardens. They belonged to those women and men who could devote their care to such exotic flowers with their colourful waxy petals which required time and water, resources that required a certain level of development in terms of urban infrastructure and economic surplus that allowed for leisure.

Begonias' physical adaptability also made them ideal for the Australian natureculture. For white settlers whose families all came from 'somewhere else' these plants with their pedigree linked them to the old countries, and to European botanical natureculture. Even if they came from many places, discovered and transported, these plants merged into the sense of success enjoyed by white settler histories in the garden displays of rural towns and suburban Australia of what was called the 'lucky country'. As one pamphlet states, 'these plants will be happy in many different locations […] you have a most attractive family of plants suitable for many different climates, situations and applications' (Valin. n.d). Begonias are depicted as adaptable and cheerful, ideal companions for white settlers who had the time for domestic pleasure (Sharp n.d). My great grandmother and grandmother, women who were devoted to their gardens, enjoyed designing spaces to grow and display begonias along with other exotic species like orchids, and their vegetable gardens.

Begonias were flowers for pleasure, not only featured in the domestic arena but also in displays in Australian botanical public gardens. In Ballarat my grandfather was among a group of successful business men who developed the town during the early twentieth century and who founded the Ballarat Begonia Festival. This festival was an early community cultural festival founded in 1953 and was inspired by British festivals that my grandfather had visited during and immediately after the war years. The festival was a post-Second World War effort to enhance cultural activities in a small rural town through the care and display of the 700 begonia plants. The begonia had been growing in the botanical gardens since 1896; new grounds were created around the lake and there was much fanfare when the young English queen visited the festival in 1954.

By the 2000s, the Ballarat Botanical Gardens records show how the numbers of begonias stored and grown in the Botanical Gardens' nursery has reached 2,500 plants, all of which require daily care for nearly ten months of the year. In late September the tubers are potted and placed in a heated glasshouse to initiate growth. They are given daily small amounts of water until growth takes off and by late October/November cuttings can commence. Stems are thinned down to leave only one or two, and by December they are re-potted to their final pot containing slow release fertiliser and moved to an unheated glasshouse. The plants are watered by hand at each stage and require daily checks.

As I delved deeper into the care shown for this non-native Earthother, I found there are several Australian based websites devoted to explaining how to grow and care for particular types of begonia.[5] The descriptions are loving in their sensuous detail. For example, the leaf colourings of the Rex Begonia imported from Assam in India are described as 'running the gamut of shades of precious metals' and its leaf textures are described as 'beautiful fabrics of silk, satin, velvet, brocade, crepe, tweed and soft woollens' (The Victorian Begonia Society n.d.). Cultorum Begonias are described as the 'most generous givers of themselves of all the begonias.' They need to be treated gently 'as with all begonia seed, it is very fine so try not to breathe too heavily when working with it. Do not cover seed with mix after planting, just press gently so the seed touches the seed-mix' (The Victorian Begonia Society n.d.). This evidence of interspecies care, which echoed the shared love of my grandmother and my uncle for the century-old fibrous Begonia Semperfloens with its large pink double flowers, pushed me to ponder further.

As I looked at the websites, historical essays and pamphlets produced by the men and women working in Australian botanical gardens or belonging to begonia societies, I wondered what do these hours of gardening and caring for plants in communities of care indicate about the evolution of this particular form of Australian capitalism? How do we read the pleasure, love and care for plants in private gardens or on display in botanical gardens? What possibilities are there for the future built on the generations of care by white settlers for Earthothers, for the exotic and beguiling begonia? How does all this caring activity mark a particular form of natureculture?

But then again, what does it hide, displace or erase?

Going back to my earlier awareness of the otherwise of my childhood home, Adelaide, there is another, far less caring side to the story of the founding of Ballarat and the surrounding countryside. This story, I discovered, was far from what I had been told as a child as I viewed the splendour of the begonias in the botanical gardens and admired them in the garden of my grandmother.

Once again, I tried to uncover what I could about the thousands of years of settlement that has been erased, and is now being re-acknowledged.

Before white settlers arrived in the 1830s, the area around Ballarat was home to 25 Aboriginal tribes known as the Wathaurong or Watha wurrung people. Each tribe occupied its own areas in the region, living off and caring for the land, joining together for ceremonial occasions or to trade.

European occupation of Wathaurong lands in 1835 was one of violent dispossession. This frontier violence is captured in Ian Clark's book *Scars in the Landscape: A Register of Massacre Sites in Western Victoria, 1803–1859* (1995) which provides a detailed study of massacres in the region. These are horror stories of how indigenous people were hunted and killed in order to make way for sheep farming. The chronicles of the time hide the massacres of the indigenous people as white settlers set out to tame the land and recreate the agriculture of home, introducing foreign flora and fauna which destroyed the indigenous species from singing birds to the stag, hare, rabbit, fox and sparrow, which quickly became pests. An infamous example of ecologically disastrous agricultural experiments of colonial Australia, in both ecological and economic terms, is the introduction of the rabbit into rural Australia. As one chronicle states, rabbits:

> devastated millions of acres of grass and grain lands, robbed the farmers of their harvests, lowered the value of land, and the Legislature has intervened with special laws for the lessening of the plague, which still prevails, however, to an alarming extent in some parts of the colony.
>
> (Withers 1887)

Such damage of naturecultures was integral and considered simply inevitable in the stories of the white European adventure. It is also highly racialised. As the white settlers explore and push West, violence is barely recorded as indigenous people are encountered and pushed aside, though the violence is evoked in names such as Murderous Valley, and there are notes on the 'side' of deaths of indigenous groups due to small pox. These racialised accounts focus on the white settler development of the town of Ballarat and the discovery of gold and squatters creating pastoral holdings.

The pastoral expansion of Victoria happened rapidly after the expedition of 'explorer' Major Thomas Mitchell in 1836. There was an attempt to control frontier violence between settlers and Aboriginal people in the 1840s, but the impact of gold brought huge changes both in terms of environmental damage and hardship to indigenous peoples. Indigenous people also took part in the gold rush, employed to guard the gold and participating in the boom that came to Ballarat where the largest minefields were struck.

But the narrative is of economic boom and progress; little space is given to what happened to indigenous cultures on the frontiers. Glimpses of interaction can be made out in the naming of landscapes borrowing from indigenous languages, the occasional interest in indigenous peoples' lives and knowledge, but there is rarely concern about the use of the land by indigenous people, what the loss meant, including the meaning of their gatherings and ways. Mostly there is a casual mention of native deaths as they were driven off the land to make way for sheep 'runs.' Or wonderment expressed about why didn't they know of or use the gold? There is a grumbling about 'laziness' and the demands for food (flour and sugar) handouts for work done on the farms. The unstated assumption in these narratives is that this land was for the taking, the indigenous peoples were a race that were ignorant, dying out and were, inevitably, being replaced by civilisation as the land was usefully and prosperously peopled by members of the British Empire in the (inevitable) march of history.

## Learning to tell Gaia stories[6]

We are responsible for telling these stories of care, and violence, and how they inform each other. How do these histories of this 'foreign' plant species fit in the violent history of white settlers and their brutal treatment of Aboriginal populations as Other and the different stories of (sometimes lack of) care reflect 'bigger scheme of things'? These histories intermingle with the soil where the begonias grow, where my grandparents are buried, where memories are being rekindled. My story of the begonia is not so innocent. Below the care and love of the delicate begonia there are the damaging effects of introducing such foreign flowers into indigenous pre-colonial Australian ecological systems which went hand in hand with the capitalisation and appropriation of the begonias themselves.

If a common liveable world is to be composed bit by bit, we need to learn to tell Gaia stories aware of such uncomfortable histories that inform our times. How do we live with such histories, as we find answers to the present troubles? As a feminist political ecologist, I would like to learn both from the violence and from the stories of the love of begonias as I search for new understandings of economies and ecologies, that take on board diverse matters of fact, concern and care. I am interested in how to build lives that take on board the care for begonias and the need to respect the loss of the culture and nature of those peoples who knew and lived with the land otherwise, as we search for new forms of worlding. How do we align with different forms of care and to take responsibility for the entangled mess of the capitalocene?

If we are to find more inclusive freedom and quality of life for humanity living with other species, it means pulling back and scaling down. It means stopping to understand what are our relations to our histories and to Earthothers. We need stories that help us to reworld, reimagine, relive and reconnect with each other in multispecies well-being.

We need to question these early histories of progress and modernity in order to relationally unmake capitalocene and find the otherwise in capitalist economies. Such a project means acknowledging and challenging the narratives of white settler colonies, in order to live new ways of being and to transform ways we deal with the world.

This chapter is just a beginning of how to see and understand the care which informs historical white settler framing of nature, ecology, culture and how to include cultural histories of specific non-market driven forms of living with nature that were destroyed in the making of the world which defines natureculture relations in Western Victoria. So how is the story of care for begonias part of the story of colonial, capitalist power and the struggle over the ecosystem and land of this particular natureculture?

Unfortunately, I have more questions than answers – but nevertheless – what kinds of disclosing are possible? How can I tell this story of caring for begonias by generations of white settler families and the uncovering of the violence and loss of indigenous peoples and species that are part of the untold story behind the development of farms, botanical gardens, artificial lakes and suburban settlements?

## Interpreting histories

Such an interpretation requires imagination. Seeing possibilities can be difficult to do given the level of violence uncovered in the conflicting stories of hope and suffering in the Australian stories of 'development' with its erasure of and violence to people, environment and thousands of years of natureculture.

In order to interpret this history, I need to digress again, but not to delve into archives, oral histories and dreamings, art and documentaries. Instead I instinctively turn to the insights of fictional stories that build imaginatively on painful stories of displacement, violence and the search for belonging that marks white Australian natureculture.

I turn to two books which imagine ways to bring together Australia's histories of care and violence. The first, the novel *The Secret River* (2005) by white Australian Kate Grenville, depicts the deep wounds when local black indigenous Australians are viciously murdered leaving 'the dirt trampled and marked with great stains. And a great shocked silence hanging over everything' (Grenville, 2005: 309). The story is one of care that went wrong when a newly arrived white settler family was unable to read the clash of different cultures and the diverse understandings of the land between indigenous peoples and white settlers. Grenville captures the deep unease of white settler compliance and guilt at the huge violence wrecked on 'the blacks.' She shows the horrors of the erasure, the violence and the unshakeable sense of white superiority to claim the right to destroy. At the same time, she depicts the struggle of the white settlers to nourish the land once they have taken it, and the pain felt as the one remaining unspeakably wounded indigenous Australian watches.

Exotic plants also figure symbolically in the novel, as a newly arrived white immigrant woman tries unsuccessfully to plant a newly staked out garden with roses and daffodils that shrivel and fail to take root: 'In spite of her care the garden did not thrive [...] The only plant that flourished was a bush of blood-red geraniums' (Grenville 2005: 319) which grew from a cutting her neighbour gave her, knowing that the hardy geranium would survive.

Grenville paints a desolate picture as the woman seeks to find some sense of belonging on a land reeking of violence as she tries to recreate something of the British nature she knows. The woman, Sarah, represents how Australians feel such deep guilt and unease, not only because of the horrific violence which enabled her to stake claim to the garden, but also because of her lack of knowledge about what could grow in the heat of the Australian bush. The only flower that survives is the hardy geranium, imported from the Mediterranean. Though smelling of dust it thrives, symbolically bearing the red blood colour of the massacre. The colour and hardiness of the flower is a reminder of the violence which happened on the land in which it now takes root. But the act of planting the geranium also hints at possibilities of a new community as it grows from a cutting that the neighbour gives, her knowing what flowers can survive. Symbolically the garden hints at the importance of care among white settlers on the blood of the murdered indigenous people.

In Grenville's story, exotic flowers are symbols of the British culture taking root in what the settlers see as the harsh landscape of Australia. They fail to learn from the indigenous people they kill, but at the same time, Grenville narrates how there is a love of the actual land which offers possibilities for former convicts and those seeking space in the new world of Australia as the settlers struggle together to create a space for gardens in the bush, defying its inhospitality for white skins and delicate foreign flowers.

Grenville points to the importance of care of flowers and gardens as symbols of survival and possibility. The care of begonias follows this storyline as an important symbol of development – of wealth and time – of technical ability and skill to care for water-needy exotics – linking Australians to other places of civilisation as they lovingly reproduce a natureculture which celebrates exotic beauty while at the same time overrides other histories and nature.

The history of white settlers and their love of the land is the subject of another book by a white Australian, Peter Reid. His study of *Belonging: Australians, Place and Aboriginal Ownership* (2000) is a personal ethnography which sets out the feelings of white Australians for the land. His book asks how can 'we non-Indigenous Australians justify our continuous presence and love for this country while the Indigenous people remain dispossessed and their history unacknowledged' (Reid 2000: 3). He argues that white Australians' emotions and intuitive love for place are part of deep belonging. His book is based on interviews with white Australians of different ages, histories and backgrounds who speak of their love for 'country.' Learning from indigenous Australians he takes 'country' itself as a living being. He depicts all Australians as caretakers in a prefigurative sense of the future, recognising that the history and future of Australia is informed 'by the sites of evil as well as good' and 'believing that belonging means sharing' place, land and the contradiction it brings (Reid 2000: 223).

The message from Reid is that belonging to a country (or land or place) requires care and sharing with others and knowledge of the natureculture. Most of all, it requires care and a sense of both a history and a future.

## Feminist imaginaries and scientific fabulations

As J.K. Gibson-Graham states, 'feminism's remapping of political space and possibility suggests the ever present opportunity for local economic transformation that does not require (though it does not preclude and indeed promotes) transformation at larger scales' (Gibson-Graham 2008: 656).

Learning from the fictional retelling of white settlers' invasion of others and taking hope from Reid's study of white Australians' love of country, my chapter's stories sketch out how we can tell tales otherwise as we work out ways to survive climate change, economic crisis and social disorder of the capitalocene.

It is a time for the telling of new stories both true and fabulous as Tsing shows in her story of the art of living on a damaged planet. In these stories nature is not just a backdrop for the story of humanity. It is the stuff of our stories that requires serious discussions among social scientists, economists, ecologists and feminists as we learn that care for life requires the interplay of many kinds of beings, and many understandings of the possibilities of coexistence with environmental loss, disturbance and survival.

If we are to find our collaborative survival we need to see how cross-species interact, how ecologies are about how many species live together – not necessarily in harmony nor in conflict and conquest. My stories of the begonia are rooted in violent and disturbing histories but also in species interaction and in care for and by white Australians. The story of my grandmother and uncle is one of care for Earthothers as well as of love and care for humans. They are complicated stories, of sensuous pleasure, of empire building, of erasure and yet, perhaps, of possibilities.

In this chapter I have not gone deep enough into the species interaction in the natureculture of white settler Australia. I have a hunch that there are many struggles to be seen in these historical landscapes strewn with ruin (Tsing 2015) but at the same time they could show how to care by looking in the past, and to the future, we might find 'models of living and dying worlds and their critters' (Haraway 2016: 32).

But which ideas, which relations, which activities are ultimately important in our modelling of new lifeworlds? Can my tentative story of the begonia, of the care of flowers in white settler Australia, be a Gaia story making a 'hot compost pile for still possible pasts, presents and futures' (Haraway 2016: 31)?

My search is how to transform and build on these stories of care, as prevalent and viable. How can these stories help to transform local economies into everyday ethical and political practice of constructing communities of care for natureculture in the face of deep erasures, violence, climate change and urban developments which deny the importance of care?

## Natureculture otherwise

It seems the story of care of the begonia is complicated further as I kept digging and find that alongside the begonia and orchid societies are movements to encourage gardeners in Western Victoria to love and care for indigenous plants. As one website reassures gardeners: 'You can never stop learning, and if you stop and notice the subtle things, they can be just as appealing as the showy exotic plants (Federation University 2018). The local technological university teaches about indigenous species and local clubs plant native shrubs and bushes.

The process of reconciliation extends to the recognition of indigenous cultures. Ballarat has now four signs of welcome and goodbye in the Wathaurang language of the traditional owners of the lands around Ballarat. According to Karen Heap, the chief executive officer of the Ballarat and District Aboriginal Co-operative (BADAC), 'Kim barne barre Wathaurong' (Welcome to Wathaurong country) and 'Kungadee' (goodbye) are translations into written word of an oral language handed down the generations. Such signs are a recognition of the need for change as they aim to 'enabl[e] the broader community to understand that there were Aboriginal people living here and there still are' (Peake 2009). BADAC was established in 1979 as a co-operative to deliver health, social, welfare and community development programs to local Aboriginal people (BADAC 2018). Along with services for indigenous people there are cultural education support programmes, museums and heritage centres built by 'Aboriginal people for Aboriginal people' with the further aim to 'stamp out negative stereotypes about the city's 1200-strong Aboriginal population.'[7]

The embrace of the native plant and movements towards reconciliation among the community living on Wathaurong land are on the fringes of mainstream (white and prosperous) Ballarat economy and society. However, such activities are part of a shifting politics of location and relations. They are creating possibilities of new collective conditions from which agency, experience and awareness of others can emerge in what Aimee Carillo Rowe identifies as 'differential belonging' (2005: 16). Differential belonging recognises that we learn to care through relations of belonging determined by political conditions that bind us to others often in ways which are not always visible. In these small shifts of care for indigenous natureculture the effects of colonial modernity and histories of erasure are being acknowledged, and the idea of belonging allows a politics of engagement.

## Conclusion: Differential belonging

My story requires more research and reflection. It radiates out of my personal questioning about my own sense of belonging to a blighted history, and natureculture which thwarts my sense of justice and community. It is also based on an aspiration to take up cross-species care in a country that is trying to acknowledge and learn from precolonial naturecultures.

As Carillo Rowe suggests, '[t]he sites of our belonging constitute how we see the world, what we value, who we are becoming' (2005: 16). In writing this story I am engaging in research which investigates and makes more transparent interspecies and transracial belongings. I do so with the hope that such research can feed into political forums which rework power across lines of difference. As Chandra Talpade Mohanty states:

> [A]s we develop more complex, nuanced modes of asking questions and as scholarship in a number of relevant fields begins to address histories of colonialism, capitalism, race, and gender as inextricably interrelated, our very conceptual maps are redrawn and transformed.
>
> (1991: 300)

It is a small beginning. I am still asking more questions than finding answers. How can I redraw these conceptual maps in ways that have political impact? How can I be accountable for the processes which continue to produce my privilege? How do I navigate across boundaries of difference in order to build intimate knowledge which lies between self and other? How do I find ways to heal histories and cross lines that divide, separate and wound?[8] What kind of active listening can I do that takes me beyond my own worlding and be in solidarity with First Nations epistemologies of listening, listening and refusal, listening and decolonising methodologies in order to expose the uneven flows of power and privilege invested in unjust social and political arrangements of which others know, and feel and live? As Megan Davis eloquently states: 'Most destructively, Australia has rejected self-determination – freedom, agency, choice, autonomy, dignity – as being fundamental to Indigenous humanness and development' (Davis 2016).[9]

As a feminist political ecologist shaped by my white first-world experience and knowledge of natureculture, I am trying to 'disembark from the colonial constraints of my belonging' and to reconfigure the relationship between histories of the 'coloniser' and 'colonised' in Australia's natureculture (bell hooks 2000 cited in Carillo Rowe 2005: 25). Can the concept of differential belonging allow me to interrogate both privilege and oppression, recognise the pain of trying to reconnect people with care for the Earth while acknowledging the ongoing damage of colonial violence? My rewriting of this particular historical narrative of erasure, of struggle and violence, of care and reconciliation, I hope, suggests new connections and invites new meanings that reach across colonial violence and racism as well as entertaining interspecies interactions. Such transracial histories and futures, such Gaia stories, are necessarily bound up in caring for Earthothers as we continue to embrace relations of belonging in contingent ways.

## Notes

1　I am deliberately echoing Donna Haraway's invitation to stay with the trouble (Haraway 2016).

2　I use the term 'otherwise' following Catherine Walsh (2016) and other Latin American scholars who question the 'other' meanings of key terms, in the case of Walsh of gender, in order to point to non Eurocentric understandings of concepts which we tend to universalize from western systems of knowledge.

3  Val Plumwood helps us understand how we need to re-imagine ourselves ecologically as we link environmentalism and social justice, understanding our connection with the world of animals, plants and minerals – what Plumwood poetically calls Earthothers (Plumwood 1993, p. 137).

4  See in particular her moving story published posthumously 'The Eye of the Crocodile' where she reflects on surviving a crocodile attack (Plumwood 2012).

5  There are five state wide websites which have a further listing of regional clubs see https://begoniaaustralis.wordpress.com/begonia-sites/ [Accessed 23 September 2018] and the website of the Melbourne Begonia Society (Melbourne Begonia Society n.d.).

6  The term Gaia Stories comes from Donna Haraways' book *Staying with the Trouble* (2016) and refers to telling imaginative stories that consider how the Earth is to survive given all the damage humanity has wrecked upon it (and our livelihoods). It is a reference to the Goddess Gaia who in ancient Greek Mythology is one of the first deities and a divine personification of the Earth.

7  Note the total Ballarat population in 2018 is 100,000 (Population Australia 2018).

8  See Carillo Rowe 2005: 38 for a very succinct and useful way to go about looking at these questions of whiteness and privilege as a Chicana feminist engaging in the politics of belonging.

9  Megan Davis is Pro Vice Chancellor Indigenous and Professor of Law at the University of New South Wales who delivered the 2017 'Uluru Statement from the Heart' from the national constitutional convention at Uluru' (Referendum Council 2017).

# References

Adelaidia, n.d. South Australian Government, Adelaide [online]. Adelaide: South Austrian Government. Available from: http://adelaidia.sa.gov.au/subjects/kaurna-people [Accessed 14 June 2018].

Afflick, R., 2012. BADAC opens new cultural museum in Ballarat. *The Courier* [online]. 3 April. Available from: https://www.thecourier.com.au/story/63154/badac-opens-new-cultural-museum-in-ballarat/ [Accessed 14 June 2018].

Bartrop, E.M., 2000. In Loving Memory of Madge Evelyn Bartrop [online]. Available from: http://www.australianorchidfoundation.org.au/madge-evelyn-bartrop/ [Accessed 5 June 2017].

Bassel, L., 2017. *The Politics of Listening: Possibilities and Challenges of Democratic Life.* London: Palgrave.

Carillo Rowe, A., 2005. Be longing: toward a feminist politics of relation. *NWSA Journal*, 17 (2), 15–46.

Clark, I., 1995. *Scars in the Landscape: A Register of Massacre Sites in Western Victoria, 1803–1859.* Canberra: Aboriginal Studies Press.

Davis, M., 2016. Listening but not hearing: process has trumped substance in Indigenous affairs. *The Conversation* [online]. 21 June. Available from: https://theconversation.com/listening-but-not-hearing-process-has-trumped-substance-in-indigenous-affairs-55161 [Accessed 3 June 2018].

Escobar, A., 2008. *Territories of Difference: Place, Movements, Life, Redes.* Durham, NC: Duke University Press.

Escobar, A. and Harcourt, W. 2005. Practices of difference: introducing 'women and the politics of place'. *In:* W. Harcourt and A. Escobar, eds., *Women and the Politics of Place.* Bloomfield, CT: Kumarian Press, 1–19.

Federation University Australia, 2018. Indigenous plants for Ballarat gardens. Ballarat: Faculty of Science and Technology. [online] Available from: https://federation.edu.au/faculties-and-schools/faculty-of-science-and-technology/community-engagement/indigenous-plants-for-ballarat-gardens [Accessed 14 June 2018].

Gibson-Graham, J.K., 2008. Place-based globalism: a new imaginary of revolution. *Rethinking Marxism*, 20 (4), 659–64.

Grenville, K., 2005. *The Secret River*. Melbourne: Text Publishing.

Haraway, D.J., 1991. A cyborg manifesto: science, technology, and socialist-feminism in the late twentieth century. *In*: D. Haraway, *Simians, Cyborgs and Women: The Reinvention of Nature*. New York: Routledge.

Haraway, D.J., 2015. Anthropocene, capitalocene, plantationocene, Chtulucene: making kin. *Environmental Humanities*, 6, 159–65.

Haraway, D.J., 2016. *Staying with the Trouble. Making Kin in the Chthulucene*. Durham, NC: Duke University Press.

Harcourt T. 2018. 'From the Goldbergs to the Icebergs: a family history.' Unpublished paper.

Harcourt, W. and Escobar, A., eds, 2005. *Women and the Politics of Place*. London: Zed Books.

Iltis, J. 1966. Chisholm, Caroline 1808–1877 [online]. Canberra: Australian National University, Available from: http://adb.anu.edu.au/biography/chisholm-caroline-1894 [Accessed 18 June 2018].

Melbourne Begonia Society, n.d. Links. [online] Available from: http://www.begoniasmelb. org.au/ [Accessed 5 June 2017].

Mellor, M., 1997. *Feminism and Ecology: An Introduction*. New York: New York University Press.

Mies, M. and Shiva, V., 1993. *Ecofeminism*. London: Zed Books.

Mohanty, C.T., 1991. Cartographies of struggle. *In*: C.T. Mohanty, A. Rosso and L. Torres, eds., *Third World Women and the Politics of Feminism*. Bloomington, IN: Indiana University Press, 1–49.

Peake, J. 2019 Welcome in Wathaurong. *ABC* [online] 19 January. Available from: http://www.abc.net.au/local/stories/2009/01/19/2468958.htm [Accessed 14 June 2018].

Plumwood, V., 1991a. Ecofeminism: an overview and discussion of positions and arguments. *Australasian Journal of Philosophy* [online], 64 (1), 120–38. Available from: doi:10.1111/j.1527-2001.1991.tb00206.x JSTOR 3810030 [Accessed 26 May 2018].

Plumwood, V., 1991b. Nature, self, and gender: feminism, environmental philosophy, and the critique of rationalism. *Hypatia* [online], 6 (1), 3–27. Available from: http://dx.doi.org/10.1080/00048402.1986.9755430 [Accessed 26 May 2018].

Plumwood, V., 1993. *Feminism and the Mastery of Nature*. London: Routledge.

Plumwood, V., 2012. *The Eye of the Crocodile*. Canberra: Australian National University E-Press.

Population Australia. 2018. Ballarat Population 2018 [online]. Available from: www.population.net.au/ballarat-population/ [Accessed 14 June 2018].

Referendum Council, 2017. Uluru Statement from the Heart [online] Available from: https://www.referendumcouncil.org.au/sites/default/files/2017-05/Uluru_Statement_From_The_Heart_0.PDF [Accessed 3 June 2018].

Reid, P., 2000. *Belonging: Australians, Place and Aboriginal Ownership*. Cambridge: Cambridge University Press.

Salleh, A., 1997. *Ecofeminism as Politics*. London: Zed Books.

Sharp, P. n.d. Begonias [online]. Available from: http://ibegonias.filemakerstudio.com.au/PeterSharp/ [Accessed 5 June 2017].

Shiva, V., 1988. *Staying Alive: Women, Ecology and Development*. London: Zed Books.

South Australian Museum. 2013. Australian Aboriginal cultures. [online] Available from: http://www.samuseum.sa.gov.au/explore/museum-galleries/australian-aboriginal-cultures. [Accessed 14 June 2018].

Stevens, M., 2002. *Begonias*. Richmond Hill, ON: Firefly Books.

Tebbit, M.C., 2005. *Begonias: Cultivation, Identification, and Natural History*. Portland, OR: Timber Press.

The Ballarat and District Aboriginal Co-operative (BADAC), 2018. Our Services [online]. Available from: http://www.badac.net.au/services/ [Accessed 14 June 2018].

The Begonia Society, n.d. Cultural Notes [online]. Available from: https://begoniasvictoria.wordpress.com/cultural-notes-2/ [Accessed 5 June 2017].

Tsing, A., 2015. *The Mushroom at the End of the World: On the Possibility of Life in the Capitalist Ruins*. Princeton, NJ: Princeton University Press.

Valin, C., n.d. Down To Earth With Begonias [online]. Available from: http://www.bigbegoniarevival.com/charles-valin/breeding-history-begonias/ [Accessed 5 June 2017].

Walsh, C. 2016. On Gender and Its 'Otherwise'. *In:* Harcourt, W., ed., *The Palgrave Handbook of Gender and Development: Critical Engagements in Theory and Practice*. London: Palgrave, 34–47. Available from: https://link.springer.com/chapter/10.1007/978-1-137-38273-3_3 [Accessed 23 September 2018].

Warren, K., 1997. *Ecofeminism: Women, Culture, Nature*. Bloomington: Indiana University Press.

Wikpedia, 2018. Begonia [online] Available from: https://en.wikipedia.org/wiki/Begonia [Accessed 14 June 2018].

Withers, W.B. 1887. *The History of Ballarat, from the First Pastoral Settlement to the Present Time* [online]. Reprinted online by the Ballarat Acclimatisation Society. Available from: http://gutenberg.net.au/ebooks13/1304971h.html#Image34 [Accessed 7 June 2017].

Wolfe, P., 2006. Settler colonialism and the elimination of the native. *Journal of Genocide Research* [online], 8 (4), 397–409. Available from: DOI:10.1080/14623520601056240 [Accessed 26 May 2018].

# 4 Environmental feminisms

## A story of different encounters

*Karijn van den Berg*

## Introduction: Living in the 'Anthropocene'

Since Paul Crutzen reintroduced the term 'Anthropocene' scientists and scholars increasingly use it to describe the current epoch that 'we humans' are living in (Crutzen 2006). The Anthropocene is used in popular discourses to refer to the current geological epoch as being marked by the significant global impact that humans have on the planet. Negative geological developments, such as climate change and 'global warming,' in this frame are viewed as a result of human domination. It assumes a growing influence and domination of humans over nature, and refers to how the human seems to put itself at the centre of the earth.

The Anthropocene age is gaining attention within critical theory, including in feminist theorising, with the renewed interest in the environment, posthuman and non-human subjects or matter. This chapter will look into the responses of ecofeminism, new materialism, posthumanism and Feminist Political Ecology (FPE) in order to explore how feminist concerns come together with and encounter environmentalist concerns. This discussion is of particular importance as environmentalists, scientists, activists and farmers are looking at environmental change in ways that are reinforcing power relations along gender, race and class lines.

Different feminist schools of thought such as ecofeminism, feminist new materialism, posthumanism and FPE think differently about the environment, discussed as naturecultures (Haraway 2003) in times of *capitalist-patriarchy* (Mies and Shiva 1993) as an *intra-action* (Barad 2008). These diverse approaches that are both environmentalist and feminist help us to rethink nature–human relations in relation to patriarchal, Eurocentric, capitalist and anthropocentric assumptions. These theoretical positions can be viewed also from activist feminist and environmentalist frameworks. It is important to recall that feminism and environmentalism were both practices first and theory second.[1]

## The Anthropocene and environmentalism

Reflecting on the Anthropocene, postcolonial scholar Dipesh Chakrabarty argues in his article 'The climate of history: four theses' (2009), that what is at stake is a negative development in which the environment is used and adapted to the needs of humans, who through their use of fossil fuels and other related activities have become a 'geological agent' on the planet (Chakrabarty 2009: 209).[2] It places the human at the centre of the Earth, superior to all other species and nature itself. As a result of this development a fall-back on the Enlightenment ideal of reason has taken place among scientists as a possible 'solution' to stop climate change and the further 'ruination' of 'planet Earth' by humans. Vassos Argyrou argues that this ideal of reason is part of a larger 'modernist paradigm' in which much environmentalist thought is currently embedded.

In his book *The Logic of Environmentalism: Anthropology, Ecology and Postcoloniality* (2005) Argyrou argues that although modernity's understanding of nature and culture has now been superseded by that of environmentalism, the power to define the meaning of both, and hence the meaning of the world itself, remains in the same (Western) hands. Argyrou analyses and criticises the extent to which environmentalism, both as a movement and as a school of thought, still reiterates the logic of the 'modernist paradigm' that is white, male and rational. Although nature in this modernist logic was considered something to be mastered, now it is increasingly seen to be something at risk, something vulnerable that needs to be protected. However, Argyrou argues that this can be considered a reiteration of the same approach, as it remains very anthropocentric with its focus on protecting and preserving 'nature' as a resource for humans. Argyrou points out that environmentalism is very much a result of modernist and humanist lines of thinking (2005: 5). For instance, if we follow the notion that Europeans did not hold the 'right' approach in mastering nature, as it is now decaying, it often follows that we need to 'return' to 'traditional' knowledges that are now labelled as 'indigenous' as they might hold more holistic and 'better' approaches to preserve 'nature.' According to Argyrou, such discourses might seem to focus on the particular value of the knowledge and experience of indigenous populations as tools in current geopolitical times, but often overlook or fail to specify what such tools might be. Therefore, it might be that it is in fact not so much about this knowledge and experience, but rather what these populations are meant to represent, 'namely, the ideal of living in "harmony with nature"' (Argyrou 2005: 70). Demanding these 'indigenous' Others to educate a Western, modern non-indigenous audience thus not only exoticises them, but is refraining from taking any responsibility for climate change and dealing with 'nature.' Preserving and encountering the environment then becomes something for the indigenous Other to take on.

Argyrou's critique is useful when looking at environmentalism and feminism as movements or schools of thought, and more generally when looking at discourses surrounding climate change as these often continue to conceptualise the environment or 'nature' as a passive entity. Nature continues to be there for 'us' humans to use and cultivate. It is important to take into account power relations among humans, as well as between nature and humanity. A feminist focus to environmentalist thinking brings into account such gender, race and class power relations, and furthermore does not take hierarchies between humans and nature for granted.

## Why environmentalism needs feminism (and vice versa)

There is an expanding variety of feminist scholars who include environmental concerns in their feminist theory. One of the first was Vandana Shiva, an Indian feminist scholar working on issues of colonialism, ecology and development within a feminist and environmental justice framework (Shiva 1997, 2010, Mies and Shiva 1993). Shiva argues that feminist theories should implement an environmentalist framework in order to avoid the dominant reductionist philosophy of a constructed nature, since it would contribute to a passive and invisible understanding of nature, organisms and non-human actors: '[I]n a reductionist approach to bio-technology, issues of social justice also vanish along with a concern for ecology' (Shiva 1997: 25). Vice versa, environmental theorists need to look critically beyond the anthropocentric, capitalist and patriarchal discourses on climate change and environmental issues, and include feminist analyses that take different power relations into account as well when looking beyond strictly human realms.

For instance, in 'Sustainable food and privilege; why green is always white (and male and upper-class)' Janani Balasubramanian (2015) calls out the whiteness and inherent privilege of many green movements that reiterate this modernist and liberal logic. Balasubramanian points out the ways in which the food reform movement today is largely predicated on privilege and rather shaky foundations as to how it deals with gender and race 'with its focus on a largely white and privileged American dream' (2015: 399). This is not to indicate that such activists are not concerned with issues of identity, but rather to point out how their discourse prevents conversations on history, justice, race and food in various ways. This is problematic as food and environmental justice are mostly issues of class and race, aspects that are often not taken into account.

Likewise, environmentalist feminist Stacy Alaimo alerts that this social justice dimension of environmentalism is often not taken into account. According to Alaimo, it is important to continuously work through discursive critique in order to explore the language used to refer to nature, the implications this language use has for environmentalisms and how it is entangled with notions of gender, class, race and sexuality (Alaimo 2010: 70). This discursive critique can be applied by looking at the rhetoric that different environmentalist feminist scholars and approaches use. One feminist strand in which this might be most obvious is ecofeminism that links 'women' and 'nature.'

## Ecofeminism: Women and nature

Ecofeminism is concerned with intersections of gender, socio-economics and the environment. Many feminist theorists describe how during the enlightenment, the mind became associated with reason and masculinity, while the body was linked to an irrational female nature. All modes of thinking seemed to have become dualistic: subject/object, mind/body, male/female, nature/nurture, black/white (Fausto-Sterling 2014: 298). The unmarked category was thereby constituted in the figure of the 'Man of Reason' (Lloyd 1984): the normative position that the white, European, able-bodied, rational man holds as the ideal universal and liberal subject of science and humanism (Braidotti 2013: 24). The 'mastery of nature' became an aspect of this humanist European man, one of his achievements as proof of European cultural superiority, a mark of civilisation as ground and legitimisation of colonialism (Argyrou 2005: 4). Vandana Shiva explains in her work how views on gender, nature and colonialism came together in the idea of 'development.' According to Shiva, this idea of development is a continuation of colonisation as it exploits and excludes women, degrades and exploits nature, and exploits and erodes other cultures (2010: 2). Such ecofeminist analysis has pointed out that views of nature are linked to colonialism and racialised and gendered ideologies.

Ecofeminism is not a singular theory, movement or approach, and different focal points can be identified within ecofeminism. Anne Fausto-Sterling distinguishes four different strands of ecofeminism: liberal, Marxist, cultural and socialist. Liberal ecofeminism accepts the idea of a passive nature, which is subject to engineering attempts to control and manipulate it. In this view, humans are seen as rational subjects that are able to dominate the earth. Marxist ecofeminists also see this domination or control over nature as important for humans, in this case more collectively, but in their theory it is more related to human freedom: 'nature provides the material basis (food, raw materials, and so on) upon which we build human life' (Fausto-Sterling 2014: 299). Thirdly, there are cultural ecofeminists, who view nature as spiritual and personal. They see human domination and control as the cause of environmental issues, rather than the cure or solution. They celebrate the perceived connection between women and nature, in the belief that male-dominated environmental movements overlook environmental threats to the female production (Fausto-Sterling 2014: 300). Lastly, although comparable to the Marxist ecofeminists, socialist ecofeminists distance themselves from the other ecofeminist movements, which in their view fail to recognise nature as an active participant. Rather, they see 'the concept of nature' as more socially and historically constructed. They strive towards an equal partnership between humans and nature, and examine the effect of colonial domination over women, indigenous inhabitants and nature (Fausto-Sterling 2014: 301).

By addressing the gendered view of nature in relation to capitalism, Anne Fausto-Sterling points out similarities with larger debates within contemporary feminist theories, such as thinking in terms of sex/gender. By using the figuration of nature to point out the limitations of this gender distinction – the reiteration of a masculine/feminine dichotomy – she shows that we can produce knowledge departing from nature as our starting point, and that theories that discuss the nature of the body are of particular relevance today.

This alignment of modernity, capitalism and patriarchy is also at the heart of the book *Ecofeminism* by Maria Mies and Vandana Shiva, as they write in their introduction:

> Our aim is to go beyond this narrow [capitalist-patriarchal] perspective and to express our diversity and, in different ways, address the inherent inequalities in world structures which permit the North to dominate the South, men to dominate women, and the frenetic plunder of ever more resources for more unequally distributed economic gain to dominate nature.
>
> (1993: 2)

However, in their efforts to criticise capitalist patriarchal frameworks through this alignment, Mies and Shiva sometimes continue or reinforce these dichotomies, when continuously speaking in terms of North/South, men/women, culture/nature, despite their attempt to 'express our diversity' (Mies and Shiva 1993: 2).

In her article 'Economic globalization, ecological feminism, and sustainable development' (1997) Shiva points to the emergence of an 'ecological feminism' that sees the current trend of globalisation as 'the ultimate concentration of capitalist patriarchy' and its violence done to nature and women. Shiva discusses other feminists who argue that both 'nature' and the 'nation' are social constructs of patriarchy that use a reductionist constructivism. This view can be very restrictive, Shiva explains, for it supports 'the erosion of national sovereignty and any form of people's protection,' instead of using the nation as an inclusive figuration of feminist ideology for all members in society (Shiva 1997: 22). Therefore, Shiva proposes a feminist reinvention of nature that leaves the capitalist and patriarchal construction of nature as passive and feminine (and thus as easily dominated) behind. She argues that an environmental framework is especially significant for feminist theories in order to avoid the dominant reductionist philosophy of a constructed nature, since it is contributing to a passive and invisible idea of nature, organisms and nonhuman subjects: '[i]n a reductionist approach to bio-technology, issues of social justice also vanish along with a concern for ecology' (Shiva 1997: 25). Feminism thus needs to become more environmental, which entails rethinking some of the terms and categories that were previously used, as Shiva explains:

> The postmodern discourse was supposed to question the privilege of the white male individual and to enable recognition of other forms of historical experience. Much western academic feminist thinking, however, is converging closely with the perspectives of the global patriarchal elite. It is reinstituting the world view of powerful white males as a norm in an era where concern for preserving diverse forms of life, both biological and cultural, is emerging as a major challenge.
>
> (1997: 26)

Thus, Shiva shows how environmental feminists need to look at themselves and their theories critically, and avoid the use of capitalist, patriarchal discourse so as to be open to diverse forms of life and challenge the normative position of the white rational man.

Not only are gendered dynamics present in the aforementioned models of modern, rational thinking, 'nature' itself has been subject to much gendered language-use as well. However, this gendering does not only happen with/in the capitalist and patriarchal framework that Mies and Shiva criticise, but within ecofeminist writing as well. Fausto-Sterling observes how nature is often personified as female, which explains the often-occurring comparison between 'nature' and 'women' in ecofeminist theories that see them as dominated by Man in the same ways, an aspect which has been criticised for various reasons (Fausto-Sterling 2014: 300). One of the limitations of this approach is that it has a tendency to reinforce the binary between men/women, by taking women as a category for granted, and leading from a somewhat essentialist idea of sexual difference. Seeing 'nature' and 'women' as being in the same predicament already implies that they are 'oppressed' in the same ways and makes them both passive actors. Even if one takes 'women' as a category, 'women' cannot always be used as a universal category, since there are many (power and privilege) differences between women, including different struggles and many differently layered power differences, as black feminists and intersectional theorists have stressed upon, whilst acknowledging that 'identity politics takes place at the site where categories intersect thus seems more fruitful than challenging the possibility of talking about categories at all' (Crenshaw 1991: 1299). Ever since, many critiques of intersectionality and elaborations of the approach have stressed the importance of looking beyond male/female to tick the box of 'gender,' to also include queer, trans and gender non-conforming subjects, as well as LGBTQIA+ sexualities. How queer and trans perspectives relate to ecofeminism's tendency to focus on the category of 'woman' women is a significant query for further research.[3]

Ecofeminism has been criticised by different scholars for seeing nature as passive and in need of preservation, as opposed to an active, superior human destroyer of nature. Although ecofeminism can be criticised for its alliance between women and nature and reinforces essentialist, homogenising and passive ideas of both 'categories,' ecofeminism should not be essentialised itself. As Fausto-Sterling has pointed out, ecofeminism consists of different strands, which see nature and its possible alliance to women in different ways.

Environmental feminist Stacy Alaimo critically reflects on ecofeminism in an affirmative way in her work and argues in her article 'Cyborg and ecofeminist interventions: challenges for an environmental feminism' (1994) that 'articulating women and nature as agents in a mutual struggle' can still strengthen ecofeminism in envisioning nature as active force, while at the same time recognising that the Mother Earth' metaphor linking women and nature and frequently used by ecofeminists, feeds into patriarchal and capitalist discourse (Alaimo 1994: 133). In her assessment of ecofeminism, Alaimo points to the danger of reducing both women and nature to homogeneous, universalised, essentialist entities in need of either help or preservation. She further argues that envisioning ecofeminist politics through metaphors could also distract from real and urgent matters and therefore miss the political relevance of the movement. More specifically, the imagery of 'Mother Earth' that has both been used by ecofeminists as well as others (now increasingly in the context of 'green' corporations) can be criticised and seen as harmful for various reasons as well. Alaimo argues that it continues the feminised idea of nature – bringing along connotations as passive or primitive – and this view of nature has also been used by capitalist, patriarchal narratives: 'portraying the earth as a mother strengthens a patriarchal discourse harmful not only to women but also to the environment' (1994: 136). According to Alaimo this metaphor codes the earth, and by feminine association also women, 'into passive victims at the same time that it depicts polluters as mere naughty boys, thus making the problem personal and familial instead of political and systemic' (Alaimo 1994: 137). In addition, as earlier pointed out, it is problematic to be speaking of a monolithic category of 'women,' because it erases differences of gender, race, class, sexuality, age, ability and more. Therefore, much of ecofeminist thinking could benefit from a more intersectional approach and politics, in order to inhabit both the interests of environmental as well as feminist (including anti-racist, classist, homophobic, heterosexist, anthropocentric) aims.

However, the use of the 'feminine' or the focus on 'woman' has been considered by Hélène Cixous as more complex than an essentialist approach to the subject of feminism, which could apply to ecofeminism as well. As Cixous has argued in *The Laugh of the Medusa* (1975), this use of the feminine can also be seen as a reclaiming of this position, rather than as essentialist:

> If woman has always functioned 'within' the discourse of man, a signifier that has always referred back to the opposite signifier which annihilates its specific energy and diminishes or stifles its very different sounds, it is time for her to dislocate this 'within,' to explode it, turn it around, and seize it; to make it hers, containing it, taking it in her own mouth, biting that tongue with her very own teeth to invent for herself a language to get inside of.
>
> (1975: 1953)

Taking Cixous' argument into account, the discourse of ecofeminism can also be considered a powerful reclaiming of the feminine position and its vulnerability to subvert and challenge power differences through the women-nature analogy. According to Alaimo, ecofeminism should therefore not be dismissed; its essentialist label can be challenged, as it should not be assumed as a universal and homogeneous movement. As said, one of the reasons this essentialist label has been put on ecofeminism is because of its focus on nature, and because nature and the discipline of biology have been understood as 'the ground of essentialism' (Alaimo 2008: 302). Alaimo also gives ecofeminism credit for effectively challenging the 'mutually constituting discourses' that gender nature 'to denigrate it and naturalise "woman" to debase her' (Alaimo 2008: 301). She affirms that articulating women and nature 'as agents in a mutual struggle instead of as passive victims, celebrating an activist alliance between women and nature could hamper the appropriation of other ecofeminist connections into narratives of domination' (Alaimo 1994: 150).

Nevertheless, Alaimo asks whether combining feminism with environmentalism could reinforce the sense that 'men are disembodied, or exist within more solid body-boundaries that protect them from environmental risk,' questioning some particular environmental issues might not be 'more indicative of race and class' (Alaimo 2008: 301)[4] than gender. Feminism from an intersectional perspective argues that race or class always plays a role and cannot be analysed separately from gender issues. Jasbir Puar's expansion of intersectionality is useful here as she uses the flexible notion of 'assemblage' to show that subjects are not constituted by different layers or differentiations of power, but rather embodied and always in process rather than fixed. This helps to consider categories, such as race, gender, sexuality, class, nation and disability, as events or encounters between bodies, 'rather than simply entities and attributes of subjects' (Puar 2013: 58) and exemplifies that environmental issues cannot easily be identified with gender, race or class but instead need to be understood as entangled and intertwined.

Analyses of environmental issues therefore benefit from an intersectional and feminist approach that avoids essentialism, challenges power relations and explores agency among different actors.

## Feminist Political Ecology

Another approach that links feminism and environmentalism is offered by FPE. FPE started out as a movement and approach to add feminist analyses and perspectives to the domain of political ecology, as a move away from dominant capitalist, rational and patriarchal approaches to environmentalism. Dissatisfied with the modernist, humanist focus of many mainstream environmental discourses, FPE focuses on gendered relations to the environment, combined with critiques of capitalism and bringing practices of the everyday into the scope of analysis. The book *Feminist Political Ecology: Global Issues and Local Experience* (1996) edited by Dianne Rocheleau, Barbara Thomas-Slayter and Esther Wangari provided a key point and founding text for establishing FPE as a theoretical field and approach (Harcourt and Nelson 2015: 1). Ever since, the field of feminist political ecology has been evolving and expanding. This is exemplified in contemporary accounts of FPE that demonstrate that FPE does not merely provide a theoretical framework and approach but is more about 'a feminist perspective and an ongoing exploration and construction of a network of learners' (Rocheleau 2015: 57). FPE offers tools for how to think and do research differently by building on an intersectional approach, focusing on everyday activities and practices, and engaging in 'situated empirical practice' (Nelson 2015: 40). Rather than a static theory FPE can be considered as a process and 'evolving practice' (Harcourt 2015: 255) 'of doing environmentalism, justice and feminism differently' (Harcourt and Nelson 2015: 9). This involves a continuous interplay of theories, practices, politics and policies, connecting activism, policy-making and academia through the 'mixing of various combinations of gender, class, race, ethnicity, sexuality, religion, ontologies and ecologies, with critique of colonial legacies and neoliberal designs' (Rocheleau 2015: 57).

However, it should be acknowledged that FPE does not exist in isolation and has been influenced by, builds on and is connected to other approaches and perspectives that link environmentalism and feminism (and even within FPE there are likely contradictions, frictions, overlaps and a variety of focal points). One example is FPE's ambiguous relationship to ecofeminism, as it both connects with and builds on ecofeminism in some ways, but also rejects some aspects of this approach (and of course different feminist political ecologists do so differently and to varying extents). Both FPE and ecofeminism aim to challenge and disrupt dominant hierarchies between humans/nature, men/women, North/South and focus on the relation between the exploitation of both nature and women through critiques of (patriarchal) capitalism (albeit in different ways). Not surprisingly, ecofeminist writing and thinking is used by feminist political ecologists, even though much of FPE is critical of ecofeminism for reasons earlier discussed in this chapter. FPE offers valuable contributions to the debates surrounding ecofeminism, and aims to avoid the essentialist critique that ecofeminism has received by actively including approaches of intersectionality, situated knowledge, decoloniality and queer ecologies. Harcourt, Knox and Tabassi for example discuss the potential of using queer ecologies within FPE in order to disrupt and challenge ecofeminism's earlier mentioned 'heterosexist and essentialist limitations' following the example of queer ecofeminist theorists like Greta Gaard (Harcourt *et al.* 2015: 289). FPE also recognises the nuances and differences within ecofeminism (as described by Fausto-Sterling earlier in this chapter) and looks for ways to open up the subjects of feminism and FPE beyond that of the (white, cis-gendered) 'woman' (Harcourt *et al.* 2015: 287–9).

This kind of constructive engagement and opening up to other debates in the larger scene of environmental feminisms is one of FPE's characteristics. By acknowledging frictions, contradictions, overlaps and shortcomings, scholars and activists that practise FPE engage in conversations and ways of thinking that are 'staying with the trouble(s)' (Haraway 2008). This is exemplified in contemporary FPE scholarship that is both exploring and actively inviting approaches surrounding decoloniality, queer ecologies and posthuman approaches (Harcourt and Nelson 2015: 6).

FPE's engagement with new materialist and posthuman approaches is shown for instance by thinking through Donna Haraway's naturecultures (2003). But FPE has only just begun to engage in feminist new materialism and posthumanism, which could be another fruitful encounter for FPE's future.

Considering that feminist new materialism and posthumanism are expanding prominent environmental feminist approaches, a more detailed account of these approaches and what they offer might be valuable input into the process of FPE.

## Feminist new materialism and posthumanism

Rather than assuming the passivity of a landscape that is possessed, commodified, mapped and read, various environmental feminist approaches that have been identified as new materialism or posthumanism have argued for approaches to nature that are more egalitarian, as they refer to naturecultures (Haraway 2003) or an intra-action between different actors (Barad 2008) through posthuman accounts (Braidotti 2013). Recognising 'nature' as active agent helps to reconceptualise it beyond essentialist terms, which helps to destabilise dichotomies such as passive/active, resource/researcher, object/subject and potentially that of nature/culture too (Alaimo 2008: 302).

A posthuman approach that is embedded in feminist thought is helpful in unwrapping and dismantling such questions and divisions that place the human on a pedestal, distinct from the environment and other species. According to Braidotti and other posthuman thinkers, envisioning politics as human only continues a bias and discrimination *vis-à-vis* animals, non-humans, the environment and other species that are incorrectly assessed as mere resource, restraint or context. Such approaches challenge the continued belief in human exceptionalism and dismantle theories of democracy that consider the world divided in active subjects versus passive objects, especially as such divisions are appearing 'as thin descriptions at a time when the interactions between human, viral, animal and technological bodies are becoming more and more intense' (Bennett 2009: 108). Braidotti argues that posthumanism provides a 'fast-growing new intersectional feminist alliance. It gathers the remains of poststructuralist anti-humanism and joins them with feminist re-appraisals of contemporary genetics and molecular biology in a nondeterministic frame,' thus conceptualising it as a powerful intersectional feminist tool and approach (2005: 12).

Post-humanism can also be rethought differently, as exemplified in the work of Karen Barad, one of the key thinkers in feminist new materialism. She describes posthumanism not as a blurring of boundaries between human and non-human and to cross out the differences *per se*, but rather as a way 'to understand the materializing effects of particular ways of drawing boundaries between "humans" and "nonhumans"' (Barad 2012: 31). In 'Nature's Queer Performativity' (2012) Barad is interested in the phenomenon of 'anthropomorphizing' as an intervention 'for shaking loose the crusty toxic scales of anthropocentricism, where the human in its exceptional way of being gets to hold all the "goodies" like agency, intentionality, rationality, feeling, pain, empathy, language, consciousness, imagination, and much more' (27). She conceptualises the environment as more than a resource or 'our surroundings'; she sees it an actor in itself. This way Barad aims to interrogate the binaries that back up the humanist ideal – or modernist paradigm – and proposes to use the current anthropomorphic moment to fracture 'the presumptions of the "anthropos" of "anthropocentrism", and in so doing open up a space for response' (2012: 27–8). This does not merely entail the inclusion of non-human as well as human actors in political analysis and discussion, but also exploring 'ways to think about the nature of causality, agency, relationality, and change without taking these distinctions to be foundational or holding them in place' (Barad 2012: 32). Such an account acknowledges the environment as well as the body and materiality in 'the fullness of their becoming' without reducing the human to a position of either being pure cause or pure effect and remaining accountable for the role 'we' (as humans) play 'in the intertwined practices of knowing and becoming' (Barad 2008: 130). As such this approach offers productive ways for these scholars to analyse environmental issues and helps to decentralise the human subject of the modernist paradigm.

Rather than seeing it as a getting rid of or coming after the human, the 'post' in posthumanism can be interpreted as indicating a positive movement beyond the human realm. Not to say that the humanist project is 'over,' but rather to expand analysis and research and to not restrict it to the human only. Considered in this way posthumanism can be seen as an active reaction against the anthropocentric development that Chakrabarty (2009) alerts to, that additionally blurs multiple dichotomies and helps in undoing the humanism of the transcendental self/other and nature/culture relation. This is eloquently done by Barad who opens up and deconstructs binaries not of assumed categories, but rather of their assumed characteristics such as agential/ non-agential, active/passive. Through such deconstructing, or reconfiguring, she shows that humans, often thought to be part of culture as opposed to nature, have been part of nature all along: '[w]hat if we were to understand culture as something that nature does?' (Barad 2012: 47). Nature and culture are intertwined and intra-active in her account and might be comparable to the 'naturecultures' that Haraway proposes in her book *When Species Meet* (2008). The accounts of Haraway, Braidotti and Barad offer ways to think beyond the 'anthropos' in the Anthropocene, and take the different power relations – between human/environment, culture/nature, West/Rest – into account and help to think of ways to take the environment seriously.

Alternatives are offered by new materialist and posthuman approaches that have criticised this anthropocentrism. Alaimo argues for 'insurgent vulnerability' as an ethical political approach that involves a 'recognition of our material interconnection with the wider environment' and counters the 'hegemonic masculinity of aggressive consumption' and impenetrability of big science (2009: 26). She uses the concept of *trans-corporeality* (Alaimo 2009, 2016) which blurs the boundaries of the human as such and reconsiders the aims of environmental preservation and protection, not merely referring to resources for human use but considering different human and non-human actors as valuable in and of themselves. Referring to new materialist theories, Alaimo asserts that such

> emerging models of materiality are crucial for developing an eco-criticism that does not replicate nature/culture dualisms or reinscribe nature as a blank slate for the imaginings of culture, but instead, seeks to account for the ways in which nature and environment, as material forces, act, interact, and profoundly affect cultural systems, texts, and artifacts.
>
> (2010: 71)

In this way, a different feminist approach to both humanness and the environment is developed, one in which what is 'human' is undecided, and the so-called 'non-humans' must be dealt with as existents too (Stengers 2010: 3).

Nevertheless, like ecofeminism, new materialist and posthuman approaches are rarely unconditionally embraced by environmental feminists. The main criticism is that such approaches might be dehumanising and that the focus on interactions with the non-human might fail to acknowledge the importance of 'real-life activity,' disregard feminism's complicated history with matters of biology and risk encompassing the (racialised and gendered) bodies and subjectivities that are affected by environmental issues (Ahmed 2008, Jackson 2015, Tompkins 2016). The philosophical language that is often used in new materialist and posthuman approaches is difficult to translate into other contexts in which climate change might be deeply felt. In *Staying Alive*, Vandana Shiva argues that '[s]ocially, the world of scientific experiments and beliefs has to be extended beyond the so-called experts and specialists into the world of all those who have systematically been excluded from it – women, peasants, tribals' (2010: 36). In this sense the 'verification and validation of a scientific system would then be validation in practice, where practice and experimentation is real-life activity in society and nature' (Shiva 2010: 36). This is precisely what new materialist and posthuman accounts do not yet focus on sufficiently. Barad might talk about real-life activity in terms of 'lightning's stuttering chatter' (Barad 2012: 27), the 'queer performativity' of atoms and analyse amoebas (Barad 2008, 2012), and Haraway might explore the feminist potential and value of human–animal encounters (Haraway 2008: 62). Yet, it is unclear what the relevance of such conceptualisations is for subjects that engage with the environment and climate change on a daily basis when '[t]he killing of people by the murder of nature is an invisible form of violence which is today the biggest threat to justice and peace,' an urgent issue that should not be overlooked and needs the inclusion of everyday lived struggles (Shiva 2010: 36).

## Conclusion

As the approaches discussed in this chapter have shown, feminist theory is an important contribution to the current debates about the Anthropocene, exposing the differently layered power dynamics at play in environmental issues.

FPE shows how an environmental framework is important for feminist and environmental theories in order to avoid the dominant reductionist philosophy of a constructed nature: 'In a reductionist approach to bio-technology, issues of social justice also vanish along with a concern for ecology' (Shiva 1997: 25). Simultaneously, FPE shows how environmental theorists and activists need to look critically beyond capitalist and patriarchal discourses. The relevance of feminism is required by environmentalists in order to come to a more multi-faceted analysis (that takes gender, race, class, nationality, anti-capitalism into account), and the relevance of environmentalism for feminism is required in order to include global environmental issues in feminist politics and aims. FPE is one theory that brings together these issues.

New materialist and posthuman perspectives provide another, most uncharted approach for FPE, focusing on alternative subjectivities and humanisms, such as the cyborg and the posthuman, that reconceptualise nature as no longer a ground for essentialism, but as an active force in itself. In this theorisation, recognising 'nature' as active agent helps to destabilise dichotomies such as passive/active, resource/researcher, object/subject, and potentially that of nature/culture too. From this point of view, FPE could move towards a more inclusive, intersectional and multi-faceted politics. Post-humanism and new materialism resist the assumptions that restrict and control both the ethical as well as the political – or ethico-political – deliberation of the human realm. A feminist lens is concomitantly needed, for it helps to contest ethics and politics that guarantee human exceptionalism.

Still, the challenge remains as to how to apply such theorising to everyday lived realities as experienced by local communities affected by climate change and other environmental issues. In this regard the ecofeminist alliance between women and nature should not be dismissed as essentialist all together: instead, environmental feminisms can provide fruitful encounters by 'envisioning women and nature as political allies,' in order to both 'emphasize the importance of women as political activists and stress the agency of nature' (Alaimo 1994: 150).

## Notes

1  For instance, ecofeminism can be considered a political movement as well as a theoretical approach, and Feminist Political Ecology is as much of a practice as it is an approach informed by theory.
2  Still it is important to ask which humans are referred to here. Which 'anthropos' is the 'Anthropocene' referring to? Which humans are doing the damage? The Anthropocene might frame humans as the 'destroyer' of the planet but does not account for which humans 'do the damage' and which humans are unequally affected by it. Moreover, the idea that humans are so dominant might be assuming an anthropocentric position in itself, and might be taking any possibility for 'nature's agency' away, as new materialist feminist Karen Barad argues (2003).
3  Scholars such as Greta Gaard are conceptualising a queer ecofeminism (1997).
4  In her later work (2016) Alaimo specifies that she resists a unison of feminism and environmentalism, and is instead more interested in frictions within and between the

two (p. 12). As she points out, feminists should be wary of embracing environmentalism because of its links with colonialism, racism, sexism and many 'essentialisms' (p. 11) and that taking into account that much of feminist and queer theory is not environmentally oriented, an alliance between the two cannot be taken for granted or assumed (p. 11). Still, I would argue that there is not one singular way to practise and think environmentalism and feminism together (hence the plural 'environmental feminisms'): The range of approaches from ecofeminism, to Feminist Political Ecology, new materialism and posthumanism shows that there are many practices and ways of thinking involved here and that there might be no natural alliance, but that there are many ways in which such alliances can be thought.

## References

Ahmed, S., 2008. Some preliminary remarks on the founding gestures of the 'New Materialism'. *European Journal of Women's Studies*, 15 (1), 23–39.

Alaimo, S., 1994. Cyborg and ecofeminist interventions: challenges for an environmental feminism. *Feminist Studies*, 20 (1), 133–52.

Alaimo, S., 2008. Ecofeminism without nature? Questioning the relation between feminism and envrionmentalism. *International Feminist Journal of Politics*, 10 (3), 299–304.

Alaimo, S., 2009. Insurgent vulnerability and the carbon footprint of gender. *Kvinder, Køn og forskning*, 3 (4), 22–35.

Alaimo, S., 2010. Material engagements: science studies and the environmental humanities. *Ecozon@: European Journal of Literature, Culture and Environment*, 1 (1), 69–74.

Alaimo, S., 2016. *Exposed: Environmental Politics and Pleasures in Posthuman Times*. Minneapolis: University of Minnesota Press.

Argyrou, V., 2005. *The Logic of Environmentalism: Anthropology, Ecology and Postcoloniality*. New York: Berghahn Books.

Balasubramanian, J., 2015. Sustainable food and privilege: why green is always white (and male and upper-class). *In*: M. Anderson and P.H. Collins, eds., *Race, Class and Gender: An Anthology*. Boston, MA: Cengage Learning, 399–400.

Barad, K., 2008. Posthumanist performativity: toward an understanding of how matter comes to matter. *In*: S.J. Hekman and S. Alaimo, eds, *Material Feminisms*. Bloomington, IN: Indiana University Press, 120–54.

Barad, K., 2012. Nature's queer performativity. *Kvinder, Køn og forskning*, 1 (2), 25–53.

Bennett, J., 2009. *Vibrant Matter: A Political Ecology of Things*. Durham, NC: Duke University Press.

Braidotti, R., 2005. A critical cartography of feminist post-postmodernism. *Australian Feminist Studies*, 20 (47), 169–80.

Braidotti, R., 2013. *The Posthuman*. Cambridge: Polity.

Chakrabarty, D., 2009. The climate of history. *Critical Inquiry*, 35, 197–222.

Cixous, H., 1975. The laugh of the Medusa. *In*: V. Leitch, ed., *The Norton Anthology of Theory and Criticism*. New York: W.W. Norton & Company.

Crenshaw, K., 1991. Mapping the margins: intersectionality, identity politics, and violence against women of color. *Stanford Law Review*, 43 (6), 1241–99.

Crutzen, P.J., 2006. *The "Anthropocene"*. Berlin: Springer.

Fausto-Sterling, A., 2014. Nature. *In*: G. Herdt and C.R. Stimpson, eds, *Critical Terms for the Study of Gender*. Chicago, IL: University of Chicago Press.

Gaard, G., 1997. Toward a queer ecofeminism. *Hypatia*, 12 (1), 114–37.

Haraway, D.J., 1988. "Situated knowledges: the science question in feminism and the privilege of partial perspective." *Feminist Studies*, 14 (3), 575–99.

Haraway, D.J., 2003. *The Companion Species Manifesto: Dogs, People, and Significant Otherness.* Chicago, IL: Prickly Paradigm Press.

Haraway, D.J., 2008. *When Species Meet.* Minneapolis, MN: University of Minnesota Press.

Harcourt, W., 2015. The slips and slides of trying to live feminist political ecology. *In:* W. Harcourt and I.L. Nelson, eds, *Practising Feminist Political Ecologies: Moving Beyond the 'Green Economy'.* London: Zed Books, 238–59.

Harcourt, W., Knox, S. and Tabassi, T., 2015. World-wise otherwise stories for our endtimes: conversations on queer ecologies. *In:* W. Harcourt and I.L. Nelson, eds., *Practising Feminist Political Ecologies.* London: Zed Books, 286–308.

Harcourt, W. and Nelson, I.L., 2015. Are we 'green' yet? And the violence of asking such a question. *In:* W. Harcourt and I.L. Nelson, eds, *Practising Feminist Political Ecologies: Moving Beyond the 'Green Economy'.* London: Zed Books, 1–28.

Jackson, Z.I., 2015. Outer worlds: the persistence of race in movement 'beyond the human'. *GLQ: A Journal of Lesbian and Gay Studies,* 21 (2–3), 215–18.

Lloyd, G., 1984. *The Man of Reason: 'Male' and 'Female' in Western Philosophy.* London: Routledge.

Mies, M. and Shiva, V., 1993. *Ecofeminism.* London: Zed Books.

Nelson, I.L, 2015. Feminist political ecology and the (un)making of 'heroes': encounters in Mozambique. *In:* W. Harcourt and I.L Nelson, eds., *Practising Feminist Political Ecologies: Moving Beyond the 'Green Economy'.* London: Zed Books, 131–56.

Puar, J., 2013. 'I would rather be a cyborg than a goddess': intersectionality, assemblage, and affective politics. *Meritum,* 8 (2), 371–90.

Rocheleau, D., Thomas-Slayter, B. and Wangari, E., 1996. *Feminist Political Ecology: Global Issues and Local Experiences.* New York: Routledge.

Rocheleau, D., 2015. A situated view of feminist political ecology from my networks, roots and territories. *In:* W. Harcourt and I.L. Nelson, eds, *Practising Feminist Political Ecologies: Moving Beyond the 'Green Economy'.* London: Zed Books, 29–66.

Shiva, V., 1997. Economic globalization, ecological feminism, and sustainable development. *Canadian Woman Studies,* 17 (2), 22–7.

Shiva, V., 2010. *Staying Alive: Women, Ecology and Development.* 2010 edition. London: Zed Books.

Stengers, I., 2010. Including nonhumans in political theory: opening the Pandora's box? *In:* B. Braun and S.J. Whatmore, eds, *Political Matter: Technoscience, Democracy, and Public Life.* Minneapolis, MN: University of Minnesota Press, 33–4.

Tompkins, K.W., 2016. On the limits and promise of new materialist philosophy. *Lateral,* 5 (1). Available from: http://csalateral.org/issue/5-1/forum-alt-humanities-new-material ist-philosophy-tompkins/ [Accessed 22 September 2018].

# 5 Climate change, natural disasters and the spillover effects on unpaid care

## The case of Super-typhoon Haiyan

*Maria S. Floro[1] and Georgia Poyatzis*

## Introduction

Natural disasters that are increasingly associated with climate change represent negative externalities that have significant impacts on vulnerable populations. To date, economic studies regarding their adverse effects have mainly focused on loss of life and livelihoods, damage to infrastructures and housing, and economic costs such as decline in agricultural outputs, productivity and growth etc. Not surprisingly, the emphasis of impact assessments using simulations has been on both short-term and longer-term impacts on loss in Gross Domestic Product (GDP) and household consumption as a result of decline in incomes.

Such studies on the effects of droughts, typhoons and severe climatic conditions like global oceanic warming do not adequately capture the social costs.[2] As climate change impacts intensify, there is growing recognition among governments and international agencies such as the International Red Cross that traditional efforts for dealing with shocks and managing risks through emergency response are inadequate and there is a need to build the resilience and adaptive capacity of communities by gathering better information including that on social vulnerability (Agrawal 2008, Canevari-Luzardo *et al.* 2017). This requires enhancement of our knowledge about the effects on human welfare not only in terms of deaths and decline in productivity but also increases in morbidity and demand for medical services as well as for care services, paid and unpaid.

This chapter argues that there are significant effects of extreme climate events on the care sector of the economy, particularly in terms of additional demand for unpaid care labour, that need to be taken into account in impact appraisals and in the design of effective, gender-aware response systems. Natural disasters such as super-typhoons, which are likely to recur at increasing frequency and intensity with climate change, have social costs that remain statistically invisible. Therefore, these costs are likely to be given little or no attention in damage assessments, disaster emergency response system design and post-disaster recovery planning and management. Natural disasters are also windows that showcase existing gender inequalities in society including the unequal share of the care workload in households. While disasters put communities, households and their members at risk of losing their homes, livelihoods and even their lives, natural disasters also have gender-differentiated impacts that amplify prevailing gender-based inequalities.

To date, the effect of extreme weather events such as super-typhoons on the demand for care has yet to be clearly identified and measured. This chapter addresses this gap and makes a contribution towards a more comprehensive picture of the welfare effects of global greenhouse gas emissions using the case of Super-typhoon Haiyan that hit the Visayan region of the Philippines in November 2013. The Philippines ranks third in the 2014 UN World Risk Index for exposure (storms, earthquakes, flood, droughts, sea-level rise) and second for overall risk (exposure and vulnerability of people) out of 171 countries (Birkmann *et al.* 2014). Using the 2015 Global Climate Risk Index, the Philippines ranks fifth for countries most affected by weather-related events from 1994 to 2013 (Kreft *et al.* 2014). The main point here is that all affected people and all services need to be taken into account in impact assessments. These include the short-term and longer-term health effects and the unpaid care work burden.

The chapter is essentially exploratory in that it provides a framework for examining the impact of climate change-related events such as natural disasters on the unpaid work burden and introduces a methodology for assessing their effects on care provisioning. Given the paucity of data, the authors use a variety of information on morbidity, health facilities, time allocation and barriers to the utilisation of health services to examine the effect of Super-typhoon Haiyan on the demand for unpaid care for illustration purposes. It builds upon a relatively small but growing literature on ecological feminist economics (Nelson 2009, Bauhardt 2014). This sub-discipline analyses the degree to which the ecological crisis is linked to the gender order and contributes to the crisis of social reproduction, or the under-provision of care for people who depend on it (Bauhardt 2014). The crisis concerns the excessive demands on those who carry responsibility for social reproduction, the vast majority of whom, given the gendered division of labour, are women. Not only do women bear the responsibility for those in need of care – the additional costs ensuing from the ecological crisis are also dumped on their shoulders (Bauhardt 2014: 61).

The chapter is organised as follows: first, it provides an analytical framework for examining the extent to which the unpaid work of family members could be stretched as a result of the health consequences of natural disasters. Second, it introduces a methodology for measuring the level of unpaid care work brought about by health shocks (illnesses) in the post-disaster period using the case of Super-typhoon Haiyan. Given data limitations, the chapter illustrates the method of accounting for care needs in the aftermath of a natural disaster by means of projections. The estimates are based on a combination of datasets, reports and medical information on specific health conditions. It also examines the time use of women and men in the Visayas Region. Third, the chapter discusses the out-of-pocket, health-related expenses shouldered by affected families in the post-disaster period. A summary and discussion of policy implications conclude the chapter.

## Conceptual framework: Relationship between climate change, natural disasters and care work

Disasters with both natural and anthropogenic causes are a global concern, for they have been shown to displace, kill and injure large numbers of people; put pressure on food, water and energy supplies; disrupt economic systems; and cause massive destruction of infrastructure. Disasters also pose serious threats to health and the situation can be aggravated with political exigencies and lack of informed or evidence-based health responses, as in the case of the 2010 Haiti earthquake.

A crucial aspect of post-disaster situations faced by households are health shocks requiring the provision of care services to their sick members. In both developing and industrialised countries, female family members have been a major source of caring labour. Extreme weather events such as super-typhoons not only lead to deaths but also illnesses that put stresses on households' primary caregivers. When increases in care work lead to intense overwork for women, especially when combined with economic distress, the tensions between roles as income earners and care providers are likely to intensify. These role conflicts are further heightened when medical facilities are damaged and emergency response systems do not take into account the care needs of the sick, thereby making women and men, especially in poor households, both 'time-poor' and 'income-poor.' Attempts to balance the time demands of rebuilding their livelihoods and providing care for the sick and disabled can lead to long hours of work, thus imposing significant costs on caregivers' well-being. The invisibility to policymakers and in climate change policy discourses of the care sector and its importance in post-disaster recovery only reinforces the notion that affected families can find their own solutions to deal with added care responsibilities. The added care burden during post-disaster periods makes it imperative to bring unpaid care work out of statistical shadows.

### Climate change and Super-typhoon Haiyan

Recent climatological research has led to a better understanding of the relationship between the intensity and frequency of natural disasters and climate change.[3] A typhoon or a tropical cyclone is one of the most potentially destructive extreme weather events. In the last decade or so, research has provided a better understanding of the links between climate and occurrence of stronger (super) tropical cyclones (TCs). Although there were questions regarding causation between anthropogenic climate change and extreme weather events such as super-typhoons a few years ago (Intergovernmental Panel on Climate Change 2013), recent evidence indicates that 'in many cases of extreme weather, we are now in a position to answer that the human contribution is significant' (Corry 2017: 480). By carefully measuring a typhoon's potential destructiveness over its lifetime, Emanuel (2005) and Takayabu et al. (2015), for example, demonstrated that typhoons' occurrence is highly correlated with the observed increasing trend in sea surface temperature (SST) during the same period.

Super-typhoon Haiyan, or Yolanda as it is known in the Philippines, is considered to be the most catastrophic tropical cyclone ever to land in Western Pacific Ocean. It struck the Visayas (Western, Central and Eastern Visayas) region of the Philippines on 8 November 2013, devastating many impoverished areas.[4] Several scientific studies indicate that the occurrence of this super-typhoon is associated with the rise in ocean global warmth.[5] Haiyan has been cited in the Warsaw International Mechanism (WIM) as an example of loss and damage due to climate change (James *et al.* 2014: 938).[6] Although a wide range of losses that can reliably be attributed to climate change were identified as priorities for the WIM to deal with – including loss of life, livelihood and cultural heritage and resulting migration and displacement concerns – the WIM overlooks a fundamental issue: health-related care needs.

### Assessing the impact on care work

The impact of Haiyan has been devastating. The super-typhoon and its associated storm surge killed more than 6,300 people and destroyed more than a million homes (National Disaster and Risk Reduction Recovery Management Council 2014). It struck the Visayas region where poverty incidence is high, ranging from 22.7 per cent in Cebu province to 39.2 per cent in Leyte province to 63.7 per cent in Eastern Samar (Novales 2014).[7] Around 3.4 million families (16 million individuals) were affected across 12,139 villages/communities. A reported 890,895 families (4 million individuals) were displaced. Of these, 21,000 families (about 100,000 individuals) were served inside evacuation centres. The total cost of damages has been estimated at US$864 million, with US$435 million for infrastructure and US$ 440 million for agriculture in the affected regions (McPherson *et al.* 2015: 1).

Conventional impact assessments of natural hazards and calamities typically rely on damage functions, which are used to translate the magnitude of extreme events to a quantifiable damage. The focus is on damage in infrastructures (housing, roads, airports, health centres, businesses, schools etc.), declines in output such as agricultural crops and GDP. These so-called damage function models typically serve as bases for designing policies and associated empirical research investigations that provide evidence.[8] For example, the Philippine government assessed the social-sector costs and damages from Haiyan based on 'repair and reconstruction of structures and provision of necessary equipment and supplies of education, health and housing subsectors' according to the final report of the National Disaster and Risk Reduction Recovery Management Council (NDRRMC 2014: 62–3).[9] The Department of Health reported that US$16 million in damages was caused to 571 health facilities in typhoon-affected areas. About 40 per cent of the rural health units (RHUs), 69.3 per cent of Barangay Health Stations (BHS), and 37.6 per cent of hospitals in the Visayan region were either damaged or destroyed (Novales 2014).[10] In two of the worst hit provinces, Samar and Leyte, as much as 44 per cent of the population do not have access to health facilities; access is worse in the poorest areas in Eastern Visayas, with up to 58 per cent of the population without access.

Recent research however reveals the limitations of these damage functions and their inadequacies as climate policy tools. As pointed out by Pindyck (2013) in his survey of the impact assessment models (IAMs) of climate change, such models have flawed assumptions and are built on arbitrary selection of values such as the discount rate. The damage function models used for example to identify the loss function in terms of change in GDP or outputs of an economic sector such as agriculture or forestry are ad hoc and 'can say nothing meaningful about the kind of damages' particularly in terms of decline in human welfare as a result of catastrophic events (Pindyck 2013: 866–8). The limitations of the damage and loss functions used in impact assessments of climate-related natural hazards are echoed by Prahl *et al.* (2016). These functions seldom consider the impact on other dimensions of people's well-being such as increased work burden and social inequalities.

In recent years, a growing number of assessments of climate-related events have gone beyond monetary costs and are more encompassing. These studies examined the effects on human health (morbidity), social interactions (including violence) and demographic responses such as migration. For example, Enarson and Chakrabarti (2009) and Novales (2014) explored the gendered ways in which the impact of natural disasters affect women and men, girls and boys differently. Novales (2014) used interviews and participant observation to uncover gender biases in the months after Haiyan's landfall. Gender gaps in access and control over assets tend to be amplified in the aftermath of disasters: poverty and anguish are intensified by inaccessibility to health services, compromising life and health situations of pregnant mothers, the disabled and the sick, and family needs, now more intense in post-disaster period, pull women into the home for care work (Novales 2014: 6–7).

To be sure, the causation between natural hazard events and observed effects such as an increase in mortality rates is anything but simple.

> First, weather events are drawn from the probability distribution that defines the climate. Each event generates some direct effect on a population where these direct effects can be described by a dose-response function f(X) where specific 'doses' of a weather parameter X (e.g. rain) generate 'responses' within the population (e.g. getting wet […]). This sequence of direct effects combined with non–climatic factors on the social outcome to produce the distribution of observed social data.
>
> (Carleton and Hsiang 2016: aad9837–42)

In other words, if an extreme weather event such as a super-typhoon occurs, this will alter the observed social data (e.g. number of illnesses, migration, etc.). Note that the social outcome such as occurrence of illness such as acute water diarrhoea (AWD) may also be caused by the household's frequent use of surface water (from rivers, etc.) for drinking prior to the occurrence of the event, in this case the super-typhoon. Hence the structure of the dose-response function leading to a shift in the distribution of outcomes should be the difference between the ex-ante distribution of AWD incidence (prior to the event) and the resulting ex-post distribution of AWD. So, while damages in infrastructures brought about by coastal floods and storm surges can be verified using probabilistic risk frameworks, social costs in the form of deaths or illnesses in affected populations, for example, are more difficult to attribute to distinct causes, given the multiplicity of other possible factors (Prahl *et al.* 2016).

Given this caveat, it is important nonetheless to broaden the policymakers' understanding of the welfare effects in the aftermath of climate change-related events that goes beyond the economic costs such as change in agricultural outputs, etc. The impact on the care sector in terms of increase in morbidity and the associated demand for care services, paid and unpaid, needs to be part of the discussion regarding the impact of climate change and the evaluations of response systems, programs and policies addressing it.

The impact of a natural disaster on health occurs through several channels. The first – and the most visible – channel is the effect on mortality.[11] Secondly, there are various injuries, brought about by the disaster. This impact is compounded if rehabilitation services for people with disabilities and injuries ceased or decreased, as in the case of Haiyan (Martinez *et al.* 2015).[12] A third channel involves the increased incidence of non-communicable diseases resulting from lack of food, destruction of infrastructures providing safe water, sanitation and sewage disposal systems and exposure to the elements due to damage or loss of housing. Illnesses such as acute watery diarrhoea, are likely to increase as a result. Fourthly, post-disaster conditions such as stagnant water, broken sewers, open sewage etc. can bring about the spread of mosquito vector-borne diseases such as malaria and dengue and can intensify their rate of infection in the affected areas where malaria and dengue are already endemic. Fifth, natural disasters can delay the treatment and recovery period of elderly with pre-existing chronic illnesses as well as the rehabilitation of people with disabilities due to the damage on health facilities. The limited access to or absence of health facilities also affect the health of pregnant women, mothers and the very young through pregnancy-related and birth complications. In the case of Super-typhoon Haiyan, 270,338 pregnant women and 180,225 breastfeeding mothers with 0–6-month-old babies were affected (DOH and WHO 2014).

Given the damage to many hospitals and health facilities,[13] the need to care for the sick, disabled and injured is mostly met by unpaid family labour. Statistically invisible and presumed by policymakers and emergency health officials to be of infinitely elastic supply, this significant demand for care labour is ignored in most climate change impact analyses or environmental assessments. As with decline in household incomes, households employ coping mechanisms that involve greater reliance on unpaid work whenever a family member becomes ill or his/her healthcare needs are unmet.

In a country with few safety nets and adequate health insurance, natural disaster occurrences also lead to increased health expenditures. As a result, affected households substitute unpaid care work for services that are not afford-able. The study by Espallardo *et al.* (2015) of self-reported health costs in the aftermath of Super-typhoon Haiyan indicated that many affected households often incurred large, out-of-pocket health expenses for consultations, medical tests, medicines and transportation costs. And in parts of the Philippines where poverty rates averaged at 37 per cent in 2012, these prohibitive costs served as main barriers to health service utilisation even among those who have access to a health facility (Espallardo *et al.* 2015). Those that were able to utilise the services ended up borrowing from friends or moneylenders, using up their sav-ings and/or selling their assets.

The above discussion illustrates why a comprehensive assessment of 'loss and damage' needs to account for the increased demand for unpaid sick care. While health is an important concern in disaster emergency response frame-works, it is generally treated in damage function or cost assessment models as a 'non-produced component.' When health issues are discussed, they usually refer to healthcare services that are performed by skilled professionals.

The unpaid care labour dimension of disaster impacts has significant impli-cations for women who typically devote more time to caregiving than men do. The unpaid care needed for health recovery must be an integral part of the impact assessment and design of emergency response systems and longer-term recovery plans. Omitting the effects on the time allocation and provisioning of unpaid care work services is likely to have an adverse impact on women's well-being. Women are then compelled to make difficult sacrifices, such as lengthening their workday to accommodate both paid work and care work or engaging in simultaneous work activities for prolonged periods of time, which can have debilitating effects on women's health due to stress, chronic fatigue or lack of sleep (Bauhardt 2014, Beneria *et al.* 2016).

## The case of Super-typhoon Haiyan

In this section, we estimate the care needs brought about by the incidence of illnesses in the aftermath of Super-typhoon Haiyan as a case study. We assess the likely spillover effect on unpaid care by undertaking the following steps:

a  estimating the incidence of illnesses reported in the post-typhoon relief and recovery period;
b  projecting the amount of sick care labour provided by household mem-bers; and
c  identifying the household members likely to provide care work using time use data.

We also provide indirect reasons as to why the spillover effects are likely to be disproportionately shouldered by women.

The following exercise is admittedly limited due to data availability issues. In particular, the lack of data on pre-existing health conditions in the affected areas does not allow the measurement of the net change in the demand for sick care labour brought about by the illnesses in the aftermath of the natural disaster. Instead, we provide gross estimates of the unpaid care labour in this section using a combination of different available information and data from the Department of Health (DOH), World Health Organisation (WHO), National Disaster and Risk Reduction Recovery Management Council (NDRRMC), International Social Survey Program (ISSP), Philippine Statistics Authority and medical reports.

### Identification strategy for measuring the impact on unpaid care

*Estimating the incidence of illnesses in the aftermath*

About 26 million individuals or 16 per cent of the Philippine population were affected by the super-typhoon; 90 per cent of those affected live in the Visayas area, which comprises of regions VI (Western Visayas), VII (Central Visayas) and VIII (Eastern Visayas). Over 6,340 confirmed fatalities were associated with Super-typhoon Haiyan, with an additional 1,061 people missing, 4.1 million people displaced and 1.1 million homes damaged or destroyed.

The estimation of the incidence of specific health conditions (injuries or diseases) after Haiyan makes use of two sets of public health data provided by the Department of Health and the World Health Organisation (WHO). The first dataset provides real-time syndrome information collected through the Surveillance in Post Extreme Emergencies and Disasters (SPEED) program (Salazar *et al.* 2016). The SPEED program enables the early detection and monitoring of health threats or diseases. The second dataset involves the Early Warning Alert and Response Network (EWARN) public health records. Under EWARN, health facilities in the Philippines coordinate reporting to detect disease outbreaks and other environmental conditions affecting public health. Table 5.1 provides a list of various syndromes and their corresponding diagnoses, which are categorised as non-communicable diseases, infectious or communicable diseases, and injuries. The top ten causes for morbidity in the 150 days after the typhoon include acute respiratory infections (ARI), pneumonia, bronchitis, fever (influenza), tuberculosis, AWD, injuries (open wounds, bruises and burns) and hypertension (high blood pressure) (Salazar *et al.* 2016: 4). Using medical studies and reports, Table 5.2 provides the average number of days the person (adult or child) is likely to be ill for each of these syndromes.

Next, we examine the syndrome rates for Super-typhoon Haiyan. A syndrome rate refers to the crude percentage ratio of total consultations for a syndrome or syndrome group divided by the total population in the catchment area of the reporting health facility. Salazar *et al.* (2016) estimated the syndrome rates for 150 days in the aftermath of Haiyan using the SPEED data collected from operating health facilities and the 2010 Philippine Census population data for each municipality or city in the catchment area of the reporting health facility.[14] Table 5.3 provides the typhoon-based syndrome rates per 10,000

*Table 5.1* SPEED syndromes and health condition initial diagnosis

| Type | SPEED Syndromes | Health Condition Initial Diagnosis |
|------|-----------------|-----------------------------------|
| A. | Communicable | |
| 1 | Loose stools with visible blood | Acute bloody diarrhea |
| 2 | Floppy paralysis of the limbs which occurred recently in a child <15 years who was previously normal | Acute flaccid paralysis |
| 3 | Fever with spontaneous bleeding | Acute hemorrhagic fever |
| 4 | Yellow eyes or skin with or without fever | Acute jaundice syndrome |
| 5 | Cough, colds or sore throat with or without fever | Acute respiratory infection |
| 6 | Loose stools, three or more in the past 24h with or without dehydration | Acute watery diarrhea |
| 7 | Animal bites | Animal bites |
| 8 | Eye itchiness, redness with or without discharge | Conjunctivitis |
| 9 | Fever | Fever |
| 10 | Fever with other symptoms not listed above | Fever with other symptoms |
| 11 | Skin disease | Skin disease |
| 12 | Fever with headache, muscle pains and any of the following: eye irritation, jaundice, skin rash, scanty urination | Suspected leptospirosis |
| 13 | Fever with rash | Suspected measles |
| 14 | Fever with severe headache and stiff neck in children 12 months and older/ Fever and bulging fontanels or refusal to suckle in children < 12 months | Suspected meningitis |
| 15 | Spasms of neck and jaw (lock jaw) | Tetanus |
| B. | Non-Communicable | |
| 16 | Difficulty of breathing and wheezing | Acute asthmatic attack |
| 17 | Visible wasting, with or without bipedal pitting edema | Acute malnutrition |
| 18 | High blood pressure (≥140/90) | High blood pressure |
| 19 | Known diabetes | Know diabetes mellitus |
| C. | Injury | |
| 20 | Fractures | Fractures |
| 21 | Open wounds and bruises/burns | Open wounds and bruises/burns |

Source: Table 1, Salazar *et al.* (2016: 3).

individuals with 95 per cent confidence intervals for two periods: within two months and after two months of the super-typhoon. Overall, the total syndrome rate for Haiyan is 59.2 per cent (95 per cent confidence interval with a probability range between 50.6 per cent and 67.8 per cent) (Salazar et al. 2016: 2). In the first two months of the post-disaster period, there were 84.5 per cent, 10.9 per cent and 10.3 per cent rates for communicable diseases, injuries and non-communicable diseases respectively. There was a significant decline in the syndrome rates, especially for communicable diseases, after two months as shown in Table 5.4.

Table 5.2 Average number of care days for health conditions

| Health Syndromes Identified by SPEED | Average No. of Days Needing Care (adult:child) | Remarks | Reference |
|---|---|---|---|
| ABD: Acute bloody diarrhoea | 3:3 | amoebic cysts identified | Holtz 2009 |
| AFP: Acute flaccid paralysis | 17:17 | median days hospitalisation | Staples, 2014 |
| AHF: Acute hemorragic fever | 21:21 | possible epidemic causing diseases such as dengue, yellow fever, and others | WHO 2016c |
| AJS: Acute jaundice syndrome | 28:28 | Hepatitis E | WHO 2016a |
| AMN: Acute malnutrition | 0:3 | child only | WHO 2016b |
| ARI: Acute respiratory infection | 14:21 | Pneumonia, bronchitis | American Lung Association 2016 Thompson 2013 |
| AWD: Acute watery diarrhoea | 14:14 | caused by contaminated water | Cleveland Clinic 2013 |
| FOS: Fever with other symptoms | 3:3 | care days reported for fever only | Mayo Clinic 2016 |
| LEP: Suspected leptospirosis | 21:21 | without treatment, can lead to kidney failure, meningitis or even death | CDC 2014 |
| MEA: Suspected measles | 10:10 | isolation period of 4 days | CDC 2016b |
| MEN: Suspected meningitis | 1:1 | requires immediate medical attention, can be fatal in hours | CDC 2016c |
| TET: Suspected tetanus | 28:28 | no 'cure', complete recovery can take months | Immunization Action Coalition 2016 |

Sources: Holtz (2009); Staples *et al.* (2014); WHO (2016c); WHO (2016a); WHO (2016b); American Lung Association (2016); Thompson (2013); Cleveland Clinic (2013); Mayo Clinic (2016); CDC (November 2014); CDC (July 2016); Immunization Action Coalition (2016).

*Table 5.3* Typhoon syndrome rates per 10,000 individuals with 95 per cent confidence intervals, comparing within two months and after two months after Haiyan

| Typhoon Disaster | Communicable diseases | Injuries | Non-communicable diseases |
|---|---|---|---|
| ≤ 2 months post-disaster | | | |
| Typhoon (*N*=1,614) | 84.5 (69.5–99.4) | 10.9 (8.3–13.5) | 10.3 (8.4–12.2) |
| > 2 months post-disaster | | | |
| Typhoon (*N*=1,811) | 14.2 (12.5–15.8) | 1.4 (1.1–1.7) | 2.3 (1.9–2.6) |
| Difference between ≤ 2 months and > 2 months post-disaster | | | |
| Typhoon | 70.3 (p<0.01) | 9.5 (p<0.01) | 8.0 (p<0.01) |

Data gathered from Visayas Regional health facilities that were in operating status in the aftermath of Haiyan.

Source: Table 2, Salazar *et al.* (2016: 4).

Using post-typhoon reporting on health consultations from EWARN data, we then estimate the disaster-related care needs of the sick in the Visayas region. Unfortunately, the data do not provide information on the severity of the different syndromes. The number of consultations instead is used as a crude indicator. It should be noted that the EWARN reports only came from operating health facilities, which on average had a catchment area covering only 58 per cent of the population in the Eastern Visayas (region VIII), and roughly 20 per cent in Western and Central Visayas (regions VI and VII) (Novales 2014).

A total of 342,157 consultations were reported in the period November 2013–March 2014 following the super-typhoon. Of these, we have information on the specific reasons for the consultation in 202,925 cases (59 per cent). The breakdown of this full-information subsample by province and type of health syndrome is given in Table 5.4 and Figure 5.1. Overall, the highest number of consultations involved ARI, open wounds, high blood pressure and fever (influenza). The EWARN statistics also indicate that 30 per cent of the health consultations concerns children less than 5 years of age.

By projecting the 2010 Population Census data using annual provincial population growth rates, we obtain the estimated number of households for 2013.[15] Assuming that each ill person is from a different household, we find that about 3.1 per cent of Visayan households in the EWARN-covered areas had to provide care for a person with ARI syndrome. Another 2.3 per cent of the Visayan households had a sick member with AWD, tetanus fever etc., bringing the total to 5.4 per cent of Visayan households that had a family member suffering from injury, communicable or non-communicable diseases.

These estimates however are likely to be underestimated. First, the applied population denominators did not take into account the outmigration of affected people. Hence, the true populations within the affected areas are likely to be lower than the reported population statistics. Information on outmigration is not available however. Second, these estimates only covered 42 per cent of Eastern Visayas (about 1,800,174) and 80 per cent of those in Central (5,769,728) and Western Visayas (5,920,444) populations (WHO 2014); the

Table 5.4 Incidence of identified health conditions post-Haiyan (November 2013–March 2014) based on number of consultations, by province

| | ARI[a] | W/B[b] | HBP[c] | Fever[d] | SD[e] | AWD[f] | Total |
|---|---|---|---|---|---|---|---|
| **Western Visayas Region VI** | | | | | | | |
| Aklan | 2039 | 1,235 | 463 | 443 | 253 | | 4433 |
| Antique | 3139 | 499 | 424 | 389 | 285 | | 4736 |
| Capiz | 11519 | 3,910 | 2,385 | 2,113 | 1,165 | | 21092 |
| Iloilo | 5780 | 1,930 | 1,481 | 786 | | 627 | 10604 |
| Negros Occidental | 227 | 84 | 51 | 32 | | 29 | 423 |
| **Central Visayas Region VII** | | | | | | | |
| Cebu | 8057 | 4,058 | 1,770 | 1,297 | 862 | | 16044 |
| **Eastern Visayas Region VIII** | | | | | | | |
| Biliran | 127 | 108 | 204 | | 164 | 127 | 730 |
| E. Samar | 17238 | 3,656 | 2,787 | | 2,394 | 1,941 | 28016 |
| Leyte | 65992 | 17,140 | 8,445 | 8,717 | 9,651 | 5,976 | 115921 |
| W. Samar | 524 | 133 | 86 | 47 | 59 | 77 | 926 |
| Total Consultations | 114,642 | 32,753 | 18,096 | 13,824 | 14,833 | 8,777 | 202,925 |
| *% Households, Visayas[g]* | *3.1%* | *0.9%* | *0.5%* | *0.4%* | *0.4%* | *0.2%* | *5.4%* |
| *% Adjusted Visayas Households[g]* | *4.2%* | *1.2%* | *0.7%* | *0.5%* | *0.5%* | *0.3%* | *7.4%* |

Sources: Philippine Statistics Authority (PSA 2010), WHO 2014.

a ARI, acute respiratory infection
b W/B, open wounds and/or bruises
c HBP, high blood pressure
d Fever and rash
e SD, skin disease
f AWD, acute watery diarrhea
g Author's calculation. Total number of households based on projected 2013 population using 1990–2010 average province level population growth rate and 2010 Census population data

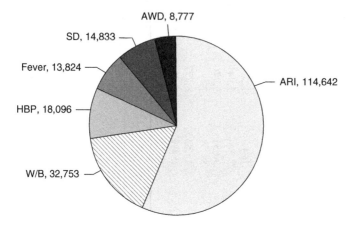

*Figure 5.1* Total number of consultations for identified health conditions post-Haiyan in Visayan region (November 2013 – March 2014).

Source: WHO (2014).

Notes:

ARI: Acute respiratory infection (3.1% of households)
W/B: Open wounds and/or bruises (0.9% of households)
HBP: High blood pressure (0.5% of households)
Fever: Fever and rash (0.4% of households)
SD: Skin disease (0.4% of households)
AWD: Acute watery diarrhea (0.2% of households)

rest presumably had no access to any health services due to transport problems and/or damage of the nearest health facility. If this is the case, the adjusted population denominators should only cover catchment areas where the population had access to a health facility.

Using the average household size of 4.9 in the Visayan region, we estimate the adjusted household–population denominator, AVH:

$$\text{Adjusted Visayan Household} \left( \text{AVH} \right) = \frac{\sum_{n=1}^{3} P_n}{4.9}$$

$$= \frac{\left[ 1,800,174 + 5,769,728 + 5,920,444 \right]}{4.9}$$

$$= 2,753,132$$

where n refers to the region in the Visayas, and $P_n$ refers to the relevant population in that region that are within the catchment area of functioning health facilities. Using the estimated AVH, we then obtain a more accurate measure of the proportion of Visayas households that sought consultation for specific illnesses. The adjusted incidence rate is 7.4 per cent, for identified illnesses involving 202,925 consultations (Table 5.4).

*Estimating the amount of time (hours) to care for the sick*

The above measurement of the amount of care (time) provided by household members in this study takes the following data limitation into account. Ideally, a time-use survey data among affected households can provide a more accurate measure of the amount of care hours provided by family members to the sick, with an accompanying health module that records the type of syndrome affecting the sick member. In the absence of such data, we provide here an estimate of the total care hours for the full-information subsample of 202,925 persons that sought consultation in a health facility. We then perform sensitivity tests to estimate the total amount of hours spent on unpaid work to care for the sick. First, we assume that sick children require about eight hours of passive and active minding (care) per day while sick adults require eight hours on average. We also estimate care hours based on alternative assumptions that the ill children/adults require 12 or 16 hours of minding per day. Second, we assume that children and adults in each region are affected by each health condition in the same proportion as they are represented in the overall health consultations. We obtain the estimated total unpaid care hours provided in the five-month (150 days) post-disaster period:

$$\text{Total Care Hours in Post} - \text{Haiyan Period} = \sum_{a=1}^{2}\sum_{c=1}^{6} R_{a,c}\, N_{a,c}\, P_{a}$$

where R is the number of required care hours per sick adult or child (subscript $a$) for each health condition (subscript $c$) using the information on the average number of sick days per adult or child for each syndrome in Table 5.2. N refers to the number of reported cases, and P is the proportion of children to adults represented in the EWARN data.

Table 5.5a provides the estimated total care hours for each person (adult or child) with an identified syndrome; Table 5.5b provides the summary of the total estimates under each assumption. The figures in Table 5.5a indicate that by far, caring for a sick child is more time-intensive than for an adult; those with ARIs, such as bronchitis and pneumonia, accounted for the largest amount of care time, followed by those with AWD. The total amount of unpaid care hours per week over the five-month post-disaster period ranged from 16.25 million hours to 32.35 million hours, depending on the daily care requirement assumptions (Table 5.5b). Figure 5.2 provides a comparison of the estimated total sick-care hours under various assumptions.

Table 5.5a Estimated amount of sick care required per health condition per person, hours per week, under various assumptions

| Health Condition | Assumption 1[g] | | Assumption 2 | | Assumption 3 | | Assumption 4 | | Assumtion 5 | | Assumption 6 | |
|---|---|---|---|---|---|---|---|---|---|---|---|---|
| | Adult: 8 hours | Child: 8 hours | Adult: 8 hours | Child:12 hours | Adult: 8 hours | Child: 16 hours | Adult:12 hours | Child: 12 hours | Adult: 12 hours | Child: 16 hours | Adult:16 hours | Child: 16 hours |
| ARI[a] | 112 | 224[h] | 112 | 336 | 112 | 448 | 168 | 336 | 168 | 448 | 224 | 448 |
| W/B[b] | 3 | 3 | 3 | 3 | 3 | 3 | 3 | 3 | 3 | 3 | 3 | 3 |
| HBP[c] | 1 | 1 | 1 | 1 | 1 | 1 | 1 | 1 | 1 | 1 | 1 | 1 |
| Fever[d] | 24 | 24 | 24 | 36 | 24 | 48 | 36 | 36 | 36 | 48 | 48 | 48 |
| SD[e] | 3 | 3 | 3 | 3 | 3 | 3 | 3 | 3 | 3 | 3 | 3 | 3 |
| AWD[f] | 112 | 112 | 112 | 168 | 112 | 224 | 168 | 168 | 168 | 224 | 224 | 224 |

Sources: Philippine Statistics Authority (2010), WHO (2014).

a  ARI, acute respiratory infection or pneumonia. Most healthy people recover from pneumonia in one to three weeks, but it can be life-threatening. American Lung Association (2016). Under Assumption 1, 14 days * 8 hours per day = 112 hrs; children's recovery takes much longer. Authors' estimate based on treatment plan from the Centres of Disease Control and Prevention (CDC 2016a).

b  W/B, open wounds and/or bruises. Authors' estimate based on Tempark et al. (2013).

f  AWD, acute watery diarrhea. Authors' estimate based on Cleveland Clinic (2013).

c  HBP, high blood pressure. One hour is used here to represent time required for medical consultation. Other care time required for high blood pressure is difficult to estimate based on reported data.

d  Fever and rash. Authors' estimate based on Mayo Clinic (2016).

e  SD, skin disease.

f  Acute water diarrhea.

g  Each assumption refers to the number of hours per day of care for ill adult or child.

h  Authors' estimate based on Thompson et al. (2013), a systematic review of literature on duration of symptoms of earache, sore throat, cough, bronchiolitis and the common cold in children.

Table 5.5b Sensitivity estimates of total sick care hours provided by Visayan households required per health condition per week, Post–Haiyan period under various assumptions, by type of health condition

| Type of Health Condition | Assumptions regarding required care time per sick adult or child per day (in hours) | | | | | |
|---|---|---|---|---|---|---|
| | (1) | (2) | (3) | (4) | (5) | (6) |
| | Adult 8, Child 8 | Adult 8, Child 12 | Adult 8, Child 16 | Adult 12, Child 12 | Adult 12, Child 16 | Adult 16, Child 16 |
| ARI[a] | 14,779,003 | 17,687,652 | 20,596,301 | 22,168,505 | 25,077,154 | 29,558,006 |
| AWD[b] | 983,024 | 1,131,482 | 1,279,939 | 1,474,536 | 1,622,994 | 1,966,048 |
| W/B[c] | 98,259 | 98,259 | 98,259 | 98,259 | 98,259 | 98,259 |
| HBP[d] | 18,096 | 18,096 | 18,096 | 18,096 | 18,096 | 18,096 |
| Fever[e] | 331,776 | 381,881 | 431,986 | 497,664 | 547,769 | 663,552 |
| SD[f] | 44,499 | 44,499 | 44,499 | 44,499 | 44,499 | 44,499 |
| Total | 16,254,657 | 19,361,869 | 22,469,080 | 24,301,559 | 27,408,770 | 32,348,460 |

Notes:
a ARI refers to acute respiratory infection diagnosed by medical practitioner (doctor or nurse)
b AWD refers to acute watery diarrhea
c W/B, refers to open wounds and/or bruises
d HBP, refers to high blood pressure
e Fever (requiring medical exam) and rash
f SD, skin disease

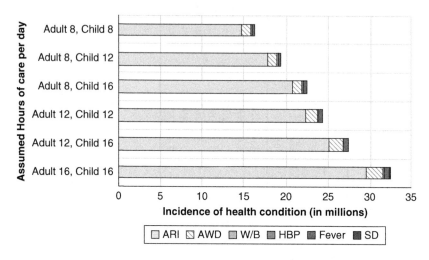

*Figure 5.2* Sensitivity estimates of total care hours in Post-Haiyan Visayan Region November 2017 – March 2018 under various assumptions, by type of health condition.

Although these are only rough estimates, there are several reasons as to why the figures provided in Tables 5.3a and 5.3b are likely to be low. First, our estimates ranging from 16.25 to 32.35 million sick-care hours are based solely on the 202,925 observations where we know the specific condition that received medical examination. They do not include the other consultations involving 139,232 health conditions whose syndromes have not been specified in the EWARN report. Second, the estimations provided in Tables 5.3a and 5.3b do not take into account the affected population in the catchment areas where the health facilities were damaged (Novales 2014: 24). Damage to health facilities, along with typhoon-related transportation difficulties meant that a significant proportion of the population that suffered injury, communicable or non-communicable disease is likely to require even longer care due to absence of health or medical treatment.

On the other hand, the estimated total hours of required care given in Table 5.5 cannot be attributed solely to the effect of Super-typhoon Haiyan. It is possible that a proportion of those who sought consultations have pre-existing health conditions (before Haiyan) such as high blood pressure, respiratory illness etc. Unfortunately, the absence of a regular collection of health data in the region prevents us from identifying the increase in sick care hours due to the increased incidence of injuries or illnesses in the typhoon aftermath.

### Household distribution of unpaid work

As in other countries, the majority of care work in Philippine households fall on women. Time-use surveys provide information on how people allocate their time across various activities including care work and household work.

In order to identify the trends in the division of labour in Visayan households, our study uses the 2012 ISSP module on Family and Changing Gender Roles collected by the Social Weather Stations, a private, well-respected public opinion organisation. The ISSP is a cross-national annual survey which covers mostly European countries and some Asian countries including the Philippines. Each year the survey is focused on one topic and 2012 was the fourth year to focus on 'Family and Changing Gender Roles.' The Philippine sample consists of 600 male and 600 female respondents. Each respondent was asked how many hours on average they spend caring for children, the elderly and the sick in their household, and how many hours they spend doing other household work.

For our study purpose, we focus on the sample data collected in the Visayan region of the Philippines, in November–December 2012, or less than one year before Super-typhoon Haiyan (Yolanda) made landfall (Gendall *et al.* 2016). The Visayan subsample consists of 300 voting-age adults, 150 males and 150 females. The survey was conducted in face-to-face interviews, with an interpreter or translator and visuals. The survey respondents were chosen through a multi-stage process using a Kish grid method with Barangays as the sampling frame. About 20 per cent of interviews were back-checked and there was a 41.8 per cent response rate.

Table 5.6 provides information regarding the characteristics of the Visayas sample respondents. More than 70 per cent have a partner (either wife or husband); nearly two-thirds of the male respondents are employed, compared to 38 per cent of female respondents. In terms of schooling, although there are very few male (2.67 per cent) and female (1.33 per cent) respondents who have no formal education, more women (20.66 per cent) than men (18.67 per cent) however receive at least some college education. Nearly two-thirds of the male respondents and three-fourths of the female respondents live in the rural areas; most (76–78 per cent) live in households with at least one child aged 0–18 years old.

We next analyse the determinants of time spent on housework and care work using the Ordinary Least Squares (OLS) regression method. We estimate the time spent per week by individual $i$ in household $j$ on a work activity $Y_{ij}$:

$$Y_{ij}^{\star} = X_{ij}\beta + Z_j\gamma + \varepsilon_{ij}$$

where $Y_{ij}^{\star}$ refers to the amount of hours per week that a person $i$ spends in doing housework, care work or both. $X_{ij}$ and $Z_{ij}$ are vectors of observable characteristics at the individual and household levels respectively, which influence the dependent variable. These include household size, sex, age, years of education, and labour force status (with employed as base dummy). Additionally, the reported partner's housework time (Model 1), the partner's care work time (Model 2) and partner's combined household work time (Model 3) are included in the estimations. Both $\beta$ and $\gamma$ are unknown parameters to be estimated.

*Table 5.6* Characteristics of ISSP Visayas sample respondents

| | No. of Respondents | | % of Total, by Sex | |
|---|---|---|---|---|
| | *Male* | *Female* | *Male* | *Female* |
| Is a partner present? | | | | |
| Partner living in same household | 107 | 112 | 71.3 | 74.7 |
| Partner living in different household | 3 | 3 | 2.0 | 2.0 |
| No partner | 40 | 35 | 26.7 | 23.3 |
| *Total* | *150* | *150* | *100.0* | *100.0* |
| Main work status | | | | |
| Paid work | 97 | 57 | 64.7 | 38.0 |
| Unemployed | 17 | 31 | 11.3 | 20.7 |
| In school | 9 | 3 | 6.0 | 2.0 |
| Sick/disabled | 12 | 4 | 8.0 | 2.7 |
| Retired | 6 | 5 | 4.0 | 3.3 |
| Performing domestic chores | 8 | 48 | 5.3 | 32.0 |
| Other | 1 | 2 | 0.7 | 1.3 |
| *Total* | *150* | *150* | *100.0* | *100.0* |
| Education level | | | | |
| No formal education | 4 | 2 | 2.7 | 1.3 |
| Elementary | 46 | 51 | 30.7 | 34.0 |
| High school | 59 | 53 | 39.3 | 35.3 |
| Vocational | 13 | 13 | 8.7 | 8.7 |
| Some college | 16 | 17 | 10.7 | 11.3 |
| Completed college | 12 | 14 | 8.0 | 9.3 |
| *Total* | *150* | *150* | *100.0* | *100.0* |
| Urban/rural | | | | |
| Big city | 9 | 9 | 6.0 | 6.0 |
| Suburbs or outskirts of a big city | 10 | 8 | 6.7 | 5.3 |
| Town or small city | 26 | 17 | 17.3 | 11.3 |
| Country village | 100 | 112 | 66.7 | 74.7 |
| Farm or country home | 5 | 4 | 3.3 | 2.7 |
| *Total* | *150* | *150* | *100.0* | *100.0* |
| No. of children 0–17 years in household | | | | |
| 0 | 36 | 32 | 24.0 | 21.3 |
| 1 | 42 | 32 | 28.0 | 21.3 |
| 2 | 27 | 36 | 18.0 | 24.0 |
| 3+ | 45 | 50 | 30.0 | 33.3 |
| *Total* | *150* | *150* | *100.0* | *100.0* |
| Household size | | | | |
| 1-2 | 19 | 15 | 12.7 | 10.0 |
| 3-4 | 51 | 57 | 34.0 | 38.0 |
| 5-6 | 55 | 43 | 36.7 | 28.7 |
| 7-8 | 17 | 28 | 11.3 | 18.7 |
| 9+ | 9 | 7 | 5.3 | 4.7 |
| *Total* | *150* | *150* | *100.0* | *100.0* |

Source: Authors' calculation. Data from International Social Survey Programme: Family and Changing Gender Roles IV – ISSP 2012. GESIS Data Archive.

Models 1 and 2 estimate the time spent in domestic chores or housework, care work including childcare, elderly care or sick care respectively, while Model 3 estimates the total household work (care and domestic chores). We also run the extended models (Models 4–6) with the number of children aged 0–5 years old and the number of children aged 6–18 years old included as control variables instead of household size.

The OLS model estimates are given in Table 5.7. In all six models, women spend significantly more hours in housework (over nine hours on average per week) and care work (over ten hours on average per week) than men. Those living in rural areas however spend about six hours less than those in the urban areas. Interestingly, those who are more educated spend more time in care work, suggesting that education helps emphasise the importance of care in the well-being of dependent members. Not surprisingly, having young children increases the hours spent in care work.

*Table 5.7* OLS results: Determinants of housework and care work hours

| | *(1) housework* | *(2) care work* | *(3) combined* | *(4) housework* | *(5) care work* | *(6) combined* |
|---|---|---|---|---|---|---|
| Hhsize | -0.28 | 1.04★★★ | 0.76 | | | |
| | (-1.32) | -3.53 | -1.81 | | | |
| female | 9.18★★★ | 10.20★★★ | 19.56★★★ | 9.23★★★ | 10.02★★★ | 19.43★★★ |
| | (9.19) | (7.23) | (9.83) | (9.21) | (7.20) | (9.83) |
| rural | -2.69★★ | -3.34★ | -6.04★ | -2.65★★ | -3.77★★ | -6.43★★★ |
| | (-2.73) | (-2.40) | (-3.07) | (-2.68) | (-2.75) | (-3.30) |
| age | 0.08★ | -0.14★★ | -0.06 | 0.09★★ | 0.09 | -0.00 |
| | (2.58) | (-3.11) | (-1.00) | (2.76) | (-1.87) | (-0.03) |
| educyrs | 0.04 | 0.44★ | 0.47 | 0.04 | 0.50★ | 0.53 |
| | (0.29) | (2.06) | (1.57) | (0.28) | (2.38) | (1.78) |
| unemploy | 0.81 | 3.43 | 4.57 | 0.70 | 3.50 | 4.50 |
| | (0.60) | (1.81) | (1.71) | (0.52) | (1.87) | (1.70) |
| NILF | 2.16 | 7.16★★★ | 9.61★★★ | 2.04 | 6.53★★★ | 8.85★★★ |
| | (1.90) | (4.46) | (4.24) | (1.78) | (4.11) | (3.91) |
| ptnr_hw | 0.09★★★ | | | 0.09★★★ | | |
| | (4.77) | | | (4.71) | | |
| ptnr_care | | 0.16★★★ | | | 0.15★★★ | |
| | | (7.58) | | | (7.07) | |
| ptnr_tot | | | 0.15★★★ | | | 0.14★★★ |
| | | | (8.18) | | | (7.68) |
| Young chld | | | | 0.18 | 4.90★★★ | 4.96★★★ |
| | | | | (0.34) | (6.69) | (4.76) |
| Older chld | | | | -0.25 | 0.61 | 0.30 |
| | | | | (-0.65) | (1.16) | (0.41) |
| _cons | 12.10★★★ | 10.02★★★ | 21.16★★★ | 10.58★★★ | 8.82★ | 18.77★★★ |
| | (4.40) | (2.59) | (3.86) | (4.07) | (2.45) | (3.66) |
| N | 1199 | 1196 | 1196 | 1199 | 1196 | 1196 |
| r2 | 0.10 | 0.14 | 0.16 | 0.10 | 0.16 | 0.17 |
| F | 17.38 | 23.25 | 27.54 | 15.29 | 25.06 | 27.06 |

*t* statistics in parentheses
★ $p<0.05$, ★★ $p<0.01$, ★★★ $p<0.001$

Table 5.8 and Figure 5.3 provide the self-reported average time spent by all male and female respondents in care work and housework (n=299) and by those with partners living in the same household (n=218). Table 5.8 also shows the respondents' report on the time spent by the partner on these activities. Female respondents report nearly 1.5 times the amount of care work than those reported by male respondents; the difference in female:male time spent in housework however is smaller, about 4.5 hours per week on average. Using the perceived amount of time spent by their partners, female respondents in couple households (or with partners) report a lower amount of time spent by their husbands in care work (11.5 hours) and housework (11.7 hours) than the average male respondent's self-reported time in these

*Table 5.8* Self-reported and partner-reported care work and house work, ISSP Visayas sample

|  | All Respondents | | Subsample: Respondents with partners living in same household | |
|---|---|---|---|---|
| **A. Hours Per Week, Self-reported** | | | | |
|  | Male | Female | Male | Female |
| Care work | | | | |
| Mean | 17 | 28 | 19.9 | 31.8 |
| Std. Dev | 18 | 26.8 | 19.2 | 27.4 |
| N | 148 | 148 | 105 | 110 |
| House work | | | | |
| Mean | 18.4 | 23.9 | 20.2 | 24.8 |
| Std. Dev | 16.9 | 17.8 | 18.2 | 18.1 |
| N | 150 | 149 | 107 | 111 |
| **B. Hours Per Week, Self-reported** | | | | |
|  | Sex of Respondent's partner | | | |
|  | Male | Female | Male | Female |
| Care work | | | | |
| Mean | 11.5 | 19.2 | 15.5 | 26.6 |
| Std. Dev | 15.8 | 23.5 | 16.6 | 23.8 |
| N | 147 | 148 | 109 | 105 |
| House work | | | | |
| Mean | 11.7 | 21.4 | 15.6 | 29.6 |
| Std. Dev | 13.8 | 21.3 | 13.9 | 19.5 |
| N | 148 | 149 | 110 | 105 |

Source: Authors' calculations. Data from International Social Survey Programme: Family and Changing Gender Roles IV – ISSP 2012. GESIS Data Archive.

Note: Data drawn from responses to the following ISSP 2012 Survey questions: \Q16a On average, how many hours a week do you personally spend on household work, not including childcare and leisure time activities?"; \Q16b On average, how many hours a week do you spend looking after family members (e.g. children, elderly, ill or disabled family members)?"; \Q17a And what about your spouse/ partner? On average, how many hours a week does he/she spend on household work, not including childcare and leisure time activities?"; \Q17b And on average, how many hours a week does he/she spend looking after family members (e.g. children, elderly, ill or disabled family members)?"

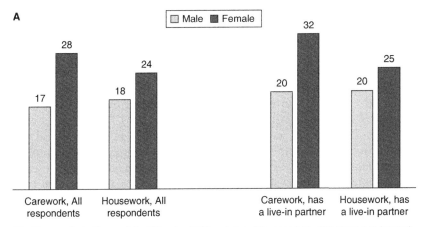

\*For All respondents: Care work (n=148 males, 148 females) and Housework (n = 150 males, 149 females). For subsample of respondents who have a live-in partner: Care work (n=105 males, 110 females) and Housework (n=107 males, 111 females.)

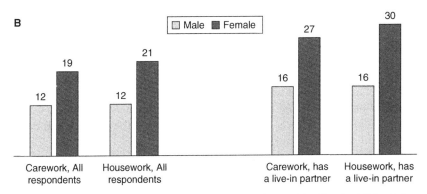

\*For All respondents: Care work (n=147 males, 148 females) and Housework (n= 48 males, 149 females). For subsample of respondents who have a live-in partner: Care work (n=109 males, 105 females) and Housework (n=110 males, 105 females.)

*Figure 5.3* a) Average care and household work hours per week, Self-reported, by sex of respondent and household type. b) Average care and household work hours per week, Respondent's report for partner, by sex of partner and household type.

activities. Male respondents in couple households also report a lower amount of time spent by their wives in care work (26.6 hours) but higher amount of housework time (29.6 hours).

If the above trends in the allocation of time within the Visayas households provide some indication on the division of care work, then women are more likely to shoulder the brunt of the additional sick care in the aftermath of natural disasters like Super-typhoon Haiyan.

## Health expenditures faced by affected households

Affected households not only face a surge in demand for time spent in caring for the sick; they are likely to also be confronted with medical expenses. In this section, we provide indirect evidence suggesting that poor households are more likely to provide longer hours of sick care due to their inability to meet these costs. We use the survey results of Espallardo *et al.* (2015) study on the out-of-pocket health expenses incurred by households during the response phase (one week after) and the recovery phase (seven months after). The surveys were conducted in the Eastern Visayas (region VIII) in 2014 where Haiyan had the greatest impact. A study team from the Department of Family and Community Medicine of the University of the Philippines and Philippine General Hospital conducted interviews on a small purposive sample of 35 individuals in two rural communities in Samar and Leyte provinces. They also reviewed hospital and PhilHealth data on claims and costs of health services, including professional fees, laboratories and medicines to validate the results.

Table 5.9 provides the main reasons cited by the survey respondents for not accessing health services. In the week after Haiyan made landfall, availability of funds for consultation and transportation was cited as the main barrier for 52 per cent of the respondents; another 47 per cent cited the distance or poor road conditions as the main problem. During the seven-month period after the typhoon however, inadequate funds to access health facilities was the main problem for 98 per cent of the respondents, due to depletion of savings, decline in earnings, and incidence of consumption shocks including out-of-pocket expenses for home repair and out-of-pocket health expenses. This implies that unattended illnesses are likely to be even higher among the poor, which prolongs the time spent in caring for the sick.

Table 5.10 provides the healthcare costs, out-of-pocket expenses during the emergency response phase (one week after the typhoon) and the transition to recovery phase (seven months after) using Espallardo *et al.* (2015) survey data. Direct healthcare costs are defined as the costs of labour, supplies, medicines and equipment to provide patient-care services. Indirect healthcare costs

*Table 5.9* Barriers to utilisation of health services, sample survey interviews, Sta Fe, Leyte and Guiuan, Eastern Samar, Eastern Visayas (*n*=35)

| Reasons | One week after | | Seven months after | |
|---|---|---|---|---|
| | *Frequency* | *Percent (%)* | *Frequency* | *Percent (%)* |
| Health facility is too far | 7 | 16% | 3 | 12% |
| Health facility is closed | 2 | 4% | 0 | 0% |
| No money for transportation | 13 | 28% | 9 | 36% |
| No money for consultation | 10 | 24% | 13 | 52% |
| Poor road conditions | 13 | 27% | 0 | 0% |

Source: Table 2, Espallardo *et al.* (2015: 98).

*Table 5.10* Self-reported out-of-pocket expenses, one week and seven months after Typhoon Haiyan, sample survey interviews, Sta Fe, Leyte and Guiuan, Eastern Samar, Eastern Visayas (*n*=35)

| Type of Expense | One week after | | Seven months after | | Ratio of mean expenses |
|---|---|---|---|---|---|
| | Mean ($US) | Range ($US) | Mean ($US) | Range ($US) | |
| Professional fee | 11.40 | 0 | 302 | 5-1177 | 6 |
| Laboratory | 19.51 | – | 191 | 5-35 | 52 |
| Medicines | 24.89 | 3.5-71 | 124 | 5-1177 | 5 |
| Hospital stay | 0.00 | 0 | 501 | 7-1177 | 0 |
| Transportation | 1.91 | 0.5-9 | 19 | 0-82 | 19 |

Source: Table 2, Espallardo *et al.* (2015: 98).

Note: All figures in $US at exchange rate of $US 1.00= PhP 42.47 (2 June 2014). Values without range represent those with only one respondent.

include non-medical components of obtaining healthcare including transportation, lodging and home services.

In public health facilities, minimal out-of-pocket or user fees were charged to those with PhilHealth insurance. Private health facilities, however, charged an additional amount outside the PhilHealth insurance coverage, which range from US$11 to US$21 per visit.[16] All patients, whether using public or private health facilities, were required to pay for medicines and supplies, which averaged about US$25 one week after the typhoon. But seven months after the typhoon, the reported costs of medical treatment had increased, with professional fees averaging about US$302 and US$191 for laboratory services During this time, most international and local non-governmental organisations and foreign medical volunteer teams had left along with their free medicine and free consultations, and most of the donor funds and medicines had been used up. The highest out-of-pocket costs are for hospital stays (US$501 on average). A review of hospital records and PhilHealth Insurance reimbursements seven months after the typhoon confirms the high costs. These expenses are considered to be 'catastrophic' considering the fact that 57 per cent of the survey respondents earn an average monthly income below US$94.

## Concluding remarks

We argue in this chapter that a comprehensive post-disaster assessment can benefit from a gender-sensitive awareness of the amount of care work demanded by an increase in morbidity rates. Such an approach requires gathering information and data about the care needs of the affected population. As long as unpaid care work remains statistically invisible, policymakers are likely to treat the unpaid care labour provided by families to be infinitely elastic and tasks for meeting the healthcare needs can be perceived as less urgent. Our empirical analysis shows a marked rise in health conditions in the aftermath of Haiyan. By means of projections, we provide estimates in the amount of unpaid work to care for the sick and injured. Time-use trends among Visayas households suggest that women are more likely to provide sick care. They face persistent tensions between the various demands for their time during the post-disaster period: on one hand, the increased demand for their time to help rebuild their livelihoods and earn income and on the other hand, an increase in the demand for care. The poor are more likely to provide longer hours of sick care due to inability to access healthcare facilities and/or to pay for medical expenses.

This study provides some key lessons for designing disaster response systems and recovery plans. One is the importance of incorporating care needs as part of the impact assessments and recovery planning. Moreover, social protection mechanisms are needed to ensure that affected households, especially the poor, can access healthcare beyond the period when free services and medicines are provided by international donors and humanitarian organisations (Espallardo *et al.* 2015: 79). Preparedness should include development of a comprehensive social health insurance to ensure protection in the event a disaster.

Ultimately, frameworks for examining climate change must incorporate the inevitable increase in care work that it precipitates. Damage functions that focus on GDP and economic output fail to adequately measure the decline in welfare precisely because the care economy is left out. This requires further research on the manner in which aspects of care work are affected by climatic conditions, directly and indirectly. There is also need for coordinated efforts across sectors of societies: households, governments and businesses to meet the demand for care in a way that reduces women's workload and redistributes the responsibility across society. Just as there is need for cooperation to effectively manage the use of natural resources so that they meet the needs of future generations. Such an agenda requires developing attitudes and viewpoints that the well-being of children, the sick, disabled and elderly are our collective responsibilities and that the ecosystem of which we are part is a set of common property resources that we all are responsible for, one way or the other.

## Notes

1 Corresponding author. The authors would like to thank the Philippine Statistics Authority officials for providing some of the data, Stephan Lefebvre and Valerie Lacarte for their research assistance, and Julie Nelson and Christine Bauhardt for their helpful comments.
2 See Pindyck 2014 and Prahl *et al.* 2016
3 The evidence provided by recent studies has illuminated key linkages between complex natural and human systems (Carleton and Hsiang 2016: 1).
4 In the devastated Tacloban City, the capital of Leyte province, an estimated one-third of the population were squatters (Yamada and Galat 2014: 433).
5 Balaguru *et al.* (2016), Takayabu *et al.* (2015), Kang and Elsner (2015) find that effects of climate change e.g. ocean freshening and increasing ocean temperatures have increased the intensity of typhoons and super-typhoons.

6  In 2013, the United Nations Framework Convention on Climate Change (UNFCCC) established the Warsaw International Mechanism to address loss and damage in developing countries from the impacts of climate change.

7  Province-level poverty incidence based on the 2012 Family Income and Expenditure Survey (FIES) data.

8  Models for estimating the costs and benefits of different global climate change policies take as inputs various 'damage functions' that describe how social and economic losses accrue under different future climate change scenarios.

9  The estimated cost of the typhoon-related damage is US$ 2.005 billion, using the exchange rate of 1 US$ = 44.67 Philippine peso (NDRRMC 2014: 63).

10  RHUs are small health clinics in rural municipalities and are part of the national public network of health centers that has its roots in the 1954 Rural Health Act. Barangay Health Stations (BHSs) are community-based organisations in both rural and urban areas that provide first aid and primary health care.

11  See McPherson *et al.* 2015 and Barreca *et al.* 2015.

12  Limited services were resumed a few weeks after the super-typhoon with the help of volunteers and the establishment of temporary facilities such as field hospitals.

13  About 40 per cent of rural health units (RHUs), 69 per cent of Barangay Health Stations (BHSs), and 38 per cent of hospitals were damaged. By May 2014, WHO had reported that 61 per cent of health facilities were partially functional or fully functional, an improvement from 49 per cent in January 2014 (WHO 2014).

14  As of March 2014, a total of 403 health facilities reported through the Department of Health and World Health Organization (DOH-WHO) EWARN system; these include 145 Rural Health Units (RHUs), 131 Barangay Health Stations (BHSs), 63 hospitals, as well as 38 newly constructed mobile clinics, 20 evacuation centers and six hospitals run by foreign medical teams (WHO 2014).

15  We use the following population growth equation to estimate the 2013 household-population for in the Visayas region:

$$ r = \frac{\log\left(P_{t+n} / P_t\right)}{n \star \log_e} \star 100 $$

Where,

r       = annual rate of population growth
$P_{t+n}$  = population in the year of interest
$P_t$      = population in base census period
n       = number of years between census and year of interest, Pt and Pt+n
e       = the natural logarithm, value of approx. 2.718

16  According to the 2013 Philippines National Demographic and Health Survey, 30.3 per cent of individuals in Western Visayas have no health insurance, and the figures for Central and Eastern Visayas are 44.0 and 29.9, respectively (PSA-USAID 2014). The percentage of individuals using PhilHealth, the national health insurance program, accounts for the vast majority of those who do have insurance (66.6 per cent Western Visayas, 53.8 per cent Central Visayas, and 69 per cent Eastern Visayas).

# References

Agarwal, A., 2008. *The Role of Local Institutions in Adaptation to Climate Change.* Washington, DC: World Bank. [online] Available from: http://documents.worldbank.org/curated/en/234591468331456170/The-role-of-local-institutions-in-adaptation-to-climate-change [Accessed 15 February 2017].

American Lung Association, 2016. *Pneumonia.* [online] Available from: http://www.lung. org/lung-health-and-diseases/lung-disease-lookup/pneumonia/ [Accessed 2 February 2017].

Balaguru, K., Foltz, G.R., Leung, R.L. and Emanuel, K.A., 2016. Global warming-induced upper-ocean freshening and the intensification of super typhoons. *Nature Communications,* 7: 13670. [online] Available from: doi:10.1038/ncomms13670. [Accessed 15 February 2017].

Barreca, A., Clay, K., Deschênes, O., Greenstone, M. and Shapiro, J.S., 2015. Convergence in adaptation to climate change: evidence from high temperatures and mortality, 1900–2004. *The American Economic Review,* 105 (5): 247–51.

Bauhardt, C., 2014. Solutions to the crisis? The green New Deal, degrowth, and the solidarity economy: alternatives to the capitalist growth economy from an ecofeminist economics perspective. *Ecological Economics,* 102: 60–8. [online] Available from: doi:10.1016/j. ecolecon.2014.03.015. [Accessed 15 February 2017].

Beneria, L., Berik, G. and Floro, M.S., 2016. *Gender, Development, and Globalisation: Economics as if All People Mattered.* New York: Routledge.

Birkmann, J., Garschagen, M., Mucke, P., Schauder, A., Seibert, T., Welle, T., Rhyner, J., Kohler, S., Loster, T., Reinhard, D. and Matuschke, I., 2014. *World Risk Report 2014.* Berlin: Alliance Development Works and Bonn: United Nations University – Institute for Environment and Human Security.

Canevari-Luzardo, L., Bastide, J., Chouet, I. and Liverman, D., 2017. Using partial participatory GIS in vulnerability and disaster risk reduction in Grenada. *Climate and Development,* 9 (2): 95–109. [online] Available from: doi:10.1080/17565529.2015.10675 93 [Accessed 15 February 2017].

Carleton, T.A. and Hsiang, S.M., 2016. Social and economic impacts of climate. *Science,* 353 (6304): aad9837. [online] Available from: doi:10.1126/science.aad9837 [Accessed 16 June 2018].

CDC, 2014. *Leptospirosis.* Atlanta, GA: Centres for Disease Control and Prevention. [online] Available from: https://www.cdc.gov/leptospirosis/ [Accessed 2 February 2017].

CDC, 2016a. *Emergency Wound Management for Healthcare Professionals.* Atlanta, GA: Centres for Disease Control and Prevention. [online] Available from: https://www.cdc.gov/ disasters/emergwoundhcp.html [Accessed 2 February 2017].

CDC, 2016b. August 2016. *Measles (rubeola).* Atlanta, GA: Centres for Disease Control and Prevention. [online] Available from: https://www.cdc.gov/measles/hcp/index.html [Accessed 8 July 2016].

CDC, 2016c. July 2016. *Meningococcal disease.* Atlanta, GA: Centres for Disease Control and Prevention. [online] Available from: https://www.cdc.gov/meningococcal/about/ symptoms.html [Accessed 2 February 2017].

Cleveland Clinic, 2013. *Acute diarrhoea.* Cleveland, OH: Cleveland Clinic. [online] Available from: http://www.clevelandclinicmeded.com/medicalpubs/diseasemanagement/gastro enterology/acute-diarrhea/ [Accessed 8 July 2016].

Corry, R., 2017. Did climate change cause that? *In*: A. Lippert-Rasmussen, K. Brownlee and D. Coady, eds., *A Companion to Applied Philosophy.* Hoboken, NJ: John Wiley and Sons, 469–83.

DOH and WHO, 2014. Typhoon Yolanda. *Philippines Health Cluster Bulletin,* 19 (16 May 2014).

Emanuel, K., 2005. Increasing destructiveness of tropical cyclones over the past 30 years. *Nature* [online], 436 (7051): 686–8. Available from: doi:10.1038/nature03906 [Accessed 15 February 2017].

Enarson, E. and Charabarti, P.G.D., eds., 2009. *Women, Gender and Disaster: Global Issues and Initiatives*. London: SAGE.

Espallardo, N , Geroy, L.S., Villanueva, R., Gavino, R., Nievera, L.A. and Hall, J.L., 2015. A snapshot of catastrophic post-disaster health expenses after Typhoon Haiyan. *Western Pacific Surveillance and Response Journal*, 6 (1), 76–81.

Gendall, P., Joye, D. and Sapin, M., 2016. *Family and changing gender roles IV: study monitoring report*. ISSP Report 2012. Manila: International Social Survey Program (ISSP) Research Group.

Holtz, L.R., Neill, M.A. and Tarr, P.I., 2009. Acute bloody diarrhoea: a medical emergency for patients of all ages. *Gastroenterology*, 136 (6), 1887–98.

Immunization Action Coalition, 2016, *Tetanus: Questions and answers* [online]. St. Paul, MN: Immunization Action Coalition. [online] Available from: http://www.immunize. org/catg.d/p4220.pdf [Accessed 16 June 2018].

Intergovernmental Panel on Climate Change (IPCC), 2013. *Climate Change 2013: The Physical Science Basis: Contribution of Working Group 1 to the Fifth Assessment Report of the Intergovernmental Panel on Climate Change*. T. F. Stocker, D. Qin, G. K. Plattner, M. Tignor, S. K. Allen, K. Boschung, A. Nauels, Y. Xia, V. Bes, and PM Midgley, eds, Cambridge, UK: Cambridge University Press. [online] Available from http://www/ IPCC.ch/pdf/assessment report/ar5/wg1AR5_ALL_FINAL.pdf [Accessed 16 June 2018].

James, R., Otto, F., Parker, H., Boyd, E., Cornforth, R., Mitchell, D. and Allen, M. 2014. Characterising loss and damage from climate change. *Nature Climate Change* [online], 4 (11): 938–9. Available from: doi:10.1038/nclimate2411. [Accessed 15 February 2017].

Kang, N.Y. and Elsner, J.B., 2015. Climate mechanism for stronger typhoons in a warmer world. *Journal of Climate* [online], 29 (3): 1051–7. Available from: doi:10.1175/ JCLI-D-15-0585.1 [Accessed 15 February 2017].

Kreft, S., Eckstein, D., Junghans, L., Kerestan, C. and Hagen, U., 2014. Global Climate Risk Index 2015: Who Suffers Most From Extreme Weather Events? Weather–Related Loss Events In 2013 And 1994 To 2013. Berlin: Germanwatch.

Martinez, R.E., Quintana, R., Go, J.J., Marquez, M.A., Kim, J.K., Villones, M.S. and Salazar, M.A., 2015. Surveillance for and issues relating to noncommunicable diseases post-Haiyan in Region 8. *Western Pacific Surveillance and Response*, 6 (1), 21–4.

Mayo Clinic, 2016. *Fever* [online]. Rochester, NY: Mayo Foundation for Medical Education and Research. Available from: http://www.mayoclinic.org/diseases-conditions/fever/ basics/definition/con-20019229 [Accessed 2 February 2017].

McPherson, M., Counahan, M. and Hall, J.L., 2015. Responding to Typhoon Haiyan in the Philippines. *Western Pacific Surveillance and Response* [online], 6 (1). Available from: http://ojs.wpro.who.int/ojs/index.php/wpsar/article/view/404 [Accessed 15 February 2017].

NDRRMC, 2014. *Final Report re Effects of Typhoon 'Yolanda' (Haiyan)* [Online]. Quezon City, Philippines: National Disaster Risk Reduction and Management Centre, Camp Aguinaldo. Available from http://www.ndrrmc.gov.ph/attachments/article/1329/ Update_on_Effects_Typhoon_YOLANDA_(Haiyan)_17APR2014.pdf [Accessed 16 June 2018].

Nelson, J.A., 2009. Between a rock and a soft place: ecological and feminist economics in policy debates. *Ecological Economics* [online], 69 (1). Available from: https://works. bepress.com/julie_nelson1/12/ [Accessed 15 February 2017].

Novales, C.L., 2014. *Haiyan Gender Snapshot: Leyte, Eastern Samar & Northern Cebu*. Quezon City, Philippines: Oxfam.

Philippine Statistics Authority-United States Agency International Development (PSA–USAID). 2014. *Philippines National Demographic and Health Survey 2013*. Manila: Philippine Statistics Authority.

Pindyck, R.S., 2013. Climate change policy: what do the models tell us? *Journal of Economic Literature* 51 (3): 860–72.

Prahl, B., Rybski, D., Boettle, M. and Kropp, J.P., 2016. Damage functions for climate-related hazards: unification and uncertainty analysis. *Natural Hazards Earth Systems Science* [online], 16: 1189–203. Available from: www.nat-hazards-earth-syst-sci. net/16/1189/2016/doi:10.5194/nhess-16-1189-2016 [Accessed 15 February 2017].

PSA, 2010. *2010 Census and Housing Population* [online]. Manila: Philippine Statistics Authority. Available from: http://web0.psa.gov.ph/old/data/pressrelease/2012/PHILS_summary_pop_n_PGR_1990to2010.pdf [Accessed 17 June 2016].

Salazar, M.A., Pesigan, A., Law, R. and Winkler, V., 2016. Post-disaster health impact of natural hazards in the Philippines in 2013. *Global Health Action*, 9 (1): 31320.

Staples, J. E., Shankar, M. B., Sejvar, J. J., Meltzer, M. I. and Fischer, M., 2014. Initial and long-term costs of patients hospitalised with West Nile virus disease. *The American Journal of Tropical Medicine and Hygiene*, 90 (3): 402–9.

Takayabu, I., Hibino, K., Sasaki, H., Shiogama, H., Mori, N., Shibutani, Y. and Takemi, T., 2015. Climate change effects on the worst-case storm surge: a case study of Typhoon Haiyan *Environmental Research Letters* [online] 10 (6): 64011. Available from: doi:10.1088/1748-9326/10/6/064011 [Accessed 15 February 2017].

Tempark, T., Lueangarun, S., Chatproedprai, S. and Wananukul, S., 2013. Flood-related skin diseases: a literature review. *International Journal of Dermatology* [online], 52 (10): 1168–76. Available from: doi:10.1111/ijd.12064 [Accessed 2 February 2017].

Thompson, M., Vodicka, T.A., Blair, P.S., Buckley, D.I., Heneghan, C. and Hay, A.D., 2013. Duration of symptoms of respiratory tract infections in children: systematic review. *BMJ* [Online], 347, f7027. Available from: http://www.bmj.com/content/347/bmj.f7027 [Accessed 2 February 2017].

UNFCCC, 2013. *Report on the structured expert dialogue on the 2013–2015 review* [online]. Report FCCC/SB/2015/INF.1. New York: United Nations. Available from: http://unfccc.int/resource/docs/2015/sb/eng/inf01.pdf [Accessed 15 February 2017].

WHO, 2014. *EWARN weekly summary report: Post-typhoon Yolanda week 18 (reporting period: 10th November 2013 to 8th March 2014)* [online]. Technical report, 2014. Available from: http://www.wpro.who.int/philippines/typhoonhaiyan/media/EWARN-10Nov2013-8Mar2014.pdf. [Accessed 29 January 2016].

WHO, 2016a. *Hepatitis E.* [online] Available from: http://www.who.int/mediacentre/factsheets/fs280/en/ [Accessed 2 February 2017].

WHO, 2016b. *Management of severe acute malnutrition in infants and children.* [online] Available from: http://www.who.int/elena/titles/full_recommendations/sam_ management/en/index4.html [Accessed 2 February 2017].

WHO,2016c. *Recommended surveillance standards.* 2nd ed. [online]. Available from: http://www. who.int/csr/resources/publications/surveillance/whocdscsrisr992syn. pdf [Accessed 2 February 2017].

Yamada, S., and Galat, A., 2014. Typhoon Yolanda/Haiyan and climate justice. *Disaster Medicine and Public Health Preparedness* [online] 8 (5): 432–35. Available from: doi:10.1017/dmp.2014.97. [Accessed 15 February 2017].

# 6 Care-full Community Economies

*Kelly Dombroski, Stephen Healy and Katharine McKinnon*

## Introduction

In this era of human-induced environmental crisis, it is widely recognised that we need to foster better ways to sustain life for people and planet. For us – and other scholars drawing on the Community Economies tradition – better worlds begin in recognising the diverse and interconnected ways human communities secure our livelihoods. Community Economies scholarship is a body of theory that evolved from the writings of geographers J.K. Gibson-Graham, which, for more than 30 years, has inspired others (including the three of us) to rethink economy as a space of political possibility. In this chapter we explore some of the common threads between Feminist Political Ecology (FPE) and Community Economies scholarship, highlighting the centrality of care work – women's care work in particular – in the intellectual and empirical heritage of Community Economies Collective (CEC). We argue that an ethic of care has always been central to Community Economies thinking. The question of how to transform our economies in order to allow human and more than human communities to 'survive well together' places care for planetary companions at the heart of our endeavours (Gibson-Graham *et al.* 2013). In this chapter we focus, however, on the role of care work within Community Economies thinking. For us, transforming the economy begins with the feminist project of recognising and revaluing a broader network of care-relationships that are central to all ecologies and economies. We argue that scholarship must *begin* with making visible the care work involved in transforming the economy for people and planet. Here Joan Tronto's definition of care is helpful. Tronto views care as:

> a species activity that includes everything that we do to maintain, continue, and repair our 'world' so that we can live in it as well as possible. That world includes our bodies, our selves, and our environment, all of which we seek to interweave in a complex, life-sustaining web (Fisher and Tronto, 1990: 40 cited in Tronto 2017: 31, emphasis in original).

With this expansive definition we might see care work as already distributed and ubiquitous in maintaining and continuing and repairing our world, but making this more visible is also to show how care work is potentially a distributed and ubiquitous start point in transforming our ecologies and economies. The work of care is required across the wide spectrum of all that is caught up in what Tronto calls the 'life-sustaining web' of our world. Who it is that does this work is an important consideration – particularly in terms of gender – but so too is the task of thinking about how care work might be shared out and proliferated in an effort to transform the relationships between humans, more-than-humans and our shared ecological context. In other words, making visible *who* is doing the care work necessary in transforming our political economies and ecologies is only the first step. Scholars also need to consider *what* this care work now entails, and *how* we might – collectively, across gender and other lines of class, sexuality, culture, species – both redistribute and proliferate the work of care for the sake of the human species and the rest of our planetary companions (Dombroski 2018). It is in these ethical negotiations around everyday care practices and care concerns that community economies of care emerge. In this chapter, we have set ourselves the task of detailing a care-full approach to community economies. We believe a sense of *the who, what and how* of care is already present in the work of CEC scholars and seek to articulate this scholarship and bring it into dialogue with FPE in a way that clarifies our shared concerns. We start with *who* by exploring a topic that might be closest to home, the gendered care work of intimate infant care. But even here we see that the 'who' caring is a lot more complicated than what it might first appear to be. We extend this further with *what,* by exploring a geography of the commons as a way of understanding the breadth of what we care for – those things, processes, knowledges, ecosystems and properties that we can (only) share in common. Finally, we look at *how* we do care work, specifically the role that scholarship can play in both acknowledging and revaluing care work in the context of beginning to transform ecologies and economies.

## Common threads: CEC and FPE

The work of the CEC and feminist political ecologists have parallel intellectual traditions that are particularly evident through the work of feminist political ecologist, Dianne Rocheleau, and the founding authorial persona of Community Economies, J.K. Gibson-Graham. Our reading of these authors and their associated fields reveals similarities in the shifts taken from second wave feminist strategies which focus primarily on women to third wave feminist strategies which draw on queer theory and thinking to pay attention to all kinds of marginalised others. We see these kinds of feminist strategies informing a commitment to scholarly care work across the two traditions.

Where political ecology focuses on the interrelationships between social, political and economic factors in shaping environmental change, feminist political ecology is widely understood as placing gender at the centre of the analysis. This is particularly the case in relation to understanding how decision-making practices and socio-political forces influence environmental laws and issues, as well as access to and control over resources (Rocheleau *et al.* 1996).

Contemporary FPE is, however, doing much more than just adding gender into the mix. Diane Rocheleau recently reflected on 30 years of FPE scholarship, recounting her initial insights from feminist Marxism, early 1990s critiques of Western science and, later, post-development and decolonial theory (Rocheleau 2015). Rocheleau signals an important expansion in describing FPE as an 'ongoing exploration and construction of a network of learners' rather than 'a fixed approach to a single focus on women and gender' (Rocheleau 2015: 57). Her encounters with indigenous cosmologies transformed the way women's lives and care work are understood as core concerns for FPE. Feminism here (and across the 'third wave') is not just about women anymore, but about all kinds of 'Others' – sexual, cultural, class, ethnic, indigenous and more – whose perspectives are essential to a process of engaging with diverse ontologies and decolonising knowledge.

We see a similar transformation taking place in the scholarly trajectories of Julie Graham and Katherine Gibson, central figures in the community economy tradition who came to write under the name J.K. Gibson-Graham. As J.K. Gibson-Graham, Katherine and Julie formulated a theory of diverse economies and have fostered scholarship and activism around community economies. Diverse economies theory asks us to pay attention to the ways in which human livelihoods around the world are secured by a plethora of different modes of economic engagement – many of which are not capitalist. Thus 'the economy' is not made up of capitalism with a smattering of alternative 'other' economic practices – lining up much like gender and sexuality into a binary. Instead, what we have is a diverse (or 'queered,' non-binary economy), where diverse capitalisms co-exist and rely upon various forms of market and non-market transactions, multiple forms of labour and remuneration, and complex arrays of systems for owning and managing property (Cameron and Gibson-Graham 2003). Recognising the already-existing diversity of our economies is a foundational step in fostering what Gibson-Graham termed 'community economies': that is, the particular combinations of work, exchange, production, distribution, investment and ownership that help our communities to survive *well* (rather than just survive) (Gibson-Graham 2011, Gibson-Graham *et al.* 2013).

Gibson-Graham (1996, 2006) have described in several places their movement from a realist, empiricist strain of research and anti-capitalist politics to a feminist-inflected politics of economic difference and economic possibility. Their work took insights from queer theory, post-structural theory and psychoanalysis to theorise diverse economies based in a recognition of and appreciation for the existence of the many different and varied modes of economic engagement, what we might also call a politics of difference. These insights were later followed by a sustained engagement with actor network and vital materialist theories, theorisations of the commons, as well as insights from ecological humanities and decolonial theory. Each of these have had a deep impact on a politics of economic difference in a now-expanding network of theorists who share a similar orientation, in particular the Community Economies Research Network.

Given Gibson-Graham's transformative encounters with theories less obviously feminist, some might wonder where women might be in all of this (see, for example, Bauhardt 2014). For us it is instructive that women's lives in illustrative examples are a foundation, or perhaps the starting-point, for an enactment of a politics of difference in much of Gibson-Graham's work. In *The End of Capitalism* it was the domestic lives of Sue and Bill that were used to illustrate the idea that the same people could be party to multiple class processes outside and inside the household. In *Postcapitalist Politics* the diverse economy of childcare is used to explain the diverse organisational forms, labour practices and market exchanges that compose an economy. Sue and Bill return again in *Take Back the Economy* to help the reader understand that moving through daily life means encountering diverse forms of private, public and common property. Each of these examples serves to illustrate the ethical dilemmas and political possibilities in daily life and in our interactions with others. Like FPE, Community Economies scholarship both recognises and revalues the centrality of women's care work in our economies and ecologies and scholarship. Recognising the significance of these contributions has provided a starting point for recognising and valuing the contributions of many diverse Others in securing livelihoods and well-being. Ultimately the recognition of diversity provides the starting point for a hopeful politics of transformation.

## Who cares?

Like FPE, Community Economies scholarship seeks to make explicit *who* is doing the caring work that societies, economies, human life and even more-than-human life depend on. The gendered nature of much of this care work is crucial, and at the same time, Community Economies scholarship is arguing that the explicit acknowledgment of a *broader* understanding of 'who cares' is also important. CEC scholar Oona Morrow and I (Kelly), for example, argue that while everyday practices of provisioning and care work of (mostly) women in the US and China can reproduce capitalist social relations, they also hold the possibility for altering, undermining and undoing those relations in both contexts (Morrow and Dombroski 2015). Likewise, CEC scholar Gradon Diprose's work on timebanking in Aotearoa, New Zealand draws explicitly on a feminist ethic of care to analyse the exchanges of care labour by (mostly) women in a timebank with an eye to fostering radical equality (Diprose forthcoming).

In a care-full community economy, we aim to take the labour and know-how of women, who have done the majority of care work in human societies, and think about how it might be multiplied and shared by an increasing array of actors and an expanded understanding of who it is that cares. The gendered nature of care can thus become a starting point for different sorts of global norms. In paying attention to the non-capitalist and alternative capitalist labour of women, it is possible to see how this women's work is both ubiquitous *and* full of 'post-capitalist' possibility. The post in post-capitalist signals not an 'after' capitalism but already the presence of a 'more' than capitalist that in turn has implications for our desires, and renewed possibilities for collective actions that produce something other than capitalism. We think of women's lives as therefore able to show possibility for a different sort of world built on a feminist ethic of care, a care-full community economy. What can be brought to this then, is a politics of increasing and redistributing caring work, not of shutting down or avoiding care work. This includes redistributing 'intuitive' care work to more men (Dombroski 2018) but also using vibrant material-ist thinking to extend the 'who' that cares beyond the human (Puig de la Bellacasa 2017).

For us, identifying who it is that cares must take into account the complex and interconnected nature of what it takes to care, which, as Tronto states, must incorporate 'our bodies, our selves, and our environment' (Tronto 1993: 103). Community Economies scholarship recognises that the work of care is being done by diverse gatherings, not only of people but of many other ele-ments that assemble to enable care work to be undertaken.[1] These additional elements include technology and infrastructure, place and territory, bodies and cultures that inflect the doings of women and men. What this means is that we need a broader concept of the 'who' of caring, that takes us beyond gen-der relations towards an understanding that care work requires the conjoined actions of *collectives*, the living and non-living things that assemble in order to enable (and sometimes disable) care.

Gerda Roelvink (2016) investigates the collective gathered around the World Social Forum (WSF). Through the WSF, different forms of social change are produced that build on feminist and radical principles, performing care for the multiple economic possibilities latent in the social movements gathered. For Roelvink, one of the central features of the collective is its *hybridity*. The hybridity of this collective action

> includes all that made the WSF possible (such as technologies required for dialogue, tents, and food markets), participants of the WSF and the collectives they represent and more. Taking this point further, the hybrid collective [...] reaches out to touch a broader assemblage, including debates in the research fields of social movements studies, actor network theory, neuroscience and pedagogy, and the academic infrastructure through which this knowledge travels.
>
> (Roelvink 2016: 106)

Roelvink reveals how the WSF hybrid collective pushed her to drop a criti-cal stance that sought always to 'reveal' how social movements were 'really' being co-opted by neoliberalism. In learning to be affected by – and care about – the work of the hybrid collective of which she was now a part, Roelvink began to revise her role as critic. Instead she began to see herself as highlight-ing and proliferating the alternative economic experimentation already under way. The force of the hybrid care collective 'lies in the act of participation and the arousal of hope for new worlds [...] [and] the experience of learning to be affected in collectives and thereby contributing to the differentiation and proliferation of [...] possibilities for action' (Roelvink 2016).

Understanding this array of actors as part of hybrid human–nonhuman collectives pushes third wave feminism into more-than-human territory (Gibson-Graham and Roelvink 2009, Gibson-Graham 2011), perhaps even into a fourth wave (Munro 2013). This engagement with human–nonhuman collectives is picked up in my (Kelly's) work around the informal/domestic environmental activism enacted through the collective work of the online forum Oznappyfree. On this forum, users discuss their experiments with a nappy-free form of infant hygiene known as elimination communication. In my analysis, I invoke a hybrid collective where care work is enabled not just by the human actors involved in care work (mothers, fathers, grandparents, infants), but also the material elements engaged (potties, nappies, water and so on). Through the Oznappyfree forum mothers and others use the internet to experiment with and share knowledge about how to 'read' or 'hear' their infants' preverbal communications about impending urination or defecation. These communications produce different assemblages of potties, nappies, water, microbes that are less resource intensive than common assemblages based on using disposable nappies (Dombroski 2015, 2016, 2018). The human and non-human actors that assemble around practices of elimination communication form this hybrid collective, through which the work of care, activism and experimentation is distributed. The women involved in my study drew my attention to how their everyday, often home-based, practices of care and activism could make a broader contribution – for example, in habituating themselves and their children into less environmentally problematic hygiene norms, through developing attunement and empathy through embodied practice that spreads well beyond this one example and home, and through making more possible for more people previously taboo hygiene practices, among other things (Dombroski 2016).

From one point of view the membership of Oznappyfree could be considered to just be individual actors in their homes. Via the online forum, however, a collective subject formed around a set of important environmental and social concerns. Thus the 'who' that acts was no longer a set of individual subjects, but a hybrid activist collective, formed through the assemblage of human and more-than-human actors. The Oznappyfree forum offers a contrast to critical feminist readings focused on how women's environmental work constitutes yet another labour performed in an individualist, neoliberalised context. Instead, narratives of home-based activism on the forum allow us to see the work women do in the home as part of broader, hybrid collective of environmental and political action.

In the context of a care-full community economy, it is important that we identify which of the diverse 'whos' of caring are *collective*, so we might see and respond to not only processes of individualisation of care work brought about by capitalist economic structures, but also see and proliferate collectivisation in care work. In a care-full community the 'who' that cares is a *hybrid* collective, and we might come to value the diverse actors involved (human andnon-human) and diverse sites and modes of engagement (across global-domestic spheres, with different forms of direct action and everyday politics), helping us recognise the diversity of identities and interrelationships in action at the heart of care-full work.[2]

## What do we care for?

If the hybrid collective is the 'who' that is at work caring in the context of community economies, then what is being cared for? For us, the concept that best captures what is being cared for is that of 'the commons.' For example, what members of the Oznappyfree collective are *caring for* can be understood as a commons. Members of the collective are, of course, caring for their infant-members. But their infant hygiene practices are also a way of caring for ecologies by reducing the flow of household waste, benefiting human and more-than-human communities in the process. Further, as the collective freely shares alternative baby hygiene techniques with a broader public via the webgroup, the capacity for collective actions expands beyond the collective itself. In our view, Oznappyfree's care work around the waste stream, infant and parent attachment and communication, and the sharing of this knowledge illustrates a post-capitalist politics of commoning.

For many the term commons is associated with pre-capitalist communities that were often sustained by access to commons, in the form of forests, fields and fisheries to which commoners had rights of access and use. Like feminist political ecologist Christa Wichterich (2015), Gibson-Graham, Cameron and I (Stephen) (2013) emphasise the important relationship between the commons of the past and commoning in the present. Contemporary commons are physical resources, knowledges and cultural practices that are distinct from private property in that access, use and benefit, but also responsibility and care, are widely distributed (Linebaugh 2008, Barbagallo and Federici 2012, following Bollier 2002). This focus on the *sociality* that defines commons draws our attention away from 'the commons' and towards a process of commoning.

We define common*ing* as a set of social processes and protocols that establish the rules of access, use and benefit in relation to commons – whether those commons are, for example, areas of oceans, the internet or a public library (see Figure 6.1, The Commons Identikit). In addition, commoning processes set rules over who is responsible for the care of that which is commoned (Bollier 2002, Linebaugh 2008, Barbagallo and Federici 2012).

Focussing attention on the *process* of commoning opens up our understanding of what might be held in common: open-access resources like the atmosphere and oceans may be commoned through the establishment of the rules of use and care; the digital-knowledge commons may be defended from forces of neglect or enclosure; and even private property may be partially commoned in the interest of community and ecological well-being. Many scholars in the

| | Access | Use | Benefit | Care | Responsibility | Ownership |
|---|---|---|---|---|---|---|
| Commoning enclosed property | Narrow | Restricted by owner | Private | Performed by owner or employee | Assumed by owner | Private individual |
| | | | | | | Private collective |
| | | | | | | State |
| Creating new commons | Shared and wide | Negotiated by a community | Widely distributed to community and beyond | Performed by community members | Assumed by community | Private individual |
| | | | | | | Private collective |
| | | | | | | State |
| Commoning unmanaged open-access resources | | | | | | Open access |
| | Unrestricted | Open and unregulated | Finders keepers | None | None | Open access |
| | | | | | | State |

*Figure 6.1* The Commons Identikit.

Source: Gibson-Graham, J.K., Cameron, J. and Healy, S., 2013. *Take Back the Economy: An Ethical Guide for Transforming Our Communities*. Minneapolis, MA: University of Minnesota Press.

CEC and beyond are, however, identifying common resources such as fisheries (St. Martin and Hall-Arber 2008), non-timber forest products (Emery and Barron 2010) and healthy soils (Roelvink 2016) as commons both used, and cared for, by human communities. While commons and their commoning communities are easier to spot when they are a natural resource, commoning and commons can also be seen elsewhere when we know what to look for.

One such example of commoning in the city occurs in Fairmount Park, Philadelphia, one of the largest urban-parks in the US. From its initial establishment in 1851, there was an ongoing struggle over how the park space was to be accessed, used and to whose benefit, and who would exercise care and responsibility for it (refer also to Figure 6.1., Gabriel 2011, Gabriel 2016). Urban planners, at the time, understood parks as recreational spaces that helped the turn of the century industrial city to function effectively, by providing a defined place for leisure away from industry. The photographic record developed during this same period of time re-enforced an image of the park-as-recreation by excluding other contending uses of park space. In fact, the park was also a site of self-provisioning: fruit and nut gathering, hunting, commercial ice harvest in winter, firewood gathering and even milling for timber. While these productive uses of park-space were later discouraged, the fruit and nut trees were never removed from the park and in the present-day many of Philadelphia's newest residents still gather resources from the park.

Like many cities in the minority world, Philadelphia has since experienced wholesale industrial decline and abandonment. Some of the empty space left behind has been filled with commons and their communities. Community Economies scholars have examined a number of different forms of emerging city-based commoning practices in a variety of places, including Philadelphia. Commoning practices include the creation of community gardens (Cameron *et al.* 2011, Morrow 2014, Borowiak, 2015, Sharp *et al.* 2015), maker spaces (Loh and Shear 2015), commoned forms of housing (Crabtree 2006, Huron 2015) and community-based approaches to low carbon energy systems (Cameron and Hicks 2014). Such collective efforts distribute the burden and benefits of remaking city space through practices of commoning.

What can be learned from examples of commoning in the city is that through collective action we have the capacity to care on a scale that exceeds the local. In a community economy of care, hybrid collectives gather to care for commons that, in turn, sustain the collective. A commoning of the atmosphere is one such collective act of care to 'sustain the collective.' Commoning the atmosphere as a response to climate change seems like an almost impossible task. Yet even here it is possible to look back at recent history to see a community of carers assembling that may prove commensurate with the task.

Cameron, Gibson-Graham and I (Stephen) describe an example of intergenerational atmospheric commoning that gives us reason to hope. In industrial communities such as Newcastle, the coal and steel industry choked the air with a thick smog of particulates. As early as the 1930s, communities comprised of both working class and management began to measure particulate levels in their communities, pressuring local councils to be early adopters of regulatory frameworks that aimed to improve local air quality. These frameworks prefigured national clean air legislation passed in Australia and the UK in the 1950s and 1960s followed by the US in the 1970s. A still-larger hybrid collective was required to first discover and then counter the threat posed by ozone depleting chemicals such as chlorofluorocarbons. While researchers in Australia and elsewhere had begun sounding the alarm about the integrity of upper atmospheric ozone depletion, it was not until spectral satellite data actually made visible the extent of the damage that the Australian public pressured the government to take decisive action. The Australian government played a key role of brokering between minority and majority worlds, including establishing a differential timetable and terms of financial support for the Montreal Protocol passed in 1987. While this effort at an internationalisation of care for the upper-ozone commons was crucially important, other efforts were equally so: in the 1980s, the union of plumbers and pipe fitters in Australia refused en masse to install any fire suppressant system that contained ozone destroying chemicals – which in turn ultimately pressured real estate developers to then pressure manufacturers for an alternative.

The story we tell here is of a range of social actors coming together in an ongoing and evolving assemblage in order to enact change. Responding to the perceived threat to their own health and the larger environment, different groups found a reason to care enough to act, to enact a care work of atmospheric repair. The commons in question only came into view as an object through scientific inquiry; the communing community – in this case a hybrid collective – only came into being in response to the threat the inquiry revealed. The collective that came into being acted on concerns that stretched beyond any one interest group. Furthermore, the work of atmospheric caring will stretch well beyond a single generation. Ozone-destroying chloro–fluoro carbons (CFCs) were first synthesised in 1911 and the ozone hole is unlikely to be completely repaired until 2085 – meaning the practice of atmospheric care stretches over seven generations. Both the scale and concerted intergenerational effort required to respond to the challenge of climate change will span our lifetime and those that will come after us.

In tracing this trajectory, we see a repeating pattern where new understandings of the nature and extent of the problem can elicit a response: a shared concern develops, a call to action is heard and a response envisioned and enacted through the work of care. Caring for the atmospheric commons in response to climate change will require the assembling of a far greater hybrid collective still, one that will be undaunted by setbacks along the way. While some government actions (such as carbon pricing) have suffered reversal in Australia in recent years, other changes (such as the profusion of photovoltaic technologies combined with home battery energy storage) have remade energy markets. Consumers of these technologies have organised into a political constituency of solar citizens that may make this emergent distributed energy technology harder to dislodge or undermine politically, while simultaneously new forms of financing for their installation on commercial and residential properties may allow them to spread further. Photovoltaic energy generation, new forms of storage, new forms of financing, the organisations sharing these innovations and an emergent civic conscience can together become a powerful hybrid collective that allows for people in Australia and elsewhere to common the atmosphere by means of caring for it.

While the challenges of addressing issues such as the anthropogenic origins of climate change are significant, what this example shows us is that it is possible to bring into being new collectives who undertake commoning around broadly defied shared interests. Even if some are motivated to participate in this emergent collective for purely 'selfish' reasoning, such people are part of a larger and ongoing practice of atmospheric commoning, performing care work. Awareness of the relationship between complex-assemblage actors and the commons they constitute and care for may help innovative practices to spread farther and more quickly than they otherwise might. In a care-full community economy, as commons are identified that require care, they call into being the collective-community that both makes use of and cares for them – we can see this trajectory through responses to commoning the ozone layer, and we see the beginnings of a parallel trajectory emerging to common the atmosphere more generally.

**How do we care?**

While care may happen through collective action that emerges consciously or unconsciously, in this chapter we wish to pay attention to how we, as academics, researchers and writers, may care. For Community Economies scholars, commoning and contributing as part of collectives that care are not just practices that happen outside the academy, driven by those whom might be counted as research participants. As for FPE, feminist research methods highlight the political dimension of scholarly research, reminding us that our everyday practices as scholars researching and teaching in the academy also have performative effects. The performativity of research has been a central feature of diverse economies critique, ever since Gibson–Graham argued that repeated invocation of the hegemonic power of global capitalism serves only to reinforce and re-inscribe that power (1996). Constantly seeking to line up analysis in certain patterns works to perform and re-perform the very structures we might wish to oppose and disrupt (Roelvink 2016). The methods researchers choose to describe reality also work to amplify the particular reality described (Law 2004, Werner 2015, Roelvink 2016). Thus, care-full work in the academy comes with selecting of methods that, for example, distribute control to participants and 'consumers' in knowledge production. Community economies of care can be supported by researchers working to connect small-scale projects in community building and community empowerment to the bigger pictures that participants are envisioning (Werner 2015). This provides discursive space for these experimental projects to be amplified beyond the local.

Reflecting on their work with community gardens in Newcastle, Australia and alternative food economies in the Philippines, Community Economies researchers Jenny Cameron, Katherine Gibson and Ann Hill explore 'the role that research might play in fostering and caring for new community food economies' (Cameron *et al.* 2014: 4). They focus on three techniques of hybrid collectives: gathering, re-assembling and translating. In Newcastle, the Newcastle Community Garden Project engaged members of community gardens from across the city, joining together in a bus trip to visit each other's gardens and bringing together the different knowledge and know-how that emerged from this hybrid collective of gardeners, plants, compost heaps, garden beds and more. Cameron and her collaborators approached the project with a care to strengthening community food economies, adopting 'a stance of openness so we are ready for possibilities to arise, especially those that realise our research intentions and start to make fragile, imaginative constructions of the new more durable' (Cameron *et al.* 2014: 13).

'Reassembling' is performed, in this case, by utilising the fruitful exchanges that emerged during the garden bus trip as the foundations for co-theorisation with research participants. The process involved literally reassembling and amplifying the reflections and utterances from the bus trip, providing voice-over narration in a film about the gardens. This recrafting of 'raw data' is a familiar process for a researcher, but involving the gardeners themselves in the process provided an opportunity to amplify the performative potential of knowledge-making. This was an 'important means of reframing and clarifying' (Cameron *et al.* 2014: 16) what the garden project was doing, connecting gardeners to the broader significance of their efforts. They use the term 'translation' to describe the process through which outcomes are relayed through indeterminate networks and connections, because they are 'translated' for use in other contexts and places beyond the participants who contributed to original gatherings and re-assemblages. The 'translated' academic papers, popular films and other forms of communication can be taken up by other groups in ways that are unpredictable.

These three methodological interventions – gathering, reassembling and translating – are deliberate strategies to undertake an action research approach that seeks to 'participate in bringing [economic food] futures into being' (Cameron et al. 2014: 22). But this is participating without controlling, enacting an ethical decision to do research in the spirit of openness, practicing care for Earthothers through co-creation of outcomes that have a life of their own, spreading in ways which, the authors hope, 'might increase the chances of community food economies becoming more visible, more interconnected and thus more robust' (Cameron et al. 2014: 24). In describing the messy and unpredictable processes involved in hybrid research collective methods, Cameron, Gibson and Hill are describing a way in which researchers find ways to care for others. In this case, care involves establishing caring relationships with research participants, in part through a co-production and co-theorisation process that accords participants respect and control. Care is also entailed by the intention to give outcomes a life of their own, encouraging them to be translated outwards.

As Tronto (2017) states, the identification of how we care also can involve translating between context-specific understandings of how to care. These dynamics came to the fore in a project focused on gender equity and economic empowerment in the Pacific, which I (Katharine) worked on (McKinnon et al. 2016). In this project the research team was tasked with working with communities to develop community-based indicators for gender equity. The tools already available to track the potential impacts of proposed Pacific free trade agreements on household economies are unable to account for the range of livelihood strategies that many Pacific and Melanesian communities rely on. Furthermore, existing gender equity indicators are based on normative visions of gender equity based in Western European conceptualisations of individual rights (McKinnon et al. 2016). The Community Economies scholars involved in this project wanted to avoid simply translating existing conceptualisations for the local context. Instead we sought to facilitate the emergence of place-based conceptualisations of gender equity. These could then inform a Pacific-wide toolkit for tracking gender equity and economic developments in a way that was meaningful in the Pacific context and could contribute to a version of 'women's economic empowerment' on their own terms.

In partnership with the International Women's Development Agency and local NGOs in Fiji and the Solomon Islands, Katherine Gibson, Michelle Carnegie and I (Katharine) ran participatory workshops to explore gendered economies with community members (Carnegie et al. 2012). The research explored the role of informal and social economic activities in people's livelihoods. Informal market exchange, unpaid labour in the household, subsistence production, volunteer work and gift exchange across wider family and community networks were found to form the core of people's livelihoods. Explorations of local diverse economies also uncovered a gendered economy, in which the roles and responsibilities of women and men were complementary. While participants were concerned about instances of inequity, most advocated a vision of complementarity in gendered work, and the expression of aspirations for gender equity tended to not be about sameness but about having the different contributions of women and men equally respected and valued.

Based on the understandings of gender equality and the gendered economy developed through community engagements, we developed a set of indicators that could be used to track important changes to livelihood practices and gender (Carnegie *et al.* 2012). An important component of this is recording and keeping track of the ways that people care for one another, and the equitability of care work provided by women and men. Unpaid care for children and elders was a part of this, so too was the care given to community when men volunteered to build and maintain church infrastructure, or women laboured to make flower displays for weekly church services. Turning insights of the interdependent economies of women and men into measurable indicators, this work provides a way to begin to make visible and to value the diverse livelihoods of Pacific communities, and the networks of interrelationships that provide for individual, household and community well-being. We might see this as part of the work of both sustaining social and knowledge commons, the circuits of care that constitute and sustain the collective. Care-full community economy scholarship, in addition to recognising the hybrid collectives who care and the commons that we care for, deploys the tools of social research to contribute to building community economies of care. We agree with feminist political ecologists that it is critical to establish 'the connection between exploitation of women's labour and the abuse of planetary resources' as a precondition for caring for those people and things neglected and abused (Mellor 2005: 123 cited in Bauhardt 2014: 61). But this is only a beginning. This care-full critical scholarship may allow us to also enlarge the 'we' who cares, deepen our shared commitment to the commons that sustain us and to continuously learn through a process of engaged research.

## Conclusion

In this chapter, we have presented a particular imagining of what constitutes the collective, what constitutes the more-than/other-than/non-human Earthothers who are cared for in commoning practices and what practices we can engage to care in, and through, our research. But economies of care are not just made up of collectives, commons and Earthothers larger than ourselves. The picture is always more complex – for one, collectives are made up of singular human beings, with subjectivities ascribed and claimed in different ways. What they seek to act upon may not be held in common or may not be recognised as part of a being-in-common (or in fact a desirable inclusion in a commons).

Research sometimes has to serve other goals and desires, fulfilling criteria and priorities of funding agencies among them. All of these activities are undertaken by, in and through bodies that are positioned differently in place and relation of power, and are often (always) unruly 'leaky' containers for human agency (Longhurst 2001). Caring involves, as Puig de la Bellacasa puts it, 'everyday doings' that are neither straightforward nor coherent: we need to ask 'how to care' in each situation (2011).The who, what and how of a community economy of care are always open to ongoing negotiation and redefinition.

Our discussions in this chapter have focused on questions of who it is that provides care, and for whom, and how we as researchers can contribute to this while remaining open to an ongoing process of negotiation. The work of hybrid collectives and attentiveness to commons is at the core of how we see and practice community economies of care. Throughout, we have begun to articulate what a Community Economies approach to care looks like as we build on foundations provided by second and third wave feminism, as we seek to not just critique but *create* care-full practices.

With the FPE tradition, Community Economies scholars are concerned for the complex and multiple dynamics through which societies, economies and environments interrelate, and for the gendered nature of all this. Yet, the feminism much Community Economies scholarship is informed by is decidedly third wave – it is about much more than thinking with and through the perspectives of women. Rather it is learning to see and think differently with all the perspectives, experiences and concerns that might be side-lined as 'Other' to the dominant mode.

The 'community' in our community economy of care is understood to include a multiplicity of others with whom being-in-common is negotiated. This includes not just women, and indeed not just the human actors, but a diverse range of other-than-human actors. A community economy is now being envisioned as something that incorporates a complex ecology in which human livelihoods, planetary well-being and care for the more-than-human are understood as interconnected and mutually dependent (Dombroski *et al.* 2016, McKinnon *et al.* 2016). The shared work of building community economies involves actively caring for, and recognising the agency of, human and non-human, identifying diverse ways of being from which caring economies can be fostered. It also involves finding ways to make the work we do as researchers and academics productive of the types of community economies we wish to foster. In a community economy of care, an ethical stance of openness to difference and diversity makes appreciative investigation possible, in which alternatives and the unexpected sources of learning are not foreclosed by the imposition of 'strong theory' (Sedgwick 1994). In a community economy of care, the relationality of livelihoods and economies are foregrounded, allowing us to focus on the ways that practices of economy create opportunities to care for human and non-human others. In a community economy of care, how we conduct ourselves, as citizens and as researchers, provides daily opportunities to perform alternative futures.

## Notes

1 Our use of the term 'assemble' here is deliberate, and we intend it to signal out engagement with actor network theory and materialist perspectives that explore ideas of assemblage, see Law, J., 2004. *After Method: Mess in Social Science Research*. London: Routledge. Space does not allow us to elaborate more deeply.
2 See Dombroski 2016 for further discussion of this politics of the everyday act.

## References

Barbagallo, C. and Federici, S., 2012. Introduction: care work on commons. *The Commoner* [online], 15, 1–21. Available from: http://www.commoner.org.uk/ Accessed [11 June 2018].

Bauhardt, C., 2014. Solutions to the crisis? The green new deal, degrowth, and the solidarity economy: alternatives to the capitalist growth economy from an ecofeminist economics perspective. *Ecological Economics*, 102, 60–8.

Bollier, D., 2002. *Silent Theft: The Private Plunder of Our Common Wealth*. New York: Routledge.

Borowiak, C., 2015. Mapping social and solidarity economy: the local and translocal evolution of a concept. *In*: N. Pun, ed., *Social Economy in China and the World*. New York: Routledge, 17–40.

Cameron, J. and Gibson-Graham, J.K., 2003. Feminising the economy: metaphors, strategies, politics. *Gender, Place and Culture: A Journal of Feminist Geography*, 10, 145–57.

Cameron, J., Gibson, K. and Hill, A., 2014. Cultivating hybrid collectives: research methods for enacting community food economies in Australia and the Philippines. *Local Environment*, 19, 118–32.

Cameron, J. and Hicks, J., 2014. Performative research for a climate politics of hope: rethinking geographic scale, 'impact' scale and markets *Antipode*, 46 (1), 53–71.

Cameron, J., Manhood, C. and Pomfrett, J., 2011. Bodily learning for a (climate) changing world: registering differences through performative and collective research. *Local Environment*, 16 (6) 493–508.

Carnegie, M., Rowland, C., Gibson, K., McKinnon, J., Crawford, J. and Slatter, C., 2012. *Gender and Economy in Melanesian Communities: A Manual of Indicators and Tools to Track Change*. Melbourne: University of Western Sydney, Macquarie University and International Women's Development Agency.

Crabtree, L., 2006. Disintegrated houses: exploring ecofeminist housing and urban design options. *Antipode*, 38 (4), 711–34.

Diprose, G., 2016. Negotiating interdependence and anxiety in community economies. *Environment and Planning A*, 48 (7), 1411–27.

Diprose, G., forthcoming. Radical equality and labour in a community economy. *Gender Place and Culture*.

Dombroski, K., 2015. Multiplying possibilities: a post-development approach to hygiene and sanitation in Northwest China. *Asia Pacific Viewpoint*, 56, 321–34.

Dombroski, K., 2016. Hybrid activist collectives: reframing mothers' environmental and caring labour. *International Journal of Sociology and Social Policy*, 36 (9/10), 629–46.

Dombroski, K., 2018. Learning to be affected: maternal connection, intuition and 'elimination communication'. *Emotion, Space and Society*, 26, 72–79.

Dombroski, K., McKinnon, K. and Healy, S., 2016. Beyond the birth wars: diverse assemblages of care. *New Zealand Geographer*, 72, 230–9.

Emery, M.R. and Barron, E.S., 2010. Using local ecological knowledge to assess morel decline in the U.S. Mid-Atlantic region. *Economic Botany*, 64, 205–16.

Gabriel, N., 2011. The work that parks do: towards an urban environmentality. *Social and Cultural Geography*, 12, 123–41.

Gabriel, N., 2016. Visualising urban nature in Fairmount Park: discipline, economic diversity and photography in nineteenth century Philadelphia. *In*: A.C. Braddock and L.T. Igoe, eds., *A Greene Country Towne: Art, Culture, and Ecology in Philadelphia*. University Park, PA: Penn State University Press.

Gibson-Graham, J.K., 1996. *The End of Capitalism (As We Knew It)*. Minneapolis: University of Minnesota Press.

Gibson-Graham, J.K., 2006. *A Postcapitalist Politics*. Minneapolis: University of Minnesota Press.

Gibson-Graham, J.K., 2011. A feminist project of belonging for the Anthropocene. *Gender, Place & Culture*, 18, 1–21.

Gibson-Graham, J.K., Cameron, J. and Healy, S., 2013. *Take Back the Economy: An Ethical Guide for Transforming Our Communities*. Minneapolis, MN: University of Minnesota Press.

Gibson-Graham, J.K. and Roelvink, G., 2009. An economic ethics for the Anthropocene. *Antipode*, 41 (1), 320–46.

Huron, A., 2015. Working with strangers in saturated space: Reclaiming and maintaining the urban commons. *Antipode*, 47 (4), 963–79.

Law, J., 2004. *After Method: Mess in Social Science Research*. London: Routledge.

Linebaugh, P., 2008. *The Magna Carta Manifesto: Liberties and Commons for All*. Berkeley, CA: University of California Press.

Loh, P. and Shear, B., 2015. Solidarity economy and community development: emerging cases in three Massachusetts cities. *Community Development*, 46 (3), 244–60.

Longhurst, R., 2001. *Bodies: Exploring Fluid Boundaries*. London: Routledge.

McKinnon, K., Carnegie, M., Gibson, K. and Rowland, C., 2016. Gender equality and economic empowerment in the Solomon Islands and Fiji: a place-based approach. *Gender, Place and Culture*, 23, 1376–91.

Morrow, O., 2014. Urban homesteading: diverse economies and ecologies of provisioning in Greater Boston. Dissertation (PhD). Clark University.

Morrow, O. and Dombroski, K., 2015. Enacting a post-capitalist politics through the sites and practices of life's work. *In*: K. Meehan and K. Strauss, eds., *Precarious Worlds: Contested Geographies of Social Reproduction*. Athens, GA: University of Georgia Press, 82–98.

Munro, E., 2013. Feminism: a fourth wave? *Political Insight*, 4, 22–5.

Puig de la Bellacasa, M., 2011. Matters of care in technoscience: assembling neglected things. *Social Studies of Science*, 41, 85–106.

Puig de la Bellacasa, M., 2017. *Matters of Care: Speculative Ethics in More Than Human Worlds*. Minneapolis, MN: University of Minnesota Press.

Rocheleau, D., 2015. A situated view of feminist political ecology from my networks, roots and territories. *In*: W. Harcourt and I.L. Nelson, eds, *Practising Feminist Political Ecology: Moving Beyond the Green Economy*. London: Zed Books, 29–66.

Rocheleau, D., Thomas-Slayter, B. and Wangari, E. 1996. Gender and environment: a feminist political ecology perspective. *In*: D. Rocheleau, B. Thomas-Slayter and E. Wangari, eds, *Feminist Political Ecology: Global Perspectives and Local Insights*. New York: Routledge, 3–23.

Roelvink, G., 2016. *Building Dignified Worlds: Geographies of Collective Action*. Minneapolis: University of Minnesota Press.

Sedgwick, E.K., 1994. *Tendencies*. London: Routledge.

Sharp, E.L., Friesen, W. and Lewis, N., 2015. Alternative framings of alternative food: a typology of practice. *New Zealand Geographer*, 71 (1), 6–17.

St. Martin, K. and Hall-Arber, M., 2008. The missing layer: geo-technologies, communities, and implications for marine spatial planning. *Marine Policy*, 32, 779–86.

Tronto, J., 2017. There is an alternative: homines curans and the limits of neoliberalism. *International Journal of Care and Caring*, 1, 27–43.

Tronto, J.C., 1993. *Moral Boundaries: A Political Argument for an Ethic of Care*. London: Psychology Press.

Werner, K., 2015. Performing economies of care in a New England time bank and Buddhist community. *In*: G. Roelvink, K. St. Martin and J.K. Gibson-Graham, eds., *Making Other Worlds Possible*. Minneapolis: University of Minnesota Press, 72–97.

Wichterich, C., 2015. Contesting green growth, connecting care, commons and enough. *In*: W. Harcourt and I.L. Nelson, eds., *Practising Feminist Political Ecologies: Moving Beyond the Green Economy*. London: Zed Books, 67–100.

# 7 Care as wellth

## Internalising care by democratising money

*Mary Mellor*

Central to the feminist critique of care is that it is externalised and marginalised by the main/male-stream economy. It is externalised by being unpaid and unrecognised. It is marginalised by being low paid and associated with low social status. Where economies rely on and exploit unpaid or underpaid work, this results in social injustice and inequality (Picchio 2003). This does not only impact on women, but other socially marginalised people. Feminists have long campaigned to get this work recognised and end the social injustice it represents. The case for recognition is that caring activities are vital for human societies as they create the conditions for well-being and flourishing. At the same time, responsibility for care work can be seen as hampering women's participation in the labour market, preventing them from developing and using their potential capabilities (Nussbaum 2000).

### The ecofeminist critique of the externalisation of care

The perspective I adopt, ecofeminist political economy, broadens the critique of the externalisation of the work and lives of women to include the externalisation of nature. That is, using the 'free' resources of nature and not taking account of the damage it sustains. Ecofeminist political economy sees the externalisation of the environment and women's care work as materially linked and ecologically dangerous (Salleh 1997, Perkins and Kuiper 2005, Mellor 2009).

What is important about the exclusion of women's lives from the notion of the economic is that women's work has become the repository of the inconvenience of human existence in nature. Domestic and caring work reflects the material conditions and impact that the embodiedness of humanity entails. This embodiedness, in turn, reflects the embeddedness of humanity within the natural environment (Mellor 2013). This does not imply an essentialist link. Women are not closer to nature, but care work is largely concerned with the daily cycle and lifecycle of human existence.

Ignoring the materiality of human existence as embodied beings enables a seemingly transcendent construct to emerge: 'Economic Man' (who may be female). Economic Man appears to be able to escape the limitations of human embodiment and 'his' embeddedness in nature. Economic Man can live in the artificially constructed world of 'the economy' where 'he' is not young or old, sick or unhappy, and does not have caring responsibilities (Mellor 1997). 'He' can also ignore the ecological impact of 'his' activities on the natural world and more vulnerable communities.

As Biesecker and Hofmeister (2010) argue, it is vital to look at the processes of mediation between society and nature, in particular the work of re/productivity that would recognise that 'the processes involved in the regeneration and restoration of human and non-human life are intrinsic to each and every process involving the production of goods and services' (2010: 1707). Ariel Salleh (2009) advocates recognition of what she calls 'embodied materialism,' and the 'meta-industrial' work carried out by women and other subordinated groups that creates 'metabolic value.' Salleh sees capitalism as owing a 'debt' at three levels: social debt to exploited labour, embodied debt to reproductive labour and ecological debt for damage to the natural metabolism, that is, nature itself (2009: 24). I will argue that these externalities can be resolved by a model of internalisation that puts care work and the sustainability of the natural environment at the centre of provisioning. I use the word provisioning because it embraces the range of services, paid and unpaid, people need in order to flourish.

## Internalising care

As Nancy Folbre challenged more than 20 years ago: who pays for the kids? (1994). A minimal level of internalisation would be some recognition that care work is a charge upon the economy. History has offered some answers. When organised labour became powerful enough to demand higher wages, this was assumed to be a family wage that would cover the costs of reproduction. Industrialisation saw labour leave the home for the factories, while what remained behind was categorised as domestic work where the female body was 'turned into an instrument for the reproduction of labour and the expansion of the workforce, treated as a natural breeding-machine, functioning according to rhythms outside of women's control' (Federici 2009: 49).

In the 1970s Marxist feminists proposed that as capitalism benefitted from women's unpaid work, capitalism should pay wages for housework (Gardiner 1997). This was opposed by radical feminists who thought it would trap women in domestic work. The suggestion also foundered on the theoretical problem of exactly how Marx's notion of surplus value could be extracted from women's domestic work. Eventually, the concept of a family wage withered with the waning of (male) trade union power and women's claims for equal treatment in the workplace (yet to be achieved).

The other main mechanism of internalisation was the development of welfare states. These addressed some of the problems of social injustice and inequality associated with care but did not fundamentally challenge the priority of the market in determining the framework of the economy. It was assumed that the building of welfare states depended upon wealth created in the market place. This wealth was then taxed to enable public expenditure. As I will argue below, this fundamentally misunderstands the monetary role of the state with dire consequences.

Neoliberalism was able to turn the initial entitlement approach to welfare into a system where 'social assistance was not a right but, instead, intrusive, conditional, inadequate and often punitive' (Bakker 2003: 75). Welfare was no longer seen as a social right, but a burden of the unworthy and work-shy on the 'hardworking taxpayer.' On the assumption that states depended on money extracted from the private sector (despite the fact that the public sector also pays tax) the claim was made that high levels of state expenditure were a drain upon the market. States should therefore shrink as a proportion of GDP through privatisation and expenditure cuts. Particular concern was raised over state deficits and borrowing which led to the imposition of austerity to 'balance the books' (Mellor 2015).

In the 1980s Marilyn Waring took a different approach. Rather than starting from the need to pay for women's unpaid labour and other 'free' goods such as the environment, she approached internalisation through the issue of recognition. Her critique was of public accounting. In her capacity as chair of the Public Expenditures Committee of the New Zealand Parliament she 'found it virtually impossible to prove [...] that child care facilities were needed. Non-producers (housewives, mothers) who are 'inactive' and 'unoccupied,' cannot apparently be in need' (1989: 2). She also describes herself as 'gasping for breath' when told that women's work in subsistence production had no value because it was not sold on the market. The argument was made that 'primary production and the consumption of their own produce [...] is of little or no importance' (1989: 78). Subsequently Waring fought a long campaign to have women's work taken account of in the United Nations System of National Accounts (UNSNA). Her demand that non-market subsistence economies should be recognised has also been echoed by ecofeminists (Bennholdt-Thomsen and Mies 1999).

Twenty years later Waring reported that 'feminists have strategised to force global and national accounting to make women's economic contribution visible in their data' (2009: 165). 'If you are invisible as a producer in a nation's economy, you are invisible in the distribution of benefits (unless they label you a welfare "problem" or "burden")' (2009: 165). Care services do not count unless they are carried out by the market, government or voluntary agencies. She points out that 'the UNSNA fail[ed] to grasp there is no demarcation for women in the subsistence household between production inside or outside the consumption boundaries' (2009: 166). Consumption boundaries refers to those goods and services produced and consumed within the household. The question then is how to value women's work.

Waring rejects a proposal to have 'satellite' accounts that put a notional value on such activities as 'ascribing monetary values to labour results in a loss of detail and specificity in policy analysis' (2009: 174). She argues instead for non-monetary data such as time use and quality of life. Bennholdt-Thomsen and Mies (1999) also oppose using money to internalise subsistence provisioning. This reflects a major concern of Feminist Political Economy and Feminist Political Ecology that capitalist markets are internalising exploited 'others' through the interweaving of gender, class, caste, race, ethnicity, colonialism and imperialism (Wichterich 2015). Neoliberal globalisation is drawing in women, indigenous people, informal and precarious workers, small-scale farmers and producers of commodities and services into global value chains. Women farmers are losing their autonomy (Pionetti 2005), while care is a growing driver of transnational migration (Yeates 2012). Meanwhile, neo-market solutions to the problem of development such as microcredit have proved problematic, leading to problems of over indebtedness (Mellor 2010a).

A new path could be to organise economies without money as Anitra Nelson and Frans Timmerman propose (2011). They see money as the main agent of capitalism driving inequality and exploitation. Even working within a seemingly more benign framework of money such as fair trade, ethical investment or carbon trading, they argue, is a delusion as it does not escape capitalist markets. Instead they envisage a money-free, market-free, class-free and state-free society based on collective production through 'sharing economies' where people collectively plan, produce, share and care for one another.

Nelson and Timmerman's radical proposal is based on their conception that money is solely related to the capitalist market. An alternative approach is to see money as existing in a variety of contexts (Zelizer 1994). Gibson-Graham argue that there are many types of economy, including those based on time, gifts and care; the capitalist market economy is just one among many (2006). McMurtry agrees, among the many are 'the community exchange market, the traditional public market, the non-monetised barter market, the socialist market, the local exchange-currency market and so on' (2002: 91). As Harcourt argues, the many alternatives leave space for non-market communal initiatives (2014). One such communal initiative is people creating money for themselves.

## Social money

There are many examples of citizen-generated alternative monetary systems that aim to decentralise currencies to the lowest level possible (Seyfang 2006, Cato 2012). Social money is often described as local, parallel or complementary to the official currency. The aim is to encourage exchange based on mutual benefit and principles such as sustainability, rather than profit. The social money is bought (with national currency) or earned or distributed in some way. The face value of the money is generally the same as the national currency. An alternative to having parity with the national currency is to base the currency on time.

In 1991 a time-based currency, 'Time Dollars,' was established in the town of Ithaca in New York state. 'Ithaca Hour' notes were issued denominated by time, from quarter-hour to two hours, but also valued at the national average hourly wage. Ithaca Hours enter the economy by being issued as loans or grants to charities, or payments to those who advertise in the movement's directory of local businesses (Raddon 2003: 13). They still circulate today. In the same year a highly successful time currency based on elderly care was launched in Japan. Hureai Kippu (caring relationship tickets) enabled care-givers to accumulate healthcare credits for their own use, or transfer them to others, for example to obtain care for their relatives living in another part of the country (Douthwaite 1999: 5). There are now hundreds of branches.

Local exchange of goods and services can also be achieved without a circulating currency. The best-known example is a Local Exchange Trading System (LETS). LETSs are membership organisations where people carry out tasks or trade with each other co-ordinated by a central record (Raddon 2003, North 2007). However, there are limitations to local trading systems. If they require records to be kept of each interaction, they cannot cope with large numbers. Local initiatives also face the problem of scale. As North points out, local alternative exchange systems can only work within those resources and activities they can harness (2007: 178). This tends to be personal services and small-scale production. The problem of control of most resources by the main public or commercial sectors remains. Unless the mainstream economic structures can be challenged, the problem of being on the outside still stands. Also, if the aim is to develop subsistence production this may mean that the work becomes very hard, especially for women if they still have responsibility for care work. Moreover, women may not want to spend their lives in local communities; they may want more freedom and mobility.

This is not to detract from the successful social money systems that do exist. An important aspect is that they provide an understanding of how money systems can be created and organised. However, by definition, they are limited to their social framework. Unlike public currencies, they are not universal structures. For that we need to return to the potential of the public currency for internalising care work in the wider economy. One suggestion is to have a basic income.

## Internalisation through a basic income

Ailsa McKay (2005) has made the case that a universal basic income could address the gender inequality around care. Unlike traditional welfare systems it would not separate out women's work. The benefit of a basic income is that it would break the link between income and work. Paid work would not be the criterion of inclusion; instead, there would be a basic right to livelihood through money distribution. The benefit of a basic income is that it would not just apply to care work but would be available to everyone. It would be universal and unconditional. As Annie Miller (2016) argues, a basic income 'provides a foundation for a different type of society, which values the individual, helping him or her to meet material needs and offering choices and the opportunity to develop and flourish' (2016: 174). The choice a basic income would open up is not just payment for care work; it could also reduce dependence on earning money. This might enable (and encourage) men to participate in unpaid provisioning work.

Caitlin McLean (2016) sees ethical, economic and political benefits and problems for a basic income. Ethically it could encourage individual freedom but might limit reciprocity and collective endeavour. Economically it could address inequality and provide a means of livelihood, but traditional economic thinking raises questions of economic feasibility and impact on employment incentives. Political implementation would not be easy given the neoliberal attack on the welfare state and challenge to existing welfare benefits. However, there are some contemporary examples. Iran and the state of Alaska in the US have a form of basic income (2016: 182). Hanlon *et al.* (2010) also report examples of money distribution in South Africa, Brazil, Indonesia and Mexico, although these are not universal as they are targeted to alleviate poverty. Paradoxically, the economic crisis and market failures of neoliberalism have opened up the potential for a basic income, with countries such as Finland and The Netherlands conducting experiments.

The weakness of most proposals for payment of a basic income is that they envisage funding through general taxation based on rolling up current welfare payments. This raises the problem of the level of payment. Spreading the available money universally may mean that those in most need might see a drop in income. Those unable to access other forms of income may still require means-tested benefits. Also, it would not challenge the difference in status between the public and commercial economies and unpaid care work. A basic income would still be seen as dependent on the 'wealth creating' sector, requiring high levels of taxation if a level of income was to be provided that created real choice.

The politics of a basic income also needs to be kept in mind. An early proponent was the right-wing economist Milton Friedman (1962). He proposed a negative income tax that would be implemented in place of all direct welfare payments and services. The aim was to solve the demand problem for capitalism. There would always be money in circulation, but it would leave people at the mercy of the market relying only on charity to relieve need. While neoliberalism has not reached this extreme, it has undermined the legitimacy of the welfare state.

## Privatising money and feminising the state

The second half of the twentieth century saw the growth of market fundamentalism which has led to a feminising of the state. Neoliberal ideology claimed that as money for state expenditure was only generated in the commercial 'wealth producing' sector, states were equivalent to households, having to live on what the 'wealth creator' could afford. States were to 'live within their means' like good housewives. Failure to do so leads to deficits and must be punished by austerity. States must avoid debt and never, ever, 'print money'; that is, issue and spend money independently of the market sector. Women and other disadvantaged groups bore the brunt of this ideology as they lost public services, financial support and job opportunities in the publicly funded sector (healthcare, childcare etc.).

Meanwhile the private financial sector took control of the creation and circulation of money. Under an increasingly deregulated banking system, a huge amount of money was created as debt, most notably mortgages. This was new money conjured out of thin air at the click of a keyboard. Much of this lending went to the financial sector which went on an orgy of speculation (much of it based on mortgages) until the whole system crashed in flames in 2008 (Mellor 2010a). Suddenly the ability of states to 'print money' out of thin air was rediscovered as central banks pumped billions into the banks to save them from collapse. Unfortunately, the neoliberal assumptions about markets as the source of money were not punctured. The public sector and 'left behind' communities continued to be starved of resources through austerity policies, leading to anger and resentment that have had dangerous political consequences.

What is needed is to ask more fundamental questions about the creation and distribution of money. Who controls money?

## Where does money come from?

Proposals for socially beneficial activities are often met with the response 'that is all well and good, but where is the money to come from?' The implication is that money is 'made' in the commercial sector and taxed into the public sector. If that is the case, why do public employees such as teachers pay tax? As the only source of the teacher's pay is public expenditure, effectively public sector workers are returning a portion of the public money they have been paid. The expenditure has come first (teacher's pay) and the tax has been collected out of that money. Teachers cannot pay their taxes if they have not first been paid. Taxation in this case is not raising the money to pay teachers but retrieving money from teachers. Similarly, part of the tax raised from the private sector can also be seen as a retrieval of public money that has been spent by the public sector into the commercial sector (including the teacher's personal expenditure). So where does money come from, is it created in the private or the public sector? In terms of money creation and circulation, is the public sector dependent on the private sector or is the private sector dependent upon the public sector?

Money does not spontaneously appear in economic circulation; it has to be created. Individuals or businesses cannot just mint coins, print notes or add numbers to their bank accounts. Although all money is now 'fiat' – that is, there is no pretence that there is another superior form of money behind it – it does have to be authorised. As I have explained more fully elsewhere (2015) there are only two sources of new publicly recognised money: bank lending or state spending. Other forms of money do exist such as citizen created social currencies or private monies such as Bitcoin, but they do not have the remit of public currencies (pounds, dollars, euros).

Historically, publicly recognised currencies have been circulated mainly by rulers or other state authorities. This was particularly so since the invention of coins around 600 BCE. The main use of money was expenditure by rulers and elites, much of it spent on conflict, prestige projects or funding ruling households. The main focus of circulation was taxation and the Treasury. Today, states and/or central banks still retain the monopoly of the creation of cash (notes and coin). However, they have not retained control of the dominant form of money in capitalist economies, bank accounts generated through bank lending. In the UK today 97 per cent of all money exists only as a bank account. Only 3 per cent is notes and coin.

Bank accounts emerged through the need to finance trade. While merchants did use various ruler authorised currencies, most of their transactions were verbal or written agreements. These grew into a formal banking system in Europe in the sixteenth century. Bank loans and transactions developed a system of bank notes (promises to pay) that passed from hand to hand. What mattered was that the bank or trader would honour the note in due course. As the banking system expanded over the centuries, the notes proliferated and many of the banks failed. The solution was to regularise the notes by recreating a monopoly of note issue through central banks.

Banks could no longer issue their own notes, but this did not stop them creating bank accounts through loans designated in the national currency. As long as account holders were happy to transfer money from account to account it was not necessary to use the national bank notes. Effectively this meant that banks were privatising the creation of the national currency through the creation of bank account loans. Banking theory said this was not real money – it was only 'credit money.' However, as the 2008 banking crisis showed, the state via the central banks had to step in to guarantee that high-street bank accounts would be honoured. When the US let a non-high-street bank fail (Lehman Brothers) it nearly brought the Western banking system down, showing that public responsibility extended to the speculative investment sector (Mellor 2010a).

The irony of the situation was that states that had ceased to create and spend their own money, had ended up guaranteeing the money created by the banks. By the second half of the twentieth century, commercial bank lending became the main source of new public currency in leading capitalist economies with state monetary authorities (central banks) playing a supporting role, including bank rescue. Any independent monetary activity by the state was derided as 'printing money.' An important difference between the two ways of creating money is that bank-issued money is always created as debt while publicly created money can be circulated debt-free through direct public expenditure. Commercially issued money is therefore always threatened by a crisis of indebtedness where people or businesses can take no more debt. State-issued money is free of debt but is threatened by inflation if the taxation mechanism for retrieval breaks down or if there are problems in the economy generally, particularly a dramatic slowdown or collapse.

This is why proposals for funding the care economy through a basic income needs to be seen in the context of how money is sourced in the economy. If new money emerges through debt in the commercial sector, extracting tax income will always be uncertain. If a basic income were to be funded by state-issued money, its implementation would depend on the expenditure priorities of the state. A major limitation on such social and public spending is the view that money is in short supply, that there is somehow a 'natural' limit on the number of coins, notes or bank accounts. There is certainly a problem if there is too much money, leading to inflation. This would be because of too much bank lending, or too much state spending with ineffective taxation, or a lack of availability of assets, goods or services. However, there is no 'natural' limit to fiat money.

## Reclaiming money from the market

Under neoliberal ideology, the state must not create its own money; it must rely on taxing the wealth-creating sector, that is, the market. I have already pointed to the fallacy in this argument: that the public sector also pays taxes. Neoliberal ideology is wrong to say that states do not, or should not, create money. There are two processes of money creation and circulation in modern economies. Banks create a circuit of money with a constant flow of loans and repayments. States create a circuit of money through public expenditure and taxation. As these are circuits of money, identifying the source of that money depends on where the circuit is observed.

If the focus is upon tax, that seems to come first (tax to spend). If the focus is upon public expenditure, that can be seen as the starting point (spend to tax). Starting from bank deposits, it would seem that they provide the money to make loans (banks merely link savers and borrowers) until it is seen that banks lend the money that creates those deposits. Banks could not expect repayments if they had not first made loans. They do not rely on prior deposits. If that were the case, it would be necessary to identify a separate source of money for those deposits and there is no such source apart from the state. This would imply public money is funding the private banking sector. The conclusion must be that bank lending is constantly creating new money while repayment of loans is removing that money from circulation.

The public circuit of money has a similar dynamic. Money is constantly being circulated through public expenditure and collected through taxation. The question is which comes first, the expenditure or the tax? The existence of deficit indicates that it must be expenditure that comes first. States allocate budgets on the expectation of tax returns (well-named); they do not spend a pre-existing 'pot' of money. Recognising this public circuit of money is a direct challenge to neoliberal market fundamentalism. Money does not emerge only from the market sector. In fact, the creation of money through debt in the private sector is a constant source of potential instability. Publicly created money has the benefit of being able to be circulated free of debt.

Seeing money in a social and public context creates the space for more socially oriented approaches. Rejecting the emphasis on money's role in market exchange enables a view of money that sees it as a useful means of account in many different contexts, including social and public arenas. The different meanings attached to money will affect how it is seen as operating in its role of representing value. While commercial views of money will always stress value in money terms as profit (money invested to make more money), social and public forms of money can address outcomes in terms of social and public benefit.

Money can mean very different things; it can mean a gift, a fine or a commercial payment. This stance requires different ways of assessing value. While commercial value is judged in the marketplace, social value will be judged in terms of personal relationships, while public value can be judged at the ballot box or in public debate. There is no reason why the values of the commercial sector should be given priority. A thoughtful but inexpensive gift may be more highly valued than an expensive but inappropriate one. Value may be exchanged with no notion of maximising profit. Money or some kind of notation is merely a convenience where the aim is not to maximise money value, but to maximise social or ecological value. Rather than profit in the market, public money could enable ecologically sustainable sufficiency provisioning. Debt free public money could be created and used to fund caring activities on a not-for-profit basis.

## Care as wellth

An important contrast is between wealth expressed in terms of the pursuit of money and assets and wellth as well-being expressed as paid and unpaid activities aimed at social and individual flourishing. If the aim of society was the pursuit of wellth, the security of social, environmental and ecological conditions would not just be internalised within money-enabled provisioning systems but be at their heart.

In modern economies, wealth is valued as both the creation and result of economic activity. The assumption is that wealth will directly or indirectly create employment and prosperity. Profitable sectors of growth such as the car industry, electronics, services or knowledge are seen as a source of new money that can be spread into the wider economy. This creates the illusion that money can only emerge through wealth creation in the private sector. Such an assumption reflects the specific history of entrepreneurial industrial economies.

A longer historical view would see rulers as major employers, mainly of mercenary soldiers or builders of palaces, castles and cathedrals. It is the concentration of money in the 'growth area' that is the key element, not the economic framework as such (capitalism, imperialism etc.). Both the private and the ruling/public sector can be a source of monetary energy. In contemporary societies, there is no reason why the provision of care should not be the energy of the economy through the creation and circulation of money as wellth rather than wealth. The older industrial nations are facing a demographic crisis of care. Instead of a problem, this could be seen as a major opportunity to redirect provisioning priorities and monetary energy.

Neoliberalism claims that new money only originates in the context of capitalist activity. This is not true. Concentration of money draws on three sources: previously circulating money, borrowing new money (bank loans) and public money (created by public monetary authorities). A decision to concentrate money on care need not mean privatisation and profit-seeking; it could be based on socially created money or publicly created money. Care-giving would be the engine of the economy through focussing existing and new money on care work. This money would then flow out into the wider economy. Prudent taxation would prevent this being inflationary.

Unlike wealth which tends to concentrate in a few hands, wellth spreads through society. The more people providing goods and services for each other, the wellthier the society (assuming the production of goods takes account of ecological limits, conditions of employment etc.). However, creating wellth would need to be accompanied by the redistribution of wealth, if inequality is to be reduced and democracy achieved.

## Democratising money

'Money is contrived by a group to measure, collect and redistribute resources' (Desan 2014: 6).

There is nothing natural about money. The form of money and the means and control of its creation and circulation are socially constructed. Evidence from anthropology is that most human societies have some means of measuring comparative value often expressed in terms of tributes, gifts, dowries or injury payments. Nations and empires have also used a variety of money forms, most usually coins or paper. As Desan (2014) points out, historical evidence shows rulers had to struggle hard to maintain sufficient trusted coinage to enable state and market expenditure. In modern economies, particularly under neoliberalism, states have ceded control of their money supply to the banking sector. New money only emerges as personal, commercial or governmental debt. I would argue that debt-based money is socially, politically, ecologically and economically unstable.

It is socially unstable because access to new money is only available to those deemed to be creditworthy. Money therefore gravitates towards the most financially viable or those who promise the greatest speculative returns. The poorest are financially excluded and those in the middle find themselves burdened with debt. It is politically unstable because the lack of direct access to new money undermines public expenditure which in turn causes social discontent. Under neoliberal orthodoxy, state spending is constrained on the grounds that it 'wastes' money that could be better spent in the market sector.

Ecologically, it is unstable because commercial control of the money supply drives growth and consumption. The market does not have a mechanism that can recognise 'enough' or 'sufficiency.' It must move forward or die.

Finally, bank-led money systems are economically unstable because basing a money supply on debt must end in crisis. There inevitably comes a point when the system can take no more debt. At that point the money supply starts to shrink. No more debt is created, while existing debts either default or continue to be paid, shrinking the supply of money further. At this point the state steps in and returns to its historical role of creating and managing the money supply. This has been clearly demonstrated following the 2008 crisis (Mellor 2010a, 2015).

If the state is to step in to rescue the banks, why can it not step in to rescue the people or the planet? Rather than leaving the money supply to the priorities of the banks, why not base the money supply on the priorities of the people or the needs of the environment? Why not spend new money first on public and social goods and services and then let it flow through to the market? Banks would then be left to do what they claim to do, take in money for investment and lend it out on a commercial basis. There would no longer be need for state borrowing and therefore no national debt. Taxation would not be seen as raising money for public expenditure, it would be reclaiming money already spent. Direct public expenditure means there would be no need to grow the commercial economy in order to increase tax income. Nor would there be the need to conform to market priorities. Quite the opposite, the market sector would be made subject to social and ecological regulation.

Budgets are critical to the monetary role of the public economy. Neoliberal economics would claim that the market needs to determine the level of public expenditure. Democratising money would mean that the people would determine the level of public expenditure they require. As I have proposed more fully elsewhere, central to the democratic control of money would be participatory budgeting (Mellor 2015: 85–6). Communities would put forward their own local budgets, while larger-scale infrastructure would have regional and national mechanisms for agreeing expenditure needs.

Public participation in public budgeting is likely to see public expenditure rising substantially. This would bring concerns about possible inflation in the market sector. To avoid this, I propose that an independent monetary authority makes an overall recommendation on the total level of taxation necessary to prevent inflation in the market sector. This independent assessment would not determine the overall level of public expenditure or how the necessary tax would be raised. The level of retrieval taxation needed would depend on the level of social and public expenditure relative to the size of the market sector. It is important to understand the importance of the reversal of taxation here. Public expenditure is not based on the 'taxpayer's money.' Instead, public expenditure creates and circulates the money that ends up in the taxpayer's pocket. The taxpayer is giving it back.

For this reason, public scrutiny of both the state and the banking sector as they create and circulate money is essential. States left to their own devices can be as destructive as markets. The strength of the case for democratising money is that there is nothing to 'back' the money, whether created by the bank or state, other than the people, their resources, their labour and their trust in each other.

## Conclusion

This chapter has made the case for internalising unpaid care activities and uncosted environmental damage and misuse, through a rethinking and reorientation of the money system. Failure to recognise that money is a social and public phenomenon has allowed the commercial sector to hijack the money supply and hold the social and public sectors to ransom. The vulnerability of the current system was demonstrated by the 2008 crisis and the subsequent public rescue of the banking sector. The contradictions of private benefit and public rescue need to be exposed. The case must be made for a monetary system oriented to promoting wellth rather than the accumulation of wealth. To do this, money creation and circulation must respond to democratically determined priorities, not market forces. Reorienting the money system in this manner would mean that care and other externalised 'women's work' would then become the major focus of wellth, the use of monetary exchange to promote well-being. Scarcity/austerity economics must be replaced by sufficiency provisioning with the aim of achieving social justice and ecological sustainability (Mellor 2010b).

Money is not the prerogative of the market or the state. It represents the entitlements and obligations that people have towards each other. At present the lack of democratic control of money means that entitlements have been harnessed by the rich and obligations placed upon the poor. The only way to access money is paid work or debt. The right to money needs to be established as a democratic right, as it represents the right to livelihood. This right should also be shared by the non-human environment; there should be an allocation of money for the preservation and autonomous development of the natural environment and other species.

It is the argument of this paper that money for wellth, a debt-free public money supply providing direct expenditure, could be the basis of an 'economics of care.' In modern economies there is a choice between a money system based on debt and the search for profit, and a debt-free money system as a public resource (Mellor 2010a, Mellor 2015). The existence of that resource has been made evident in the state rescue of the banks following the 2008 financial crisis. Instead of creating huge sums to rescue a flawed banking system, the public power to create money should be harnessed through participatory democracy, to build a socially just and ecologically sustainable provisioning system with care at its heart.

## References

Bakker, I., 2003. Neoliberal governance and the reprivatisation of social reproduction: social provisioning and shifting gender others. *In*: I. Bakker and S. Gill, eds, *Power, Production and Social Reproduction*. London: Palgrave, 66–82.

Bennholdt-Thomsen, V. and Mies, M., 1999. *The Subsistence Perspective*. London: Zed Books.

Biesecker, A. and Hofmeister, A., 2010. Focus: (re)productivity: sustainable relations both between society and nature and between the genders. *Ecological Economics*, 69, 1703–11.

Cato, M.S., 2012. *The Bioregional Economy: Land, Liberty and the Pursuit of Happiness*. London: Routledge.

Desan, C., 2014. *Making Money: Coin, Currency and the Coming of Capitalism*. Oxford: Oxford University Press.

Douthwaite, R., 1999. *The Ecology of Money*. Cambridge, UK: Green Books.

Federici, S., 2009. The devaluation of women's labour. *In*: A. Salleh, ed., *Eco-Sufficiency and Global Justice*. London: Pluto Press, 43–57.

Folbre, N., 1994. *Who Pays for the Kids?* London: Routledge.

Friedman, M., 1962. *Capitalism and Freedom*. Chicago, IL: University of Chicago Press.

Gardiner, J., 1997. *Gender, Care and Economics*. Basingstoke, UK: Macmillan Press.

Gibson-Graham, J.K., 2006. *A Post-Capitalist Politics*. Minneapolis, MN: University of Minnesota Press.

Hanlon, J., Barrientos, A. and Hulme, D., 2010. *Just Give Money to the Poor: The Development Revolution from the Global South*. Sterling, VA: Kumerian Press.

Harcourt, W., 2014. The future of capitalism: a consideration of alternatives. *Cambridge Journal of Economics*, 38 (6), 1307–28.

McMurtry, J., 2002. *Value Wars: The Global Market Versus the Life Economy*. London: Pluto Press.

McKay, A., 2005. *The Future of Social Security Policy: Women, Work and a Citizen's Basic Income*. London: Routledge.

McLean, C., 2016. Debating a citizen's basic income. *In*: J. Campbell and M. Gillespie, eds, *Feminist Economics and Public Policy*. London: Routledge, 177–88.

Mellor, M., 1997. Women, nature and the social construction of 'economic man'. *Ecological Economics*, 20 (2), 129–40.

Mellor, M., 2009. Ecofeminist political economy and the politics of money. *In*: A. Salleh, ed., *Eco-Sufficiency and Global Justice*. London: Pluto Press, 251–67.

Mellor, M., 2010a. *The Future of Money: From Financial Crisis to Public Resource*. London: Pluto Press.

Mellor, M., 2010b. Could the money system be the basis of a sufficiency economy? *Real-World Economics Review*, 54, 79–88.

Mellor, M., 2013. The unsustainability of economic man. *Ökologisches Wirtschaften*, 4, 30–33.

Mellor, M., 2015. *Debt or Democracy: Public Money for Sustainability and Social Justice*. London: Pluto Press.

Miller, A., 2016. A citizen's basic income and its implications. *In*: J. Campbell and M. Gillespie, eds., *Feminist Economics and Public Policy*. London: Routledge, 164–76.

Nelson, A. and Timmerman, F., 2011. *Life Without Money: Building Fair and Sustainable Economies*. London, Pluto Press.

North, P, 2007. *Money and Liberation*. Minneapolis: University of Minnesota Press.

Nussbaum, M., 2000. *Women and Human Development: The Capabilities Approach*. Cambridge: Cambridge University Press.

Perkins, E. and Kuiper, E., eds., 2005. Explorations: feminist ecological economics [special issue]. *Feminist Economics* 11 (3), 107–48.

Picchio, A., 2003. A macroeconomic approach to an extended standard of living. *In*: A. Picchio, ed., *Unpaid Work and the Economy*. London: Routledge, 11–28.

Pionetti, C., 2005. *Sowing Autonomy: Gender and Seed Politics and Semi-Arid India*. London: International Institute for Environment and Development.

Raddon, M.B., 2003. *Community and Money*. Montréal: Black Rose Books.

Salleh, A., 1997. *Ecofeminism as Politics: Nature, Marx and the Postmodern*. London: Zed Press.

Salleh, A., 2009. From eco-sufficiency to global justice. *In*: A. Salleh, ed., *Eco-Sufficiency and Global Justice*. London: Pluto Press, 291–312.

Seyfang, G., 2006. Sustainable consumption, the new economics and community currencies: developing new institutions for environmental governance. *Regional Studies*, 40, 781–91.

Waring, M., 1989. *If Women Counted*. London: Macmillan.

Waring, M., 2009. Policy and the measure of woman. *In*: A. Salleh, ed., *Eco-Sufficiency and Global Justice*. London: Pluto Press, 165–79.

Wichterich, C., 2015. Contesting green growth, connecting care, commons and enough. *In*: W. Harcourt and I.L. Nelson, eds., *Practising Feminist Political Ecologies: Moving Beyond the 'Green Economy'*. London: Zed Books, 67–100.

Yeates, N., 2012. The globalisation of paid care: labour migration. *In*: S. Razavi and S. Staab, eds., *Global Variations in the Political and Social Economy of Care*. London: Routledge, 241–56.

Zelizer, V.A., 1994. *The Social Meaning of Money*. New York: Basic Books.

# 8 Diverse ethics for diverse economies

## Considering the ethics of embodiment, difference and inter-corporeality at Kufunda

*Pamela Richardson-Ngwenya and*
*Andrea J. Nightingale*

## Introduction

Today's globalised world throws up new economic and environmental challenges, as well as new opportunities for transformation. Striving for a sense of empowerment and reconnection, many people are keen to experiment with alternative ways of conceptualising and organising economic activities in order to undermine the dominant logic of the global capitalist economic system. In capitalism, economic transactions and markets have conventionally been framed as exchanges governed by rational principles, based on a calculation of value. An insistence on rational self-maximisation under the presumably objective 'invisible hand of the market' (Smith 1937) is contested by critics, often on the grounds that such a system has unethical outcomes (see Ricard 2015). Many popular readings of alternative economies such as fair trade, implicitly rest on the notion of putting 'ethics' back into international economies (Trentmann 2007, Varul 2009, McEwan *et al.* 2017). Such assumptions, however, articulate a reformist approach that does not challenge the underlying logic of capitalist exchange and furthermore, does not engage with the question of what it might mean to become 'ethical' (Richardson-Ngwenya 2012a).

Emerging from these critiques, 'Community Economies' are put forward as a viable alternative, as many of the chapters in this volume explore. Proponents of community economies insist on a different systemic framing of economic activity that embraces alternative notions of value, exchange and growth (Massey 2005, Bauhardt 2014, Bollier 2017). As we review in more depth below, community economies often purport to be driven explicitly by moral concerns, articulating principles of solidarity, caring for environment, animal welfare and social justice as organising features of economies. Further, conceptualisations of community economies are often 'guided by a distinctive ethical stance' (Gibson-Graham 2005: 4) or an 'ethical orientation to the world' (Gibson-Graham 2008: 618): it would seem that community economies abound with 'ethical practices,' 'ethical choices,' 'ethical decisions,' 'ethical visions,' 'ethical projects,' 'ethical interventions,' 'ethical transformations' and 'ethical commitments' (Gibson-Graham 2008: 618). Despite this emphasis on ethics as one feature of community economies, 'ethics' has too often been incorporated without a clear and robust theorisation of what is meant by the term 'ethical' or how such a view of ethics is conceptually derived (Miller 2013). Without conceptual clarity, there is a risk that well-intentioned efforts at creating alternative economies will fail due to fundamental misunderstandings and conflicts around what it practically means to produce and reproduce ethics in such economic spaces and what additional challenges emerge in trying to promote them across scales (see Gibson-Graham 2006).

In this chapter, we hope to contribute to the alternative and community economies literature by exploring some of this ambiguity around 'the ethical.' Our main contribution is to develop an understanding of ethics that shows how embodied, more-than-human relations are a central part of why diverse ethics emerge within alternative economies – and how ethics is fundamentally a dynamic and contested sphere. We suggest that by looking at such economies as driven by alternative moral rationalities, greater conceptual clarity of the (diverse) ethics of diverse community economies emerges. Our approach builds on a Foucauldian assumption that economic spaces are *always* simultaneously ethical spaces, firstly (following Foucault) in that they are performatively governed, formally or informally, by codes of conduct (or values/principles). And secondly, (following Levinas 1969) that such spaces are always already constituted ontologically by ethical relations between entities/subjects. An underlying premise then is that 'economies' are ethical spaces, not simply in terms of normative rationalities that aim to create a 'good life' through 'good practices' (Muraca 2012, Harcourt 2014), but also (by viewing ethics through a poststructuralist, feminist lens) as a space in which embodied, inter-subjective, more-than-human relations immanently unfold and practically constitute value-in-the-making (Bollier 2017).

Applying this open and pluralist engagement with ethical thought, our chapter is exploratory. We begin by thinking through relevant conceptualisations of ethics and how they have been applied in diverse economies literature to date. Through this exploration, we seek to develop a research trajectory and engage with reflexive questions: what difference does practising a diverse conceptualisation of ethics make to our understanding of alternative economic spaces? What can this contribute to debates in feminist political economy and political ecology? How might such a 'pluriform' (*cf.* Escobar 1998) understanding of economic ethics translate into a research agenda and collaborative engagement that is relevant or useful to the communities involved?

The next section lays out the intellectual context of community economies, ethics and feminist interventions in ethical thought that guides this line of questioning. We then illustrate these ideas through a brief case study of a village in Zimbabwe: Kufunda Village. Firstly, we look at the core principles that shape the community economy. Kufunda Village consciously positions itself as an alternative to the mainstream; rather than existing as a collection of households seeking a livelihood, Kufunda villagers ('Kufundees') are 'learning our way into what it takes to build a healthy and vibrant community' (Kufunda

Village n.d.a). After introducing Kufunda and the alternative principle (an ethic of learning) that guides their community economy agenda, we look at some of their practices through the lenses of three prominent themes in feminist ethical thought: embodiment, difference and inter-corporeality.

The empirical example draws attention to the embodied materiality of economic practice, highlighting how Kufundees cultivate a sense of (the ethical) self and community that is immanent and relational. Their testimonies describe how the group practice of jewellery-making reconstitutes 'economy' in ways that are different from a rational calculation of surplus/exchange value, and that also transcends a simple 'fair trade' logic of monetary compensation. While this may at first seem to naïvely romanticise community economies (Aguilar 2005), we emphasise how living with sensitivity to (inter-corporeal and interspecies) difference can equally result in problematic, antagonistic relations between the (socio-environmental) self and community, tensions which can be even more pronounced when trying to 'scale up' community economies. It is for this reason that we are wary of essentialising 'an ethic of care' within community economies; rather, we suggest there is a need to destabilise the emphasis on care. We rather argue that an alternative feminist economics needs to embrace the ambiguity and inter-corporeality of caring relations, as well as acknowledge the important relations of competition and strife that together shape the success of such experiments in community economies. We use this experiment in applied ethical philosophy for thinking through the difference that such ideas can make to heterogeneous, alternative economy-building processes (Harcourt and Nelson 2015).

## Community and diverse economies

Community economies are often self-defined alternatives to hegemonic capitalism and organised in a way that seeks to transcend the emphasis on extraction of surplus value that is so characteristic of mainstream capitalism (Bauhardt 2014). Many experiments in community economies focus on barter, alternative currencies and community-based volunteer efforts to generate new forms of value. Community economies are both grassroots initiatives and part of a growing research agenda interested in conceptualising life-giving alternatives, rather than simply engaging in academic critique (Gibson-Graham 2005, 2008). Intellectually, Gibson-Graham have been crucial to this debate beginning with their seminal contribution, *The End Of Capitalism (As We Knew It): A Feminist Critique of Political Economy* (1996). In much of their work, they have sought to deconstruct the notion of a hegemonic capitalist economy that subsumes all other forms of economic activity. Rather, they theorise how different social relations and means of exchange serve to constitute multiple capitalist forms. Conceptualising 'diverse economies' opens up our imaginations to alternative logics of economic exchange and drives us to empirically investigate creative forms of exchange and social reproduction (Cameron and Gibson-Graham 2003).

For our purposes here, there are two contributions that emerge from the literature that help to build a more robust conceptualisation of the ethics of community economies. First, ontologically, economies are conceptualised as performative, always in the making or becoming (Gibson-Graham 2008). Rather than social and economic relations being structured, a performative ontology highlights the importance of everyday relations between people and things that serve to (re)shape economies. Drawing from the work of Jean-Luc Nancy, Gibson-Graham highlights how the community is best approached not as a model, identity or essence but as the relationship of 'being-in-common' or the 'commonality of being' (81–2). Instead of 7.5 billion people in the world being subservient to capital, people have the power to recreate the economic forms they want by how they choose to engage with each other, and we would add, with other species and things. By recognising that economies result from the socio-natural relations that produce and *are produced by* particular ways of understanding, knowing and being in relation to an economy and ecology, it is possible to reimagine other ways of engagement. The community economy is thus not a single economic form but rather emerges uniquely from place-based relations of exchange that transcend simple monetary interactions (Gibson-Graham 2006).

The second relevant theoretical insight that underpins ideas of community economies is that the local and the global are inherently relationally constituted through interactions between humans and non-humans. Massey developed this idea in her work on space and place, insisting that space is not simply a container for social relations, but rather that social relations serve to constitute space and place (Massey 1994, 2005). Places in turn are constituted by their socio-economies – the everyday relations that serve to bring together and transform people, things and other species – as well as by their connections to other places; a concept that both encompasses but also goes well beyond simple economic exchange (Massey 2005). Rather, places become the locus of possibility, the material manifestations of worldviews, knowledges, virtual and physical transactions, and the relational performance of subjectivities.

Conceptualising place in this manner opens up the possibilities for a transformative politics of place. As Harcourt (2014) has highlighted, place-based politics may be about resistance but they are also about re-appropriation, re-construction, and re-invention of practices and possibilities (Harcourt 2014). Harcourt draws from the insight of Mohanty and Miraglia (2012) that 'places act as prisms that refract global economic and governance structures, bending and shaping them in ways that make sense within the politics of particular sites and in different communities' (Mohanty and Miraglia 2012: 122–3). When the economy is conceptualised as heterogeneous and diverse, it is easier to imagine alternative possibilities for productive activities, such as those that foster spaces where collective economic decision-making, based on counter-hegemonic principles, is encouraged (Burke and Shear 2014).

The community economies debate has increasingly segued into an interest in commoning; indeed, there is considerable conceptual and political overlap between these literatures (see also Dombroski *et al.* this volume). In the current debate, 'commons' signals far more than simply property regimes developed to manage common pool resources that Ostrom (1990) sought to valorise. Rather, commons represent collective efforts to (re)imagine social, economic and cultural relations between people and the places they live. Commoners seek to own and control something that belongs to them in the first place, rather than re-distribute wealth generated by markets (Bollier 2007b). The difference between the standard economic theory of value and a commons-based one is that the latter is explicitly based on relationality (Bollier 2017). Importantly, in a commons, value is an event. It is something that needs to be enacted again and again. Commons offer alternative ways of explaining how significant value can be created and sustained outside of the market system (Bollier 2007a). And vital to our argument here, most commoning efforts need to be understood as ongoing projects that reflect explicit desires to produce alternative means of exchange and relations of value creation.

The literature on community economies and commoning often places an emphasis on care and social reproduction. Feminists have long sought to highlight the importance of (non-monetised) reproductive labour that fundamentally supports capitalist economies (McDowell 1991, Federici 2011, Harcourt 2014). This has led feminist political ecologists to argue for giving greater attention to care, the household and personal relations in economic analyses that link ethics, nature and culture (Harcourt 2014). Commons, as a form of community economy, are not only about collectivisation, but also about positioning care as the driving force of economic value creation (Morrow and Dombroski 2015). Such care extends well beyond the human community to include other species and serves to frame new socio-natural ontologies. Wendy Harcourt summarises this post-capitalist concern:

> to find ways to live with and redefine capitalism aware of social and ecological limits and to see how to change our economic values to include care and respect for our families, communities, other knowledges and cultures. The concept of living economies proposes that we redesign our economies so that life is valued more than money and power resides in ordinary women and men who care for each other, their community and their natural environment. The challenge for the future is to build a broad platform for living economies or alternatives building up from community needs, which are inter-generational and gender aware, based on an ethics of care for the environment.
>
> (Harcourt 2014:18–19)

While we are supportive of these efforts to reimagine the relations necessary to produce more vibrant and life-giving material-discursive ontologies (Barad 2003), we believe this project can benefit from a deeper conceptual engagement with ethical philosophies. If we are to adopt an understanding of ethics – like the above conceptualisations of community economy – which is fundamentally performative and relational, then ethics as fixed beliefs or values held are rendered entirely unstable. Below, we work through a pluriform understanding of ethics. We mobilise the concepts of embodiment, difference and inter-corporeality, looking at how these ideas have been deployed in feminist ethical theory in order to unpack how the 'ethics' of community economies can be more critically and diversely understood.

## Unpacking the diverse ethics of community economies

Building on Gibson-Graham's (2008) argument for a critical conceptualisation of economies as ethical spaces, we begin here to delve into what that might mean. As discussed above, community economies are positioned as 'ethical' alternatives to hegemonic capitalism. In conjunction with the community economies literature, which proposes a recognition of plural, diverse economic modes and practices (Cameron and Gibson-Graham 2003), we propose to consider 'ethics' as a plurality of modes, concepts and ontologies, and to explicitly situate 'the ethical' within feminist debate. We now unpack and journey through the four ethical concepts that will then frame our engagement with the empirical activities of Kufunda.

### Ethics as an articulation of mind: Principled subjects

It is commonly recognised that modern capitalist concepts of the economy have been imbued with a Cartesian ethics (Colebrook 2005). A Cartesian perspective understands life as shaped by a mind-body dualism: 'The thinker who recognises herself as alienated from the mechanistic material world comes to objectify this material world, and, through such objectification, to see it as an instrument that she should effectively control to achieve her own rational goals' (Wee 2002: 257).[1] A Cartesian metaphysics thus constructs a non-thinking material world as reigned over by disembodied, thinking minds. The mind, from this perspective, becomes the source of all moral reasoning and ethical action, leaving little room for emotional connections that underpin many relations, for example those based on caring.

Capitalism, argues Claire Colebrook (2005), is 'based on competitiveness, quantification and the ruthless extension of individual reason' (Colebrook 2005: 11). Proponents of such an economic system (and particularly neoliberalists) reject 'external' modes of ordering the economy: the transactional relation between units (material uniform equivalents) is 'king'; 'human individuals emerge as independent social units only in this "egalitarian" relation to capital; it is the capacity to sell one's labour that both defines one's social position and determines the social as such' (Dumont 1977: 84 cited Colebrook 2005: 3). Similarly, Gibson-Graham (1996) present globalisation as a discourse that constructs its subjects as 'citizens' of capitalism: they are entrepreneurs, or employees, or would-be employees; they are investors in capitalist firms; they are consumers of (capitalist) commodities.

Such a system thus assumes the interaction of rational individuals, exchanging material units of value, following the transactional rules of capital. Social and environmental costs are largely excluded from the valuation process. Capitalist business and bureaucracy function to sap the sense of responsibility and agency from the subject (Bauman 1993: 13). Without wishing to suggest a bimodal view of economy (i.e. capitalism versus everything else), we can say in general that community economies aim to recognise, reduce and account for the social and environmental costs of economic production and thus explicitly adopt a rather different set of ideals based on various notions of responsibility, care, rights and justice (Bauhardt 2014, Harcourt 2014). These call for a different set of ethical values to govern behaviour.

But community economies are diverse and cannot be reduced to a singular definition. Echoing an Aristotelian stance, Fairtrade, for example, implies that we should develop *better* values, or virtues, in order to create a healthier, more 'ethical' economy or 'conscious capitalism' (Fyke and Buzzanell 2013). Yet, the ultimate test of such values is assumed to play out in terms of monetised exchange: producers get better prices and consumers are willing to pay more for 'ethical' products. In contrast, Gibson-Graham argue that community economies can be viewed as spaces that do not subject themselves to the logic of 'the bottom line' or the 'imperatives of capital' (1996). In Gibson-Graham, Cameron and Healy (2013) the following principles are put forward:

- surviving together well and equitably;
- distributing surplus to enrich social and environmental health;
- encountering others in ways that support their well-being as well as ours;
- consuming sustainably;
- caring for – maintaining, replenishing and growing – our natural and cultural commons; and
- investing our wealth in future generations so that they can live as well.

They explain that 'an Economy centred on these ethical considerations is what we call a community economy' (Gibson-Graham *et al.* 2013: xix). These principles are thus pitched as the alternative *ethics* of community economies.

As well as putting forward ethical principles, Gibson-Graham's early work engages Foucault's notion of 'ethical subject' formation, endorsing the cultivation of our capacities to imagine, desire and practise non-capitalist ways to be. The ethical subject refers here to an idealised 'self-formed subject' that emerges from 'working on our local/regional selves to become something other than what the global economy wants us to be' (Gibson-Graham 2003: 56). Here, ethical subjectivity implies the capability and possibility for a subject to question their own conduct and to question the dominant moral codes. In Gibson-Graham's theorisation of community economics, local/regional actors self-create an 'ethical subject' through a critique, questioning and ultimately remaking of the moral codes that structure relations of economy and society (Gibson-Graham 2003).

From this perspective, ethical subjectivity is based on an ethics that derives from the mind, from conscious and rational processes. It requires an analysis of how one's life is located within the global system and an identification of proactive steps to combat that positioning. Ethical subjectivity here is then a contained, fairly exclusive position. The formation of ethical selves is predicated upon the autonomy and individual agency of subjects who are able to contest dominant (ethical) principles and values governing socio-economies. Feminist philosopher Rosalyn Diprose (2002), however, has argued that the notion of a subject with pre-defined borders denies the primary ambiguity of the subject (2002: 96). Rather, ethical subjectivity arises from embodied, relational dynamics whereby we are unavoidably entangled in inter-corporeal (more-than-human) relationships. In this case, we should assume firstly, that the subject is co-produced in the context of an inherently ambiguous and relational debt to the Other and secondly, that the emergent, ambiguous subject may not know what they need to question or how to position themselves in a stance that is reliably, for example, anti-capitalist. In other words, ethical subjects (and stances) are rarely fixed, but rather shift as their boundaries and interrelations shift. This calls for a continual re-positioning – and embodying – of ethics in space, place and relation. Diprose and other feminists have articulated this notion of (inter-corporeal) ethical subjectivity through a sustained engagement with the concept of embodiment, outlined below.

### Ethics as embodied spatial practices

Conceptualising ethics as codes of conduct, norms or virtues has also been challenged by feminists who have recognised that codes, norms and virtues are political modes of socialisation that result in enhancing the power of certain embodied individuals, whilst often oppressing and disenfranchising other kinds of bodies (Foucault 1985). For example, through a binary logic, historically women (but not only women) became associated with bodies, nature and emotions to the detriment of their political and ethical subjectivities, unable to vote, participate in paid employment, higher education and suchlike. Through recognition of the partial nature of such codes and the politics of embodiment, feminists have taken issue with Cartesian philosophy and with the ethics that emerge therefrom: Moira Gatens argues that '[p]hilosophers have typically ignored the corporeal aspects of being human' (Gatens 1996: viii) and Luce Irigaray laments that '[t]he whole historic and historical analysis of philosophy shows that being has yet to be referred to in terms of body or flesh [...]. Thought and body have remained separate' (Irigaray 1993: 74). This intellectual bifurcation of mind and body, Diprose argues, is related to the fact that philosophy 'has been a male-dominated enterprise [...] formulating concepts that address the lifestyles of men [...] affirming the existence and status of men' (Held 1993, Diprose 2002: 130, Noddings 2013). It has thus been postulated that 'Man is the model and it is [...] his reason which is taken for Reason; his morality which is formalised into a system of ethics'

(Gatens 1996: 24). In response to this, the mind-body dichotomy at the root of modern notions of abstract, disembodied and universalisable ethical codes have been deconstructed and contested by feminists conceptualising ethics not as disembodied rules/virtues, but as concrete embodied practices. Hence, embodiment has become one of the key concepts through which feminists have critically intervened in moral philosophies.

This recognition of the importance of embodiment prompts basic ontological questions about what it means to have a body, or to be embodied. Rather than postulating the body and thought as separate incommensurable entities, feminists have argued that all experience is embodied: The self is a 'corporeal cultural artefact' (Diprose 2002: 21). Further conceptualisations of the body, described by Sharp and McDowell (2014) include:

> a surface to be mapped, a surface for inscription, as a boundary between the individual subject and that which is Other to it, as the container of individual identity, but also as a permeable boundary which leaks and bleeds and is penetrable.
>
> (3)

Robyn Longhurst (1997) has argued that our bodies are at the core of our experience of the geographies we inhabit. We live our lives as embodied creatures; feeling, sensing and thinking through the body (Rodaway 1994). Judith Butler (1990) and Gillian Rose (1993) present embodiment as a performative condition: a specific physicality of being/becoming that is central to experience and to the production of knowledge. The ethical norms described above thereby come to inhabit, configure and be performed by bodies (Gatens & Lloyd 1999). Moreover, the body becomes the site of emergent ethical practices, the physical and symbolic space where ethical relations between self and other are immanently co-constituted. From this perspective, our bodies – the sockets of our eyes, the lining of our stomachs, the lingering of our fingertips – are always already implicated in the articulation of our 'ethical selves.'

Moving on, much of the community economy literature helpfully reconstitutes the economy as an ethical *space* (Gibson-Graham and Roelvink 2010) as opposed to being described as, or constituted by, an ethical *subject*. This 'ethical space' discourse centralises embodied *practices* of community coexistence and place-making (see also Dombroski *et al.* this volume). While not always emphasising the embodied dynamics of this coexistence, Gibson-Graham and Roelvink (2010) articulate a notion of community and economy as co-produced through everyday practices of negotiating co-existence and interdependence (including working together, eating together, monetary transactions etc.). A community economy is defined here a 'space of decision making where we recognize and negotiate our interdependence with other humans, other species, and our environment. In the process of recognizing and negotiating, we become a community' (Gibson-Graham *et al.* 2013: xix). From this perspective, ethics are constituted in the space *between* bodies, through practices that can be understood to produce new ethical values (such as health and enjoyment) in the dynamic, inter-relational spaces of community.

Harcourt (2016) draws on Gibson-Graham (1996, 2006), but also on Rocheleau (2016) and Haraway (2011), to explore the relation between changing gender dynamics, ethical values and livelihoods in Bolsena, Italy. Through three women's narratives, Harcourt shows how everyday practices (of caring for goats, making cheese, providing hospitality, singing songs and creating occasions for people to enjoy organic wine) participate in the formation of new ethical values and economic imaginaries, grounded in their search for 'the good life.' The women speak of their embodied and emotional attachments to the town, the lake, the Tuscan landscape and their cultural practices, as they intertwine new technologies with the historically bound material realities of Bolsena in both their livelihood and enjoyment practices. Their embodied practices and experiences thus participate in the creation of emerging, alternative visions of a place-based economy that promotes health and joy, as well as a means of sustenance.

Rearticulating ethics as embodied and spatial practices, as implied through Harcourt's (2016) case study, destabilises the de facto power and self-righteousness of governing principles and processes of 'ethical selving,' described in the previous section. Principles and associated subject positions become objects of critique, as the material politics behind them is made clearer and attention to the specificity and ambiguity of *different* embodied relations is enhanced. In terms of community economies, this urges us to find ways to consciously integrate this ambiguity into our analyses of socio-economic ordering and also to give more critical attention to embodied practices.

### Ethics as emergent: Relational difference

An important trope in poststructuralist feminist theory, which undoubtedly stems from a focus on the body, is the primacy of multiplicity and difference: bodies are specific, plural, non-binary entities that cannot be made equivalent to each other (Kirby 1989). Influenced greatly by Merleau-Ponty's (1945) *Phenomenology of Perception*, such analyses centre on the 'flesh' as the pre-personal matter in which the mind is embedded and from which a perceptual structuring of the world emerges. The flesh anchors our personal subjectivity, our intersubjective relationships and our inter-corporeal relations with the world. However, the flesh is not regarded as a uniform sameness: rather, the flesh is a communal interface (and the locus of inter-subjective sensual experience) through which a divergence between self and other is necessitated. Cohabiting the same world, perceiving and responding differently, the Other as Difference then has the power to surprise, disorient and transform the Self (McCann 2011). Approaching an Other with a sense of wonder renders one unable to negate or subsume them; rather, each subject appreciates the value of the irreducible difference presented (McCann 2011). Following this logic, an 'ethical breach' (in other words, an injustice) then results when one person subsumes the other into their own identity, for example by assuming that one person can represent the other (Irigaray 1993).

The conceptual implications of this insistence on relationality, difference and multiplicity are profound. This is not simply recognition of embodied diversity in terms of gender, race, ability etc. It is a deeper acknowledgement of infinite and fluid difference that precedes and disrupts identity-formation (Deleuze 1994). The feminist contributions to this stance are evident in the acknowledgement of the profound unknowability of the other and simultaneously, a commitment to empathy, care and responsibility (Bondi 2003). Significantly, the centring of difference disrupts earlier socio-ecological ethics that built on female solidarities and, through ecofeminism, reified the 'woman–nature nexus' (Merchant 1996). Gender-based unity, highlighting commonalities of gendered experience (of inequality/domination/violence), have been reinterpreted as a problematic (unethical) subsuming of the other (Okin 1994, Flax 1995). Careful sensitivity to the diversity of perceptions, experiences and positionalities is demanded and ultimately, the question remains regarding how to integrate difference into a system of justice or a process of political transformation (Okin 1994).

An ethics of accepting embodied difference as primal has interesting implications for an alternative rendering of economic exchange: If different interacting bodies can never be reduced to equivalence, then trading and transacting on the basis of equivalence is rendered impossible/unjust. Can an alternative economic rationality take account of this poststructural feminist ethic of irreducible difference – difference that also requires a recognition of the inter-corporeal, more-than-human foundations of ethics? This is arguably evidenced in some community/local economic exchange systems, where, operating without money, contributions of labour, goods and services are valued and exchanged in terms of time and contributions to well-being. Further, communities that espouse an approach of 'wonderment' (Bennett 2001, Henare *et al.* 2007), in other words, a respect for unique individuality of humans as well as of 'things' could also be considered as practicing an 'ethics of difference.'

We have briefly explored various ways in which ethics have been theorised: Firstly, in terms of guiding principles of mind; secondly, as embodied, spatial practices; and now, as an attentiveness to and ultimate respect for emergent, irreducible difference. For Emmanuel Levinas (1969), this embodied difference constitutes an unavoidable vulnerability and is the ontological precondition of ethics (Diprose 2002, Popke 2003, Harrison 2008). In these terms, ethical relations are constituted by inter-corporeal attachments and connections: we 'are kin, tied to each other by the passage of bodily substance' (Haraway 1997: 22). This lays an important foundation for thinking of ethics in more-than-human terms, which we explore below.

### Ethics as an ontological condition of life in a more-than-human world

While much of the feminist work on embodied ethics evokes maternal, reproductive and sexual metaphors, more recent work has expanded and disrupted this implicitly anthropocentric ontology (Bennett 2001, Gibson-Graham and Roelvink 2010). As Gibson-Graham and Roelvink (2010: 324) point out: 'We are at the brink, in this welcoming posture, of recognising Earthothers as not-other than ourselves; as we are just a hair's breadth away from acknowledging our co-constituted being as body-world.' This is not to subsume difference however: in his 'How to talk about the body' article, Bruno Latour (2004) 'depicts a dynamic, changing, living body-world, proliferative and differentiating rather than stable and monolithic' (Gibson-Graham and Roelvink 2010: 325). Focus has been placed on the 'being-in-common of humans and the more-than-human world' (Gibson-Graham and Roelvink 2010: 320) or the ethical 'entanglements' between water, fish and fishers, for example (Probyn 2014, 2016).

Such approaches recognise agency (the capacity to act) as distributed through multiple materialities: '[a]gencies are everywhere, making 'things.' They make economies, they make rationalities, they even make natures [...]. These agencies are collective matters, made up of all manner of humans and non-humans, technologies and biologies' (Hinchliffe *et al.* 2007: 260). These ideas force us to understand economies as diverse assemblages of humans and non-humans (Latour 2000, 2004) constituted through interactive processes of giving/taking, producing/consuming, moving/staying, working/resting, growing/decaying, and so on (DeLanda 2006). It is in this conceptual move that we see economies as relational configurations of human and non-human interactions.

Inter-corporeality, or the co-becoming of more-than-human bodies, is central to this conceptualisation (Gibson-Graham and Roelvink, 2010), which is prefigured as an inescapable ontological condition as well as a stance or orientation to the world. While such an approach might raise questions regarding the ethical capacities or considerabilities of non-human lifeforms (Whatmore 1997, Bennett 2001, Bingham 2006), the louder call is for an 'ethics of visceral attachment' (Whatmore 1997, Mol 2008). This is a stance that lacks a fixed normative code to guide behaviour, instead signalling an (admittedly vague) human striving for attentiveness and responsiveness to (and thereby a responsibility for) more-than-human inter-corporeal relations (Richardson-Ngwenya 2012b, Krzywoszynska 2016).

Thus far, we have charted a conceptual course through various ways of theorising ethics, focussing on principles, embodiment, difference and (more-than-human) inter-corporeality. In the spirit of poststructuralist feminism, we believe that it is important to engage with a diversity of 'ways of seeing,' not least to enhance capacity for empathy and understanding, but also, to perform a scholarly 'ethics of difference' ( Irigaray 1993, Flax, 1995, Smith 2000). This is then a feminist move in itself: allowing and exploring a plurality of positions. It is thus highly appropriate to pose 'diverse ethics' as a conceptual agenda.

However, it is important at this point to note that although the narrative map of ethical concepts drawn above *implies* a somehow linear journey – from disembodied mindful principles, to embodied relationality, followed by divergence and differentiation, finally extending ethical thought into a cosmopolitan, posthumanist lifeworld – it is of course not a smooth trip from one conceptual territory to another. Ethical principles, for example, are not left behind. Rather, these concepts nest together in topological space, surfacing and shaping the lifeworld terrain in concert. For example, even when we choose to situate ethics in the nexus of embodied, interactive practice, or in the co-constitutive relations of more-than-human life, we can continue to posit and hold on to ethical principles that help us to (dys/functionally) navigate, govern and discipline our relations and emotions. Moreover, accepting diverse ethics and giving them analytical space to live together is important given the tendency in the feminist economies and political ecologies literatures to focus on particular kinds of ethics – most especially caring relations – without necessarily reflecting on how ethical relations are primarily conceptualised, or considering how the different concepts matter.

To briefly recap, up to this point we have reviewed how the literatures on community economies and commoning draw the attention to ethics. And while we are broadly supportive of such moves, when we delve more deeply into feminist and related critiques of how ethical subjectivities emerge, the need to re-theorise ethics in feminist political economies and political ecologies is clear. The literature on ethics brings us to emphasise three key dimensions of ethical practices: one, ethical practices are embodied, but this does not imply that they are individuated. Rather, the body, as a relational inter-corporeal assemblage, is a space where ethical relations between self and other are immanently co-constituted. For community economies theorists, this means that (diverse) ethics are constituted through the body, but are not reducible to autonomous individuals who take on a 'caring ethical stance' – a point we suggest too often remains implicit in new feminist work on political economies and political ecologies. Two, feminist work on ethics and subjectivities highlights the inherent unknowability and fluidity of difference. Difference always emerges relationally and precedes identity formation, requiring community economy proponents to attend to how footloose attempts at promoting new subjectivities are. 'Emancipatory' or 'community-minded' practices produce shadows: the Others and exclusions that by necessity emerge when new subjectivities are claimed. Three, ethical practices are produced within and productive of more-than-human relations. From this standpoint, ethics do not precede or impact upon ecologies; rather, ethical relations are inherently inter-corporeal, embodied and more-than-human, meaning that ecologies are already involved as ethics emerge. This insight demands that feminist political economists rethink the boundaries of economies – 'ecologies' cannot be compartmentalised within their analyses – and demands that new feminist political ecologies recognise how ethical practices emerge from within socio-natures. What happens now if we look at a material example of an alternative economy with this pluralist view of ethics in mind? We explore this question by journeying through some of the material-economic practices at Kufunda Village, bringing them into conversation with the different conceptions of ethics charted above.

## The community economy of Kufunda Village

Kufunda Village is a village and hosting centre located approximately 40 kilometres from Harare.[2] The village was founded in 2003 as an experiment in community-building and sustainability. Project initiator, Maaianne Knuth, is Zimbabwean-Danish and having conceived of the idea for the village/centre, negotiated to utilise part of her mother's family farm in Ruwa to begin the task of materialising this vision. An initial team of more than 20 volunteers was composed of both local and international 'Kufundees.' Their learning and hosting activities cover two primary domains: (1) the practical physical domain of a sustainable healthy community, and (2) the less tangible but equally important domain of culture, learning and collective leadership, which enables a community to thrive. In 2017, there were 25 people living and working at Kufunda Village with their families. The author first came into contact with this community in 2011, while living and also conducting research on sustainable agri-food initiatives in Zimbabwe (Ngwenya 2013a). An initial research visit sparked the beginning of a longer-term (ongoing) more personal engagement, which has included several short stays and various arts and youth outreach activities (Ngwenya 2013b).

The village is arranged with a community garden and communal buildings at the centre, surrounded by different households, with the fields at the outer edges. The villagers produce much of their own food communally, using 3–4 hectares of land as a commons for production of millet and sorghum, inter-cropped with nitrogen fixing legumes and sunflower. In addition to community labour (everyone is obliged to work together on community tasks for 2–4 hours per week), casual labourers are employed to assist at peak times, such as weeding and harvesting. In 2015, the community managed for the first time to produce enough grain to feed themselves for the entire year, having previously struggled with poor maize harvests. This food is received through the community kitchen; communal cooking takes place for much of the year at least once a day. For household cooking, families must buy grain from the community store and each family also has a garden to produce vegetables for their own use. The adults work in small teams, focused on the different tasks/areas including permaculture and organic farming, health and nutrition, ethno-botany, eco-building, education, and renewable energy. Although the resident population is quite small, Kufunda hosts up to 60 visitors at a time (mostly local youth and community leaders who come to attend workshops or courses, as well as occasional foreign volunteers and trainees), which increases demand for resources and requires careful organisation.

### The alternative economic principle of learning

'Kufunda' itself means 'to learn' and learning is an overarching ethic that underlies the founding, function and focus of this Zimbabwean community.

As their website homepage states: 'We are learning our way into what it takes to build healthy and vibrant community. Our journey is one of exploring and seeking to live what we believe to be possible [...]' (Kufunda Village n.d.a).

Learning at Kufunda is encouraged through hosted training programmes and 'learning camps' covering topics such as leadership, permaculture and movement, as well as through organised educational institutions now including a kindergarten and a Waldorf-inspired school (Kufunda Village 2017a). The ethic of learning acts as a guiding principle that gives purpose and shape to the activities of Kufunda. As in any community, economic activities are integral, being central and necessary for people to survive and generate income.

At Kufunda, learning itself is commodified to an extent as an experience to be sought and bought: 'Join us for our second Learning Camp with the focus on diving into the experience of Being Village. Step in with us to a taste of Belonging in the heart of Africa' (Kufunda Village 2017b). The cost of this ten-day learning experience is US$ 1,200–3,000. Social learning is thus for sale as a means of generating income to sustain and consolidate the centre, but importantly, it is also offered freely to those who seek it and do not have money to contribute:

> If $1,200 is still beyond your pocketbook right now, please e-mail us and let's talk. If you are able to fit this within a training budget and can afford more, please e-mail us and let's talk as well. This is an experiment. Let's see what it takes to be in right relationship.
>
> (Kufunda Village 2017c)

However, this is not simply an offering to others; an ethic of learning guides how the village makes plans, so that it implements activities not only intending to generate livelihood but also for the community members to strive towards fulfilment: 'for this to be real, *we* need to be learning as well' (Knuth in Ngwenya 2013c).

While the above paragraph might give the impression of an organisation that functions like a community college, this is not the case. At Kufunda, learning is not simply about organised studies or the acquisition of knowledge; learning is rather articulated as an ever-unfolding journey, exploration and movement of the material and immaterial body-self, in relation to the world(s) in which it dwells, 'to enable that soul to fully land in this body, becoming enabled to fulfil his or her purpose on Earth' (Kufunda Village 2017a). The poetry of co-founder Maaianne Knuth expresses this notion of learning in terms of her dance practice. Here, learning is experienced as the becoming of an integrated and knowing self, achieved through the practice of dance:

> mind needs not be too anxious in getting it all right
> body knows, soul knows
> and then mind can serve the clarity that can arise from that
> powerful combination
> The practice, the practice, the practice
> All else flows from there
>
> (excerpt from Knuth 2014a, *Practice is Integration*)

This decentred, fluid notion of learning through mind-body praxis resonates with the concept of learning put forward by Gibson-Graham and Roelvink (2010: 322): 'Momentous as it may sound and mundane as it may actually be, this learning is a process of co-constitution that produces a new body-world.' So while learning is an alternative, guiding ethic or principle that brings the people of Kufunda together and shapes their socio-economic activities, it is also an embodied sensibility. This brings us nicely to our next conceptual engagement with ethics, as a conditionality and outcome of embodied practice.

### The embodied ethics of beading together

A few years ago, in times of financial difficulty, a group of women at Kufunda got together to bead as a means of trying to generate income. As Tsitsi Mayakaza explains:

> the project started when Kufunda was still 'young' and we didn't have proper salary to live. Thanks to the jewellery we managed to pay all the necessary costs for the family and it helped me to pay the examination fees for my children.
>
> (Kufunda Village n.d.b)

Today, the monetary aspect of jewellery making is still an important motivation, but the embodied practice of beading together has proven to have value in itself. Some testimonies (all sourced from Kufunda Village n.d.b) from group members describe their experiences of this economic practice:

> When I started I firstly thought at the advantage of incomes, but during the process of creating jewelleries something has changed. Hence I am now involving my family and beading became a way to share time with them. So I consider beading as gift for my family. Today I even teach this art craft to the kids to help them to develop art, creativity and sustainability at the same time. When I bead alone I focus on the manual work and it has become a good way to lose stress. Sometimes I even create jewellery when I have some challenges in my life, it helps me to calm down and see the things differently.
>
> (Patricia Mutsvandiani)

> I discovered this passion of using my hands and creating art out of them. I like to use my creativity to do something that can even help my family financially.
>
> (Loveness Tenis)

> Sometimes I bead alone and sometimes in the group, but I don't very much like to work alone because when I'm on my own a lot of thoughts

come in my mind that are not always pleasant. For me it is much better to work in the group.

(Sekesayi Mariyapera)

The above quotes from the beaders at Kufunda give a clear sense of how the embodied, communal experience of creating value is *valued in itself*. This obviously does not resonate with a version of economy that rests on the rational calculation of surplus value. The working of hands with natural materials, the material crafting of beauty and the embodied experience of sitting together as women, are central to how this economic practice is conferred value by the 'producers.' Thinking of their beaded products, we can grasp an understanding of how the ethics of this economic practice are embodied, emotional and produced in community, in a way that clearly relates to Bollier's (2017) conceptualisation of value as a relational event. In other words, the 'making' of value involves not just the act of beading but is a relational co-production of self and society that inheres in the communal, performative practice and space of beading:

Making jewellery brings out the beauty inside me, it is a way to express my art and my creativity. While I bead I have my own space where I can meditate and where I can find joy and quietness in me. I became more aware about the importance to create space for myself with the years. Beading is also a way to bring Kufunda's women together. It is a moment where we question each other, where we share time and interest and where we get to know each other better.

(Sikhethiwe Mlotsha (Kufunda Village n.d.b))

Here, we can sense how the space of beading practice, where women learn about each other and about themselves, can be re-thought as a site of emergent and embodied ethics (McCormack 2003). The questioning, sharing and knowing relations that emerge between the beader and her companions immanently unfold, as jewelled patterns emerge between their fingers, giving a value to the practice that surpasses any monetary payment that might be received.

## Making sense of difference

The above account of beading suggests a rather harmonious interaction whereby subjects are open to and respectful of each other. But what of the ethics of *difference* that Luce Irigaray (1993) locates as central to, produced by and productive of human inter-subjectivity? Interestingly, there seems to be a strong positive emphasis on human diversity and uniqueness at Kufunda. This is clear first in how the communal tasks at Kufunda are divided and delegated according to who has interest and talent in the particular area:

Some of us are working with permaculture and organic farming, others are working with health and nutrition and making good herbal remedies out of locally grown plants. Some are into eco-building, others into renewable energy, some are into working with children.

(Kufunda Village n.d.c)

Secondly, a sensitivity to difference is evidenced in their approach to co-learning:

> At their essence, our programmes are all about nurturing and releasing each person's unique and creative gift and talent in community. We believe in community and in what becomes possible when whole, or free, people come together for learning and co-creation.
>
> (Kufunda Village n.d.d)

Such attention to difference and community has resonance with McCann's (2011) insight that 'possibilities for creative and cooperative transformation spring from the flesh's communality and its ongoing processes of divergence' (501).

Thirdly, we can see attentiveness to difference in the way in which fees are assigned for course attendance: 'One of the things we've been learning in Zimbabwe over the last decade is how to dance with many different economies at the same time' (Kufunda Village 2017c). Most of the programmes at Kufunda are residential and cost money. However, instead of prescribing a fixed fee for all, a flexible and responsive invitation to pay according to financial capability is extended:

> The reality is that most in Zimbabwe cannot (afford the full fee) at this time, and so this campaign is essentially enabling us to have full diversity, and enabling us to offer this to the women with less resources, but as big a heart and purpose as any of us. Everyone will contribute, whatever their reality – but for many of the women the contribution may come in the form of crops that they bring from their fields, instead of money.
>
> (Knuth 2017)

The willingness to respond to different human capabilities, as well as a conscious emphasis on bringing people together to generate creative transformation, are ways in which we can positively view an 'ethics of difference' in this community economy.

Importantly, difference is also a source of conflict and contestation. The struggle between a 'we' and a 'me' is ongoing and present in daily life at Kufunda. The imperative for self-disciplining and commitment to the notion of a common good is constantly at stake, as inter-subjective differences arise. Expressions of the tension generated through difference can result in full blown conflicts, or more mundanely as insidious disapprovals or controversies. For example, the community experience of food production has been that maize is not an appropriate crop for the climate and soil, whereas drought-resistant millet and sorghum lead to more reliable and greater harvests, capable of feeding everyone. Therefore, the community agricultural practices emphasise millet and sorghum. However, individual preferences for eating maize result in some expressions of discontent and leads to individuals buying it for home consumption.

Another example of how differences in perception can result in conflict, concerns the keeping of free-range chickens, which frequently invade the community permaculture garden and cause damage. The 'chicken advocates' argue that the garden is not very productive and it is more important to have chicken to eat. From the garden team perspective, this is considered to be selfish and irresponsible. The contention seems to be about whether the garden is more important or the chickens. However, such contestations emerge in the context of the broader striving for a clear, common understanding about what the 'common good' should look like and how it can be achieved. This is not an easy question, nor does it have a stable answer. What the 'common good' is can shift depending on the viewer and also over time and space. Maize and chickens are 'good' in some contexts and for some eaters, but 'bad' for others who may prioritise other issues.

Journeying with this concept of difference, we can also discern some ways in which more structural ethical relations of gender difference are negotiated at Kufunda. While community and human uniqueness are celebrated, it is also recognised that

> it is a time in which we need to discover new approaches to old imbalances and injustices that are reaching levels of undeniable crisis. It is our belief and experience that there are aspects of women's ways and women's leadership that have been pushed into the background for far too long. It is time to call those ways into new being.
>
> (Knuth 2017)

Disputing the hegemonic production of gender inequities is a clear example of how Kufunda is actively making (new) sense of embodied difference, and attempting to productively shift the ethical relation between men and women, asking 'how do we want it? And how do we honour the tradition, but still live together in a way where we also honour that we're each strong and unique individuals?' (Knuth, author interview, Knuth, 3 May 2012). One clear attempt to disrupt dominant gender relations is through the *Women are Medicine* programme, which invites 'every woman to step in as more choice-full, conscious co-creators of our future' (Knuth 2017).

This programme catalysed a perceived shift in the ethics of (gendered) difference, performed during a village workshop, as profoundly expressed through the poem of participant, Bev Reeler:

> Something happened at the end of the year in our Women are Medicine workshop at Kufunda.
> Well many, many things happened.........
> but the story that stays with me at the end was about the men.

Some of the Kufunda men said they wanted to be part of this workshop
so they offered to cook for us.........................
A group of young men and boys from the youth group
gathered in the kitchen every day
chopping and laughing and singing to loud music
a different harmony
It was the best food we have ever tasted at Kufunda
and for 4 days, we were nourished by their extraordinary care
and generosity


On the closing morning we invited them into the circle
and they stood in the centre
in a circle facing outwards
We welcomed them with a Hopi Indian salute
and the women spoke to them of the gratitude they felt
for the nourishment and care they had given.
Their eyes shone
one of the younger boys shot his fist into the air
'YES'
Then we asked them to teach us aikido
(for they have been doing it for years now)
to 'make the cut'.........
to draw our swords and cut our place into the present
cutting away what was no longer helpful and bringing our power
into being
Young boys teaching their sisters and wives and grandmothers
how to draw our swords
bringing, with deep focus, our intention in the world
When we were ready we came back to the circle
and as each woman made her cut
there was a young man holding our back
They brought their warriorship
fed us
held the babies
As I drew my sword
a young man 50 years my junior stood behind me
it was an extraordinary experience
some new meeting of energies
combining into a powerful force
Something magic happened
Something that we have never touched
in all years of gender circles
about equality, abuse of women, rape, wife beating
some new energy shifted into place
as they made their cut into the centre of the circle

to 'hold our backs'
bring their support to this co-creation of feminine and masculine energy
and a new possibility opened up.

(Reeler 2014, Women are Medicine, Men are Magic)

The participant's description of a perceived shifting of energies and new possibilities for relating emerging through the encounter is comparable to McCann's (2011) description of an ethics of difference:

> This relational field, the flesh, is a milieu of constant, transformative exchange. Sensuous and spatial things and places transform me moment by moment, from small adjustments of pupil size and heart rate to sudden flashes of meaning. Interaction with human others transforms me as well, as they present new possibilities for interpreting and interacting with the world. […] The other's speech or action, a different style of being in response to my own perceived world, has the power to surprise, disorient and transform me. These possibilities for creative and cooperative transformation spring from the flesh's communality and its ongoing processes of divergence.

(2011: 501)

The perceptual emphasis on energies, forces and flows, evident in the poem, illustrates how embodied practices of community economy can bring forth new, affective articulations of difference (Grosz 2005, Colls 2012). Such practices are quite unusual, as compared to more conventional ways of addressing gender inequalities, for instance through changes in policy, protocol or law. The potential of creating transformative difference through such embodied practice is, in this way, evidenced at Kufunda and now forces us to consider how such affective attunement can extend into a more-than-human cosmological space, where philosophers conceive of ethics as generated through visceral attachments and trans-species inter-corporeality.

### More-than-human ethical cosmologies

We cannot separate from others,
Animals, rivers, trees, soil
We are part of the land
It is our body
It's me. It's you.

(excerpt from Fafi 2015, To be is to inter-be)

Through the story of Kufunda, we have moved from an ethics grounded in the mind to one grounded in the body, and now we want to extend this into the world, to encompass interspecies relations, or 'being-in-common of humans and the more-than-human world' (Gibson-Graham and Roelvink 2010: 320).

This emphasis in the community economies literature stems from observations of world-making practices and popular narratives, and can indeed be found echoing through the discursive productions of Kufundees. The poetry quoted in this section expresses wonder, attentiveness and responsiveness to visceral attachments with the more-than-human world, thereby conveying an articulation of the 'ethical stance' described in Gibson-Graham and Roelvink (2010).

> I have often appreciated Bev's garden
> But yesterday I met it in a way I have not before
> And I wondered, and I wonder
> how much of the gifts and miracles of life
> pass me by
> as I move through my life
> with my awareness turned inward
> moving through the stories and the dramas of my own delightful mind
> I am learning something about the quality of Relationships
> And that I am in relationship with all of life – not only human beings:
> The earth beneath my feet,
> The Trees that grow in my garden
> The many birds that nest above me, the wind, the rain, the butterflies,
> the bats, the rocks,
> And it is my choice how conscious I wish to be about those relationships
> As with all relationships as I engage with them,
> I discover new gifts, immense beauty.
> I am discovering a world of magic,
>
> Just waiting for me to reach out and touch it
> What does it mean to be human?
> In a world full of magic
> To truly be human in a world full of magic …
> I suspect the answer is something so much vaster
> than what I have been living until now
> Like the unfurling of a new shoot
> I open myself and reach out
> into a fresh new world

(excerpt from Knuth 2014b, *Nurturing my Relationship(s) with all of Life*)

Knuth, we suggest, articulates in her poem and practise the notion put forward in posthumanist philosophy of 'learning to be affected' (Latour 2004). While the relationships she celebrates in the poem are familiar, she marvels at how to 'know' them in a new, more fully embodied manner. However, it is important to highlight that the romance of these new encounters is not all-encompassing. As already discussed, the pragmatic, day-to-day task of creating a community economy is fraught with tensions between individual agency and the village collective. This also includes the sometimes-uncooperative agency of non-human actors. For example, returning to the 'garden versus chicken' issue, the problem here, as conveyed by Kufunda administrator Claudia Zehl-Mahachi, is inherently embedded in the specific, more-than-human context of Kufunda Village. This includes soils, trees, insects, fungi, wildlife and the nature of the underlying aquifer, which has meant that the existing boreholes have not been able to supply enough water to irrigate the community garden year-round. This has led to a question, for some Kufundees, as to whether the garden is a viable project. On the other hand, many believe that it is a matter of finding an effective way to manage the water situation.

Contextualising this issue further, most of the inhabitants are not vegetarians and meateating has cultural significance in Zimbabwe, especially in relation to community events (funerals, weddings etc.), but there is not yet any meat production on the site except for the free-range chickens. They are therefore highly valued by the owners. The garden, in contrast, is, a central feature of the project as a demonstration site for perma-culturists and source of vegetables, herbs and derived medicine. The recalcitrant (free-ranging) chickens have the 'audacity' to stray from their households into the garden, causing occasional mayhem. As a punishment to the human owners, if found in the garden, the chicken will be caught and released to the owner only following the payment of a monetary fine. The 'problem' – which was previously pitched as a simpler divergence of interest/vision – appears rather differently here. It is now understood as an outcome of a complex and specific configuration of nature-society, emerging from the encounter of different energies, actants and materials living together in a shared space. The embodied interactions in place result in the continual emergence of different relations, which requires human actors to constantly revise their intentions, desires, actions and subjectivities – and thus, their ethical stance.

This brief exploration of the potential, practical meaning of a more-than-human ethical stance in relation to Kufunda can be surmised as the performance of an attitude that is 'open to life' and yet 'does not guarantee constant joy' (Knuth 2014c). A more-than-human, cosmological ethics is articulated through the ongoing, lived process of learning to be affected by life as a Kufundee. This embodied, situated movement involves an attentiveness and responsiveness to (sometimes unwanted) visceral connections; balancing a sense of being here while becoming otherwise. Knuth poeticises this ethical stance in her poem, *Through the 10,000 Things*:

(…)
Being open to life
does *Not* guarantee constant joy.
(And wouldn't that be somewhat dull anyhow?)
Sometimes life comes through as grief,
as rage, as fear, as passion,

sometimes it scares us shitless.
The question is,
Can we keep *moving*?
*With* it?
*Without* being subsumed by it?
(…)
It's a different kind of motion than the
*relentless* doing that exists in our culture.
It is being Here Now,
All of me;
Embodied me.
Moving with what is here.
(…)

(excerpts from Knuth 2014c *Through the 10,000 Things*)

## Concluding our journey with diverse ethics: Contributions and questions

In this chapter we have argued for the need to conceptualise ethics more carefully in community economies research. Ethical principles and commitments cannot capture the embodied, multi-relational and interspecies nature of how shared, diverse ethics emerge. The case study material illustrates how the Kufunda community goes beyond the enactment of particular principles; the economy and indeed, the community itself, is conceived as constituted through embodied, inter-corporeal, interspecies practices. These practices are experienced as both valuable and challenging, precisely because of their embodied and more-than-human qualities.

A diverse, community economy therefore does not imply a lack of contradiction or a singular focus on caring and 'being in common.' Rather, it is an economy that consciously (and unconsciously) works with the tensions of negotiating inter-subjectivity and more-than-human relations, while generating value in the process. These ongoing tensions constitute an ethical ontology that is sensitive to the challenges of difference. Because of their relational and performative nature, ethical tensions can be reinforced or renegotiated through small, everyday practices, as well as at the level of community decisions (e.g. fines for wayward chickens), and inter-community negotiations across scales (e.g. differential fees for courses at Kufunda). Conflicts and tensions need to be understood as part of a broader, ongoing *striving* for a common understanding about what the 'common good' should look like given diverse economies, and how it can be achieved. *Diverse* ethical modes, discussed in this chapter, are mobilised in both conceptualising and operationalising place-based visions of the common good.

Accounting for difference and diversity, of course, has been central to the feminist project for over 30 years now (Henriques *et al.* 1984). But our analysis points to the work still to be done. At a conceptual level, we have shown how accounting for difference requires going well beyond the recognition of embodied diversity in terms of gender, race, ability, caste etc. It requires a profound acknowledgement of the infinite nature, performance and instability of difference that emerges as (fluid) embodied markers of identity. Poststructural feminists have insisted on acknowledging the profound unknowability of the other and simultaneously, the need to foster empathy, care and responsibility. As we argued above, it is the latter points that we believe need further thought if we are to take recognition of difference to another level. The Kufunda case study shows how care and responsibility are situated and unclear when put into communities of practice. While caring and responsibility are certainly at work, we have illustrated here how the *relational co-production of self and community* also emerge through embodied experiences of generating value, for example through beading in community. Another (more problematic) co-production of self and community emerges when 'free-range' chickens confront the limitations of a shared vision for community gardens.

Contributing to the wider literature, our analysis points to the need to decentre 'care' within feminist economic visions of the 'common good.' We argue that an alternative feminist economics needs to embrace the ambiguity of caring relations and acknowledge the important relations of competition and strife that together shape the success of experiments in community economies. While we do not advocate abandoning care as a feminist project, we caution against retaining it as *the* defining characteristic of new feminist economic and political ecologies. 'Care' can be experienced as highly oppressive for some people, particularly given the problematic of accounting for difference and the instability of inter-corporeal relations.

To come back to the question we posed at the beginning, *what difference do such ideas make to heterogeneous world-building processes?* We see several contributions towards, as well as questions opened, for building new feminist ethical economies and political ecologies. First, our case study adds to others documenting the embodied ways in which people are learning to live in community economies (differently). These are valuable and worthwhile stories that warrant sharing widely: there remain remarkably few of them in the literature (Bollier and Helfrich 2015). Second, it points to the importance of fostering the global performance of community economies by cultivating ourselves as new kinds of academic subjects, open to techniques of ethical thinking that can elaborate a new economic ontology (Gibson-Graham 2008: 628). Gibson-Graham called for such a shift nearly ten years ago and – while our analysis has pointed to some conceptual slippage in the community economies literature – our work is deeply inspired by theirs. For us, this means shifting away from an emphasis on care and placing the messy, contradictory and conflictual relations through which we articulate ethnical stances as central to how we comport ourselves as academics.

Third, our case study suggests a gap in how to reconnect localised community examples to wider debates. So far, community economies have failed to adequately confront the problem of scale both conceptually and pragmatically.

What would it mean to think about diverse social economies or political economies at the global level? If scale is inherently both a *product* and *productive* of inter-corporeal relations (Harris and Alatout 2010, Ahlborg and Nightingale 2012), then 'scaling up' community economies is not simply a matter of applying (our new) diverse ethics to larger scales of economic activity and populations. Rather, entrenched and historically situated inequalities that emerge from embodied differences (gender, race etc.) and from territorial differences (Global North/South), cannot be 'performed away' by enrolling global leaders in collective beading projects (or their equivalent). An intellectual and political challenge for further research thus remains over how to 'stretch out social relations' (Massey 2005) in a manner that allows for diverse ethics to flourish and co-constitute larger community economies – or at least to link smaller-scale community economies together in ways that do not subsume each other.

While certainly we do not have prescriptive answers to these questions (and indeed, such prescriptions would undermine our purpose here), our analysis takes us, finally, back to learning. The case study shows how learning in itself is a dimension of value; value that cannot be measured through metrics or economic gains. Rather, it has an attitudinal character that nevertheless can be captured through a sense of a 'better life' which for many people includes a lifetime commitment to critical, creative inquiry. 'Learning' community economies are anchored in and attendant to divergent needs and differential capacities. Holding attention to the fluid and unstable nature of relational selves, ethics and communities can only be realised through continual, active learning. It is not a state to be achieved, but rather a process to be embarked upon that deepens with each encounter. As Knuth poeticised, 'The practice, the practice, the practice: All else flows from there' (Knuth 2014a).

## Notes

1  Descartes writes: 'Through [my new physics] we could know the power and action of fire, water, air, the stars, the heavens and all the other bodies in our environment [...] and we could use this knowledge [...] [to] make ourselves [...] the lords and masters of nature' (Decartes AT 6:61–2, CSM 1:142 cited in Wee 2002: 257).
2  Please consult Raftopoulos and Alois Mlambo (2008) for an overview of the social and political context of Zimbabwe.

## References

Aguilar, F.V., 2005. Excess possibilities? Ethics, populism and community economy. *Singapore Journal of Tropical Geography*, 26 (1), 27–31.
Ahlborg, H. and Nightingale, A.J., 2012. Mismatch between scales of knowledge in Nepalese forestry: epistemology, power, and policy implications. *Ecology and Society*, 17 (4).
Barad, K., 2003. Posthumanist performativity: toward an understanding of how matter comes to matter. *Signs*, 28 (3), 801–31.

Bauhardt, C., 2014. Solutions to the crisis? The Green New Deal, degrowth, and the solidarity economy: alternatives to the capitalist growth economy from an ecofeminist economics perspective. *Ecological Economics*, 102, 60–8.

Bauman, Z., 1993. *Postmodern Ethics*. Oxford: Blackwell.

Bennett, J., 2001. *The Enchantment of Modern Life: Attachments, Crossings, and Ethics*. Princeton, NJ: Princeton University Press.

Bingham, N., 2006. Bees, butterflies, and bacteria: biotechnology and the politics of nonhuman friendship. *Environment and Planning A*, 38 (3), 483–98.

Bollier, D., 2007a. *The Growth of the Commons Paradigm*. Cambridge, MA: Massachusetts Institute of Technology Press.

Bollier, D., 2007b. A new politics of the commons. *Renewal: A Journal of Social Democracy*, 15 (4), 10–16.

Bollier, D., 2017. *Re-imagining Value: Insights from the Care Economy, Commons, Cyberspace and Nature*. A Deep Dive hosted by Commons Strategies Group in cooperation with the Heinrich Böll Foundation and David Graeber, 5–8 September 2016 Available from: www.boell.de.

Bollier, D. and Helfrich, S., 2015. *Patterns of Commoning*. Amherst, MA: Commons Strategies Group.

Bondi, L., 2003. Empathy and identification: conceptual resources for feminist fieldworl. *ACME: An International E-Journal for Critical Geographers*, 2 (1), 64–76.

Burke, B.J. and Shear, B.W., 2014. Introduction: engaged scholarship for non-capitalist political ecologies. *Journal of Political Ecology*, 21 (1), 127–44.

Butler, J., 1990. *Gender Trouble: Feminism and the Subversion of Identity*. New York: Routledge.

Cameron, J. and Gibson-Graham, J.K., 2003. Feminising the economy: metaphors, strategies, politics. *Gender, Place & Culture*, 10 (2), 145–57.

Colebrook, C., 2005. *Philosophy and Poststructuralist Theory: From Kant to Deleuze*. Edinburgh: Edinburgh University Press.

Colls, R., 2012. Feminism, bodily difference and non-representational geographies. *Transactions of the Institute of British Geographers*, 37 (3), 430–45.

DeLanda, M., 2006. *A New Philosophy of Society: Assemblage Theory and Social Complexity*. London: A and C Black.

Deleuze, G., 1994. *Difference and Repetition*. New York: Columbia University Press.

Diprose, R., 2002. *Corporeal Generosity*. Albany, NY: State University of New York Press.

Escobar, A., 1998. Whose knowledge, whose nature? Biodiversity, conservation, and the political ecology of social movements. *Journal of Political Ecology*, 5 (1), 53–82.

Fafi, 2015. To be is to inter-be. *Dancing with the Universe*, 8 August 2015 [online]. Available from: http://www.kufunda.org/single-post/2015/08/07/To-Be-is-to-InterBe [Accessed 25 July 2018].

Federici, S., 2011. Women, land struggles, and the reconstruction of the commons. *Working USA*, 14 (1), 41–56.

Flax, J., 1995. Race/gender and the ethics of difference. *Political Theory*, 23 (3), 500–10.

Fyke, J.P. and Buzzanell, P.M., 2013. The ethics of conscious capitalism: wicked problems in leading change and changing leaders. *Human Relations*, 66 (12), 1619–43.

Gatens, M., 1996. *Imaginary Bodies: Ethics, Power, and Corporeality*. London: Routledge.

Gatens, M. and Lloyd, G., 1999. *Collective Imaginings: Spinoza Past and Present*. London: Routledge.

Gibson-Graham, J.K., 1996. *The End of Capitalism (As We Knew It): A Feminist Critique of Political Economy*. Cambridge, MA: Blackwell.

Gibson-Graham, J.K., 2003. An ethics of the local. *Rethinking Marxism*, 15 (1), 49–74.

Gibson-Graham, J.K., 2005. Surplus possibilities: post-development and community economies. *Singapore Journal of Tropical Geography*, 26 (1), 4–26.

Gibson-Graham, J.K., 2006. *A Post-Capitalist Politics*. Minneapolis, MN: University of Minnesota Press.

Gibson-Graham, J.K., 2008. Diverse economies: performative practices for 'other worlds'. *Progress in Human Geography*, 32 (5), 613–32.

Gibson-Graham, J.K., Cameron, J. and Healy, S., 2013. *Take Back the Economy: An Ethical Guide for Transforming Our Communities*. Minneapolis, MN: University of Minnesota Press.

Gibson-Graham, J.K. and Roelvink, G., 2010. An economic ethics for the Anthropocene. *Antipode*, 41, 320–46.

Haraway, D.J., 1997. Modest_Witness@Second_Millennium.FemaleMan_Meets_ OncoMouse: *Feminism and Technoscience*. London: Psychology Press.

Haraway, D.J., 2011. Speculative fabulations for technoculture's generations: taking care of unexpected country. *Australian Humanities Review*, 50, 95–118.

Harcourt, W., 2014. The future of capitalism: a consideration of alternatives. *Cambridge Journal of Economics*, 38 (6), 1307–28.

Harcourt, W., 2016. Gender and sustainable livelihoods: linking gendered experiences of environment, community and self. *Agriculture and Human Values*, 1–13.

Harcourt, W. and Nelson, I.L., eds., 2015. *Practising Feminist Political Ecologies: Moving Beyond the 'Green Economy'*. London: Zed Books.

Harris, L.M. and Alatout, S., 2010. Negotiating hydro-scales, forging states: comparison of the upper Tigris/Euphrates and Jordan River basins. *Political Geography*, 29 (3), 148–56.

Harrison, P., 2008. Corporeal remains: vulnerability, proximity, and living on after the end of the world. *Environment and Planning A*, 40 (2), 423–45.

Held, V., 1993. *Feminist Morality: Transforming Culture, Society, and Politics*. Chicago, IL: University of Chicago Press.

Henare, A., Holbraad, M. and Wastell, S., eds., 2007. *Thinking Through Things: Theorising Artefacts Ethnographically*. London: Routledge.

Henriques, J., Hollway, W., Urwin, C., Venn, C. and Walkerdine, V., 1984. *Changing the Subject*. London: Methuen.

Hinchliffe, S., Kearnes, M.B., Degen, M. and Whatmore, S., 2007. Ecologies and economies of action: sustainability, calculations, and other things. *Environment and Planning A: Economy and Space*, 39 (2), 260–82.

Irigaray, L., 1993. *An Ethics of Sexual Difference*. C. Burke and G.C. Gill., trans. Ithaca, NY: Cornell University Press.

Kirby, V., 1989. Corporeogeographies. *Inscriptions* [online], 5. Available from: https:// culturalstudies.ucsc.edu/inscriptions/volume-5/vicki-kirby/ [Accessed 24 July 2018].

Knuth, M., 2014a. Practice is integration. *In: Dancing with the Universe*, 3 June 2014 [online]. Available from: https://dancinguniverse.net/2014/06/03/practice-is-integration/ [Accessed 24 July 2018].

Knuth, M., 2014b. Nurturing my relationship(s) with all of life. *In: Dancing with the Universe*, 9 November 2014 [online]. Available from: https://dancinguniverse.net/tag/presence/ [Accessed 25 July 2018].

Knuth, M., 2014c. Through the 10,000 things. *In: Dancing with the Universe*, 30 January 2014 [online]. Available from: https://dancinguniverse.net/2014/01/30/beyond-the- 10-000-things/ [Accessed 25 July 2018]

Knuth, M., 2017. *Young Women Are Medicine, 2017* [online]. San Francisco, CA: Indigogo. Available from: https://www.indiegogo.com/projects/young-women-are-medicine- 2017-leadership [Accessed 25 July 2018].

Krzywoszynska, A., 2016. What farmers know: experiential knowledge and care in vine growing. *Sociologia Ruralis*, 56 (2), 289–310.

Kufunda Village, n.d.a. *Welcome to KUFUNDA VILLAGE* [online]. Harare, Kufunda Village. Available from: http://www.kufunda.org/ [Accessed 24 July 2018].

Kufunda Village, n.d.b. *The power of women's art* [online]. Harare, Kufunda Village. Available from: http://www.kufunda.org/jewellery [Accessed 24 July 2018].

Kufunda Village, n.d.c. *Our story* [online]. Harare, Kufunda Village. Available from: http://www.kufunda.org/about-us [Accessed 25 July 2018].

Kufunda Village, n.d.d. *Communiversity Courses* [online]. Harare, Kufunda Village. Available from: http://www.kufunda.org/courses [Accessed 25 July 2018].

Kufunda Village, 2017a. *Kufunda Village School: Waldorf inspired education in Nature* [online]. Harare, Kufunda Village. Available from: http://www.kufunda.org/nyeredzi [Accessed 24 July 2018].

Kufunda Village, 2017b. *Being village: Returning to the hearth* [online]. Harare, Kufunda Village. Available from: http://www.kufunda.org/learning-camp [Accessed 25 July 2018].

Kufunda Village, 2017c. *Being village: online invitation* [online]. Harare, Kufunda Village. Available from: http://docs.wixstatic.com/ugd/7d3c10_cbc929bb07a54af9b1eb2d580bdaf6da.pdf [Accessed 25 July 2018].

Latour, B., 2000. When things strike back: A possible contribution of 'science studies' to the social sciences. *The British Journal of Sociology*, 51 (1), 107–23.

Latour, B., 2004. How to talk about the body? The normative dimension of science studies. *Body & Society*, 10 (2–3), 205–29.

Levinas, E., 1969. *Totality and Infinity*. A. Lingis, trans. Pittsburgh, PA: Duquesne University Press.

Longhurst, R., 1997. (Dis)embodied geographies. *Progress in Human Geography*, 21 (4), 486–501.

Massey, D., 1994. *Space, Place and Gender*. Minneapolis, MN: University of Minnesota Press.

Massey, D., 2005. *For Space*. Thousand Oaks, CA: Sage.

McCann, R., 2011. A sensuous ethics of difference. *Hypatia*, 26 (3), 497–517.

McCormack, D.P., 2003. An event of geographical ethics in spaces of affect. *Transactions of the Institute of British Geographers*, 28 (4), 488–507.

McDowell, L., 1991. Life without father and Ford: the new gender order of Post-Fordism. *Transactions of the Institute of British Geographers* 16 (4), 400–19.

McEwan, C., Hughes, A. and Bek, D., 2017. Fairtrade, place and moral economy: between abstract ethical discourse and the moral experience of Northern Cape farmers. *Environment and Planning A*, 49 (3), 572–91.

Merchant, C., 1996. Reinventing Eden: Western culture as recovery narrative. *In*: W. Cronon, ed., *Uncommon Ground: Rethinking the Human Place in Nature*. New York: W.W. Norton and Company, 132–70.

Merleau-Ponty, M., 1945. *The Phenomenology of Perception*. C. Smith, trans. London: Routledge.

Miller, E., 2013. Community economy: Ontology ethics, and politics for radically democratic economic organising. *Rethinking Marxism*, 25 (4), 518–33.

Mohanty, C.T. and Miraglia, S., 2012. Gendering justice, building alternative futures. *In*: D.A. McDonald and G. Ruiters, eds, *Alternatives: Public Options for Essential Services in the Global South*. New York: Routledge, 99–132.

Mol, A., 2008. I eat an apple: on theorising subjectivities. *Subjectivity*, 22 (1), 28–37.

Morrow, O. and Dombroski, K., 2015. Enacting a post-capitalist politics through the sites and practices of life's work. *In*: K. Meehan and K. Strauss, eds, *Precarious Worlds: Contested Geographies of Social Reproduction*. Athens: University of Georgia Press, 82–98.

Muraca, B., 2012. Towards a fair degrowth-society: Justice and the right to a 'good life' beyond growth. *Futures*, 44 (6), 535–45.

Ngwenya, P., 2013a. Sustainable agri-food initiatives, Zimbabwe. In: *Sustainable agri-food initiatives, Zimbabwe* [online]. Available from: https://sustainableagriculturezimbabwe. wordpress.com/category/sustainability-initiatives-some-case-studies/ [Accessed 25 July 2018].

Ngwenya, P., 2013b. Visioning a sustainable future: exploring youth participatory video and visions of the future in Zimbabwe and South Africa. In: *Visioning a Sustainable Future*, 12 May 2013 [online]. Available from: https://visioningthefuture.wordpress.com/ [Accessed 24 July 2018].

Ngwenya, P., 2013c. *Introducing Kufunda: A community of learning* [online]. Video. New York: Vimeo. Available from: https://vimeo.com/69458759 [Accessed 24 July 2018].

Noddings, N., 2013. *Caring: A Relational Approach to Ethics and Moral Education*. Oakland, CA: University of California Press.

Okin, S.M., 1994. Political liberalism, justice, and gender. *Ethics*, 105 (1), 23–43.

Ostrom, E. 1990. *Governing the Commons: The Evolution of Institutions for Collective Action*. Cambridge: Cambridge University Press.

Popke, E.J., 2003. Poststructuralist ethics: subjectivity, responsibility and the space of community. *Progress in Human Geography*, 27 (3), 298–316.

Probyn, E., 2014. Women following fish in a more-than-human world. *Gender, Place and Culture*, 21 (5), 589–603.

Probyn, E., 2016. Entanglements: Fish, guts, and bio-cultural sustainability. In: E.J. Abbots and A. Lavis, eds., *Why We Eat, How We Eat: Contemporary Encounters Between Foods and Bodies*. London: Routledge, 289–300.

Raftopoulos, B. and Mlambo, A., eds., 2008. *Becoming Zimbabwe: A History from the Pre-colonial Period to 2008*. Oxford: African Books Collective.

Reeler, B., 2014. Women are medicine – men are magic. In: *Dancing with the Universe* [online], 5 January 2014. Available at: https://dancinguniverse.net/tag/men/ [Accessed 25 July 2018].

Ricard, M., 2015. *Altruism: The Power of Compassion to Change Yourself and the World*. London: Atlantic Books.

Richardson-Ngwenya, P., 2012. Negotiating fairness in the EU sugar reform: the ethics of European-Caribbean sugar trading relations. *Ethics, Policy & Environment*, 15 (13), 341–67.

Richardson-Ngwenya, P., 2012b. A vitalist approach to sugar-cane breeding in Barbados: in the context of the European Union Sugar Reform. *Geoforum*, 43 (6), 1131–9.

Rocheleau, D., 2016. Rooted networks, webs of relation, and the power of situated science: bringing the models back down to Earth in Zambrana. In: W. Harcourt, ed., *The Palgrave Handbook of Gender and Development: Critical Engagements in Feminist Theory and Practice*. London: Palgrave Macmillan UK, 213–31.

Rodaway, P., 1994. *Sensuous Geographies: Body, Sense, and Place*. London: Routledge.

Rose, G., 1993. Progress in geography and gender: or something else. *Progress in Human Geography*, 17 (4), 531–7.

Sharp, J. and McDowell, L., 2014. *A Feminist Glossary of Human Geography*. London: Routledge.

Smith, A., 1937. *The Wealth of Nations* [online]. Adam Smith Reference Archive ed. New York: Random House. Available from: https://www.marxists.org/reference/archive/ smith-adam/works/wealth-of-nations/ [Accessed 24 July 2018].

Smith, D.M., 2000. *Moral Geographies Ethics in a World of Difference*. Edinburgh: Edinburgh University Press.

Trentmann, F., 2007. Before 'fair trade': empire, free trade, and the moral economies of food in the modern world. *Environment and Planning D: Society and Space*, 25 (6), 1079–102.

Varul, M.A., 2009. Ethical selving in cultural contexts: fair trade consumption as an everyday ethical practice in the UK and Germany. *International Journal of Consumer Studies*, 33 (2), 183–9.

Wee, C., 2002. Self, other, and community in Cartesian ethics. *History of Philosophy Quarterly*, 19 (3), 255–73.

Whatmore, S., 1997. Dissecting the autonomus self: Hybrid cartographies for a relational ethics. *Environment and Planning D: Society and Space*, 15 (1), 37–53.

# 9 Striving towards what we do not know yet

## Living Feminist Political Ecology in Toronto's food network[1]

*Carla Wember*

## Introduction

It is a Saturday in Toronto's early autumn. Summer's heat has yet to make way for the chilly days to come. I take the subway and then a bus to the city's northern border where I meet Laura[2] on the farm she manages. It is a farm in a community where supermarkets are scarce and in them no fresh vegetables are to be found. She shows me around, and for an hour we talk about what the farm means to her, about the difficult challenge of convincing authorities that it needs to be established and maintained, and about the progress being made in Toronto food politics toward advancing the needs of residents of communities like hers. At the end of our interview she cautions me:

> It is really important to stay in touch. How can the project benefit as well? Don't just say 'I get my stuff and I am gone,' letting the research sit in a dusty room. We need access to it. I think research plays a key role in helping us to move forward.

Her comments speak to an urge to overcome limitations – to change, to transform. All of my interview partners, I believe, share her sentiment. This push for transformation into more just, equitable and sustainable food systems mirrors broader multifaceted attempts, struggles and ideas to reject the current hegemony of a neoliberal capitalism that oversteps ecological boundaries and exploits people.

Laura indicates two things: first, the important role that research possesses for developing alternative thought, and second, the need for interconnectedness and reciprocity between research and practiced alternatives. Since the 1980s, new strains of theory like environmental economics and ecological economics have challenged neoclassical economic research to think about planetary ecological boundaries, externalities, value of ecosystems and thus the need for transformation. While the first mainly remains within neoclassical logics and methods, the latter asks for more holistic socio-ecological thoughts and transdisciplinary research. I start from the conviction that broader transdisciplinary knowledge and theory–building are indeed required in order to address the question of how to think and practice transformations of the economic system so that it engenders sustenance of human and non-human livelihoods. I thus turn to feminist scholars locating their thought in ecological economic theory.

I want to show first how thinking economic practices in their embodiment and embeddedness helps us see the connections between gendered structures and the economy, and ways of rethinking and redoing economic practices and systems can emerge. Toronto's food network exemplifies how economic practices of food production that seek to address the ecological crisis cannot be seen as separate from caring practices in communities, households and nature. Economic practices are instead engendered through embodied reproductive work attributed to nature and women. For this, I begin this chapter by referencing the work of Mary Mellor, which I use to contend that the central flaw of our current economic system is the subordination and externalisation of embodiment and embeddedness of human existence to women and ecosystems. I then want to exemplify, through the field of food by looking at embodiment as felt experiences, how these structures are maintained and where potentials for change lie.

Secondly, I want to draw attention to the actors of these alternative economic food practices. With theories of feminist ecological citizenship and Feminist Political Ecology, I argue that subjectivities and collectivities that practice alternatives are not pre-existent but instead emerge through their practices and experiences. This indicates how economic actors are not only producers or consumers but instead practitioners of citizenship through their contributions to socio-technical projects such as food networks. Their acts of living and practicing (feminist) ecological citizenship show how the economic is inseparably embedded in socio-ecological realities.

## Embodied gendered economies

Ecological economists and theorists pushing concepts of strong sustainability argue for conceptualising the economic system as embedded in a social system that is then part of an ecological system. This cautions against overthinking the powers of economic logics and assumptions of inherent necessities. Current economic practices externalise this embeddedness leading to ecologically unsustainable and destructive consequences, so they argue. Mary Mellor, ecofeminist scholar of social theory, sheds light on how this externalisation is connected to gendered oppression in our current economic system. She pushes ecological economists to include what she calls an ecofeminist political–economic standpoint: 'If green economists do not take on board these arguments, there will be a danger of replicating gender inequality in any future green economy' (Mellor 2006: 140). Mellor introduces the term valued economy to describe all economies that use money or prestige to value human activities (2006: 139). This indicates that the underlying concept of economy that Mellor applies is much broader. Marylin Power, for example, speaks of feminist economics by defining economy as the manner by which humans collectively organise to secure their survival (2004: 7). The capitalist market economy as one valued economy, so Mellor argues, values neither embeddedness nor embodiment. This is expressed through a devaluation of both natural lifecycles and 'body work' – that is to say, the work fulfilling the needs of our embodiment (Mellor 2001: 135). The latter finds its expression in domestic work, care for the elderly and children and emotional work. This work has historically been associated with women and femininity. Mellor thus calls this work 'women's work' and distinguishes it from work of women. She hereby firmly repels the notion of a natural link between femininity and body work and instead sees gendering of human societies as the outcome of the failure to address embodiment as a social and ecological issue. Transcendence is thereby upgraded while the immanent world of the body and the natural environment are devalued and exploited (2001: 133).

> What is important about women's work and relevant to green economics is that it is embodied and embedded. Women's work is embodied because it is concerned with the human body and its basic needs. Broadly it is the maintenance and sustenance of the human body through the cycle of the day and the cycle of life (birth to death), in sickness and in health.
>
> (Mellor 2006: 141)

Mellor argues that only this work of embodiment allowed space and time for the social – understood as transcendent – to be constructed and separated from the natural, the immanent. In this sense, the relationship between society and nature is gendered as both women's work and ecosystems are externalised in androcentric value systems, especially in economic terms (Mellor 2001: 134). Adelheid Biesecker and Sabine Hofmeister apprehend this work as 'the reproductive' and see it being incorporated as an invisible factor in the capitalist process of value creation. It becomes invisible through the system of economic valuation that distinguishes between productive and reproductive work and gives a monetary value to the one and none to the other (Biesecker and Hofmeister 2010: 58). They introduce the category (re)productivity[3] in order to overcome this division and hierarchisation and enable a perspective on 'the whole' of productivity, defining it as 'the procedural unity of all productive processes in nature and society, not separated by devaluation, yet marked by difference' (Biesecker and Hofmeister 2006: 19, own translation). It helps us decode the connection between societal relations of nature and gender (Biesecker and Hofmeister 2010: 69).

The externalisation of immanence is also expressed in a transgression of ecological and biological times (Mellor 2006: 143). While ecological time is the timescale for regeneration and renewal of ecosystems that allows for ecological sustainability, biological time is the timescale for the rhythms and needs of human existence (Mellor 1997: 136): 'It is time-consuming work often involving just being there, available, dependable, on call. It is the work for the human body and its basic needs' (Mellor 2001: 133). Yet, current economic practices expect bodies to be present, fed, cleaned, nurtured and emotionally supported and ready to be adaptable to a transcendent timescale of nine to five (Mellor 2001: 135). Thus, Mellor argues for thinking of an ecologically sustainable economy that starts from 'the embodiment and embeddedness of human lives, from the life of body and the ecosystem. This means that a provisioning economy would start from women's work and the vitality of the natural world' (Mellor 2006: 145). For her, spatial proximity is no solution, as utopias of green futures would argue, in societies that are structured by mechanisms of transcendence, separating the social from the natural both conceptually and in practice (Mellor 2001: 135). Rather, she argues for questioning concepts of the social that ignore the boundaries of the ecological: 'Embodiment is not confined to women, it is a human problem.' (Mellor 2001: 135) The analytical lens of embodiment will be a guiding one throughout this chapter. How can we grasp economic practices of food through embodiment? How can embodiment be a source of transformation?

## *Felt food economy*

In their book *Food and Femininity*, Josée Johnston and Kate Cairns enfold a comprehensive picture of how femininities are lived, expressed, imposed and rejected through food work. They start with shopping as a contradictory felt experience between pleasure, freedom, guilt and restraints; continue with maternal food work, dieting as an embodied balancing act between healthy lifestyles and societal imaginaries; and end with food politics between individual consumption and collective action. This gendering of food practices is strongly embodied. It materialises for instance in food choices like ordering in a restaurant: 'Do I pick salad or chicken wings?' This embodied decision takes place in a societal frame of possibilities and evaluation, which is for example expressed in the decision for a vegetarian diet that is often understood as a performance of femininity (Johnston and Cairns 2015: 107). There are also embodiments when thinking about regulating our body and feeling food: do we hold in or relax our stomach? How does it feel if a child rejects the food we have prepared? What feeling does it evoke to stroll the aisles of a supermarket without being able to buy food for others or me (Johnston and Cairns 2015: 25)? Johnston and Cairns argue that even the neoliberal capitalist system that embeds the gendering of food is embodied. This happens through the work with and through the body – self-regulation and self-optimisation through food, individualisation of 'healthy eating choices' and privatisation of food provision. Food ethics are also mostly located in the private sphere, deeming the individual consumer responsible for 'eating for change.' Thus, neoliberal logics and mind-sets are maintained through the feelings that are evoked by food experiences. In the tradition of feminist research, feelings are conceptualised as collectively constructed and historically situated rather than individual phenomena in the self (Boler 1999: 6). This enables a perspective on how neoliberal capitalism is reproduced but also challenged through daily food choices, practices and work. Through this analytical bridge, everyday experiences, with their felt agency on the one hand and systematic questions of oppression and inequality on the other, merge and can be observed in the same glimpse (Johnston and Cairns 2015: 34). Food work as care work then gets tangible through feelings such as devotion, pressure, limitation but also pleasure, creativity, excitement, political empowerment and pride. The intensity of those feelings in an economic system, which is characterised by individualising responsibilities, contributes to the inability to distribute food work more equally. For many women, following Johnston and Cairns, it feels confrontational and simply not worth it:

> Paradoxically, women are still positioned as gatekeepers of the kitchen, but they are now deemed responsible for their own oppression. This is a situation of women making individual choices, but one that is clearly structured by enduring gendered inequities – a situation that Beagan et al. describe as 'gender gone underground' (2008: 666).
>
> (Johnston and Cairns 2015: 166)

Ethical food work as a special form of care work fits in well: interviewees of Johnston and Cairns express a fear of being too dogmatic or unaccommodating with choices on ethical food consumption and thus are afraid of dropping out of social desirability (2015: 118). However, food practices not only create femininities but also reinforce the heteronormative family. Arlene Voski Avakian and Barbara Haber (2005) state, referencing Marjorie DeVault (1991): 'Through the work of feeding, women quite literally produce family life from day to day' (Avakian and Haber 2005: 8). Patricia Allen and Carolyn Sachs (2013) describe how the heteronormative image of the nuclear family is produced and kept up through food work and its connected responsibilities. Ethical consumption specifies the narrative of a healthy, conscious and responsible family.

Looking at ethical food work, it is dangerous to assume that the knowledge of food automatically leads to a desire for local and organic produce along with the willingness to pay the respective price. Julie Guthman (2008) describes this as a 'universalising impulse' that would set white practices as the norm and demand an assimilation to conventionally exclusive spaces. She thus calls for a 'less messianic approach to food politics' (2008: 388). Johnston and Cairns outline how ethical consumption is used as a token for distinction to feel comfortable with oneself or the group that one belongs to. The boundaries this creates can be racist as well as classist (Johnston and Cairns 2015: 121). Excluded people then often feel guilt and frustration. Thus, the 'eat for change' mantra becomes a hegemonic performance enabled through classist privilege (2015: 122). The questionability of the 'eat for change' mantra brings us to a central point of this chapter. It assumes that private consumption practices can contribute to change and are thus an incremental part of food politics. What can this tell us about places, subjects and ethics of feminist food politics?

## Living feminist ecological citizenship

The old feminist claim 'the private is political' is interesting when theorising about food and gender. As Johnston and Cairns (2015) or Allen and Sachs (2013) write, food work is conventionally seen as a private matter such that consumption choices, preparation and eating are not publicly regulated. Thus, ethical food consumption is also seen as a private decision. This decision is however perceived as a political action by many women, which Johnston and Cairns observe as a 'gendered articulation of political agency [which] needs to be recognised' (2015: 119). Still, the 'eat for change' mantra is contested among different scholars: some researchers indicate the transformative potential that could arise through consumer empowerment and emerging food movements that push for ecological and social justice (Baker 2004, Lockie 2009, Starr 2010). Others caution, however, that through those aspirations processes of neoliberalisation stay covert as the responsibility for safe and just food systems, in effect, gets devolved to self-regulating individuals (Maniates 2002, Allen *et al.* 2003, Szasz 2007, Guthman 2008). They see danger in glorifying the informed and responsible consumer in that doing so could consolidate an image of the good, neoliberal citizen (Biltekoff 2013: 93). These considerations connect to observations that, through transformations of the global economy, responsibilities generally get re-privatised and duties of citizens are emphasised more than social aspects of a state solidary system (Squires 1999: 173, Goodman *et al.* 2011: 143). Sherilyn MacGregor (2006: 107) sees – especially for the North American context – a trend since the 1980s to condition participation in society with duties to work including unpaid engagement and in return cutting services of the social state. As an example, she names the Canada Green Plan (1990), which says, in reference to achieving sustainability goals, that '[s]elf-regulation is better than government regulation, and that voluntary action is the most effective way to achieve enduring results' (Government of Canada 1990 cited in MacGregor 2006: 108). Structural problems of capitalist production are concealed, a green washing of neoliberal resistance against ecological regulation introduced and inequalities reinforced (MacGregor 2006: 109). These developments coincide with gender relations: women have less decisive power in public and are exposed to higher expectations in private, which confronts them with high individualised responsibility. Hence, following Johnston and Cairns, women also see more political leverage space in the market than in government structures:

> Thus, the gendering of ethical consumption draws upon, and can in turn reproduce, a gendered division of domestic labour and gendered realms of authority. Many women explicitly located their food politics within individual consumer practices, as opposed to social movements.
>
> (Johnston and Cairns 2015: 123)

Although green theories are starting to dismantle a common dichotomy in political theory between care as private and intimate, as well as concrete, and citizenship as public and objective, gendered divisions of labour are mostly not recognised. Care is introduced as a central value for Earth citizenship and sustainability without being embedded and discussed in the term's history, controversy and exact meaning. Bart van Steenbergen (1994), for instance, introduces care in opposition to control, whereas Robin Attfield (1999) makes references to care for nature without further explaining what this could imply. Hence, care becomes an 'unqualified good, a feeling that can easily be applied to human interactions with nature' (MacGregor 2006: 96). In return, the omission of gender relations leads to a feminisation of ecological responsibility that strongly links to the motive of motherhood. Care is naturalised as an instinctive activity being possible without specific knowledge or consideration (Code 1995: 107). Claims for a democratisation of the household, urgently needed for a just distribution of necessary (ecological) domestic work, are mostly absent in green theory (Rowbotham 1986, Phillips 1991, Lister 1997).

### *(Re-)constructing the public*

I argue that while it is important not to neglect the power that alternative consumption practices wield, we also need to extend food politics and especially feminist food politics to the public. It is necessary and hard-earned from a feminist standpoint to understand the private as a public matter. Yet, this can easily be instrumentalised by neoliberal tendencies to shift responsibilities from the public to the private. Moreover, feminist scholars caution that the complete blurring of boundaries between the private and the political could eventually eliminate the political as it would then be everything. Instead, they argue for re-drawing the boundaries of the political 'such that it no longer marginalises women, and distinguishing between democratic power and undemocratic domination such that the constraints provided by a democratic form of power might allow individual empowerment' (Squires 1999: 24). Iris Marion Young (1990) argues for a reconceptualisation of 'the public.' Conventionally, the public realm is idealised as attaining the universality of a general will and thus displacing everything particular to the private sphere. Practically, it encompasses excluding all groups embodying particularity such as women, Black people, Native Americans and Jewish people (Young 1990: 97). This results in members of those groups either being excluded from citizenship or included by repressing the particularity of their identity. Thus, 'the meaning of "public" should be transformed to exhibit the positivity of group difference, passion and play' (Young 1990: 97).

Moving away from an understanding of one public, Elisabeth Klaus and Ricarda Drüeke (2008) move to Oskar Negt and Alexander Kluge's (2001) definition of publicity as an organisational form of social experience, withdrawing the idea of one central public sphere. This resonates with Nancy Frasers's concept of subaltern publicities (1997). These are understood as parallel discursive spaces where subordinated groups can create counter discourses that allow for opposing interpretations of their identities, interests and needs.

Fraser sees those subaltern publicities as necessary for the functioning of a discursive sphere working as a corrective. Publicity thusly is a discursive space consisting of weak and strong publicities in which conflicts are staged (Fraser 1997: 81).

## Caring for justice: Ethics of feminist ecological citizenship

In political theory, an ethics of justice is often opposed to an ethics of care. This juxtaposition is rooted in the equality versus difference dilemma: while the one is founded in special, contextual relationships and is assuming a self in relation, the other is grounded in the idea of abstract and universal rights for autonomous individuals (Squires 1999: 141). Ethics of justice are reasoned within cognitive objectivism, which assumes a permanent and a-historic frame that can ultimately be adduced to determine nature and truth from a neutral view from nowhere (Squires 1999). As an antipole, maternalist theories argue for a feminised version of citizenship that is founded in virtues of the feminine private sphere, especially motherhood, featuring contextualisation and the particular (Elshtain 1981, Gilligan 1982, Ruddick 1989). Here, the distinction between care as a set of material practices and care as a disposition carrying certain values and ethics becomes blurred (MacGregor 2006: 58–9). It is argued from an epistemological perspective that we can learn from experiences and knowledge of women as caretakers when developing an ethics of Earth care (Merchant 1996).

MacGregor criticises this assumption as dangerous in an androcentric world that creates but also exploits and devalues a female capacity to care. Female experimental knowledge seemingly would not need a self-evaluation or reflexivity (2006: 79). Yet, MacGregor acknowledges, referring to Catriona Sandilands (1999), that maternalist thought fostered politicisation of women in ecological struggles and rendered visible forms of politics that the dominant ecological movements had missed. Still, she argues that care should be less idealised and instead regarded as paradoxical assemblages of practices, feelings and moral orientations embedded in particular relationships and contexts and socially constructed as feminine and private. Activities of women in public are then only considered appropriate when founded in motherhood.

Motherhood is loaded with many powerful cultural meanings offering women access to politics[4] (Sandilands 1999: 71). Sociologist Harriet Rosenberg (1995) argues that mothers are particularly addressed by ecological campaigns of corporations or governments: 'The individual mother is exhorted to accept personal responsibility for a crisis that she is said to be able to ameliorate through private practices within her household' (197). Also in relation to food, motherhood is seen as the incarnation of natural and pristine provision and care. Johnston and Cairns (2015) quote a food blogger who is critical of the corporate, industrial food system: 'Mom lost much of her authority over the dinner menu, ceding it to scientists and food marketers' (cited in Johnston and Cairns: 172). This shows how commonly understandable a reference to motherhood in connection to food responsibility is. The link is unquestioned and romanticised even, especially in discussions aiming at a fairer and more environmentally reasonable food system. MacGregor emphasises this critique especially in the context of capitalist societies in which a theoretical association of care with femininity would support a trend of devaluation, continuing feminisation and re-privatisation of care work (MacGregor 2006: 67). Here, she highlights the shock-absorbing role women often play in economic restructurings through the acceptance of unpaid privatised care work and the increasing shifting of care work to migrant and racialised people.

Referring to feminist political economists she calls these relations unsustainable and thus builds an (analytical) bridge to (feminist) struggles for ecological justice (MacGregor 2006: 70). In doing so, MacGregor connects to the question of what an ethical foundation of mutual politicisation of feminist and ecological issues could look like that she finds lacking in many ecofeminist approaches: 'The place of consciousness raising, the process whereby women look critically at their lives and question accepted norms, is necessarily diminished [...] if the assumption is that political and ecological awareness emerge intuitively (or 'naturally') from women's social location' (MacGregor 2006: 71).

She feels the need to bend thoughts away from the question of what women (and other marginalised people) *are* under current problematic circumstances towards the question of who they *can become* as political actors in a radical-democratic, non-sexist and ecologically just society (MacGregor 2006: 79). Yet how can an acknowledgment of the gendering of care work, in its pivotal role for politics and everyday life, succeed without also naturalising care workers as female and thus excluding them from political deliberation as irrelevant? Here it would be necessary to mediate the ethics of care and of justice, moving away from a maternalist perspective of only revaluing care: 'I suggest that, through the language of citizenship rather than through the language of care, a more useful ecofeminist conversation about women's eco-political engagements may occur' (MacGregor 2006: 73).

Still, the 'view from nowhere,' which in the sense of Cartesian Rationalism originates from a transcendence of experiences, feelings and needs, and which founds the classic idea of citizenship, is likewise problematic from a feminist perspective (Squires 1999: 142). MacGregor thus draws attention to approaches from feminist scholars taking up a mediating position. Joan Tronto (1993), for instance, argues for an extension of an ethics of care beyond the private sphere needing to be paralleled with a politicisation and decoupling of gender. She claims: 'Care needs to be connected to a theory of justice and to be relentlessly democratic in its disposition' (Tronto 1993: 171). She analyses the socio-historic circumstances that led to a dichotomisation of justice and care, locating the current devaluation of care in the real power that caring activities actually encompass as they indicate human vulnerability and interdependence (Tronto 1993: 123). Likewise, Patricia Hill Collins (2000) argues for the acknowledgment of an ethics of care, which she refuses to exclusively connect to femininities but also to experiences of Afro-American cultures. She thus shifts the focus from a universalising and naturalising perspective towards roots in experiences of oppression fostering the connection to care (Collins 2000: 264). Seyla Benhabib (1992) approaches the convergence of different ethics through a modification of Jürgen Habermas's communicative ethics in including both the generalised Other as a moral agent as well as the concrete Other as an individual, with important differences between the two. Through communication, a combination of both could succeed: a rational perspective on 'the Other' with equal rights and duties, as well as a contextual perspective, including history, identity and emotional constitution (Benhabib 1992: 159). Thus, she challenges the dominant assumption of incompatibility between autonomy and care.

When talking about citizenship, two broad conceptualisations are conventionally used: the liberal perspective looks at citizenship of a community as a status that adjudges rights to individuals while the civic or latterly communitarian approach looks at citizenship as an activity where a citizen participates in responsibilities (Benhabib 1992: 168). Here I would like to invoke a synthesis between both, referring to Ruth Lister (1997) and Chantal Mouffe's (1992) understanding of citizenship as both a practice involving human agency as well as a status that with political, civil and social rights protects and fosters interests of marginalised people. This entails, in a tradition of Hannah Arendt, looking at the appearance in public as citizen as allowing us to discover 'who' we are rather than 'what' we are (*cf.* Mouffe 1992). This shifts the perspective from a substantial, pre-existing individual towards the acknowledgement of a procedural embodied human being 'inevitably dependent on others for care and nurturance, including, for ecofeminists, non-human others and the natural world' (MacGregor 2006: 101). Transferred to the question of a common good, this perspective argues for a common good as something we constantly refer to but can never reach. A radical democratic vision of citizenship thus recognises the many different relations of dominations preventing liberty and equality for all. Therefore, articulation of people's differences is necessary, yet as 'relations of equivalence' (Squires 1999: 182).

Thus, neither through ethics of care nor through ethics of justice can foundations of political processes be conceptualised. Whereas one remains in a dichotomising reproduction of gender relations, the other is unable to overcome the exclusion of everything exceeding rationality: feelings, bodies or contextualisation. Instead, the focus needs to shift from the 'what' to the 'how': with the presumption that we are mutually dependent and connected beings, we need to overcome perceptions of substantial individuals and instead perceive individuals in processes of becoming, encompassing human as well as non-human beings. This calls for impartiality in the processes of deliberation that go beyond communicative ethics to include a variety of experiences in addition to mere verbal exchange. These differences in experience call for politics of 'solidarity in difference' (Benhabib 1992, Mouffe 1992, Lister 1997).

## Living Feminist Political Ecology

Turning to how this politics is done, practised and lived has become the research focus of a strain of theory emerging since the 1990s: Feminist Political Ecology (FPE). Scholars committing to FPE focus on practices as specific, historical and embedded yet shared experiences. Here too, the becoming of things is at the core of analysis and politics: how do possibilities emerge 'for becoming something and someone different – rooted in place and history – and connected to envisioning alternative futures *with* and among broader communities' (Harcourt and Nelson 2015: 7)? Thinking about those alternative futures is itself understood as a practice of living political ecology that is entrenched with power relations. Connecting to Donna Haraway's approach of situated knowledge (1988) Wendy Harcourt and Ingrid L. Nelson state: 'Such acts of imagining "green" or "just" futures come *from* the privileges, status and other features of the individual or community doing the imagining' (Harcourt and Nelson 2015: 7, emphasis in original). Thus, researchers of FPE actively embrace the partiality, contradictoriness and becoming-ness of the research process that does not progress towards an ultimate goal but 'stays with the trouble' – as Haraway puts it (2016). This helps 'generate richer, more complex theories and understandings beyond a simplistic and hierarchical God's-eye view and "ground-up" view. The question of disclosing/sharing/representing what is "known" is complex' (Haraway 2006: 15). This complexity is reflected in the underlying research commitment to asking how to sustain livelihoods. These are understood as 'attentive to everyday needs, embodied interactions and labours as well as emotional and affective relations with the environments and natures where we live' (Haraway 2006: 13). These livelihoods, so argue researchers of FPE, are gendered also in its understanding of place. Dissociating from narratives of global economic inequality merely locating women in place, 'FPE is able to shape an analysis of the global through a nuanced gendered understanding of the interlinkages between body, home, community and natural resources in the public political sphere' (Harcourt 2015: 252). Thus, Christine Bauhardt argues that instead of addressing ecological problems only through approaches of resource management that fit well into economic discourses of efficiency and productivity, a more holistic and radical approach needs to be found, one which she calls resource politics. This could enhance 'policy options far beyond the responsibility of women caring for humans and the planet and this is as it should be' (Bauhardt 2013: 371).

The normative focus is directed away from a uniform understanding of sustainable development that rests within the neoliberal core of the productive individual and environment that are assumed to be fully known through cognition. Instead, complex and multifaceted embodied and embedded systems need to be grasped through just these embodied and embedded modes of knowledge. Wendy Harcourt writes about a livelihood in Italy that she is part of: 'That [the community] allowed me to understand "on my skin" how environment is linked to culture through relations of power, agency and responsibility to human and non-human environments' (Harcourt 2015: 254). Dianne Rocheleau, a pioneer of FPE, describes how she experiences power relations inscribed in material surroundings: 'Suddenly the land lit up with gendered landscapes and land-use patterns and the material implications for water and resource management and food production' (Rocheleau 2015: 33). Both quotes show the importance of the researching subject that is assumed to be embedded in the phenomena and practices they investigate. This goes along with a critique of Western knowledge systems putting decolonial thought, especially decolonial feminism at the forefront.

> In this way I can convey my own situated and partial knowledge as part of a larger movement and a journey, a coalition and a coalescence of people seeking to decolonise themselves, their professions, social and environmental movements and the terms of encounters across distinct cultures, histories and geographies.
>
> (Rocheleau 2015: 29)

The case is made to turn towards the many complex ways gendered, colonial structures work together with exploitation of nature, thereby highlighting 'the need to decentre humans in understanding the economy and to make more visible non-Western cultures' understanding of the need to regenerate sources of sustenance' (Harcourt 2015: 254). Here, FPE goes beyond describing how socio-natural realities are intertwined in gendered and colonial structures but actively strives to decolonise and de-gender them. FPE wants to think, to reflect and to act us out of oppressive ways of being in the world.

> If it takes a village to raise a child, perhaps it takes 1000 villages and their uninvited apprentices to inform, motivate and guide a paradigm shift, and eventually a political reversal, among academics, professionals and activists involved in environment, development and social justice.
>
> (Rocheleau 2015: 31)

This directs the perspective to the act, the practice, the living of Feminist Political Ecology. This also involves a shift away from *the* right, *the* green or *the* just. Harcourt cautions, referring to Karen Barad, not to see a situating in the world as static and thus provided with definable responsibilities and privileges. Rather, embodiments put us in the world in a 'dynamic specificity. Ethics is therefore not about right response to a radically exterior/ised Other, but about responsibility and accountability for the lively relationalities of becoming of which we are part' (Barad 2007: 377). This leaves us with agency and efficacy in the world and yet with imperfect, half-done, reciprocal and hybrid outcomes of actions and non-actions. Patricia Piccinini pushes us to see the 'unexpected consequences of the stuff we don't want but must somehow accommodate. There is no question as to whether there will be undesired outcomes; my interest is in whether we will be able to love them' (Piccinini 2006, quoted in Haraway 2007).

Within the perspective of embodied gendered economies and living Feminist Political Ecologies, food plays a distinctive role. Barely anything is tied more closely to human survival and our embodiment than food. We have to relate to it on a daily basis and it is deeply bound into our everyday practices and thus in the structuring of our lives. Thus, food organising that tries to counteract a globalised agrarian system that is deeply embedded in capitalist structures seems to be more than fruitful for learning about possibilities of economic transformation that start from acknowledgement for embodiment and embeddedness.

## Restructuring food and place

Scholars and activists promoting local alternatives to an industrialised global food system often are overly optimistic that implementation of concepts like 'food-in-social context' (Hendrickson and Heffernan 2002) or 'foodsheds' (Kloppenburg *et al.* 1996) will easily create solutions to current problems. Consumers feel they are counteracting economic concentration, social disempowerment and ecological degradation when prioritising local food (Hinrichs 2003: 33). Yet, an increasingly broad scholarship criticises these normative concepts for assuming an intrinsic value of spatial proximity that would automatically translate into more environmentally sustainable food production and at the same time positive, respectful and non-instrumental social relations:

> In the local food movement there is a sense that, because people live together in a locality and encounter each other, they will make better, more equitable decisions that prioritise the common good. While this is a beautiful vision, localities contain within them wide demographic ranges and social relationships of power and privilege embedded within the place itself.
>
> (Allen 2010: 301)

To engage with alternatives to the current food system I turn to David Goodman *et al.* (2011), Erna Melanie DuPuis and David Goodman (2005) and Patricia Allen (2010) in looking at Alternative Food Networks (AFNs) more analytically. These are conceptualised as 'relational organisational expression[s] of recursive material and symbolic interactions between producers and consumers' (Goodman *et al.* 2011: 8) that emerge as constellations of production–consumption practices, inhering knowledges, routines, narratives and materiality. These socio-technical projects aim at changing orders of the socio-ecological that is currently structured by the conventional agro-industrial food supply (Goodman *et al.* 2011: 50–1). This conceptualisation explicitly takes on a practice perspective that for me points to asking about material circumstances *and* its meanings ascribed by involved actors. It means engaging with the interplay between both: touching questions of (re)distribution of land and other resources, access to (daily) food provision and material circumstances of food production in light of how involved actors make sense of it, narrate it and draw connections. Knowledge structures and routines are assumed to be mutually dependent and stabilised through communities of practices (Warde 2005).

Space is not a distinct category that exists outside of social relations but instead is an emerging socio-material process. This recognition is necessary to look at inequalities and oppression that come into play and shape answers to questions like: Who owns the land? Who lives in the place and why? Who is narrated as belonging to the place? Or simpler: Whose place is it? This shifts our perspective towards differences in recognition, participation and economic distribution in and among places (Allen 2010). To include those questions into reflections on local food, Claire Hinrichs (2003: 36) introduces the term 'diversity-receptive-localisation.' It is based on an awareness and incorporation of complex cultural, social and ecological struggles as outlined in the concept of 'politics of difference' by Young (1990: 319). The local is then conceptualised as embedded in a world community and only possible through its relational character with other localities and other spatial levels and imaginaries. The narrative and organisational foundation of this concept is an 'utopia of process' (Harvey 2001 cited in DuPuis and Goodman 2005: 369). It opposes the idea of a fixed ideal of what social coexistence needs to look like and instead turns to the process of its creation. Utopia of process focusses on communal becoming and developing in collective deliberation processes. The underlying argument is that solutions can only grow over time with involvement and need to be correctable in terms of including more experiences, circumstances and contexts. In order to create processes of diversity-receptive localisation, negotiations of neoliberal constructs and agrarian ideologies have to be part of deliberation, planning and implementation of localisation processes, which requires 'wider, more inclusive conceptualisations of alterity that effectively embrace social justice, citizenship, and democratic governance' (Goodman *et al.* 2011: 153).

## Striving towards what we do not know yet: Feminist food politics in Toronto

Toronto is the centre of Southern Ontario, a very urban region with around 12 million people, of which 40 percent live in Toronto along the shore of Lake Ontario, called Golden Horseshoe (Friedmann 2011: 169). Toronto with its 2.6 million inhabitants was built on farmland, which is the most fertile in Canada and among the best in North America (Friedmann 2001: 169). While historically the economic and cultural connections between town and farming in Southern Ontario were very strong and food was produced in the city of Toronto, this changed with the industrialisation of food and agriculture. The final push for farmers to 'get big or get out'[5] came from imports. The rich farmland around Toronto came under pressure for conversion to roads, industries, housing estates and shopping centres. Total farm area in Ontario decreased from 22.8 million acres in 1931 to 9.5 million acres in 2006.

In addition, food processing industries got out of business, reducing the number of stable buyers and resulting in what Lauren Baker *et al.* (2010) call a missing infrastructure for a regional food system.

Simultaneous to urbanisation of farmland, a 'dramatic reversal of immigration history' (Friedmann 2011: 172) took place where, unlike former newcomers, a present generation of immigrants did not have the incentive or opportunity to come to farm – coinciding with the development of global markets in food and agriculture (Friedmann 2011: 160). Today not only Toronto but the whole region is a site of transnational diasporas having ties to groups in other countries: half of the Metropolitan Toronto's population of 5.5 million are born outside of Canada (Friedmann 2011: 174). As outlined in the Report 'Fighting for Food Justice in the Black Creek Community' published by the Black Creek Food Justice Network (2015), many of them live in marginalised parts of the city where grocery stores are hardly accessible without vehicles. Moreover, a criminalisation of People of Colour in supermarkets and policing of access to food through for instance gated shelves were named as major problems. This shows that there are large differences in food accessibility along lines of race, economic situation and spatial dispersion.

The seemingly relentless urbanisation of Southern Ontario was slowed down in 2005 with a pioneering policy for environmental protection, introducing 'The Greenbelt.' It consists of 1.8 million acres of provincially protected land, covering a large part of the Golden Horseshoe. While it encompasses diverse natural landscapes and some of Canada's most valuable agricultural land, there is increasing pressure of intense speculation on the Greenbelt. Yet, Harriet Friedman states that 'the conversation has shifted and urban expansion onto farmland is no longer presumed to be "natural"' (Friedmann 2011: 169). This is also reflected in the lively food organising in Toronto with networks of small businesses in food production and retailing, a community of food activists, municipal and non-governmental organisations, and 7 billion dollars spent on food annually in the city (Friedmann 2007: 390).

In my research I found three main strategies in what was described as a bottom-up practice-oriented approach that some name a movement while others call it a scene or network. While there is a strong inclination to entrepreneurship as mirrored in local food supplying companies, private farming businesses and food boxes,[6] there is also an approach to address food organising through non-governmental work.[7] These organisations provide for instance education, lunch programs, school gardens or own food-box programs. The third approach uses commonly owned land and provides possibilities to collectively grow or provide low-barrier access to the grown food.[8] Many of the leaders of those different approaches are connected in the Toronto Food Policy Council (TFPC) or other networking efforts. In her work, Allen (2010) highlights how the TFPC is a model for other councils and 'prioritises food justice, establishing the right of all residents to adequate, nutritious food and promoting food production and distribution systems that are grounded in equity' (301). It was established in 1991 as a subcommittee of the Board of Health to advise the

City of Toronto on food policy issues. It is exceptional as it brings diverse stakeholders together by also having farmers as members. At the core of its work is the Toronto Food Strategy. In addition, it works on urban agriculture, fosters regional cooperation with the Greater Toronto Area Agriculture Action Committee and involves young food activists through a Youth Chapter, the Toronto Youth Food Policy Council (TYFPC). These efforts are embedded in the municipality and connected to institutions on regional levels like FoodSecure Canada, the Greenbelt or SustainOntario.

### *(Gendered) food inequalities in Toronto*

No matter whom I talked to in my research, connections of food (organising) and questions of social justice are primarily seen through the lens of class and race. Missing food accessibility for low-income communities, food deserts in marginalised and racialised neighbourhoods around Toronto or criminalisation of People of Colour in supermarkets are experienced and problematised. Colonial history and ownership of land were also regularly mentioned but always in connection with an insecurity of how to address these issues. The triad of often overlooked historic and current labour conditions, food insecurity and missing decision-making power, all of them structured by class and race, feel upsetting and frustrating to many. Especially from the grower's side, there is unease to grow for an 'elite bunch of people.' One interview partner calls the varieties that are grown in Toronto's local food networks for revenue's sake 'white food.' This shows how food is a place where nature and culture, material and meaning, bodies and what lies outside their borders cannot be separated. What we eat is determined by where we are positioned in society through our body and then becomes our body.

Finding answers when asked about gender relations in food (organising) was much more difficult. The majority of interviewees self-referenced to be feminist or interested in feminist politics. Yet, the connections between gender and food are experienced as difficult to grasp and hard to express. I experienced a strong reluctance out of fear to reproduce gendered notions like a naturalisation of a connection between care and femininity. The link for many was yet obvious, considering the strong majority of women being involved in local food networks in Toronto. Many talked about connections between food, gender and care. Yet the uncertainty of how to speak about the pleasure that is found in taking care through food and farming goes along with a resistance to naturalise this inclination as a feminine act or property:

> I hear a lot of people say like [disguises her voice]: 'Because women are nurturers.' And I am like: 'No.' But those are the types of things, I don't really want to perpetuate. But whether that's a socialised thing or something that you are taught to do because of patriarchy. You know, you'd have to unpack it more. It's too simple to be like: women are nurturers. I think people are nurturers. And I don't know – that's different.

There is a strong conviction that the work that is done in local food organising is incremental in creating more just, equitable and sustainable food. This goes along with a disbelief and frustration around the felt and experienced insecurity in farming. One interviewee describes how she hesitated before deciding to go into farming: 'I don't know if I can do this by myself. And I don't have the finances to do this. [...] Everything felt very unsure.' This is also associated to gendered dynamics: 'I think a lot of people would really enjoy the work but women are more used to not being paid appropriately for their work. And unfortunately that is true for farming.' Many interviewees touch upon the connection between the devaluation of women's work and the devaluation of life sustaining resources, yet there remains insecurity of how to frame and address this intersection.

This is also mirrored in the volunteer culture in the Toronto food network. One interview partner claims that it is something to be proud of, giving a project legitimacy and ensuring its outreach, another is sceptical, stressing the gendered notion around it. She argues that for women it 'doesn't feel as much of a stretch' and is actually a self-expectation to do unpaid work. Volunteer work can then be seen as extended care work deeply entrenched in self-concepts of women and structures relying on the availability of this workforce. This volunteering culture, which is deeply embedded in a North American context, inheres a tension: while on the one hand it ensures a low-barrier accessibility, creating avenues for new projects, connections and networks and thus enables a broad movement, on the other hand it builds on gendered structures of exploitation of unpaid female or feminised work. One interview partner mentions how a student nutrition program in her organisation is staffed with one man in 18 people. She explains that it started as a volunteer program serving snacks in their kids' school: 'That program is specifically related to gendered understandings of who provides food, who nurtures children and who cares about it.' Thus, a certain femininity is, as conceptualised by Johnston and Cairns (2015), produced and maintained as hegemonic that only certain groups have access to be and live. Tropes of white middle-class femininity in the food network also show through the 'privilege to be enabled to get into a field of work where you're not getting a pay check right away and having the privilege to leave the urban centre and access land,' one interviewee states.

Yet, although creating land access is mainly reserved to men in Canada as well as worldwide,[9] it does contribute to material change through local food organising. Forms of collective farming and creating community spaces that detach farming from its connection to the heterosexual family challenge the agrarian vision of the family farm. Women have (limited) access to land and decision-making structures independent of the men in their family. Yet, this does not necessarily mean that ownership is redistributed as it is mostly publicly or commonly owned lands.

Interview partners that are involved with farming express a strong resistance against tropes of femininity. Often approached with ideas of proximity of women and nature and nurturing as a main motivation for women to go into farming, those ideas are refused with frustration and anger. Motivations voiced instead are very focused on the body and emotions. Feeling strong, empowered, being challenged on different levels or experiencing emancipative potential through new bodily experiences in farming that are normally only seen as permissible for men are highlighted as motives. It is articulated how farming is perceived as a feminist act of rupturing conventional understandings of femininity. Those experiences are described as gates and mostly safe situations to include those experiences into other areas of life. Farming is also connected to feelings like joy, passion and happiness that gives room for connections between mind work and body work. This indicates that through farming, positive and emancipative feelings and concepts of the body and the self can be experienced and developed. These feelings are perceived as resistant to hegemonic ideas of femininity and social desirability. Yet, not only conceptions of the self as an individual are changed but also the perception of the personal interconnectedness and relation to the (non-)human world around. 'Food is something physical, something you can feel, something you can touch' was expressed in one of the TFPC meetings. It reflects a re-embeddedness into material cycles and new relations to the natural world that many interview partners address. Different expressions like creating 'a different way of being in the world, a completely, different relationship with nature and a different relationship with other places and with people, between people' or rejections of human life as the centre of the universe all point in this direction. This needs a learning process that can be enabled through farming. One interviewee pulls it straight: 'You are working very closely with a whole bunch of other organisms, conditions, whatever. So you kind of get that you are not the one pulling the strings.' This shows a way of working and experimenting in co-habitation with non-human beings that renounces on the one hand a mechanistic idea of domination of nature and on the other hand a conceptualisation of women being closer to nature.

### Space for politics of becoming

I experienced food to be framed as a political and public topic in Toronto rather than people connecting to it through their household practices. The bridge between private practices and approaches to food structured around access, growing and sustainability were somewhat given but not systematically included in the work for alternatives in food systems. Time regimes were for instance only addressed when talking about volunteer work but not in terms of distribution of food work in the household. When asked for change, all interview partners directed the focus mostly on issues around resource access, structural changes through policies and more diverse representation instead of revaluation and redistribution of private food work. Places for making this change were firstly seen in the creation of alternative practices of local food supply, education, catering but also changes in individual consumption behaviour. The last strategy was yet contested as challenges in the food system were mostly seen as unsolvable by individuals. While the creation of alternatives in Toronto mostly relies on individual choices, coordinating institutions with the TFPC leading the way were seen as having a major impact in changing food systems. It was especially appreciated in its function of networking, discussing issues and contributing to strategies and policies. In many interviews the political level of pushing policies and coordinating change beyond economic alternatives was stressed as crucial. Thus, disaccording with the assumption of Goodman *et al.* (2011) that AFNs are more directed at the market than at politics, the importance of political structures in organising food was strongly emphasised in Toronto.

The local as a general concept was not seen as a value in itself but was argued for from a specific organisational perspective, strongly linked to an understanding of community. Here an interesting conception of place unfolds. Toronto itself is seen as a structure or even an actor that enables conversations and learning processes. One interview partner personalises the space and gives it a distinct identity: 'Toronto taught me how to listen to people.' The space emerges through dynamic places, leaders, events and public places giving food organising a specific momentum. This specificity of Toronto as an enabling space is mostly characterised by the diversity that interview partners experience and appreciate. Thus, the place is not only characterised by a factual variety of people's origin, cultural practices and experiences of marginalisation, but the appreciation of these differences is seen as a foundational and maintaining the value of Toronto. Here the local is defined by change and difference – at least in networks of food organising. This also connects to how the issue of food is approached. It is not only perceived in a production and consumption perspective but is rather seen as a focal point for a multitude of issues like eating, growing, cooking, cultural expression, care, material marginalisation and thus a reflecting point for societal relations. Many interview partners highlight how they see the Toronto food network as developing and emerging through 'those really, really honest conversations around the local food movement' on inequalities and privileges especially concerning race as a way to 'look at it and figure out a way of moving forward [so] that we can really make any change.' Many white interviewees told me how they learned to address their privileges through food politics. One interview partner talks about reflecting on privileges in a way that puts feelings of being personally offended or becoming defensive aside and acknowledges their own entanglement in power relations:

> It is about how we bring these histories into our everyday lives despite of personal relationships and I think it is very hard for people to really acknowledge, understand and separate from that. And that is why the work is so hard.

These learning processes and involvements with one another through food organising in Toronto fostering collaboration and solidarity cannot yet be thought of without including connections of the socio–natural establishing in the Toronto food network. I argue that food organising is a place where new socio-natural orderings can be enabled. Human/non-human metabolisms can create and can be founded in exclusions but also have the potential to create inclusion and common metabolisms. When assuming that ecological and social processes of crisis are equi-primordial (Mellor 1997, Biesecker *et al.* 2010, Bauhardt 2012), new relations and appreciation of social and ecological re-productivity are necessary. The generating of new naturecultural orders and narratives can help to lay foundations that also create change on an economic level. Currently, capitalist economies rest on the socio-cultural devaluation of re/productivity of human and non-human being that upholds its exploitation and privatisation (Bauhardt 2012: 9). Creating new narratives and experiences within practices of connectedness of (non-)human re/productivity can thus contribute to delegitimising the logic of exploitation. Practices of co-habitation and work with and along natural re/productivity through farming in structures of local food organising could be effective in that. Feelings play a central role here. Johnston and Cairns describe how neoliberal processes and logics of individualisation of responsibility are embodied in collectively produced feelings of for instance guilt, ambition or joy of successfully accomplished food work. I want to capture this conceptualisation and argue that through farming in local food communities, feelings are created that can be resistant against those neoliberal mind-sets. To do work that is fulfilling and done along natural re/productivity was described as joyful and passionate by many interview partners. It was seen in opposition to striving towards profit and individual recognition. Community and collaboration between different projects filled interview partners with pride and gave them a sense of strength. Yet, there was also anger about too few resources for this work and a feeling of powerlessness when reflecting the small scale of influence and potential for change projects still have. I argue that these different embodied experiences of local food organising can be key to creating possibilities to (re)think and (re)practise socio-material connections in new, emancipatory ways and use feelings like anger and frustration to address structural mischiefs collectively.

These observations strongly connect to ethics of feminist ecological citizenship. In practising communities of (non-)human co-habitation and collaboration the perspective shifts towards the question of what we can be and what we can become. Goodman *et al.* (2011: 50–1) consider AFNs as socio-technical projects that emerge as constellations of production-consumption practices, knowledges, routines, narratives as well as material. Beyond creating new practices of production and consumption, I see political and public spaces emerging in Toronto. Klaus and Drüeke's (2008) concept of intertwining levels of public spaces can be applied to local food organising in Toronto. The rooting of local food organising in communities creates spaces of care, networking, learning from and with each other and enables personal encounters. Examples of those spaces are for instance markets and the vitalisation of commonly used spaces by the Thorncliffe Park Women's Committee, member and incubator farming programs, community gardens or volunteer work for organisations like FoodShare or The Stop. Here spaces of care for the connections between people and non-human beings emerge and enable low-barrier access into food communities and food politics. Secondly, more official – or as Fraser (1997) would say 'strong' public spaces – are created through the work of T(Y)FPC and networking organisations like Toronto Urban Growers. Here structural barriers and technical questions of legislation are addressed on a small scale. Moreover, strategies that frame the work of small projects and organisations are developed that formulate common goals and orientation. Thus, local food organising in Toronto addresses alternative practices and thus private responsibility on the one hand. Here communities take on responsibilities for care of lands and one another. On the other hand, through the connection of the TFPC to the municipality and work with other governmental institutions like Golden Horseshoe Food and Farming Alliance, policies and thus structural frames are addressed. This includes topics like land access, planning of public spaces or water supply. I argue that both levels create and are maintained by caring citizenship. In the community work, process-oriented understandings of citizenship apply where it is practiced through creating active communities, support for one another and collaboration with the land. In political institutions and in claims beyond that, which were developed through food work, rights as citizens from the state and governments were claimed and change fostered. Through citizenship practices of becoming, people can experience what they can be (leaders, volunteers, community members, food organisers, farmers etc.) and grow with the work they are doing. This shows how local food organising in Toronto goes beyond creating alternative production-consumption practices and political spaces open up to practice citizenship as becoming. Yet, as many interview partners pointed out, more resources are needed to stabilise the work that is being done and thus enable a scaling-up. Interview partners were concerned about too weak links to the municipality ('Who knows who the next health official will be?'), too little means to include residents with little resources, or too little funding and too high barriers through technical standards and political guidelines for new projects. Strategies for that still need to be found.

While interviewees describe food as an umbrella issue through which social and ecological inequalities can be addressed, gender relations are only subjected under the surface. Yet, personal, institutional and discursive structures and practices exist that could be used to advance discussions around gender and its politicisation:

> I would be interested to know more about that intersection between feminism and the environment. Because I consider myself very much a feminist. I think that was probably one of the first kind of topics I took on as a teenager. It was the most relevant to me. So, I would love to see more about that kind of thinking. What it means in an urban ag[riculture] context.

In this system, a low-barrier access for people to be involved and represented in shaping local food organising is created. Leadership can be taken on and learned. This is what many interview partners describe as a process of learning and growing into this role. Allen and Sachs (2013) argue that many women are already struggling for change in the food system but rarely connect these efforts to the aim of altering gender relations. I see this confirmed in local food organising in Toronto and yet see ample potential to make this connection. Many interview partners share experiences of learning processes and conversations around privilege concerning race and class through food organising in Toronto and are curious to talk and think about how food relations interact with gender or queer issues. This indicates that a stronger and concrete politicisation of gender relations in Toronto local food organising is possible. Hindering this is a vast insecurity of explaining gendered inequalities in the food context as well as a fear of naturalising connections between women and care. I see a connection point to commonly address gendered and ecological injustices in what interview partners explicitly as well as implicitly describe as a dilemma between sustainability and affordability in local food organising. This mirrors a structural contradiction of capitalist economy that is identified in FPE: a structural devaluation and externalisation of the reproduction capacity of humans as well as of ecosystems. The primacy given to market solutions paired with the symbolic devaluation of reproduction of life results in an asymmetric production of food. This entails overproduction, food waste and ecological degradation of soils, water and ecosystems as well as exploitative working conditions. At the same time, it externalises food work as part of social reproduction like shopping, cooking and meal-planning to the private sphere where it is expected to be accomplished unpaid. Alternative practices like the Toronto local food organising touch these systemic boundaries expressed in a dilemma between sustainability and affordability. The alternative practices still operate in a system were costs of ecological and social degradation are not systematically internalised. Thus, individual alternative practices are competing in a system where food gets cheaper and the economic inequality, produced by the same system, prevents people from accessing food that instead of contributing to the degradation of ecosystems might even make them healthier and more sustainable. Yet, the systemic degradation of ecosystems is obvious while degradation of human reproductive work is harder to grasp. Thus, alternative practices of local food organising express an individual resistance against the degradation of ecosystems. While a reorganisation of care work is not automatically addressed, there is high potential within Torontonian food networks to change this. This could then be a starting point for alternative food practices to address and politicise both the crises of social and ecological reproduction. Beyond this politicisation at a local scale, food networks can potentially be a gateway for larger movements to challenge broader societal structures.

## Conclusion

Thinking and practising food is politically and analytically extremely insightful when asking for the embodiment of economic systems and feminist ecological citizenship. It lets us come across our dependence on and interconnectedness with our social and natural relations and conditions. I investigated how local food networks in Toronto are places of embodied gendered economy and if they can be a place to jointly resist crises of ecological degradation and gendered injustices. I see three levels on which local food politics can counteract a food system that rests upon exploitation of reproductive capacities of ecosystems and feminised work of social reproduction.

Firstly, alternative economic practices are developed that mainly try to achieve the production of ecologically sustainable food and thus internalise ecological costs. Here spaces of individual choice are created that yet still compete in a system that externalises the ecological costs of food production. Moreover, there are no explicit approaches to address systemic invisibility and degradation of social reproduction. However, so I argue secondly, farming and food organising that is embedded in local structures lets new socio-ecological narratives and imaginations emerge. These are strongly fostered by and embodied through feelings such as joy, passion, anger, connectedness, frustration, empowerment or fulfilment. I argue that through these embodied narratives, (gendered) neoliberal scripts can be counteracted and new socio-ecological imaginations can be created. Collective food work can build appreciation for social and ecological re-productivity that helps to delegitimise exploitation and individualisation and enables economic change. Lastly, local food organisation in Toronto shows how beyond alternative production–consumption practices, political spaces open up, in which subjectivities and collectivities can become. Co-habitation and collaboration among humans and non-humans becomes possible beyond structural inequalities through learning processes and tough discussions around privilege and respect for difference. This example shows that through a resolute utopia of process in diversity-receptive localities, feminist ecological citizenship can be practised and lets us strive towards what we do not know yet.

## Notes

1 Many thanks to Dave Mardis and Ronna Werner for their incredibly important help and input.
2 Name changed.
3 Following Christine Bauhardt, I will use the spelling re/productivity hereafter to indicate the equivalence of reproductive and productive work included in this term (Bauhardt 2012: 12).
4 E.g. Mothers against Drunk Driving (madd) (www.madd.org) or Mütter gegen Atomkraft e.V. (http://www.muettergegenatomkraft.de/).
5 A slogan shaped in the 1970s by the US-American Minister for Agriculture Henry A. Wallace, describing the political agenda to cut subsidies so that only farms that were able to grow big enough to assert themselves on the market could survive.
6 E.g. Fresh City Farms (https://www.freshcityfarms.com/) or 100km Foods Inc. (http://www.100kmfoods.com/).
7 E.g. The Stop Community Food Centre (http://thestop.org/), FoodShare (http://foodshare.net/), Thorncliffe Park Women's Committee (http://www.tpwomenscomm.org/).

8  E.g. Black Creek Community Farm (http://www.blackcreekfarm.ca/), Toronto Community Gardens (http://tcgn.ca/).
9  In 2011, 27.4 per cent of the agricultural landholders in Canada were female (Government of Canada 2011). By tendency, this share is increasing. Compared internationally, these numbers are in the upper midfield (FAO 2017).

## References

100km Foods Inc. www.100kmfoods.com. [Accessed 17 June 2018].

Allen, P., 2010. Realising justice in local food systems. *Cambridge Journal of Regions, Economy and Society*, (3), 295–308.

Allen, P., FitzSimmons, M., Goodman, M.K. and Warner, K., 2003. Shifting plates in the agrifood landscape: the tectonics of alternative agrifood initiatives in California. *Journal of Rural Studies*, 19 (1), 61–75.

Allen, P. and Sachs, C., 2013. Women and food chains: the gendered politics of food. *In*: P.W. Forson and C. Counihan, eds., *Taking Food Public: Redefining Foodways in a Changing World*. Hoboken, NJ: Taylor and Francis.

Attfield, R., 1999. *The Ethics of the Global Environment*. Edinburgh: Edinburgh University Press.

Avakian, A.V. and Haber, B., 2005. Feminist food studies: a brief history. *In*: A.V. Avakian and B. Haber, eds, *From Betty Crocker to Feminist Food Studies: Critical Perspectives on Women and Food*. Amherst: University of Massachusetts Press, 1–29.

Baker, L., 2004. Tending cultural landscapes and food citizenship in Toronto's community gardens. *Geographical Review*, 94, 305–25.

Baker, L., Campsie, P. and Rabinowicz, K., 2010. *Menu 2020: Ten Good Food Ideas for Ontario*. [online] Toronto: Metcalf Foundation. Available from: https://metcalffoundation.com/downloads/Metcalf_Food_Solutions_Menu_2020.pdf [Accessed 17 June 2018].

Barad, K., 2007. *Meeting the Universe Halfway*. Durham, NC: Duke University Press.

Bauhardt, C., 2012. *Feministische Ökonomie, Ökofeminismus und Queer Ecologies: feministisch-materialistische Perspektiven auf gesellschaftliche Naturverhältnisse* [online]. Available from: www.fu-berlin.de/sites/gpo/pol_theorie/Zeitgenoessische_ansaetze/Bauhardtfemoeko nomie/Bauhardt.pdf [Accessed 17 June 2018].

Bauhardt, C., 2013. Rethinking gender and nature from a material(ist) perspective: feminist economics, queer ecologies and resource politics. *European Journal of Women's Studies*, 20 (4), 361–75.

Beagan, B., Chapman, G.W., D'Sylva, A. and Bassett, B.R., 2008. 'It's just easier for me to do it': rationalising the family division of foodwork. *Sociology* 42 (4), 653–71.

Benhabib, S., 1992. *Situating the Self: Gender, Community, and Postmodernism in Contemporary Ethics*. New York: Routledge.

Biesecker, A. and Hofmeister, S., 2010. Im Fokus: Das (Re)Produktive: Die Neubestimmung des Ökonomischen mithilfe der Kategorie (Re)Produktivität. *In*: C, Bauhardt and G. Çağlar, eds, *Gender and Economics: Feministische Kritik der politischen Ökonomie*. Wiesbaden: VS Verlag für Sozialwissenschaften, 51–81.

Biesecker, A. and Hofemeister, S., 2006. *Die Neuerfindung des Ökonomischen: Ein (Re) produktionstheoretischer Beitrag zu Sozialen Ökologie*. Munich: Oekom.

Biltekoff, C., 2013. *Eating Right in America: The Cultural Politics of Food and Health*. Durham, NC: Duke University Press.

Black Creek Food Justice Network 2015. *Fighting for Food Justice in the Black Creek Community: Report, Analyses and Steps Forward*. Toronto: Black Creek Food Justice Network.

Black Creek Community Farm. www.blackcreekfarm.ca [Accessed 17 June 2018].

Boler, M., 1999. *Feeling Power: Emotions and Education*. London: Routledge.

Code, L., 1995. *Rhetorical Spaces: Essays on (Gendered) Locations*. New York: Routledge.

Collins, P.H., 2000. *Black Feminist Thought: Knowledge, Consciousness and the Politics of Empowerment*. 2nd ed. New York: Routledge.

DuPuis, E.M. and Goodman, D., 2005. Should we go 'home' to eat? Toward a reflexive politics of localism. *Journal of Rural Studies*, 21, 359–71.

Elshtain, J.B., 1981. *Public Man, Private Woman: Women in Social and Political Thought*. Princeton, NJ: Princeton University Press.

Food and Agriculture Organization, 2017. *Gender and Land Rights Database* [online]. Available from: www.fao.org/gender-landrights-database/data-map/statistics/en/ [Accessed 17 June 2018].

Fraser, N., 1997. *Justice Interruptus: Critical Reflections on the 'Post-socialist' Condition*. New York: Routledge.

Fresh City Farms. [online] Available from: www.freshcityfarms.com [Accessed 17 June 2018].

Friedmann, F., 2007. Scaling up: bringing public institutions and food service corporations into the project for a local, sustainable food system in Ontario. *Agriculture and Human Values*, 24, 389–98.

Friedmann, F., 2011. Food sovereignty in the Golden Horseshoe region of Ontario. *In*: H. Wittman, A.A. Desmarais and N. Wiebe, eds., *Food Sovereignty in Canada: Creating Just and Sustainable Food Systems*. Halifax, NS: Fernwood Publishing, 169–89.

Gilligan, C., 1982. *In a Different Voice: Psychological Theory and Women's Development*. Cambridge, MA: Harvard University Press.

Goodman, David, DuPuis, E.M. and Goodman, M.K., 2001. *Alternative Food Networks: Knowledge, Practice, and Politics*. New York: Routledge.

Government of Canada, 2011. *Census of Agriculture: number of farm operators by sex, age and paid non-farm work, Canada and provinces every 5 years* [online]. Available from: www5.statcan.gc.ca/cansim/a26?lang=eng&retrLang=eng&id=0040017&pattern=0040200.0040242&tabMode=dataTable&srchLan=-1&p1=-1&p2=9 [Accessed 17 June 2018].

Guthman, J., 2008. 'If only they knew': colour blindness and universalism in California alternative food institutions. *Professional Geographer*, 60 (387–97).

Haraway, D.J., 1988. Situated knowledge: the science question in feminism and the privilege of partial perspective. *Feminist Studies*, 14 (3), 575–99.

Haraway, D.J., 2007. Speculative fabulations for technoculture's generations: taking care of unexpected country [online]. Available from: www.patriciapiccinini.net/writing/30/20/38 [Accessed 17 June 2018].

Haraway, D.J., 2016. *Staying with the Trouble: Making Kin in the Chthulucene*. Durham, NC: Duke University Press.

Harcourt, W., 2015. The slips and slides of trying to live feminist political ecology. *In*: W. Harcourt and I.L. Nelson, eds., *Practising Feminist Political Ecologies: Moving Beyond the 'Green Economy'*. London: Zed Books, 238–59.

Harcourt, W. and Nelson, I.L., 2015. Are we 'green' yet? And the violence of asking such a question. *In*: W. Harcourt and I.L. Nelson, eds., *Practising Feminist Political Ecologies: Moving Beyond the 'Green Economy'*. London: Zed Books, 1–26.

Hendrickson, M. and Heffernan, W.D., 2002. Opening spaces through re-localisation: locating potential resistance in the weaknesses of the global food system. *Sociologia Ruralis*, 42 (4), 241–53.

Hinrichs, C.C., 2003. The practice and politics of food system localisation. *Journal of Rural Studies*, 19, 33–45.

Johnston, J. and Cairns, K., 2015. *Food and Femininity*. New York: Bloomsbury Academic.

Klaus, E. and Drüeke, R., 2008. Öffentlichkeit und Privatheit: Frauenöffentlichkeiten und feministische Öffentlichkeiten. *In*: R. Becker, B. Kortendiek and B. Budrich, eds., *Handbuch Frauen- und Geschlechterforschung: Theorie, Methoden, Empirie*. 2nd ed. Wiesbaden: Springer, 237–44.

Kloppenburg, J., Hassanein, N. and Stevenson, G.W., 1996. Coming into the foodshed. *Agriculture and Human Values*, 13 (3), 33–42.

Lister, R., 1997. *Citizenship: Feminist Perspectives*. New York: New York University Press.

Lockie, S., 2009. Responsibility and agency within alternative food: assembling the 'citizen consumer'. *Agriculture and Human Values*, 26, 193–201.

MacGregor, S., 2006. *Beyond Mothering Earth: Ecological Citizenship and the Politics of Care*. Vancouver, BC: University of British Columbia Press.

Maniates, M., 2002. Individualisation: plant a tree, buy a bike, save the world? *In*: T. Princen, M. Maniates and K. Conca, eds., *Confronting Consumption*. Cambridge, MA: Massachusetts Institute of Technology Press, 43–66.

Mellor, M., 1997. Women, nature and the construction of 'economic man'. *Ecological Economics*, 2 (20), 129–140.

Mellor, M., 2001. Nature, gender and the body. *In*: A. Nebelungen, A. Poferl and I. Schultz, eds, *Geschlechterverhältnisse – Naturverhältnisse: Feministische Auseinandersetzungen und Perspektiven der Umweltsoziologie*. Opladen: Lekse and Budrich, 121–39.

Mellor, M., 2006. Ecofeminist political economy. *International Journal for Green Economics*, 1(1-2), 139–50.

Merchant, C., 1996. *Earthcare: Women and the Environment*. New York: Routledge.

Mouffe, C., 1992. Feminism, citizenship and radical democracy. *In*: J. Butler and J. Scott, eds, *Feminists Theorise the Political*. New York: Routledge, 369–84.

Mothers against Drunk Driving (madd). [online] Available from: www.madd.org [Accessed 17 June 2018].

Mütter gegen Atomkraft e.V. [online] Available from: www.muettergegenatomkraft.de [Accessed 17 June 2018].

Phillips, A., 1991. *Engendering Democracy*. Cambridge, UK: Polity Press.

Power, M., 2004. Social provisioning as a starting point for feminist economics. *Feminist Economics*, 10 (3), 3–19.

Rocheleau, D., 2015. A situated view of feminist political ecology from my network, roots and territories. *In*: W. Harcourt and I.L. Nelson, eds., *Practising Feminist Political Ecologies: Moving Beyond the 'Green Economy'*. London: Zed Books 33–66.

Rosenberg, H., 1995. 'From trash to treasure': housewife activists and the environmental justice movement. *In*: J. Schneider and R. Rapp, eds., *Articulating Hidden Histories: Exploring the Influence of Eric R. Wolf*. Berkeley, CA: University of California Press, 191–203.

Rowbotham, S., 1986. Feminism and democracy. *In*: R. Blaug, ed., *Democracy: A Reader*. New York: Columbia University Press, 321–4.

Ruddick, S., 1989. *Maternal Thinking: Towards a Politics of Peace*. Boston, MA: Beacon Press.

Sandilands, C., 1999. *The Good-Natured Feminist: Ecofeminism and the Quest for Democracy*. St. Paul, MN: University of Minnesota Press.

Squires, J., 1999. *Gender in Political Theory*. Cambridge, UK: Polity.

Starr, A., 2010. Local food: a social movement? *Cultural Studies, Critical Methodologies*, 10 (6), 479–90.

Steenbergen, B. van, 1997. Towards a global ecological citizen. *In*: B. van Steenbergen, ed., *The Condition of Citizenship*. London: Sage, 141–52.

Szasz, A., 2007. *Shopping Our Way to Safety*. St. Paul, MN: University of Minnesota Press.

The Stop Community Food Centre. [online] Available from: thestop.org [Accessed 17 June 2018].

Thorncliffe Park Women's Committee. [online] Available from: http://www.tpwomens comm.org/ [Accessed 17 June 2018].

Toronto Community Gardens. [online] Available from: tcgn.ca [Accessed 17 June 2018].

Tronto, J., 1993. *Moral Boundaries: A Political Argument for an Ethic of Care*. New York: Routledge.

Warde, A., 2005. Consumption and theories of practice. *Journal of Consumer Culture*, 5 (2), 131–53.

Young, I.M., 1990. *Justice and the Politics of Difference*. Princeton, NJ: Princeton University Press.

# 10 'The garden has improved my life'

## Agency and food sovereignty of women in urban agriculture in Nairobi[1]

*Joyce-Ann Syhre and Meike Brückner*

In this study we explore urban human nature linkages by analysing the reconnection to food through urban agriculture and its impacts on female agency and livelihood. Thereby, the interviews with female farmers in Nairobi broadened our perspectives on gender relations in society as well as helped us to reflect on existing societal perceptions of a good life and life quality.

During our stay in Nairobi we spent a longer time with one women called Fikira living in a peri-urban area of the city. Fikira's house is surrounded by a garden and located in a neighbourhood where livestock keeping seems to be part of urban life. The city centre is not far away, yet both atmosphere and air are already so different and clean. During our interview and participative observations, we got to better know Fikira. When she told us how she got here it became clear that her motivation to start urban agriculture is more unique than literature told us. Before she started farming she ran her own business and made good money. She was a businesswoman and a social worker at heart. Motherhood then became the point of turn. It made her settle down and change life priorities. Thus, starting a kitchen garden appeared logical next to taking care for her children but also to start something new for herself. Now the children are grown up but still enjoy spending time in the garden and Fikira continues to provide herself as well as people from her neighbourhood with fresh vegetables. She reflects that 'the garden has not improved my income, but it has improved my life.' Urban agriculture creates a healthier life as it not only improves the body and diet but also an urban environment. As an urban farmer, you care for it. 'Also, freedom. Nobody tells me what to do then.' She told us that in her office she had to follow a certain routine, day by day, which even bored her sometimes. Therefore, the kitchen garden created a space for herself to reflect on and create a good life.

The concept of a good life is discussed in a broader sense to question economic concepts of welfare and life quality in countries of the Global North. Thereby, living in a healthy environment also becomes part of the discussion but often in a minor way. The *buen vivir* concept in Latin American countries outlines very strong claims by including the right to a good life as well as the right of nature to be preserved in their legislation. However, how do other cultural and regional contexts define a good life? And how do female farmers in Nairobi define it while being embedded in gender structures? Harcourt (2017) therefore emphasises the urgent need for feminist perspectives in discussions on change as different gendered experiences create different visions for an alternative economy and ecology.

In our study we define urban agriculture as an alternative space and practice of cultivation and food provisioning. Since today's agri-food regime is highly industrialised and capitalised, it is necessary to envision alternative food systems in which actors who farm, field and cook meals regain a voice. In this sense we see food as a window of opportunity to politicise agrarian change without losing the connection to the everyday life of people, their practices and relationships to their land and nature, including family and the community they are living in. In the context of Nairobi, urban agriculture is mainly practised by women as a non-capitalist and non-industrialised practice which allows us to envision a localised and alternative form of food provisioning and consumption. Studying practices of urban agriculture in Nairobi gives us the opportunity to understand local livelihoods and women's attempts to act in a sustainable manner in their care for themselves, their family and community environment and in their care for nature and ecology.

According to Tronto (2013), taking care is an activity that includes 'everything that we do to maintain, continue, and repair our "world" so that we can live in it as well as possible' (p. 19). As a basic principle in ecofeminism, women (as mothers) who do the caring, nurturing and subsistence work also care for nature. In a liberal capitalist system, women's unpaid care labour and nature's work are both exploited. Thereby it can be asked whether caring as an activity is unpaid because it is deeply gendered and feminised. Consequently, we define care as an activity and ethic that is valuable to sustain life and should be practiced by all citizens. In our study, kitchen gardens create agency for female farmers. Here, women become more than mothers and care-givers; they become active citizens. As a result, care can be understood as a political ethic that is essential to both justice and democracy (MacGregor 2004).

Urban agriculture is not a new activity *per se*. As environments and local circumstances shift from rural to urban, women bring their skills and knowledge to the city. In our case study, agricultural practices are based on the long-term experience of farming in the 'rural home' and the value attached to it; therefore, farming within the city can be understood as an attempt to continue the rural agricultural traditions that the women grew up with. This continuity of agricultural practices shows sincere appreciation for and respect towards agricultural work grounded in the will of self-care and care for the environment. But this appreciation was not always reflected on a political level. Not until 2015 was urban agriculture officially declared a legal practice in Nairobi. Thus, it seems interesting to choose Nairobi as a study case seeing as legalisation recently changed possibilities for urban farmers.

In Nairobi, urban agriculture is often started and practised out of necessity to feed the family and to generate a small income. This is the narrative reproduced by many studies on urban agriculture in the Global South. But to engage in urban agriculture, as our empirical work shows, an active decision is needed by the women in order to act autonomously, to eat healthy and to individually define how their daily life should look. Therefore, we argue that it is necessary to widen the understanding of farming in the city from a strategy of survival towards a satisfying and defiant activity that allows for active decisions which contribute to a good life and personal and communal well-being.

By paying attention to crops that are planted and eaten, we aim to show that urban agriculture is a form of care on the field and on the plate. The women interviewed take the lead in deciding what is grown – in our case mostly African Indigenous Vegetables (AIVs) – and bring their knowledge of these vegetables to the garden and also to the plates of their families and friends. With this they value their traditional crops and food and further demonstrate profound respect for natural and socio-cultural resources alike. Finally, with this chapter we are interested in illustrating agricultural alternatives emerging through practiced urban agriculture in Nairobi that enable socio-ecological spaces of food sovereignty, biodiversity and agency.

Utilising a Feminist Political Ecology (FPE) and food sovereignty lens, this study aims at exploring how socio-cultural and ecological (power) relations alike play out in women's daily experiences in practising urban agriculture in Nairobi. We are interested in the knowledge, responsibility and practice in the gardens and in the wider family and community setting to examine how the women work constantly to ensure a sustainable livelihood and a good life. We use gender as an analytical and dynamic category to see how the women in our study, with their diverse backgrounds and experiences, reflect and reshape gender relations.

Nairobi is a contradictory city; one who visits it can easily capture contrasts in lifestyles, livelihoods, infrastructures and wealth demonstrating prevalent political, social and historical power relations. The city is a place of international organisations and players such as embassies, non-governmental organisations and UN agencies, but also a home and living environment to people and farmers. We understand urban agriculture as one entry point to discover the complexities of Nairobi's livelihoods and environments.

The text is structured as follows: we first briefly introduce the concepts of food sovereignty, emphasising the need of a rights-based approach that claims power for those producing and consuming food. Before coming to our empirical section, we provide an overview of the current situation of urban agriculture in Nairobi and highlight the importance of AIVs for food and meal sovereignty. Lastly, in the empirical section we share the stories of the female farmers Fikira, Chagina, Dalia and Hanya and look at their practices and actions, aiming to show how women use their gardens to (re)define their gender identity and seek agency and food sovereignty.

## The politics and cultures of food sovereignty

Harcourt (2015) proposes a creation of a global imaginary of environment that everyone can fight for. To create such a global imaginary, local and place-based initiatives such as their situated knowledge and their situated experiences are needed to get people involved in their everyday life. When talking about sustainable solutions in agrarian change, food sovereignty is such a local based initiative. As a framework, food sovereignty is rights-based by formulating the right of local communities to control their own agri-food system, including markets, ecological resources, food cultures and production modes. Additionally, the concept formulates agrarian reform with a shift towards agroecological practices, equal trade regimes, attention to gender relations and equity and the protection of intellectual and indigenous rights (Wittman 2011). In practice, this includes reforms of land-based social relations in favour of rural and urban dwellers in order to ensure: access to and control over land resources; democratic access; and control over productive resources in agriculture like seeds (Borras and Franco 2010, Rosset 2013). Seed sovereignty is hereby limited by, for example, seed patenting by transnational agribusinesses, which transformed seeds as natural base into a 'commodity and standardised product sold on global markets, dis-embedded from social relations and environmental conditions' (Bezner Kerr 2010: 138). In the context of urban agriculture in Nairobi, the topics of land availability and access to agricultural resources like seeds become especially politicised and gendered. Urban female farmers lack access to urban land because of gendered land tenure structures. Here, initiatives of collective female agency might open a window of opportunity to gain control over land.

Food sovereignty also highlights the socio-cultural values of farming and food, stressing the meaning of daily practices which can be both material and immaterial. The Nyéléni Declaration speaks about 'culturally appropriate food' when referring to the socio-cultural dimensions of food sovereignty. Although this seems to be an essential aspect of the concept, there is little understanding in literature of what this exactly means. Sampson and Wills (2013) state three reasons for that: 1) within the food sovereignty community there seems to be a consensus that culturally appropriate food is a key part of its demands; 2) material demands of food sovereignty (seeds, land or water) or claims to healthy or enough food seem to be more direct, concrete or substantial; and 3) the cultural appropriateness of food is often treated as an individual and subjective perception or preference. Based on that, we consider the approach of *meal sovereignty* as an important approach to broaden the discussion on food sovereignty from a producer and consumer perspective (Brückner and Brettin 2017). The approach seeks to dismantle the socio-cultural meaning of food by combining agricultural production and household consumption practices while stressing the entanglement with politics and economics at the same time. It specifically targets the so far under-conceptualised issue of consumer sovereignty and addresses the socio-cultural dimensions of consumption like the gendered division of labour in procuring and cooking, the symbolic meaning of food, indigenous knowledge, taste, preferences and perceptions while not losing sight of the more material resources (e.g. water, fuel) that shape meal sovereignty. Here we claim that only everyday caring activities such as producing food for a daily meal can make concrete configurations of power structures which influence meal culture and different understandings of culturally appropriate food. Urban farmers in our case study not only long for food sovereignty; they also long for meal sovereignty and thus a meal that is self-produced, healthy, safe and environmentally sound. Urban agriculture gives them the opportunity to make all of these tangible.

## Agency and the gendered urban landscape in Nairobi

In the gendered urban agricultural landscape of Nairobi, gender acts as a central structural category. Here gender is linked to the biological sex and understood as culturally defined male/female activities and responsibilities which shape the gender division of labour, gendered space and knowledge. Gender is relevant in urban agriculture in Nairobi as 64 per cent of urban farmers are female (Pasquini *et al.* 2009). They significantly constitute the food self-sufficiency of their families and contribute to family income both indirectly and directly, through saving money that would be normally spent on food and through selling surplus food (Foeken and Mwangi 1998, Mkwambisi *et al.* 2011). Thereby, women act in gendered spaces, mostly the private sphere where they plant vegetables in kitchen gardens. Generally, the separation of space functions as social and political power reproducing gender relations and distributing rights of control and access to resources (Thomas-Slayter *et al.* 1996), but in our study case gendered spaces can create agency and a good life for women in Nairobi.

To address the transformative power of women in debates on agrarian change or food sovereignty, gender and gender structures in urban agriculture need to be understood as a more dynamic process which makes the agency and creativity of women visible. Such a rebuilding approach of gender can be found in recent FPE works, especially in the work of Nightingale (2006). Here, gender is understood as process and dynamic over time and space as gender is generally unable to pre-exist its context. Related to the gender-environmental nexus this means that gender and environment are mutually constituted: the environment produces gendered struggles over responsibilities and resources, but gender also constitutes environmental change. Therefore, gender as a process needs to be analysed as both a fundamental cause and consequence of environmental issues and change (Nightingale 2006).

In the case of urban agriculture in Nairobi, everyday practices of female farmers portray internalisation of gender relations as well as resistance to them. Hereby, the concept of agency presents an approach in feminist analysis that balances these contrasts by questioning individualism or autonomy as not decoupled from collectivity and relationships to others (Abrams 1999). Mahoney and Yngvesson (1992) define agency as paradoxical in the relational context of creativity and conformity. To resist gender domination, subjects first have to recognise aspects of this domination: 'that subjects want to resist must be understood in the context not only of an acting [...] subject but of a reacting [...] subject as well' (Mahoney and Yngvesson 1992: 70). In our case, women start urban agriculture as reacting in line with the gendered division of labour and perceptions of gendered space and knowledge and build their resistance to societal constraints in relation to that. Through that, urban kitchen gardens can be regarded as places where women gain control over their lives. But being an agent also means to understand the gendered structures in social life where one is embedded in. Then, based on that pre-condition these structures can be transformed to some extent (Sewell 1992, Kabeer 1999).

An FPE agenda in research focusses on substantial issues like reclaiming access to and control over resources through collective action and social movements or changing individual gender identities through the practice of agency (Elmhirst 2011). Studies already identified such women's agency in diverse fields. Lee-Smith (1997) describes a wide set of female strategies to reclaim access to and control over land resources in Kenya ranging from collective land acquisition to change of religion as Kenyan women realised that in Islam female land inheritance is possible. Urban agriculture creates income independence for women and a greater position in intrahousehold conflicts (Slater 2001) and enables situations where women create strategies like keeping their money for their own use without the knowledge of male relatives (Maxwell 1994). Gabel (2005) demonstrates in her study on open-space cultivation in Zimbabwe that landless women cultivate land in a successful way through a complex informal land tenure system created by a web of women's support networks. Thereby, group dynamics are generally seen as way to collective redefinition of gender relations through collective action and agency in many works (Thomas-Slayter *et al.* 1996). In the context of community forestry, Agarwal (2001) identifies women's bargaining power on a state, community and household level as crucial for active participation of women. Hereby, the building of group strength and group identity is able to change social and individual female perceptions of women's work and contribution. In a study conducted in Latin America, Howard (2006) emphasises that kitchen gardens not only produce material benefits for women but also contribute to a positive social status and a respectable identity. Through their gardens, women challenge men's economic dominance which creates a greater say on the household level for them as authorised garden managers. As garden managers, female farmers also mainly contribute to agrobiodiversity as seed keepers and selectors as well as knowledge holders of plant diversity (Howard 2003). Thereby, women predominate seed use and management through the gendered division of labour which also creates gendered differences in seed selection criteria. Women's selections are more diverse and adapted to meal cultures, nutritious quality and storage requirements. Women also rather focus on traditional crops as they rather supply local markets. Consequently, they contribute to food security and sovereignty as their contribution as food managers is connected to a positive effect on the household's and children's nutrition (Sachs 2013).

## African Indigenous Vegetables as gendered and place-based cultivation practice

As FPE addresses the uneven power relations in access and control over natural resources in relations to sustainable livelihoods, the issue of agrobiodiversity is a crucial topic in theoretical and empirical debates. A number of researchers (e.g. Rocheleau 1995, Bezner Kerr 2014, Bhattarai *et al.* 2015) focus on the utilisation and conservation of local agrobiodiversity in order to understand the complex meanings for daily lived realities. Bezner Kerr (2014), for example, illustrates with a case study of the 'forgotten crops' sorghum and finger millet in Northern Malawi how gendered practices and knowledge are shifting with a change in policies towards maize production and how this affects agrobiodiversity and agricultural practices.

Agrobiodiversity is not only important for the ecosystem, it also is of socio-cultural importance. Further, the medicinal value of indigenous crops is vital as well as its non-material, spiritual value to the local community. To illustrate the importance of agrobiodiversity from an FPE perspective the work refers to AIVs, local crops produced and consumed in Kenya and across the African continent. AIVs are central in this research as they are locally adapted to the agroecological conditions and highly relevant in local production systems. Moreover, they are regularly consumed and highly appreciated as an essential part of the local meal cultures. Although the process of value chain modernisa-tion and upgrading is slowly underway, AIVs are so far barely commercialised and have not yet been exported. Therefore, we argue, that the production and consumption of AIVs constitutes an alternative for producers and consumers to move beyond the global dominance of cash crops or a wider food regime that is increasingly globalised and embedded in global power structures. As a result, AIVs are also central for the concept of food sovereignty as indigenous vegetables are a way to re-localise everyday agri-food practices. The vegetables are culturally appropriate and have the potential to contribute to autonomy and sovereignty of urban farmers and consumers.

How AIVs are grown and utilised is a result of continuous transmission of local knowledge in production and consumption, mainly passed on by women. Thereby, the history of AIVs is multifaceted and embedded in the colonial past of Kenya: in pre-colonial times, AIVs were a commonly grown crop and served as a meal accompanied by Ugali (a side dish made of maize flour). The colonial settlers discarded the indigenous leafy vegetables and introduced Western vegetables which had a direct effect on indigenous production and meal practices. Nowadays, AIVs are back in favour as their nutritional and medicinal characteristics are highlighted by research programs as well as local initiatives. Relating to our research field of urban agriculture, AIVs are one potential crop which are more competitive when grown in urban areas as compared to rural ones (de Neergaard *et al.* 2009). Examples of typical AIVs cultivated in Nairobi are Kunde, Terere, Managu, Sageti, Kanzira and Mitoo (see Table 10.1). The cultivation of AIVs in urban agriculture and especially

*Table 10.1* Commonly found AIVs in urban agriculture in Nairobi

| Common local name | Common English name |
| --- | --- |
| Managu | (Black) African Nightshade |
| Terere | Amaranth |
| Sageti | Spiderplant |
| Kunde | Cowpea |
| Kanzira | Ethiopian kale |
| Mitoo | – |

home gardens is mostly done by women who do subsistence farming for household consumption but who also increasingly combine this with selling of surpluses to create income and new possibilities for female action.

## Nairobi's policy and urban planning in urban agriculture

Even though farming practices are visible everywhere in Nairobi, for a long time there have been no urban planning policies specifically targeting urban agriculture as a means to secure food production and consumption within the city (Kawai 2003). The city government did not recognise the contribution of urban agriculture (Lee-Smith and Memon 1994) to food access and availability, nutritional and food security, and, ultimately, food sovereignty. A study by Mwangi (1995) conducted in the 1990s confirms that urban agriculture was prohibited in Nairobi: 'crop farming is not allowed within the city boundaries because crops encourage breeding of mosquitoes while tall crops such as maize act as hiding places for thugs' (p. 9). Freeman's book on the urban informal economy in Nairobi argues that also the academic discussion at that time ignored the central role of urban agriculture and specifically the important role of women in farming within the urban area (Freeman 1991). The colonial past of the city and the zoning regulations introduced during the British colonial period caused a racial segregation in the city (Charton-Bigot and Rodriguez-Torres 2006) and an allocation of different land uses in specific areas. Urban agriculture has been recognised as an activity practiced outside and not inside city borders, and therefore agricultural or livestock activities were forbidden in urban zones.

In the meantime, progress has been made and several African policies legalised urban agriculture in the last years (Simiyu 2012). Positive opportunities for example in the fields of waste recycling, air purification and decontamination of polluted waters and soils in cities have been recognised.[2] These positive effects might have contributed to increasing acceptance of urban agriculture through municipalities and the invention of urban agriculture policies during the last years (Redwood 2009). Finally, since 2015 a wider institutional framework has been in place and the Urban Agricultural Promotion and Regulation Act as a regulatory framework was accepted (Nairobi City County 2015, Lee-Smith and Lamba 2016). According to the Ministry of Agriculture, this was mostly promoted by urban farmers and organisations like the Mazingira Institute working on urban agriculture issues emphasising the importance of urban cultivation for urban food security especially for the poor and marginalised.

However, how do farmers benefit from these new regulations while the city of Nairobi is still growing and land becomes less available? Foeken and Mwangi (1998) predict unfavourable conditions for urban agriculture in Nairobi, saying that 'there is not a bright future for agricultural activities in the city' (p. 318) as open spaces become scarce. A specific problem that was clearly recognised during our empirical study is that many programs on urban agriculture (e.g. trainings or capacity building workshops) target collective initiatives rather than individuals. This is a serious problem for women who often practice urban agriculture individually, for example in kitchen gardens. Our observations are in line with a prediction Rakodi (1985) made more than 30 years ago: those who actually need the support may not profit from a formalisation of urban agriculture. Urban farmers organised in networks usually have a safety net in terms of financial reserves. Moreover, land, work and knowledge on farming can be shared. The results of our study further indicated that farmers welcome the Regulation Act and the new attention to farming in the city. However, they feel that so far the positive impact on their livelihood brought by the new policies is limited.

Hovorka's (2006) paper on practical and strategic gender needs in urban agriculture raises important questions concerning policies from a feminist perspective. Her paper focuses on the critique that urban agriculture may burden women with even more work (Rakodi 1985, Hovorka 2006) and further points out that 'it relieves state policymakers and planners of the responsibility of improving people's quality of life because individuals are taking responsibility for it into their own hands' (Hovorka 2006). On these grounds, Hovorka refers to urban agriculture as 'a double-edged sword for women' (p. 52) and therefore emphasises the need for an emancipatory agenda by focusing on strategic gender needs in urban policy. According to her, addressing strategic gender needs in policy could mean the equal involvement of women in planning, decision-making and control processes related to policies and projects on urban agriculture. In search for concrete studies referring to policies or planning regarding gender and urban agriculture, we noted a huge gap on planning approaches addressing gendered constraints and agency as key issues, so we can only refer to Hovorka's claim for practical and strategic gender needs. The women interviewed in her case study were supported through government grants as part of a Financial Assistance Policy giving them financial capital as a basic requirement. It must be noted that the grant addressed middle-income farmers and supported direct investments in infrastructure, land or labour, but did not allow for sustainable upkeep as the daily costs of farming were not covered. Rakodi (1985) also highlights the value of resource provision such as land: 'Urban agriculture is [...] essentially a survival strategy, and so it is unlikely that cultivators could afford to buy or lease' (499). However, to create opportunities of action for women and to use the emancipatory potential of urban agriculture, other criteria need to be fulfilled such as access to information, training and education. These examples show on the one hand that much needs to be done at the policy level and on the other that a wider assessment of the Regulation Act in Nairobi is needed concerning its contribution to the daily life of farmers and specifically female farmers at the local level.

## Methodological disclosure

Our research builds on several in-depth interviews with female urban farmers in Nairobi which were conducted during a research stay in 2017. Furthermore, several experts working in urban planning and county ministries as well as non-governmental organisations working on the issue of urban agriculture in Nairobi were interviewed to gather background information related to the political framework in the local context. Through in-depth interviews with female farmers, we try to understand women's everyday practices in their home gardens and the transformative potential related to gender relations based on that. By analysing the motivation to start urban agriculture, we discover strategic decision-making situations of female farmers and we also identify creativity in coping with barriers in the gendered landscape of urban agriculture. We aim to make female agency in shaping sustainable livelihoods visible through that. Furthermore, women's gardening practices are analysed according to their sustainability and the concept of food sovereignty by focussing on drivers for the cultivation of AIVs and the degree of self-sufficiency. Finally, these findings should help to define an emancipatory agenda in urban planning policy which focusses on strategic gender needs and sustainable alternatives in urban agriculture. For that we share narratives of four women living in Nairobi who gave us their time and openness. For anonymity, the names have been changed. All women have a rather rural and sometimes even farming background and migrated to Nairobi. Some of them worked in formal employment before starting urban agriculture. Their educational backgrounds are quite diverse and range from basic education to higher university degrees. The broad sample hereby enabled a diverse picture of individual practices in urban agriculture.

As white women from Europe doing research in Nairobi we considered ourselves as outsiders to the field. Therefore, we took into consideration our socio-cultural background as being different to the Kenyan context. To enable mutual exchange and create understanding on both sides, the approach of participatory research was conducted. Hereby, we visited some female farmers several times to get to know each other more deeply. Furthermore, our active participation in the garden enabled teamwork and appreciation for each other to dissolve perceived cultural differences and hierarchical relations associated with the research. Thus, we define our role as researchers as people who gather information and knowledge to act as mediators for creating understanding about certain social phenomena but also as people who get involved practically and personally. Through that, we think it is possible to trigger change and support female farmers by embedding their life experiences and knowledge in a broader FPE debate on urban planning policy and agrarian change.

## Between conformity and creativity: Gender relations in urban agriculture in Nairobi

During the visits of the female farmers and their kitchen gardens in Nairobi, we rarely met male relatives. As most of the interviews took place in the morning, most men were working in town or even farther away, while the women were at home to take care of the children or grandchildren. Therefore, the interviews mostly took place in a private space. The youngest children, not attending school yet, played around or took part in the interview. This picture illustrates the gendered division of labour found in many Kenyan families.

However, next to their role as mothers, the women also had something else in common. All of them are proud owners of a kitchen garden next to their houses or on collective gardening plots. These gardens play a central role in their lives as they offer personal opportunities for self-perception and self-realisation. Some of them earn income from the selling of vegetables and develop marketing structures in their neighbourhood to enable both selling vegetables and being at home as mothers. In other cases, the garden created a web of network activities for them to get training, support each other and make business together. Thus, we want to ask in what way do women use these gardens to (re)define their gender identity and circumstances under gendered constraints and to seek agency and (collective) action?

### Motivation to start urban agriculture

Fikira (meaning 'with deep thoughts' in Swahili) lives together with her husband in a house in the western part of Nairobi with a garden in the backyard. Her husband keeps pigs in a stable and her grown-up son is currently building another stable to keep animals for his own business. The whole family somehow seems to be involved in urban agriculture. Nevertheless, the garden is under the authority of Fikira. Here, she makes the decisions and manages the money. Already retired, Fikira told us about her home garden and the meaning of urban vegetable cultivation in her life. Before she came to this place 20 years ago, she was a rebellious woman active in the women's liberalisation movement. As a social worker she had the opportunity to spend some time in the US as well as in England for projects and working in social institutions, a possibility which is not common for most Kenyans. Afterwards she started a printing company in Nairobi and earned good money. When she met her husband, she was surprised about his eagerness to marry her as she was 'so rebellious at this time.' Then, she reflects that her marriage and especially her motherhood changed her life completely. In Kenya, women traditionally move to the husband's place after marriage to have children and focus on the family. This was also the time when she quit her job to start her home garden and produce food for the family:

> When I arrived here I started to have children and I didn't want to go and leave the children. So here is a piece of land and instead of going to work in town, look for food here, for the children.

It was her initial motivation and obvious reaction to start urban agriculture in that phase of life. As her focus was on feeding the kids, she cultivated maize, beans and potatoes at the beginning to feed her children well and to produce a solid basis of food crops. Now, she focusses on the production of traditional vegetables like most of the urban female farmers in Nairobi. Also, the other women being interviewed stated that their motherhood was a central reason for starting the garden. The garden provides them with fresh and healthy vegetables which are hard to find at local markets. As the quality of food is very important in order to provide a balanced diet for the women and their families, the cultivation of vegetables, especially traditional ones, makes them food sovereigns and active citizens in the urban agri-food system. In some cases, the women's initiative to start the home garden took place against the will of the family or their husbands. Here, especially the socio-cultural perceptions of women as not being farmers and the gendered division of labour were actively redefined and dismantled by women becoming urban farmers.

Another motivation being stated by female farmers was being able to pay education fees for their children through the gardens' income. As the home garden saves money indirectly through less food expenditures or directly through the selling of harvest surpluses, it is a great contribution to the family's income situation. Some women stated that their education was already paid through a home garden cultivated by their mothers. Fikira and the other women also generally reflected on gender relations in Kenya being the reason for unemployment among young women taking care of the children and struggling for food. Fikira described it as 'a kind of education' of Kenyan women. Behaving in another way would feel 'very awkward'. She does not 'see it with [her] father, [she doesn't] see it with [her] grandfather.' Although Fikira did not directly complain about that situation, she reflected on her position as being embedded in traditional social and cultural gender norms. During the interview, her husband joined us first as an observer but later also as an active dialogue partner in the interview. Fikira directly invited him to state his opinion after she stated hers. We perceived their way of interacting with each other as respectful and mutually appreciative. They both agreed on the aspect that working together, discussing together and understanding each other in a relationship is the best way to create a healthy and respectful relationship and atmosphere at home. He appreciates her activities in the garden and her knowledge about cultivation and marketing which is unfamiliar to him. Nevertheless, Fikira sometimes has discussions with him to receive further advice. Related to decision-making she feels free to make own decisions in her garden and her life as long as it does not hamper his activities. Also, in urban gardening they closely work together as his pigs create manure for her vegetables to grow. We visited Fikira several times and worked together with her in the garden. She is a very reflective and experienced woman who is interested in world politics and actively engages in community work in her neighbourhood to share her experiences. In her relationship to her husband she likes to present herself as a *Kenyan woman* who takes care of the children and the household: 'It's a kind of education.' However, through the garden she created herself a space where she can work freely and independently from everyone. This, she stated, is what really motivates her.

## Creating sustainable livelihoods and a good life

Chagina (meaning 'the brave one' in Swahili) grew up in a rural village near Nairobi where her mother used to farm to finance her and her sibling's education. Through the selling of maize, potatoes and cabbages her mother managed to sustain all their needs and enable them to go to the city to work in formal employment. So, Chagina moved to Nairobi to start working in a non-governmental organisation dealing with HIV. Her contract was always limited and short-term, her payment was small and sometimes even delayed. Based on that, Chagina could not sustain her needs, so she quit her job to start urban agriculture. For her farming is business and she considers herself a businesswoman. Through her income from farming, she can finance the education of her two daughters and even save money at the end of the month. Especially the growing of AIVs sustains a stable and good income for her. She describes her husband's income as 'rare' and emphasises that she works for her children:

> Me, I do work for my kids. I feel very bad when [he/she] is asking me, Mom can you buy these [...] but I can't buy anything. [...] And [now] when they ask me for something I will tell them I will buy it for you tomorrow. [...] You don't care for Papa, I will buy for you.

Men often do not see the great impact of home gardens on sustaining a family's needs. Chagina explained that it first became visible for her husband when she was sick and could not tend the garden for a week. She asked her husband for money to buy food and finance the children. He was surprised how much money she actually requires to sustain the family life; money which solely was generated from the garden before. Through that, he found his passion for supporting her in the garden. According to her mother, Chagina's decision to quit her job was risky and stupid as working in an office is connected to social prestige and success. She realised for herself that this is not true and the option of urban farming creates a better livelihood for her and her family. She describes her farm as a 'stream which never dries' as people always need to eat vegetables. According to her, having a stream or a source of stable income is important for a good life as well as to maintain her livelihood. Planting vegetables is sustainable as there is always something for you to eat although there might be no customers around. By sustaining basic needs like good nutrition, one can start to focus on enhancing livelihood opportunities for the future; expanding farming is often stated as a vision: 'If I can get a big farm I would feel very good. I could even employ myself there. I do my work there.' Also, in times of retirement urban agriculture can sustain one's livelihood. This is only possible when establishing an efficient and stable marketing network in the neighbourhood. We observed that female farmers in Nairobi successfully set up an informal marketing structure for home-grown vegetables through direct contact with their customers. These structures act independently from commercial market structures.

However, Chagina also stated that her garden is a place where she can relax and forget stress: 'I feel so good when I am here. Even if I [come] with a lot of stress, [it] will disappear.' This is similar to other narratives found in the case study, such as Fikira's which was mentioned earlier. A reflection on healthiness and happiness can be also found in another statement given by a female farmer:

> Wake up in the morning, go to the shamba³. [...] The body feels ok. The place where I was working before, I was so busy there, no resting. [...] Although I don't earn that salary I used to get, I feel happy and I thank God.

We conclude that women's home gardens generally seem to facilitate good life. A good life is connected to different aspects like health, a happy family and money to feed yourself and your family as well as being able to pay for education and be without worries. Home gardens play a major role in creating such a life since a healthy environment also belongs to a good life and sustainable livelihood: 'The minute you see green you are sure that you have fresh air around you.'

### *Choice of agricultural practices and crops*

The perception of human–nature relations among female farmers in Nairobi is quite diverse. Nature is seen as the environment we live in. Human beings must preserve their environment as we cannot survive without it. As a farmer, you work together with nature which means that you can use nature without destroying it. Farming is a space where human–nature relations are lived as well as challenged, as humans can destroy the urban environment by their practices.

Dalia (meaning 'gentle' in Swahili) lives near the city centre in the eastern part of Nairobi. The landscape here is much drier and therefore impedes the possibility of urban agriculture compared to the western parts of Nairobi. Together with her husband she lives in a small house near a main road. Her garden is beautiful although it was dry season when we visited her. The garden is located in an open space between neighbouring houses on open-space land. She told us that they are lucky because they have such a large unused area next door. They also keep different livestock like goats, indigenous chickens and rabbits. Before they moved here and created the home garden, the place was used for dumping and was unsuitable for children. Now several neighbours have joined them with small gardens to make the place productive and beautiful. Dalia worked as a typist before she married her husband and settled. The three children have already grown up and graduated from university. Coming from a rather modest background, the family home garden financed the educational career of her children. As seen in many cases, the husband is more responsible for the livestock while Dalia takes care of the garden, but they also divide most of the tasks when there is much to do. Here, she especially grows AIVs as well as a diversity of medical herbs and fruits. Dalia calls her husband by his last name, a gesture of respect according to her. In the garden it is also mostly him who makes decisions. This was not the case for other female farmers cultivating their gardens alone and not as a family farm.

The principle of their family garden is quite unique as they do not use any chemicals or even commercial seeds. Pesticides and fertilisers are not good for health, as the doctor advised to eat more organic food, she told us. For making the soil fertile naturally, they use manure from their livestock as well as compost. Composting is not performed by many urban farmers in Nairobi. They use either rabbit urine or other natural substances like ash against pests and harmful insects. Instead of buying seeds from agribusinesses like most of the urban farmers do, Dalia produces her own seeds by saving and sharing them with others. So, she is not only food sovereign and self-reliant through the food she produces but also in terms of agricultural inputs as she does not rely on commercial seeds and agribusiness products. Thereby, especially the production of AIVs as well as the agrobiodiversity in their home garden influences food sovereignty in a positive way.

In the beginning they started growing vegetables only for self-consumption. This was the case for all female farmers visited. Self-consumption is positively related to the use of natural ways for pest control and the use of manure as they only want to eat what is healthy and contains less artificial chemicals. Also, motherhood can be identified as an essential aspect for the focus on self-sufficiency as well as for the cultivation of indigenous vegetables since these are part of their meal culture, more nutritious and better for the children's diet. Therefore, women would also rather have the knowledge about how to grow, prepare and cook AIVs. The women also stated that it is mostly women who grow AIVs as they know their special value. It is common to eat mixtures of different AIVs; for the preparation, everyone seems to have their own secret recipe. Home gardens also show a greater agrobiodiversity as the small space is used to grow as many different vegetables as possible for making the household food self-sufficient, self-reliant and thus meal sovereign. As Dalia solely depends on rainwater, her home garden cannot sustain the family's food needs all year round. However, they have livestock to create income and a sustainable livelihood in dry times.

### Group farming as solution to denied access and control

Hanya (meaning 'hope' in Swahili) has a small urban farm together with other women near the Kibera Slum in the centre of Nairobi. Their women's group formed after post-election fights as a way to create peace among different ethnic groups and to grow vegetables for building up a safety net for all members. The name of the group, Tekakuliki, is symbolically formed out of the first letters of every ethnic group represented in the group. Hanya as well as the other group members come from rather poor backgrounds. She was working as a street vendor in Nairobi selling vegetables to other farmers. Now she grows vegetables on her own, has a small farm outside of Nairobi where she cultivates tea and other crops for sale, and owns three houses in Kibera for renting. This all was possible though a microcredit scheme given to her women's group in the past. Thereby, the urban group garden formed the base as it created a space to come together and give structure to the group. During the interview we had the chance to meet all group members while a regular meeting was taking place. As chairwoman, Hanya takes great responsibility and has to speak to all the members. They have known each other for a long time and successfully managed to collectively save money and receive loans which enabled several small businesses. Hanya appreciates the group work as the other members gave her new inspirations and advice in difficult times: 'to join together will make you go higher and higher. When you are alone you can't make it the way you make it together because you can't reinforce yourself.' Generally, in Kenya, it is quite common among women to form so-called chamas, women's groups to collectively save money. Women often join the chamas secretly as male relatives do not like it as one female farmer told us. The principle of chamas is as follows: all women individually save an agreed amount of money every month which will be collected by the chama. Then, every month one woman of the group receives the whole value. Through that, large amounts of money become available to women in a short time apart from formal banking institutions which often deny access to financial means to women. Chamas emerged during post-colonial times as part of a new era of women's movements. The pooling of money was used to buy things like land, water tanks, home equipment and even livestock to build a secure foundation initiated by collective action (Robertson 1996). Hanya told us that no men are allowed in her group as they are less cooperative. During the interview Hanya did not talk much about her personal life as she was eager to tell about the group's success and their idea behind it, but she mentioned that she has a family which she supports financially.

Another female farmer who is part of a large group farming on open spaces in the northeast part of Nairobi mentioned that as a group they easily have access to agricultural training and support offered by the respective county. Also, as in Hanya's case, the women's group received a greenhouse and a water tank donated by the Ministry of Water and Irrigation. In contrast to Hanya's women's group, farming on open spaces was performed by a mixed group of men and women. Thereby, men make up the majority of the group. Following the question of why there are not more women involved she said that urban farming is nothing for women as

> you are the woman of the house [...]. Now you find that this is affecting us, you don't want to come out of the house, you want to maintain who you are. You don't want to be burned by the sun, you want to remain.

She also told us that there was a lot of gossip when she joined the group as she was alone as a woman. Besides, the group mainly focusses on the marketing of vegetables rather than on self-consumption. As most of the men are young and single their strategic objections seem to be different. They also do not focus on food sovereignty and self-reliance of food like we saw it with the women. So, who is the agent here?

## Discussion: Urban agriculture as a practice of care, agency and sovereignty

In Kenya rural–urban migration created a situation in which new ways of urban food and agricultural practices and supply structures can prosper. Thereby, we show in our empirical case study that urban agriculture is not only a strategy to alleviate urban food insecurity and poverty, but also a way to create female agency and a good life, as well as to shape sustainable urban livelihoods. In our research we aimed to make this visible by finding out what motivates women in Nairobi to start urban agriculture, how this activity changes their lives and how they creatively overcome gendered barriers in the urban landscape. First, we found out that the main motivation to start urban agriculture is motherhood, independent from the socio-economic background of the women. In Kenya, women often quit their formal employment when they marry and become mothers to dedicate themselves to care work in the family. This is also the time when women start to create small home gardens to produce fresh and healthy vegetables to feed their children. Here, care and motherhood are not seen as a constraint for female agency, but as an opportunity and space to create personal freedom and self-realisation through their gardens. As indicated in the quote 'nobody tells me what to do,' women can make decisions freely and are not dependent on others. As the kitchen gardens are situated in gendered spaces and knowledge, female farmers have the decision-making power here and the possibility to practice agency. This also becomes clear as women choose urban agriculture as a perspective which contributes to their livelihood and a good life. They realised that formal employment in the city cannot always sustain all family needs while urban agriculture is considered as a 'stream of life which never dries.' With their gardens they have a long-term perspective and the possibility to shape a healthier and freer life for themselves knowing there is always something to eat for the family.

Secondly, AIVs play a central role in creating sustainable livelihood opportunities for women as they adapt well to urban cultivation and play a central role in Kenyan meal cultures. Women like to cultivate AIVs as they have the knowledge of their richness in nutrients and positive health effects; they also know how to prepare AIVs. As producers and consumers of AIVs, they also contribute to agrobiodiversity and a re-localisation of agri-food practices in urban agriculture, as well as to food and meal sovereignty through a high degree of self-sufficiency in home gardens. The aim to cultivate for self-consumption increases the awareness about ecological impact and resource protection in urban agriculture. Chemical pesticides and fertilisers are not used as the female farmers understand the impacts of these substances on their and their children's bodies. Here, motherhood again plays a central role for a sustainable way of urban agriculture where natural methods are preferred to protect the body and the urban environment. Thereby the agri-food system created through female farmers in Nairobi acts as an alternative to commercial systems focussing on cash crops and less food self-sufficiency. Consequently, female farmers play an active role in shaping socio-ecological alternatives and contributing to agrarian change in line with the concept of food sovereignty.

Thirdly, we met inspiring women who are engaged in group farming and women's groups to overcome gendered constraints in the urban landscape. Thereby, the groups constitute the space for collective agency as women get not only inspiration and strength from other women, but also the possibility to reflect on gender relations and practices. According to Abrams (1999), collectivity enables women to see themselves differently and to create competing images of women's lives. Hanya and the other group members created different fields of activity for themselves which would not be thinkable before. They managed to claim access to and control over resources collectively by strictly rejecting any male membership in their group.

However, what does this mean for the policy on urban agriculture? In what way does the Urban Agriculture Regulation Act in Nairobi take into consideration female farmers and their strategic needs? We think that it is important to place these individual and place-based narratives into a broader context of urban policy and planning. Therefore, we pledge to actively take up collective and individual agency of female urban farmers in Nairobi since women are agents of change for sustainability and food sovereignty in urban agriculture. Those women, migrating from the rural to the urban, brought their agricultural knowledge and skills to the city and adapted their practices according to the new landscape. They opened green spaces within the city and thus contribute to the urban ecology and further live their own perception of a good life which means being close to nature and caring for it. To support this potential, urban policy and policymakers need to address strategic gender needs by actively involving women in planning, decision-making and control processes, focusing on equal access to information, training and education in a collective and individual context. Now, official training and ministry support is only offered to farming groups as the impact seems to be higher here. As most of the urban agricultural activities take place on an individual level and on small plots, official support must also focus on that by directly addressing individual female farmers. It is also a strategic step to support food security in Nairobi as increasing land pressure in the future will strengthen the relevance of home gardens and individual farmers in creating food self-sufficiency in a growing city. Programs focussing on the commercialisation of urban vegetable production, especially of AIVs, exclude rather than include female farmers as most of them use informal marketing structures in the neighbourhood. Here it is important to consider all forms of vegetable marketing in urban agriculture to support already successful structures of female famers without creating new (gendered) competition. We pledge for an emancipatory policy agenda which does not dictate to female urban farmers 'what to do' but instead appreciates female agency and their transformative potential for food sovereignty created by home gardens driven by motherhood and women's willingness to live independently.

## Notes

1 This research has been carried out within the HORTINLEA Subproject 'Gender Order: Embedding Gender in Horticultural Value Chains to Close or Reduce the Productivity Gap' and 'Meal Cultures in Market Trends and Consumption Habits.' The authors thank the project for providing contacts, information and exchange of experiences.
2 See Mougeot 2005, Cole *et al.* 2008.
3 Swahili, meaning garden or small cultivated ground.

## References

Abrams, K., 1999. From autonomy to agency: feminist perspectives on self-direction. *William and Mary Law Review*, 40 (3), 805–46.

Agarwal, B., 2001. Participatory exclusions, community forestry, and gender: an analysis for South Asia and a conceptual framework. *World Development*, 29 (10), 1623–48.

Bezner Kerr, R., 2010. Unearthing the culture and material struggles over seed in Malawi. In: H. Witte, A. Desmarais and N. Wiebe, eds., *Food Sovereignty: Reconnecting Food, Nature and Community*. Halifax, NS: Fernwood, 134–51.

Bezner Kerr, R., 2014. Lost and found crops: Agrobiodiversity, indigenous knowledge, and a feminist political ecology of sorghum and finger millet in Northern Malawi. *Annals of the Association of American Geographers* [online], 104 (3), 577–93. Available from: https://doi.org/10.1080/00045608.2014.892346 [Accessed 15 June 2018].

Bhattarai, B., Beilin, R. and Ford, R., 2015. Gender, agrobiodiversity, and climate change: a study of adaptation practices in the Nepal Himalayas. *World Development* [online], 70, 122–32. Available from: https://doi.org/10.1016/j.worlddev.2015.01.003 [Accessed 15 June 2018].

Borras, S.M. and Franco, J.C., 2010. Food sovereignty and redistributive land politics. In: H. Witte, A. Desmarais and N. Wiebe, eds., *Food Sovereignty: Reconnecting Food, Nature and Community*. Halifax, NS: Fernwood, 106–19.

Brückner, M. and Brettin, S., 2017. Meal sovereignty: empirical insights on an innovative perspective. In: *The Future of Food and Challenges for Agriculture in the 21st Century: Debates about Who, How and with What Social, Economic and Ecological Implications We Will Feed the World*, 24–26 April 2017, Victoria-Gasteiz, Spain.

Charton-Bigot, H. and Rodriguez-Torres, D., eds., 2006. *Nairobi Today: The Paradox of a Fragmented City*. Nairobi: French Institute for Research in Africa.

Cole, D., Lee-Smith, D. and Nasinyama, G., eds., 2008. *Healthy City Harvests: Generating Evidence to Guide Policy on Urban Agriculture*. Lima: International Potato Centre/Urban Harvest and Kampala: Makerere University Press.

De Neergaard, A., Drescher, A.W. and Kouamé, C., 2009. Urban and peri-urban agriculture in African cities. In: C.M. Shackleton, M.W. Pasquini and A.W. Drescher, eds., *African Indigenous Vegetables in Urban Agriculture*. 1st ed. London: Earthscan, 35–64.

Elmhirst, R., 2011. Introducing new feminist political ecologies. *Geoforum* [online], 42 (2), 129–32. Available from: https://doi.org/10.1016/j.geoforum.2011.01.006 [Accessed 15 June 2018].

Foeken, D. and Mwangi, A.M., 1998. *Framing in the City of Nairobi*. ASC Working Paper 30. Leiden, the Netherlands: African Studies Centre Leiden.

Freeman, D.B., 1991. *City of Farmers: Informal Urban Agriculture in the Open Spaces of Nairobi, Kenya* [online]. Montreal: McGill-Queen's University Press. Available from: http://www.jstor.org/stable/j.ctt8169k [Accessed 11 July 2018].

Gabel, S., 2005. Exploring the gender dimensions of urban open-space cultivation in Harare, Zimbabwe. *In*: L.J.A. Mougeot, ed., *Agropolis: The Social, Political and Environmental Dimensions of Urban Agriculture*. London: Earthscan and Ottawa: International Development Research Centre, 107–36.

Harcourt, W., 2015. The slips and slides of trying to live feminist political ecology. *In*: W. Harcourt and I.L. Nelson, eds., *Practising Feminist Political Ecologies: Moving Beyond the 'Green Economy'*. London: Zed Books, 238–59.

Harcourt, W., 2017. Gender and sustainable livelihoods: Linking gendered experiences of environment, community and self. *Agriculture and Human Values* [online], 34 (4), 1007–19. Available from: https://doi.org/10.1007/s10460-016-9757-5 [Accessed 11 July 2018].

Hovorka, A.J., 2006. Urban agriculture: Addressing practical and strategic gender needs. *Development in Practice* [online], 16 (1), 51–61. Available from: https://doi.org/10.1080/09614520500450826 [Accessed 11 July 2018].

Howard, P.L., 2003. *Women and Plants: Gender Relations in Biodiversity Management and Conservation*. London: Zed Books.

Howard, P.L., 2006. Gender and social dynamics in swidden and homegardens in Latin America. *In*: B.M. Kumar and P.K.R. Nair, eds., *Tropical Homegardens: A Time-Tested Example of Sustainable Agroforestry*. Wageningen, the Netherlands: Springer, 159–82.

Kabeer, N., 1999. Resources, agency, achievements: Reflections on the measurement of women's empowerment. *Development and Change*, 40, 435–64.

Kawai, D., 2003. *Women and urban agriculture: A case study of Nairobi, Kenya*. Thesis (MA). University of Nairobi.

Lee-Smith, D., 1997. *'My House Is My Husband': A Kenyan Study of Women's Access to Land and Housing*. Lund: Lund University.

Lee-Smith, D. and Lamba, D., 2016. Implementing the right to food enshrined in Kenya's constitution. *The Star* [online], 2 January 2016. Available from: https://www.the-star.co.ke/news/2016/01/02/implementing-the-right-to-food-enshrined-in-kenyas-constitution_c1266511 [Accessed 11 July 2017].

Lee-Smith, D. and Memon, P.A., 1994. Urban Agriculture in Kenya. *In*: A.G. Egziabher, D. Lee-Smith, D.G. Maxwell, P.A. Memon, L.J.A. Mougeot and C.J. Sawio, eds, *Cities Feeding People*. Ottawa, ON: International Development Research Centre.

MacGregor, S., 2004. From care to citizenship: calling ecofeminism back to politics. *Ethics and the Environment*, 9 (1), 56–84.

Mahoney, M.A. and Yngvesson, B., 1992. The construction of subjectivity and the paradox of resistance: reintegrating feminist anthropology and psychology. *Signs*, 18 (1), 44–73.

Maxwell, D., 1994. Internal struggles over resources, external struggles for survival: urban women and subsistence household production. *In 37th annual meeting of the African Studies Association* [online], 3–6 November 1997, Toronto. Vancouver, BC: City Farmer. Available from: http://www.cityfarmer.org/danmax.html [Accessed 15 June 2018].

Mkwambisi, D.D., Fraser, E.D.G. and Dougill, A.J., 2011. Urban agriculture and poverty reduction: evaluating how food production in cities contributes to food security, employment and income in Malawi. *Journal of International Development* [online], 23 (2), 181–203. Available from: https://doi.org/10.1002/jid.1657 [Accessed 15 June 2018].

Mougeot, L.J.A., ed., 2005. *Agropolis: The Social, Political and Environmental Dimensions of Urban Agriculture* [online]. London: Earthscan and Ottawa, ON: International Development Research Centre. Available from: https://idl-bnc-idrc.dspacedirect.org/bitstream/handle/10625/28341/IDL-28341.pdf?sequence=47&isAllowed=y [Accessed 15 June 2018].

Mwangi, A.M., 1995. *The Role of Urban Agriculture for Food Security in Low-Income Areas in Nairobi.* Nairobi: Ministry of Planning and National Development and Leiden, the Netherlands: African Studies Centre Leiden.

Nightingale, A., 2006. The nature of gender: work, gender, and environment. *Environment and Planning D: Society and Space* [online], 24 (2), 165–85. Available from: https://doi.org/10.1068/d01k [Accessed 15 June 2018].

Pasquini, M.W., Assogba-Komlan, F., Vorster, I., Shackleton, C.M. and Abukutsa-Onyango, M.O., 2009. The production of African indigenous vegetables in urban and peri-urban agriculture: a comparative analysis of case studies from Benin, Kenya and South Africa. *In*: C.M. Shackleton, M.W. Pasquini and A.W. Drescher, eds., *African Indigenous Vegetables in Urban Agriculture.* 1st ed. London: Earthscan, 177–223.

Rakodi, C., 1985. Self-reliance or survival? Food production in African cities with particular reference to Zambia. *African Urban Studies*, 21, 53–63.

Redwood, M., ed., 2009. *Agriculture in Urban Planning: Generating Livelihood and Food Security.* London: Earthscan and Ottawa, ON: International Development Research Centre.

Robertson, C., 1996. Grassroots in Kenya: women, genital mutilation, and collective action, 1920–1990. *Signs*, 21 (3), 615–42.

Rocheleau, D.E., 1995. Gender and biodiversity: a feminist political ecology perspective. *IDS Bulletin* [online], 26 (1), 9–16. Available from: https://doi.org/10.1111/j.1759-5436.1995.mp26001002.x [Accessed 15 June 2018].

Rosset, P., 2013. Rethinking agrarian reform, land and territory in La Via Campesina. *Journal of Peasant Studies*, 40 (4), 721–75.

Sachs, C., 2013. Feminist food sovereignty: Crafting a new vision. *In: International Conference on Food Sovereignty: A Critical Dialogue*, 14–15 September 2013, New Haven, CT.

Sampson, D. and Wills, C., 2013. Culturally appropriate food: researching cultural aspects of food sovereignty. *In International Conference on Food Sovereignty: A Critical Dialogue* [online], 14–15 September 2013, New Haven, CT. Available from: https://www.iss.nl/fileadmin/ASSETS/iss/Research_and_projects/Research_networks/ICAS/20_SampsonWills_2013.pdf [Accessed 15 June 2018].

Sewell, W.H., 1992. A theory of structures: duality, agency, and transformation. *American Journal of Sociology*, 98 (1), 1–29.

Simiyu, R.R., 2012. *'I Don't Tell My Husband about Vegetable Sales': Gender Dynamics in Urban Agriculture in Eldoret, Kenya* [online]. Leiden, the Netherlands: African Studies Centre Leiden. https://openaccess.leidenuniv.nl/bitstream/handle/1887/20255/ASC-075287668-3255-01.pdf?sequence=2 [Accessed 16 June 2018].

Slater, R.J., 2001. Urban agriculture, gender and empowerment: an alternative view. *Development Southern Africa* [online], 18 (5), 635–50. Available from: https://doi.org/10.1080/03768350120097478 [Accessed 11 July 2018].

Thomas-Slayter, B., Wangari, E. and Rocheleau, D., 1996. Feminist political ecology: crosscutting themes, theoretical insights, policy implications. *In*: D. Rocheleau, B. Thomas-Slayter and E. Wangari, eds., *Feminist Political Ecology: From Global Issues to Local Experiences.* London: Routledge, 287–307.

Tronto, J.C., 2013. *Caring Democracy: Markets, Equality, and Justice* [online]. New York: New York University Press. Available from: https://books.google.de/books?id=8H L0IiVr2-sC [Accessed 15 June 2018].

Urban Agriculture Promotion and Regulation Act 2015 (Nairobi City County).

Wittman, H., 2011. Food sovereignty: a new rights framework for food and nature? *Environment and Society: Advances in Research*, 2, 87–105.

# 11 Transnational reconfigurations of re/production and the female body

Bioeconomics, motherhoods and the case of surrogacy in India

*Christa Wichterich*

Our first environment is our body, our children, families, communities and the earth that sustains us.

(Wiltshire 1992)

From the perspective of Feminist Political Ecology (FPE), biological reproduction is a socially, politically and economically constructed form of a societal nature relation and of embodied natureculture (Haraway 2003). The processes of pregnancy – the growth of the embryo as a living being in the uterus and delivery – are unique experiences for a woman where her own body can be perceived as the first material environment and as a way to understand the self. The female body can be understood as an agent and as a material site; simultaneously a container and a resource for the production of life. Procreation can be theorised as a bio-social process and reproduction and production are inseparably connected in a naturecultural process of doing gender and doing motherhood as a social, material, cultural and symbolic relation.

This chapter explores these themes further by adopting Donna Haraway's notion of natureculture and Haraway's metaphor of reproduction as an 'implosion of contemporary life in technoscience' (2003: 4). In order to highlight the entanglement of production and reproduction this chapter uses the notion 're/production'. In particular, it analyses how since the 1970s, assisted re/productive technologies (ART) have reshaped and reconfigured processes of biological re/production. ART has introduced a new chapter in societal nature relations in terms of human domination over the body and re/production as nature. Medical sciences and re/productive technologies through the processes of in-vitro fertilisation (IVF); prenatal and pre-implantation diagnosis; the generation and conservation of egg cells, sperm and umbilical cord blood; and surrogacy have the possibilities to control, 'correct' and 'optimise' nature. These attempts to control bodily re/production raise ethical questions about the embodied societal nature relations and the growing hegemony of ART and similar expert knowledge over bio-social processes. This chapter argues that the reconfiguration of reproduction and production of life is achieved through medicalisation and technologisation, through fragmentation and extraction of body parts and biological material and through a Taylorised division of labour involved in re/production (Gupta and Richters 2008). Re/production in these new technologies, life sciences and the respective re/productive political regime become sites and drivers of change in doing bodies and doing gender (West and Zimmerman 1987), which has a bearing on motherhood, the economics of care and re/production as well as on the division of care and re/productive labour.

The chapter looks at the ongoing transformation of bodily natureculture and the political-economic and scientific reconfiguration of re/production in transnational markets with a focus on the surrogate motherhood in India. The chapter argues that surrogacy breaks up the naturecultural nexus of sexuality, intimacy and re/production. Due to ethical concerns, commercial gestational surrogacy is highly contested viewed from the widely differing poles of autonomy and subjugation, free choice and exploitation, constructing the surrogate mother as victim or rather as agent and worker.

As the chapter shows, the surrogate mother acts at an interface of three interactive and intertwined power regimes, the repro-medical-industrial complex, biopolitics and the hegemonic heteronormative re/productive regime in society (Wichterich 2015). Key markers of these three power regimes are the categories of gender, class and/or caste, race and North/South. A leading question for the chapter is how patriarchal, class, racial and imperial/colonial power relations co-construct the new forms of re/production and of control over women's bodies. The chapter looks first at discourses around surrogacy and a possible right to one's own child. Second, it analyses the driving biopolitical and economic forces and mechanisms for the re/productive industries and their impact on surrogate labour and the reconfiguration of women's subjectivities. India is taken as a prominent case study for transnational surrogacy and the ongoing extractivism of biological resources and care work driven by market principles. In the final part of the chapter, future perspectives for surrogacy and shifting markets in Asia are explored after it had been banned in India.

The chapter adopts a multi-scalar approach to surrogacy, merging local, national and transnational dimensions and links structural analysis and discourse analysis with an analysis of agency and subjectivities. Three types of empirical sources have been used for this chapter: ethnographic studies in India, documentary films and interviews with three Indian re/productive medical entrepreneurs.[1] The overall background is my personal experience of contributing from the 1980s onwards to the feminist critique of population policies, in particular in India where I lived for several years, and of re/productive technologies. As a scholar activist I aim at bringing feminist perspectives from the South and the North into dialogue.

## From desire to right: Discourses around one's own child

Since the birth of Louise Brown, the first 'test tube baby,' in the late 1970s re/productive technologies and their respective markets have been highly contested among feminist activists and scholars. There has been a strong critique of ART linked to the medicalisation and commercialisation of women's body, fertility and procreation. Building on an ecofeminist critique of natural sciences in laboratory experiments inspired by Bacon and Newton, authors like Gena Corea (1985), Janice Raymond (1993) and FINRRAGE, the Feminist International Network of Resistance to Reproductive and Genetic Engineering, disapproved of re/productive technologies as instruments of control in male hands. Rita Arditti, Renate Duelli Klein and Shelly Minden (1984) critically discussed whether in-vitro fertilisation would reproduce gendered, class, racial and North–'Third World' relations of power and exploitation, with a perspective of 'baby farms' with 'cheap' black surrogates carrying babies for affluent white couples from the North. Their question 'What future for Motherhood?' countered Shulamith Firestone's hypothesis that radical emancipation of women would mean liberation from motherhood, pregnancy and childbirth, and (re-)production of human life outside of the body in laboratories.

At the same time, re/productive technologies and repro-medical sciences fuelled the narrative that there are technical solutions to infertility. Infertility was rediscovered and dubbed a biological disorder or even disease (Orland 2001, Inhorn and Balen 2002). The promise of technical solutions went beyond in-vitro fertilisation as correction of the stigma of childlessness to an optimisation of re/production, for example, by pre-implantation diagnosis and social freezing. This nurtured manifold desires and demands for an own child, a healthy child. ART opened scope in the middle classes for new imaginaries and constructions of gender and body, desire and needs for a life with children and in a family (Greil 2002, Inhorn and Birenbaum-Carmeli 2008). While those re/productive technosciences generate economic realms and emerging markets, people can shape along these new transnational technoscapes (Appadurai 1996) fluid repro-scapes as dreamscapes where re/production is no longer confined to one place, culture and to heteronormativity due to transnational trade and transnational tourism (Sama 2010, Waldby 2012). While the ARTs bring about a denaturalisation of re/production, the desire for one's own child became re-naturalised. The technological options offered by bio-sciences and repro-industries turned the desire for an 'own' healthy child into a right, claimed by childless couples as well as by homosexual and 'genetically risky' couples and by singles (Gupta and Richters 2008, Majumdar 2014). Many couples prefer this option over adoption as non-genetic, 'only' social parenting (Briggs 2010).

One epistemic interpretation of the potential of re/productive technologies as an instrument of modernity is the emancipation of re/production from nature and – from a queer perspective – of the heteronormative 'natureculture' of re/production (Mamo 2007). ART enables a change in societal rules over an assumed gendered embodied order of 'natural' re/production and an individual liberation from the assumed natural, heterosexual order of biological re/production and the corresponding social norms (Thompson 2005). In these debates, feminist discourses about surrogacy move between ecofeminist rejection of re/productive technologies, commodification and medicalisation of the female body on the one hand, and on the other hand the techno-optimistic claim for emancipation through self-determined control of the technology and for a change of gender norms (Bauhardt 2013).

However, re/productive options beyond sexuality, one's own gender, and biological age are highly ambivalent: they might – from a queer and emancipatory perspective – undermine social norms and binaries, give more control over re/production to LGBTIQ-persons, and foster self-organised biotechnological options of 'making bodies, persons and families' (Thompson 2005, de Jong and Tkach 2009). At the same time, repro-technologies are part of the new commercial bioeconomy with ever-new markets and companies that offer to realise the desire for a child in a commodified and consumptive form and ultimately control these processes.

Contrary to the feeling of a right to one's own child, two well-known cases in the US triggered a counter discourse on the rights and the autonomy of surrogate mothers, which challenges their victimisation as subjugated and exploited bodies. In 1986 (Baby M) a white and in 1993 a black surrogate mother demanded the newborns back from the white ordering parents, breaching their contract. In both cases, the courts gave custody rights to the genetic fathers (Markens 2007). The scandals around these care claims of the surrogate mothers led to the concept and practice of gestational surrogacy which attributes genetically and biologically defined ownership rights to the commissioning parents because the surrogate mother is genetically not related to the child. In the process, the 'naturally' felt emotional bond between a surrogate mother and the child and her desire for caring became coined a risk factor for the commercial use of the female body and for the market contract with the commissioning parents. This contract actually assumes a 'professional' rational attitude by the surrogate mother and subordinates emotions and caring as mere instruments to achieve the objective of the contract: a healthy baby as per order.

In another reaction to these events in the US, women, out of their professed joy about the physical experience of pregnancy and childbirth, offered themselves as surrogate mothers with the altruistic motive to help infertile and childless couples. This has led to a narrative of a gift economy, namely surrogacy out of solidarity and sisterhood, has been widespread in the USA. This reinterpretation of contract-based (re-)production through an altruistic discourse represents a moralising form of dealing with the discomfort of commercialisation (Terman 2010). The remuneration paid for the surrogate service is therefore officially called 'maintenance compensation' and not a wage. Where laws interdict the commodification of egg cells and sperm but allow altruistic donation, they feed into a narrative of a gift economy and a fertile altruistic woman caring for an infertile woman even though sometimes high 'compensations' are due (Schultz and Braun 2013). In general, driven by the strong desire for one's own child, social relations and practices in re/productive arenas, commercial or non-commercial, are emotionally and imaginarily laden.

Proliferation, commodification and trade in body parts, fluids and tissues raise once again the question about property rights *vis-à-vis* one's own body in terms of ownership and control over the parts and functions of the body (Dickenson 2001, Gupta and Richters 2008). So-called 'egg sharing' is an example of how the gift and the commercial economy get intertwined: women whose eggs are harvested for an in-vitro fertilisation are offered a cheaper price if they 'donate' surplus eggs for another childless couple who then pay for it (Sarojini 2014: 107).

Politically and legally controversial is the ownership of surplus biomaterial, such as frozen eggs and sperm, oocytes (unfertilised eggs from the petri dish), non-implanted embryos and umbilical cord blood. Life sciences, medical research and re/productive business identify legal loopholes to explore new re/productive options such as uterus transplantation and embryo 'donation' to a woman whose attempts with IVF were not successful but who wishes to have the experience of pregnancy and delivery.

In this context, surrogacy might become a more normalised option for affluent women who do not want to expose themselves to the rigours of pregnancy and childbirth because of age or career. This results in a variety of forms of motherhood, reinforces the inequalities between women, and creates new re/productive classes. While in most countries and cultures the natureculture of pregnancy and delivery is seen as constitutive for motherhood, in the case of gestational surrogacy the genetic mother is considered the authentic one with ownership and custody for the child according to the contract and payment made. This causes legal confusion with regard to maternity leave. In 2014 the European Court of Justice ruled that women who became mothers through a surrogacy arrangement do not have a right to maternity leave because they did not give birth. In a countermove, the UK government allows those women to claim maternity leave. Such legal fluidity shows how politics, regulation and law-making lag behind rapidly changing dynamics of naturecultures which implode in technoscience.

In the rest of the chapter I now turn from Western debates to look at how biopolitics shapes spaces for the flourishing transnational re/productive industry and the corresponding re/productive tourism, and how the economic principles of capitalist practices linked to resource- and care extractivism govern the processes of surrogacy.

## Biopower and the political regime of re/production in India

Against the background of different naturecultures of re/production, ethical considerations and a growing re/productive-industrial complex, nation states formulated laws and policies that legalise, regulate or ban ART and surrogacy. These legal provisions are part of the biopolitics of nation states which control the population, sexuality, health and re/production, gendered bodies and ultimately life and death of people (Foucault 1976). This politically constructed geography of dos and don'ts opened or closed spaces for re/productive markets and shaped the sites for re/productive tourism, thus fuelling a transnationalisation of bioeconomic investment and business as well as of fertility tourism (Waldby 2012, Gupta 2014).

Hegemonic re/productive biopolicies in countries like India in the Global South have been framed by neo-Malthusian population control policies *vis-à-vis* the so-called 'over'-population of the poor with racist and eugenic implications while in the Global North an alarmist, no less racist and eugenic discourse about the possible extinction of the white middle class spread out (Towghi and Vora 2014: 6). Surrogacy marks a paradigm shift in the appreciation of the re/productive capacities of poor women in the Global South: for decades in Western discourse, fertility and procreation of subaltern women in the Global South was constructed as backward, passive, subjugated, unruly and unplanned. Now, being placed at the service of pro-natalist policies of the countries of the global North and the global middle class, it is gaining unprecedented appreciation.

On this demographic and biopolitical background, India is an important case study for gestational surrogacy motherhood and the reorganisation of re/production, because the sector has developed quickly into a booming industry and a hub for re/productive medical tourism. The normalisation of surrogate motherhood is advanced in India and is ethnographically well documented (Marwah 2014, Pande 2014, Rudrappa 2015). In the global re/productive economy, the comparative advantage of India is the absence of regulations, the high level of techno-medical services and knowledge and the affordability of the services of surrogate mothers.

The hegemonic re/productive system in India is characterised by patriarchal and social selection mechanisms. This is marked by traditional cultural preference for sons which leads to prenatal sex determination; frequent femicide and a distorted sex ratio; and population control programmes which since the 1970s targeted poor, subaltern, Muslim and indigenous groups in society with the slogan 'Small family, happy family.' Interventions in the re/productive processes and the bodies of women have increased due to the easy accessibility of technologies for sex determination – though banned since 1994 – and sterilisation through laparoscopy. Since an attempt of mass sterilisation of men failed politically in the 1970s, the state organises regular laparoscopy camps for mothers of two children, supported by a semi-commercialised system of incentives, such as financial bonuses and penalties for government employees, medical staff and the targeted women. The Indian state favours permanent or long-lasting methods of birth control, which actually leave women with no control over their own re/production and no freedom of choice, such as implants and sterilisation (Rudrappa 2015: 25). Until recently coercive measures are enforced recklessly, resulting in health hazards or even deaths of women; for example, in a camp for tubal litigation in November 2014, 14 women died.[2] In this context, surrogacy in India means a reinterpretation of the re/productive capacity of poor, subaltern women as a valuable resource in a growing industry while otherwise the state denies re/production to these women and mistrusts their self-discipline to use birth control methods (Pande 2014: 26–37).

At the same time, since infertility constitutes a tremendous stigma in hegemonic Hindu culture, the state legalised in-vitro fertilisation (IVF) in the 1970s. From 2002 onwards, the neoliberal Indian government issued licences to 3,000 IVF clinics which offer a broad range of ARTs, including surrogacy. The state simultaneously supported the set-up of a clinical and techno-medical infrastructure in order to attract medical tourism. State support for the sector included tax exemptions and reductions of customs, which privileges domestic and foreign investors in export processing zones and other export sectors in order to promote their competitiveness. Moreover, excellence in life sciences and genetic research as well as the high quality of ART is considered to be of great political prestige in a country known for its high maternal mortality (Sunder 2006: 76).

Despite such state support, surrogacy is publicly contested. These contestations are reflected in the media; the topic is frequently discussed during talk shows on TV. Demands to regulate the growing sector and ethical controversies over how to bridge modernisation and 'traditional' Hindu-identitarian values were constantly played out in the media. In 2013, the then Hindu-nationalist government quit the *laissez-faire* policy style and introduced morally and culturally justified arguments for restricting surrogacy to heterosexual married couples, meaning excluding same sex couples and singles as was done in Russia.[3] Simultaneously, political efforts were made to revise the decriminalisation of homosexuality. For years there were public debates about whether surrogacy should be completely banned in order to avoid exploitation of the women involved (Gupta 2014). Questions were raised about whether a ban could stop the tendencies to rearticulate re/production outside of sexuality, of kinship and outside of the female body, and how to stop the expansion of exploitative bioeconomic industries.[4]

## Bioeconomies and market efficiency of baby production

Bioeconomies consist of the valorisation of body material and bio-physical processes in commercial markets based on re/productive expert knowledge and technologies (Lettow 2012). At an interface between production and re/production, private and public, the re/productive industry orchestrates a new economy of intimacy as well. Body parts, bio-material and processes become disaggregated and reified to become tradable goods and services (Gupta and Richters 2008). Biotechnologies facilitate the fragmentation of physically and socially intertwined processes such as the fertilisation of egg cells by shifting them into the laboratory and clinics. Thus, bio-industrial value chains are constructed to supply the resources, namely stem cells, eggs and sperms for the production line of regeneration and repair of bodies and of 'making' healthy children (Waldby and Mitchell 2006). These value chains are part of a techno-scientific form of capitalism based on bodily material as bio-capital and women's embodied services. It is a new form of gendered accumulation operationalised through resource and care extractivism (Sunder 2006, Wichterich 2016).

Fragmentation and splitting up are core mechanisms to prepare for surrogacy: fertilisation, pregnancy, childbirth and motherhood are fragmented into a Taylorised division of labour and outsourcing. In particular, the separation of the newborn from the delivering mother who existed together for nine months as an inseparable socio-physical and natureculture entity is a new form of reification and alienation between producer and the body product which was ordered, is paid for and owned by its genetic parents.

The proliferation of expert knowledge generated by biomedical research and life sciences and the availability and accessibility of ART raised or strengthened desires and felt needs. The fertility industry became a driving force for natureculture and bio-social processes which were considered in earlier regimes to be private, intimate and opposite to business and private accumulation to be included into capitalist markets. This acquisition of previously non-commercialised areas of society and natureculture means the conquering and capitalistic penetration of 'last colonies' (Mies *et al.* 1988) or 'accumulation through dispossession' (Harvey 2004). In the era of neoliberal globalisation this market expansion into earlier non-commercialised areas went hand in hand with the transnationalisation of the re/productive industry and its rise to become a billion-dollar business. The supply of re/productive technologies and industries is embedded in the ideology of liberalised free trade and transnational value chains, of transnational malls offering a broad range of goods and services, and of free choice of consumers. Driven by the acceleration of globalisation dynamics, the generation of human life becomes a production site and value creation chain based on the commercial provision of biological resources, scientific knowledge and care labour in various markets.

The legal framework of the individual surrogacy is a contract signed by the ordering parents, the re/productive entrepreneurs, meaning the clinic or the agency, and the prospective surrogate mother. This market contract articulates surrogate motherhood and the respective labour as a service, and the woman as a service provider. It regulates the temporary resource and care extractivism in complex unequal relations and temporarily creates a form of class/caste, ethnic and neo-colonial compromise. It claims to create a win–win situation between formally equal partners based on informed consent as an indicator for free choice. The contract presupposes the surrogate mother as the owner of her body that can be used as a means of production for income generation. However, the market view of one's own body as individual property and of women as a free market agent is at odds with the socio-cultural contexts in poverty relations in India (Majumdar 2014). Additionally, a truly informed, knowledge-based approval by the surrogate mother is illusionary due to the large gap in techno-re/productive knowledge between the medical staff and the surrogate mother.

India has become a hub for the transnational re/productive bioeconomy orchestrated by a transnational network of re/productive entrepreneurs. Sound statistics are not available but nearly 80 per cent of ordering parents are supposed to be foreigners. Package deals are offered to commissioning parents by actors networks including agencies abroad and in India that mediate IVF clinics and doctors, bio-material and logistic firms, pharmaceutical markets; hotels and sightseeing tours; legal advisors in particular for the transfer of the babies to countries where surrogacy is prohibited; and local recruiters, often former surrogates (Sama 2012, Sarojini 2014). The expansion of the Indian market heated up the competition and resulted in an increasing informalisation with falling prices and, for example, rickshaw drivers working as intermediaries.

In order to reduce the risk of eventual claims to the baby, in India the surrogate mother is not allowed to be the simultaneous provider of egg cells, meaning: genetic mother. The woman must have at least one child of her own as proof for the operability of her re/productive organs and already existing maternal emotional bonds to an own child. For the same reason, the newborn is not shown to the surrogate after delivery in order to prevent the 'natural' desire to care.

From a medical law perspective, Wadekar (2011) assumes that with the signed contract women cede their rights over their body and re/production to the re/productive entrepreneurs, mainly the clinic. Sharmila Rudrappa, who did multisite ethnographic research in Bangalore and in the US, calls it a 'reproductive assembly line' (2012). Being commercialised, the principles of capitalist markets like efficiency and rationality expand into the re/productive processes of fertilisation, insemination, implantation and pregnancy. A high dose of stimulating hormones is given to the genetic mother and to the surrogate mother in order to increase the success rate of harvesting egg cells and of embryos nesting in the uterus. The decision to provide her body as a vessel or of 'renting a womb imagined as an empty and otherwise unproductive space' for the production of someone else's baby (Vora 2013: S100) implies that the surrogate is subjected to intensive medical interventions and performance monitoring. In case the embryo implantation is not successful, surrogates have to accept further attempts. As per the contract she is not allowed to abort. The efficiency of the pregnancy is supported by regular drug and hormone administration, and checked by frequent blood and ultrasound tests in its course (Sama 2012: 63, 80). Normally, five embryos are transferred into the women's uterus. Thus, sometimes twin or triplet pregnancies occur. According to the wish of the ordering parents, one or two of the embryos are aborted, called embryo 'reduction,' often even without informing the surrogate (Pande 2015: 106). In order to fix a date for the ordering parents to pick up the baby, delivery is mostly done with a Caesarean section, called 'cutting day.'

As all commissioning parents require a healthy child, according to the contract regular quality control including testing for pelvic inflammatory disease (PID) and paediatric neurotransmitter disease (PND) is done. Embryos with a genetic disorder are immediately aborted. The role of medical treatment shifted from a 'technique of caring for the body to one of producing bodies as the instruments of service work and subjects as sites of new forms of social and medical risk' (Towghi and Vora 2014: 13). ART presumes to ensure techno-medical control of the 'natural' process, the subjugation of the biological process and the body of the woman under re/productive expert knowledge in order to optimise it. For the sake of a healthy child, many clinics ask the surrogate mothers to provide pumped milk for one or two weeks, which is then given to the genetic parents to feed the baby (Rudrappa 2015: 154).

The accommodation of the women in hostels in or near the hospital allows for constant medical intervention, monitoring and supervision (including of the diet) is an entrepreneurial strategy of governance and efficiency, similar to the accommodation of Chinese export workers in dormitories adjacent to the factory (Pande 2014: 64ff.). Analogically, Amrita Pande analyses the clinic–hostel complex as a disciplinary regime to keep the body and the mind of the surrogate mothers under control, and makes them permanently feel that it is the medical intervention, the knowledge and the skills of the doctor who enables them to produce a baby.

Using bioresources and embodied work of a surrogate to re/produce one's own child is a form of resource and care extractivism which enables middle-class couples to realise their desire for a child and parenthood. Arlie Hochschild (2012) calls surrogacy in India a 'backstage,' a rather invisible scene of the global free market and of outsourced work comparable to domestic work that is outsourced by professional women in the Global North to domestic workers and nannies from the Global South. It is part of the neoliberal configuration of the economy and of an 'imperial mode of living' (Brand and Wissen 2011). This implies a new stratification of re/production (Ginsburg and Rapp 1995) with neo-eugenic elements (Pande 2014: 104–28) and reconstructs social inequalities between women despite the temporary class/caste, ethnic and neo-colonial compromise as laid down in the contract.

## Labour and care extractivism

Recent ethnographic and micro-sociological research on surrogacy in India focused on the work and the subjectivities of surrogate mothers (Sama 2012, Pande 2014, Sarojini and Marwah 2014, Vora 2014, Rudrappa 2015). According to these case studies, through their physical and emotional labour of preparation for the embryo transfer, pregnancy and childbirth, surrogates practise a new social and bio-material form of motherhood. Based on this research, one can understand the emerging subjectivities of these women as cross-boundary workers who float between production for someone else and biological re/production, between market-based rationality and intimate embodied privacy. It is a highly emotionally and morally charged agency and labour. Women's relation to their body as the bio-physical self is at the core. In order to do justice to the agency of the surrogate mothers, the chapter now explores the kind of labour performed.

As a centrepiece of a transnational techno-medical fertility industry mediated by various brokers, the women's embodied labour encapsulates and yet also blurs categories of Marxist economics like subcontracted labour, commodification and exploitation (Floyd 2014). It also analytically challenges neoclassical economic categories of freedom of choice and freedom to use one's own body as a means of production. It demands new analytical categories, which – with an intersectional approach – take into account the emerging transnational business structures, national policies and the agency of the surrogate mothers. This re/productive labour as service for others implies resource and care extractivism is highly ambivalent, contingent or even contradictory.

The production of a human being comprises highly valuable work. This work is 'clinical,' 're/productive' and 'regenerative' work similar to the proliferation of re/productive tissues and body material for medical and re/productive sciences and business (Waldby and Cooper 2008: 59, 2010: 9f.). Kalindi Vora (2009) considers it to be outsourced care work, with considerable affective components and a commodification of 'vital energy.' The work consists of 'doing bodies' in the double sense, namely to make the female body facilitate and promote a pregnancy and childbirth, and on the other to produce another living body and to accept the growing of another person in one's own body.

Due to the hormones and other medication additional to many checks and tests done, women experience the surrogate pregnancy as more stressful and difficult than their 'own' previous pregnancies. Their embodied knowledge built in their earlier pregnancies and deliveries is largely devalued and obsolete. At the same time, many of the surrogates are conscious about the vital and energetic power of their body and are proud of their own material re/productivity and the growing foetus as a product of their body: 'They just gave the eggs but all the blood, all the sweat, all the effort is mine' (Pande 2015: 8).

Hochschild (2012: 29) sees 'emotional work' in particular done in the suppression of affection for the child growing in their bodies and in the acceptance of the separation from the child after birth. Like migrant maids from the Global South taking care of children in the Global North, surrogates are trapped in a contradiction between professionalism and emotionality, closeness and distance, productivity and re/productivity.

The disciplinary clinic–hostel regime configures the surrogate's relationship to her own body and self professionally as 'perfect mother-worker' (Pande 2015) and as entrepreneurship. 'Psychological counselling' encourages them to consider the uterus as an unused means of production for income generation. This strategy aims at generating a professional rationalised relationship of the woman to her own body. Surrogates are told to suppress an emotional attachment to the embryo, and instead to see the ordered baby as non-personalised object for others and the surrogacy as a service to 'birthing a mother' (Terman 2010) and 'making parents' (Thompson 2005).

On the other hand, the surrogate mother is constantly asked to develop a responsible, caring mothering attitude towards the embryo in her body in order to support the growth of a healthy child. This includes normalisation strategies like praying regularly for the child and performing rituals to welcome the unborn child in the family. Thus, surrogate labour requires the balancing and management of contradictory expectations to be emotional and caring, and at the same time professional and self-disciplined to avoid bonding and accept the separation of the embryo from the body.

Additionally, the agency and labour done by surrogate mothers are framed and veiled by the ideology of gift economy. As infertility is a social stigma in India, it is easy for the re/productive entrepreneurs to take up the narrative of donation and gift economy, and to launch a discourse on altruism and 'one woman helping another.' The representation of surrogacy as an altruistic and reciprocal practice justifies low payment and the absence of social protection and labour rights. Linked to narratives of pregnancy and childbirth as partly natural biological processes and partly professional labour of the medical staff, the labour of the surrogate mothers is hardly recognised. The surrogates themselves adopt this narrative, articulate their intention to 'help' as kind of compensation of their monetary motivation, thereby upgrading their own morality and themselves to 'moral workers' (Rudrappa 2015: 96).

As transnationally outsourced labour, surrogacy is highly precarious, temporary and risky. There is no social protection or insurance coverage in the contract. This mirrors the asymmetrical power relations and dependencies in which the surrogates assume all risks with their body. After receiving only small instalments in the very beginning of the clinical process and after successful implantation of the embryo, most of the time they will not receive payment in case of a miscarriage or stillbirth (Rudrappa 2015: 101).

The other side of the surrogacy relationship is the construction of motherhood and parenthood, which is part and parcel of the process (Thompson 2005, Teman 2010, Vora 2013: S99). After successful implantation of the embryo, Indian clinics inform the to-be parents: 'Congratulations. You are pregnant.' Through frequent calls, the ordering parents demonstrate their claim to monitor the progress. Regularly, ultrasound scans are sent to them so that they feel constantly involved, identify with and become attached to the embryo. Though many ordering parents are extremely grateful to the surrogate mother, the focus of the social and the commercial interaction is on the 'foetuses as persons,' and the surrogate mothers fear justly that they are turned into 'non-persons' (Rudrappa 2015: 126).

The ordering mothers are in a homologous dilemma of emotionality and rationality. Some reduce the process to the hiring of a wage labourer and explain the offshoring from the US to India: 'These women do not want my child. They want my money. That's fine for me!'[5] Others feel deeply obliged to the surrogate mother and some are embarrassed about the commercial transaction process and simulate in public the pregnancy by fixing differently sized cushions on their belly which are offered online for sale (Rudrappa 2015: 127).

The actual appropriation of the ordered 'own' child takes place during or immediately after birth when the newborn is handed over to the genetic mother. Some are allowed to observe and record the birth in the clinic from a distance,[6] others are allowed to cut the umbilical cord and thus actively separate their property from the producer (Vora 2013: S101). This means a transfer of agency and of care to the genetic mother while the surrogate mother is ousted into passivity and her labour into invisibility.

## New subjectivities and dilemmas

The ethnographic focus on surrogate mothers and their agency has enabled researchers such as Pande, Rudrappa and Sama to revise and differentiate their initial perspective of the women as mere victims of exploitation. Together with the recognition of surrogacy as work, there was also recognition of their agency and new subjectivities.

They acknowledge that despite their precarious situation, many of the surrogate mothers experience their ability to nurture a life in their body and give birth as embodied power and a vital resource, which helps them to build self-confidence. They see their bodies and their re/productive capacities enhanced by the job as surrogate. Sometimes they even mobilise subversive energies against the disciplinary regime, for example, they secretly season the tasteless food with chilli and spices. Some developed the idea of a surrogate co-operative (Rudrappa 2015: 162f). Pande sees the concept of labour as an opportunity to explore both exploitative and emancipatory dimensions. She observed that the resistance strategies have increased over the years; some surrogates even started to negotiate their payment (Pande 2014: 10).

Most of the surrogates experience the time in the clinic–dormitory complex as peaceful and relaxed, as a kind of leisure compared to their normal family or field work. For the surrogate mothers in Bangalore interviewed by Rudrappa (2015: 86ff.) the re/productive work is welcomed as a lucrative change from their labour in the textile sector which earns them 100 dollars per month. They feel 'depleted' by the daily 14 hours of work, in addition to the frequent exposure to sexual harassment and health hazards. In comparison, they appreciate the job as a surrogate as 'simple' and 'meaningful' because they 'create something new.' Additionally, they enjoy the new sisterly relationships with other surrogates (Pande 2014: 157, Rudrappa 2015: 95).

For Dalit and Muslim women, it is important to be qualified as surrogates due to the re/productive capacities of their body and not to be discriminated against because of their caste or religion. Many hospitals also accept widows or single mothers, normally stigmatised in Indian society, as surrogates. Most of the women appreciate that foreign commissioning parents – different from Indians – are not concerned about the particular sex of the baby.

The outsourcing of re/productive labour is another form of transnational extractivism of care, emotions and bodily energy, temporarily but often with lasting impact. Emotionally, the women handle the separation from the new born child very differently: some say that they never got over the pain and therefore would never do the surrogate job once again. Others secretly nurture fantasies of kinship relations. A number of them decide to embark on a second or even third surrogacy because the money earned with the first one was used up quickly or evaporated somehow.

The surrogates want their work and their subjectivities to be respected in a symbolic order that iconises and glorifies motherhood and devaluates care work. They often hide this work in the neighbourhood, fake a job as maid in another city or claim the baby died after birth because they are confronted with a whore discourse, which discredits the commercial usage of a women's body as prostitute in an economy of intimacy. The surrogates try to contest the stereotype of immorality and dirty work – 'At least I am not sleeping with anyone' (Pande 2014: 128) – and distinguish themselves from sex workers and as well from women who give away their own children for adoption. Nevertheless, after the return to the village, some women experience stigmatisation by the neighbours or even violence by their husbands despite earlier agreements. Pande sees this constant self-defence against the stigma of sex work as part of surrogacy labour between appreciation as saviour for an infertile woman and depreciation, between private and public.

In such complex intersecting power structures, surrogacy for these women is first of all a social practice in a framework of multiple dependencies and subordination, exploitation, governmentality and outside control. However, it is important to recognise that surrogate mothers are not completely powerless objects or only a bodily resource in the context of neoliberal globalisation (Floyd 2014). Rather, being agents and victims at the same time, the women form new subjectivities through their agency, motivations, perceptions and dreams in these asymmetric power relationships and structures of inequality.

Surrogacy breaks up the hegemonic patriarchal re/productive regime in Indian gender relations and results in new subjectivities which are contingent and often ambivalent because the woman provides her body not for the re/production of her own family but for strangers. She withdraws care and sexuality from her own family but returns home with a considerable income. The job earns up to ten times the annual income of a rickshaw driver or a farm worker. This new role as breadwinner boosts their self-esteem and qualifies them as a 'good' wife and in-law in the family. Their key motivation to embark on this dubious job is care for their own kids: 'I do it for my children,' in particular for their education (Marwah 2014: 271). Ultimately, this maternal ethics of care confirms the prevailing stereotype of femininity, namely the woman as self-sacrificing and serving, as a vessel and instrument for others.

## Perspectives

The multi-scalar approach to the contested complex of surrogate motherhood could not solve the inherent contradictions and dilemmas. The ongoing reconfiguration of re/production continues to range between an envisioned right to one's own child, individual freedom of choice and attempts to overcome heteronormativity and other binaries on the one hand, and on the other the prevention of economisation, exploitation and dispossession.

The recent research focus in India on surrogate subjectivities and the recognition of their work necessarily leads to the demand for employment rights (Pande 2015: 10). Humbyrd (2009) sharpened this argument by proposing 'fair trade' surrogacy by means of labour rights and social security, as if it were normal wage work. Rudrappa declares to advocate transnational surrogacy in case 're/ productive justice' can be guaranteed to the contract mothers (2015: 173). Every piece of legalisation, however, means a normalisation ignoring other substantial ethical concerns.

Presently, these controversies gain momentum because re/productive markets in India and Asia more generally, function like a chessboard, where the actors are shifted by new biopolitics and laws. These sometimes bizarre situations reveal the complexities of changes. After years of prioritisation of economic growth and neoliberal interests, in 2013 the Indian state allowed surrogacy due to moral reasons for heterosexual couples only. This triggered an unprecedented chain of action. Commissioning Israeli gay couples got their Indian surrogate mothers transferred to Nepal. After the earthquake in 2014, the Israeli government, on the basis of its pro-natalist nationalism, sent an air-craft with a rescue team to Nepal to rescue the Israeli citizens born out of sur-rogacy. The surrogate mothers stayed behind. When the Nepali government banned surrogacy in 2015, the Israeli government transferred 25 Nepalese sur-rogate mothers for delivery to Israel. Meanwhile, Israel has allowed surrogacy for same-sex couples in the country itself but there is a lack of Israeli surrogates.[7]

Thailand prohibited surrogate motherhood for foreigners after a scandal in 2015 when an Australian couple refused to accept their baby with Down's syndrome and left the baby with the surrogate. After the ban, Thai women have been transferred to Cambodia for embryo transfer and delivery but spent most of the pregnancy at home. China revised its one child policy in 2016 and allowed surrogacy, thereby potentially opening up a huge re/productive market.

In India, the Hindu-identitarian government introduced a law to ban commercial surrogacy and egg donation in 2016 after years of *laissez-faire* policy and of public debates on the transnational commercialisation of re/production and the exploitation of Indian women by foreign nationals. From May 2017 onwards, only 'altruistic' surrogacy will be allowed for Indian citizens. Thus, the cultural Hindu-chauvinist orientation and the claim of moral superiority of the current governing party have gained the upper hand over their neoliberal economic interests. Both are based in nationalism.

The media immediately showed protesting surrogate mothers because the ban would deprive poor women of a lucrative income option. The ban does not take into account that poverty is the root cause for woman who opt for surrogacy, or consider the other forms of exploitation of women in the informal economy or the stigmatisation of infertility. As a result, the ban drives women into illegality, mobile arrangements and even greater vulnerability (Nadimpally *et al.* 2016). Re/productive entrepreneurs warned that prices would go up and went underground; agencies and clinics set up branches in Cambodia. However, at the end of 2016 Cambodia also announced a provisional ban.

Australia, where surrogacy is prohibited, had urged Cambodia to stop the operation of Australian agencies in Phnom Penh. Thus, the commercial techno- and repro-spaces are reconfigured all the time and very fluid.

Techno-sceptical and leftist feminists in India welcomed the ban, while others who did research on the subjectivities of surrogate mothers criticise the ban from the perspective of women's rights (Nadimpally *et al.* 2016: 14, Pande 2016[8]). The discomfort with the ban on commercial surrogacy is directed against the obvious interest of the governing party to represent and strengthen its Hindu-identitarian, anti-emancipatory moral profile inside and outside of India while it doesn't care for women's rights or for an improvement of their economic situation.

Bans by individual nation states are not a sufficient response to surrogate motherhood as a highly paradoxical re/productive option in a neoliberal arena governed by biopolitics, bio-capitalism, and imperial lifestyles. Apart from protection against commodification of their body, women need sexual and re/productive rights as well as social, economic and livelihood rights. The recent biopolitical shifts will result in an illegalisation of surrogacy and further precarisation of the women and will trigger of a new offshoring of the re/productive industry and the emergence of new markets. Additionally, re/productive sciences are developing new bio- or gene-centred techno-solutions such as the transplantation of uterus, the fusion of the genes of the parents with those of a donor in a foetus and ectogenesis, the production of embryos in an artificial uterus. Parallel to the ongoing geo-engineering as domination-oriented intervention into nature and reorganisation of nature for the purpose of economisation, in the area of biological re/production one can speak of the advancement of body- and even of life-engineering.

Rather than stressing technical solutions, social solutions for the desire for children and for new forms of family life apart from abortion, which are already invented and lived in everyday life should be highlighted, such as LGBTI and queer families, elective affinities, kinship out of affinity, caring communities and patchwork families. They have hitherto been underrepresented in all political discourses, but could represent a counter pole to the desire for an 'own' child and the queer ambition to move beyond the heterosexual matrix. However, debates on the ongoing reconfiguration of re/production need to be multi-scalar and on a local, national and transnational level as re/production itself, and systematically bring women's rights and their voices into the debates and analysis.

## Notes

1   a) Ethnographic studies by Amrita Pande, Sama, Kalindi Vora and Sharmila Rudrappa, b) documentary films, namely four long documentaries: 'Google Baby,' 2009 by Zippi Brand Frank; 'Made in India,' 2010 by Rebecca Haimoutz and Vaishala Sinha; 'Ma Na Sapna: A Mother's Dream,' 2013 by Valerie Gudenus; 'Can we see the baby bump, please,' 2013 by Surabhi Sharma; additionally 20 short documentaries for TV, advertisement spots for agencies and clinics and two talkshows on Indian TV c) three interviews with doctors in their reproductive clinics.

2   https://www.theguardian.com/world/2014/nov/13/india-sterilisations-second
    -camp-went-ahead-and-another-woman-died
3   http://www.telegraph.co.uk/news/worldnews/asia/india/9811222/India-bans-gay
    -foreign-couples-from-surrogacy.html
4   http://www.thehindu.com/features/metroplus/society/gaps-in-surrogacy-bill/article
    5276062.ece
5   PBS News Hour, 5.8.2011
6   Future Baby, 2016, Austrian documentary by Maria Arlamovsky
7   https://www.huffingtonpost.com/2015/04/30/nepal-earthquake-israel_n_7179708.
    html
8   http://www.thehindu.com/opinion/op-ed/Surrogates-are-workers-not-wombs/article
    14594820.ece: Surrogates are workers not wombs

# References

Appadurai, A., 1996. *Modernity at Large: Cultural Dimensions of Globalisation.* Minneapolis, MN: University of Minnesota Press.

Arditti, R., Klein, R.D. and Minden, S., eds., 1984. *Test-Tube Women: What Future for Motherhood?* London: Pandora Press.

Bauhardt, C., 2013. Rethinking gender and nature from a material(ist) perspective: feminist economics, queer ecologies and resource politics. *European Journal of Women's Studies*, 20 (4), 361–75.

Brand, U. and Wissen, M., 2012. Global environmental politics and the imperial mode of living: articulations of state-capital relations in the multiple crisis. *Globalisations*, 9 (4), 547–60.

Briggs, L., 2010. Reproductive technology: of labour and markets. *Feminist Studies*, 36 (2), 359–74.

Corea, G., 1985. *The Mother Machine, Reproductive Technologies from Artificial Insemination to Artificial Wombs.* New York: Harper and Row.

Dickenson, D., 2001. Property and women's alienation from their own reproductive labour. *Bioethics*, 15 (3), 205–17.

Floyd, K., 2014. Leihmutterschaft – die neue Bioökonomie. *Debatte* [online], 30. Available from: http://debatte.ch/2014/10/leihmutterschaft-die-neue-bioökonomie/ [Accessed 21 September 2018].

Foucault, F., 1976. *The Will to Knowledge*, London/New York.: Pantheon Books.

Ginsburgh, F. and Rapp, R., eds., 1995. *Conceiving the New World Order: The Global Politics of Reproduction.* Berkeley, CA: University of California Press.

Greil, A.L., 2002. Infertile bodies: medicalisation, metaphor and agency. *In*: M.C. Inhorn and F. van Balen, eds., *Infertility around the Globe: New Thinking on Childlessness, Gender, and Reproductive Technologies.* Berkeley, CA: University of California Press, 101–18.

Gupta, J.A., 2014. Biocrossing and the global fertility market. *In*: N. Sarojini and V. Marwah, eds., *Reconfiguring Reproduction: Feminist Health Perspectives on Assisted Reproductive Technologies.* New Delhi: Zubaan Books, 177–218.

Gupta, J.A. and Richters, A., 2008. Embodied subjects and fragmented objects: women's bodies, assisted reproduction technologies and the right to self-determination. *Bioethical Inquiry*, 5, 239–49.

Haraway, D.J., 2003. *The Companion Species Manifesto: Dogs, People, and Significant Otherness* [online], Chicago, IL: Prickly Paradigm Press. Available from: http://xenopraxis.net/readings/haraway_companion.pdf [Accessed 21 September 2018].

Harvey, D., 2004. The new imperialism: accumulation by dispossession. *Socialist Register*, 40, 63–87.

Hochschild, A., 2012. The back stage of global free market nannies and surrogates. *In*: H.G. Soeffner, ed., *Transnationale Vergesellschaftungen*. Wiesbaden, Germany: Springer, 1125–38.

Humbyrd, C., 2009. Fair trade international surrogacy. *Developing World Bioethics*, 9 (3), 111–18.

Inhorn, M.C. and van Balen, F., eds., 2002. *Infertility around the Globe: New Thinking on Childlessness, Gender, and Reproductive Technologies*. Berkeley, CA: University of California Press.

Inhorn, M.C. and Birenbaum-Carmeli, D., 2008. Assisted reproductive technologies and culture change. *Annual Review of Anthropology*, 37, 177–96.

de Jong, W. and Tkach, O., eds., 2009. *Making Bodies, Persons and Families*. Münster, Germany: LIT.

Lettow, S., ed., 2012. *Bioökonomie: Die Lebenswissenschaften und die Bewirtschaftung der Körper*. Bielefeld, Germany: transcript.

Majumdar, A., 2014. The rhetoric of choice: the feminist debates on reproductive choice in the commercial surrogacy arrangement in India. *Gender, Technology and Development*, 18 (2), 275–301.

Mamo, L., 2007. *Queering Reproduction: Achieving Pregnancy in the Age of Technoscience*. Durham, NC: Duke University Press.

Markens, S., 2007. *Surrogate Motherhood and the Politics of Reproduction*. Berkeley, CA: University of California Press.

Marwah, V., 2014. How surrogacy is challenging and changing our feminisms. *In*: N. Sarojini and V. Marwah, eds., *Reconfiguring Reproduction: Feminist Health Perspectives on Assisted Reproductive Technologies*. New Delhi: Zubaan Books, 266–306.

Mies, M., Bennholdt-Thomsen, V. and Werlhof, C. von, 1988. *Women: The Last Colony*. London: Zed Books.

Nadimpally, S., Banerjee, S. and Venkatachalam, D., 2016. *Commercial Surrogacy: A Contested Terrain in the Realm of Rights and Justice*. New Delhi: Sama Resource Group for Women and Health.

Orland, B., 2001. Spuren einer Entdeckung: (Re-)Konstruktionen der Unfruchtbarkeit im Zeitalter der Fortpflanzungsmedizin. *Gesnerus*, 58, 5–29.

Pande, A., 2014. *Wombs in Labour: Transnational Commercial Surrogacy in India*. New York: Columbia University Press.

Pande, A., 2015. Global reproductive inequalities, neoeugenics and commercial surrogacy in India. *Current Sociology*, 4, 1–15.

Rajan, K.S., 2006. *Biocapitalism: The Constitution of Post-Genomic Life*. Durham, NC: Duke University Press.

Raymond, J., 1993. *Women as Wombs: Reproductive Technologies and the Battle over Women's Freedom*. San Francisco, CA: Harper San Francisco.

Rudrappa, S., 2012. Working India's reproductive assembly line: Surrogacy and reproductive rights? *Western Humanities Review* [online], 66 (3), 77–101. Available from: https://con texts.org/articles/indias-reproductive-assembly-line/ [Accessed 21 September 2018].

Rudrappa, S., 2015. *Discounted Life: The Prize of Global Surrogacy in India*. New York: New York University Press.

Sama Resource Group for Women and Health, 2010. *Constructing Conceptions: The Mapping of Assisted Reproductive Technologies in India*. New Delhi: Sama Resource Group for Women and Health.

Sama Resource Group for Women and Health, 2012. *Birthing a Market: A Study on Commercial Surrogacy*. New Delhi: Sama Resource Group for Women and Health.

Sarojini, N., 2014. Unravelling the fertility industry: ARTs in the Indian context. *In*: N. Sarojini and V. Marwah, eds., *Reconfiguring Reproduction: Feminist Health Perspectives on Assisted Reproductive Technologies*. New Delhi: Zubaan Books, 92–122.

Sarojini, N. and Marwah, V., eds., 2014. *Reconfiguring Reproduction: Feminist Health Perspectives on Assisted Reproductive Technologies*. New Delhi: Zubaan Books.

Schultz, S. and Braun, K., 2013. Procuring tissue: Regenerative medicine, oocyte mobilisation and feminist politics. *In*: A. Webster, ed., *The Global Dynamics of Regenerative Medicine: A Social Science Critique*. Basingstoke, UK: Palgrave Macmillan, 118–49.

Terman, E., 2010. *Birthing a Mother: The Surrogate Body and the Pregnant Self*. Berkeley, CA: University of California Press.

Thompson, C., 2005. *Making Parents: The Ontological Choreography of Reproductive Technologies*. Cambridge, MA: Massachusetts Institute of Technology Press.

Towghi, F. and Vora, K., 2014. Bodies, markets, and the experimental in South Asia. *Ethnos*, 79 (1), 1–18.

Vora, K., 2009. Indian transnational surrogacy and the commodification of vital energy. *Subjectivities*, 28 (1), 266–78.

Vora, K., 2013. Potential, risk, and return in transnational Indian gestational surrogacy. *Current Anthropology*, 54 (7), S97–106.

Vora, K., 2014. Experimental sociality and gestational surrogacy in the Indian ART Clinic. *Ethnos: Journal of Anthropology*, 79 (1), 1–18.

Wadekar, N.D., 2011. Wombs for rent: a bioethical analysis of commercial surrogacy in India. *Tuftscope: The Journal of Health, Ethics, and Policy* [online], 10 (3), Available from: http://s3.amazonaws.com/tuftscope_articles/documents/160/Original%20Article%20--%20Wadekar.pdf [Accessed 20 September 2018)].

Waldby, C., 2012. Reproductive labour arbitrage: Trading fertility across European borders. *In*: M. Gunnarson and F. Svenaeus, eds., *The Body as Gift, Resource, and Commodity*. Stockholm: Södertörns University, 267–95.

Waldby, C. and Cooper, M., 2008. The biopolitics of reproduction: post-Fordist biotechnology and women's clinical labour. *Australian Feminist Studies*, 23 (55), 57–74.

Waldby, C. and Cooper, M., 2010. From reproductive work to regenerative labour: The female body and the stem cell industries. *Feminist Theory*, 11 (1), 3–22.

Waldby, C. and Mitchell, R., eds., 2006. *Tissue Economics: Blood, Organs, and Cell Lines in Late Capitalism*. Durham, NC: Duke University Press.

West, C. and Zimmerman, D., 1987. Doing gender. *Gender and Society*, 1 (2), 125–51.

Wichterich, C., 2015. *Sexual and Reproductive Rights*. Berlin: Heinrich-Böll.

Wichterich, C., 2016. Feministische Internationale Politische Ökonomie und Sorge-extraktivismus. *In*: U. Brand, H. Schwenken and J. Wullweber, eds., *Globalisierung Analysieren, Kritisieren und Verändern: Das Projekt Kritische Wissenschaft*. Hamburg: VSA, 54–72.

Wiltshire, R., 1992. *Environment and Development: Grass Roots Women's Perspective*. Barbados: Development Alternatives with Women for a New Era.

# 12 Menstrual politics in Argentina and diverse assemblages of care

*Jacqueline Gaybor*

## Introduction

In the last two decades or so, menstrual activism in Argentina has been gaining widespread attention by linking several important gender, environmental and economic issues with menstruation management. Leveraging between the feminist and environmental movements, and as part of a global trend, menstrual activism brings new demands for recognition and proposals for change. This has partly been motivated by concerns raised mostly by women regarding the health risks and the negative effects on the environment that the use of disposable menstrual products entails. It has also been motivated by the growing tensions between traditional narratives that perceive menstruation as a negative event in need of hygiene, and those newer narratives that celebrate or see menstruation as a natural part of a woman's lifecycle and thereby propose sustainable ways for women to manage it.

A variety of discussions about menstruation have been attracting increasing interest of women in Argentina and are slowly becoming part of the political debate. For instance, on 28 March 2017, two bills were presented in the Senate of Buenos Aires Province proposing the free provision of disposable menstrual technologies. On 3 May 2017, one bill that proposes the provision of menstrual products for free and another that seeks to eliminate taxes on all menstrual products were presented to the National Congress (Economiafeminista, n.d.). Moreover, the local press and local academe have given space and coverage to the emergent and diverse discussions arising around the topic of menstruation. If we look at social media, there are countless websites, blogs, YouTube channels and a good number of private Facebook groups created for sharing knowledge about women's own bodies and hosting a diverse array of discussions around menstruation. At the same time, several female entrepreneurs have been locally designing, producing, importing and commercialising reusable menstrual management technologies – among them, the menstrual cup, reusable menstrual pads, sea sponges and reusable panties. At the same time, there are increasing numbers of self-organised gatherings to learn about feminine anatomy in a 'hands on' manner and do-it-yourself (DIY) workshops linked to responsible consumption, e.g. how to sew reusable menstrual pads or how to home-make gynaecological remedies.

In this chapter, I explore how these emergent and heterogeneous initiatives about menstruation are shaping the social and environmental landscape in Argentina, focussing mostly on the role of reusable menstrual technologies. My analysis uses Feminist Political Ecology (FPE), through which I explore how menstrual activists question the prevailing ways of managing menstruation, and through which I examine their leadership and action in relation to crafting responses to environmental and social problems linked to current dominant forms of managing menstruation. Following an FPE approach, I claim that these initiatives emerge from their individual life stories, their experiences, relations and choices informed by their gender, middle-class status, age, professional background and urban context. Based on interviews, focus group discussions and my participation in a number of events and workshops in Argentina, I explain that the actions and experiences of menstrual activists are expressive of an ethics of care. By understanding care as going beyond 'the narrow confines of the private sphere' (Tronto 1991: 7), I discuss how caring for the body extends to a broader relationship of caring for the environment and caring for the community and future generations. I argue that the actions of menstrual activists are a form of environmental and social activism aimed at transforming their embodied menstrual experiences, as well as producing a direct social and environmental impact. I examine the practices of care alongside Science and Technology Studies (STS), a framework useful for this discussion due to its concern with the politics of technology, which contributes 'to an understanding of social and political change by exploring how technologies and new forms of social life are co-produced' (Wajcman 2006: 707).

## Feminist Political Ecology

FPE emerged as an interdisciplinary academic field in the 1990s through the work of Dianne Rocheleau, Barbara Thomas-Slayter and Esther Wangari, when *Feminist Political Ecology: Global Issues and Local Experiences* (1996) was first published. FPE appeared as a critique of sustainable development and as a contribution to the expansion of Political Ecology. FPE 'brings into a single framework a feminist perspective combined with analysis of ecological, economic and political power relations' (Rocheleau *et al.* 1996: 287). FPE has challenged essentialist understandings, by which women are seen as being closer to the natural environment. Through this association, it is argued that there is a natural connection between women and the natural environment, which gives women an intrinsic and better understanding of the environment and how it should be protected (Shiva 1988). However, as Andrea Nightingale explains, this approach uses the blanket category of 'women' without recognising the real differences that can exist between women. Furthermore, 'it was assumed that all women would have the same kind of sympathies and understandings of environmental change as a consequence of their close connection to nature' (Nightingale 2006: 167).

FPE argues that gender differences are indeed real and they therefore shape the experiences, responsibilities and interests of people related to the environment. However, from an FPE perspective, these differences do not necessarily have their roots in biology. Rather, they stem from the social interpretation of the biological and social constructions of gender, which will vary depending on the cultural, class, racial and geographical contexts, and which at the same time are subject to individual and social change over time. In that sense, FPE rejects the theory that women are biologically closer to nature and 'advocates a poststructural position, which recognises and affirms women's socially constructed environmental knowledge, skills, associations, and values across a diverse range of contexts, including culture, class, and nationality' (Rocheleau and Nirmal 2015: 797).

FPE has been developed on the basis of a series of empirical case studies from around the world. This body of work presents an analysis of gendered experiences and responses to environmental change, problems and vulnerabilities in rural and urban areas in countries from both the Global North and the Global South. Most of the work done within FPE demonstrates how gender, race, class, caste and ethnicity, along other variables, are conceived as mutually embedded 'axes of power,' in the sense that they define the access to and control of resources, particular types of knowledge, environmental decision-making and social-political processes. By focussing on these structures, FPE provides important tools 'for arguing that men and women have differential opportunities and challenges in relation to environmental change and development' (Nightingale 2006: 169). This speaks of the importance of looking at gender and its interrelationship with social, economic and political aspects when analysing politics of control, rights to access to resources and environmental decision-making.

As pointed out by Rocheleau and Nirmal, the academic literature, the popular press and even alternative social movement media have often disregarded or actively denied women's contributions to the protection of the environment (Rocheleau and Nirmal 2015). Through a collection of empirical studies from different parts of the world, FPE aims to present evidence that enriches theory and closes this gap. As explained by Rocheleau and Nirmal, 'this matters for reasons of equity – that is, to ensure and to recognise women's leadership and contributions in ecological innovation, decisions, and the vision of possible futures' (2015: 795). Therefore, a significant contribution from FPE has been to draw attention to the asymmetry in Political Ecology studies, due to its blindness to gender and other differences. However, as pointed out by Rocheleau and Nirmal (2015), FPE goes beyond noting the presence of women in and their contributions to the different streams of Political Ecology, both in process and in content: 'feminist thought and practices challenge conventional ideas of gender, sexuality, identity, and affinity' (Rocheleau and Nirmal, 2015: 795).

Currently, FPE scholars are reflecting on the notion of sustaining livelihoods, which suggests that ecological and social change 'start from the level of the everyday life, social reproduction and ongoing people's struggles for gender-aware ecological and social justice' (Harcourt and Nelson 2015: 12). From an FPE approach, the term 'livelihoods' refers to the securing of one's needs in more ways than just financially. Livelihoods are also 'everyday, embodied and emotional relations to resources and natures' (Harris 2015: 158). Through this understanding, FPE moves away from livelihoods approaches that are narrowly focused on market-based and capitalist logics of value; by contrast, it is 'attentive to everyday needs, embodied interactions and labours as well as emotional and affective relations with our environments and natures where we live' (Harcourt and Nelson 2015: 13).

## The ethics of care

In this chapter I follow Fisher and Tronto's definition of care, which offers an understanding of care as an activity or practice – in the sense that goes beyond being a mental or an emotional concern – that is not only directed towards oneself but also toward people, things, living beings and the environment. In 'Toward a Feminist Theory of Caring,' Fisher and Tronto define care thus:

> On the most general level, we suggest that caring be viewed as a species' activity that includes everything that we do to maintain, continue and repair our world so that we can live in it as well as possible. That world includes our bodies, ourselves, and our environment, all of which we seek to interweave in a complex, life-sustaining web.
>
> (1990: 40)

It is important to disaggregate these terms in order to gain a deeper understanding of this definition. In the first place, Fisher and Tronto define care as an activity. For Tronto, this 'refers to a mental disposition or concern and to actual practices that we engage in as a result of these concerns' (Tronto 2001: 61). This is a central consideration in order to avoid over-idealising care in order to understand it as practices that go beyond emotional investments. In *Globalising Care: Ethics, Feminist Theory and International Relations*, Fiona Robinson explains that care is a contextual practice of relational nature (Robinson 1997). The practice of care is contextual insofar as its understanding and enactment will be specific to a particular environment/society. Every socio-cultural context has a particular understanding of what care is, how care should be organised, and why care is relevant. Joan Tronto also embraces this pluralistic vision in her conception of care, as she explains: 'the activity of caring is largely defined culturally, and will vary among different cultures' (1993: 103). Yet, she argues, 'despite the fact that the meanings of care vary from one society to another, and from one group to another, care is nonetheless a universal aspect of human life' (1993: 110). The understanding of what 'good care' means will depend on the socio-cultural context, the ways of life and of the people who are engaged in the caring practice. Which means that in every particular instance, caring is expressed in a unique manner that is linked to the situational setting in which it takes place. In this discussion, Lucy Jarosz's (2011) work with women farmers involved in community-supported agriculture in the US is very relevant. She demonstrates that human–care–environment interactions are socially shaped and particular to geographic and historical contexts. Her analysis then rejects the notion that women are biologically closer to nature, 'which places women as nurturers, environmental caregivers, and allies of nature' (Jackson 1993). Discussing small-scale organic agriculture, Jarosz explains that the ethics of care 'does not spring from a "special" relationship that women have with nature, [it] emerges out of conscious desire to live and think in a way that improves both the individual and the lives of others, as well as being environmentally conscious' (Jarosz 2011: 319–20).

According to Fisher and Tronto (1990) care has four separate but intertwining phases: caring about, care of, caregiving and care-receiving. Caring about involves 'paying attention to our world in such a way that we focus on continuity, maintenance, and repair' of our world (1990: 40). Limitations on resources, time and knowledge have an obvious impact on how we care about something, forcing us to make choices. The next phase is taking care of, which involves recognising one's responsibility for the identified need and defining how to respond to it. 'Taking care of requires more continuous time spent and more explicit knowledge of the situation than does caring about' (1990: 40). Caregiving, in contrast, involves 'the concrete responses, the hands-on work of maintenance and repair' (1990: 40). Here, the knowledge about 'how to care' is key, mainly because it is about choosing one course of action over another, but also because it is a matter of responsibility and accountability of consequences. The last category is care-receiving, which encompasses the effects or response (not necessarily conscious, human or intentional) of the caregiving from a thing, a person, group of people or the environment.

## Why looking into menstrual management technologies matters in an analysis of care

Menstrual management products are not usually seen as being about care, nor about technologies. One explanation is because they are so ingrained in daily lives, they are not included in definitions of technology (McGaw 2003). It can also be because technologies tend to be commonly associated with masculinity (Wajcman 2008), or maybe because technology tends to be related to complex mechanisms like sophisticated electronics and hardware, molecular combinations or rockets. However, menstrual management products have been defined as technologies since the early 2000s (McGaw 2003, Vostral, 2008). McGaw and Vostral demonstrate that bringing technologies into the analysis of menstruation allows for a wider realm of exploration; one that shows the political, economic, historical and cultural aspects of design process, its role and uses in society. As Vostral states: '[when] defined as a technology, the physical artefact, knowledge about its function, and how people use it can all be analysed' (Vostral 2008: 12). Hence, looking at menstrual products as technologies enables us to understand the various logics that went into the design and creation of technologies. We can also hereby scrutinise the multiple intended and unintended consequences of their use – by society in general as well as by the individual users. As explained by Dombroski *et al.* (this volume) 'the work of care is being done by diverse gatherings, not only of people but of many other elements that assemble to enable care-work to be undertaken.' Including technologies in this analysis allows me to see how the practices of care are mediated by human but also by non-human actors.

## Care for the body, care for the environment and care for the future generations

### Care for the body

> We women know very little of our body, at least here in Argentina. So the first time I saw the menstrual cup, I found it extremely weird. My first question was *How do I wear that? It is huge! That thing will get lost inside of my body! If so, how do I get it out?* Well, despite the doubts, I bought it. Pads and tampons started to irritate my skin and gave me allergies, so I was desperately looking for [other] options. I use [the cup] every month. [...] It became more than something to collect my blood; it became a tool to explore and know more about my body.
>
> (Natalia 2016)[1]

Like Natalia, many of the women I met in the course of this study often spoke about searching for healthy alternatives to manage menstruation as a way to take care of their body. Allergies to tampons, disposable pads, the well-known presence of dioxins in these technologies (DeVito and Schecter, 2002, Mazgaj *et al.* 2006) and the fear of getting Toxic Shock Syndrome by using tampons (Tierno 2005) motivated women on this search. Additionally, in 2015 a team of scientists at a local university (Marino and Peluso 2015) found glyphosate in tampons and sanitary pads sold in Argentina. Glyphosate is used in the fumigation of pine and eucalyptus trees, from which the absorbent material (FLUFF pulp) of pads and tampons is made (Korol, 2013). Glyphosate has gained a lot of public interest from a public health perspective. The International Agency for Research on Cancer (IARC), the specialised cancer agency of the World Health Organisation, has classified this compound as *probably carcinogenic* (IARC, 2015). In addition, local researchers have documented the negative health effects caused by human exposure to or contact with glyphosate in Argentina. These studies reveal that there is a direct relationship between glyphosate and cancer, fertility problems and malformations (Eleisegui, 2013, Sández, 2016). Marino and Peluso's (2015) study was extensively covered by the local press, which raised the population's awareness about the health risks of using disposable tampons and pads (El Federal 2015, Infobae 2015, LaVoz 2015, Telam 2015, UnoSantafe 2015). In this regard, and alerted by the presence of the pesticide, some of my participants mentioned that they started to search for alternatives that would not put their health at risk.

There are still very few scientific studies to date that analyse the safety – or danger – of reusable menstrual technologies, mainly the menstrual cup. Medical literature coming from the United States and Canada has shown that the product is harmless to women's health (Howard *et al.* 2011, Shihata and Brody 2014). However, in 2015 a medical report from Western University, Canada, documented *a rare case* in a 37-year-old woman in which the use of the menstrual cup was associated with menstrual TSS (Mitchell *et al.* 2015). To my knowledge, this is the first documented case that links the menstrual cup to TSS. Nevertheless, the menstrual cup, as with other reusable menstrual technologies, is commonly associated with healthier products. A certain positive reputation has been created around these products that frame them as safe for one's health, and increasingly more women are deciding to make a change based on this characteristic.

The use of the menstrual cup, however, demands strict hygiene practices so as not to become a vector of infections. In the framework of healthcare, those who promote this product in Argentina have been in charge of emphasising several hygiene measures – not only that a reliable water source is essential for using the menstrual cup, but also proper care, like washing hands before insertion and removal, or boiling the menstrual cup in clean water.

Going back to Natalia's opening statement, she points out that, unexpectedly, the menstrual cup became a tool for learning about her body. This was not an isolated experience; I repeatedly heard similar reflections from my participants and not only referring to the cup, but to the reusable pads and the sea sponges. For instance, my participants talked about having begun to explore their own bodies in '3D' in order to be able to use the menstrual cup and the sea sponges. Many of them talked about feeling curiosity but also fear of hurting themselves or of 'finding something unexpected' at the beginning of their self-discovery process. They also spoke about how knowing more about their bodies and sexuality made them feel self-empowered and capable of challenging and contradicting misinformation around their sexual and reproductive health.

The self-learning process, very personal and private, was supported by online discussions in private Facebook groups and online forums, as well as by short informational booklets and pamphlets circulating in different gatherings and fairs. These informational channels play an important role in explaining how to use reusable menstrual technologies, but they also go beyond that. They cover information about the functioning of the female body, female anatomy and the menstrual cycle, and offer natural home remedies recipes to help relieve menstrual cramps and heal vaginal infections.

One of my interviewees, Macarena, a sociology student, inspired by some of her friends who had switched to reusable pads, bought one of these booklets at a fair when she bought her first set of reusable menstrual pads. She explained to me that the booklet was key in the learning process about her body:

> Just two years ago, I started to get to know my body and I am 30 years old. It [the booklet] was seriously educational. It taught me about my body with far more intimacy than has been achieved through various gynaecologists that I went to throughout my life. It took me a while but I learned to examine myself and this was a gift of ownership over my body.
>
> (Macarena, 2016)[2]

An important dimension related to care comes from the observation, exploration and knowledge of the anatomy and the different processes of change that the body experiences. This dimension of care sometimes manifests itself in self-care: from the awareness about one's body to the preparation of homemade remedies and body practices or exercises to help relieve menstrual cramp pain and cure vaginal infections. At the same time, these forms of self-care seek self-management, for instance, in breaking the dependency on painkillers (especially Ibuprofen/Ibuvanol, which are prescribed in cases of menstrual cramps) as well as some women have started to give themselves vaginal and cervical self-exams.

Verona has organised several get-togethers to learn about the menstrual cycle and sexuality in different parts of Argentina. Verona is a dancer who has been learning about sexuality and the female anatomy for many years. She began investigating the causes of menstrual cramps and alternatives to reducing the pain because she suffered from very strong cramps herself. She aims to promote self-knowledge of the body that understands corporeality as encompassing more than just a physical aspect.

> The body is a territory of a great memory – memory of the places where I have been, of my relations with others and of my entire lineage. In my body is the violence and love that I have felt. Everything is there, I see it without denial, receive it; but I also have the ability to transform it. We all do.
>
> (Verona 2016)[3]

To understand the body as such implies what authors like Yvonne Underhill-Sem (2005), Elizabeth Grosz (1994) and Helen Keane and Marsha Rosengarten (2002) have argued: bodies are not just inert and passive matter where biological and social categories are ascribed. Rather, the body is itself a site of knowledge, resistance and empowerment, where traditional or modern practices and narratives can be challenged. What I could observe is that categories generally associated with the menstrual body in Argentina such as *ill*, *weak* and *dirty*

(Rohatsch 2013, Felliti 2016) were challenged with different and even sometimes, opposing discourses. On the one hand, some of my interviewees seek to speak about menstruation without censorship, as something normal and not as a debilitating bodily illness. For them, this is key for opening the space to problematise the health, the environment and the economic effects related to the dominant practices of menstrual management. On the other hand, some of my participants had a more radical view with respect to reversing these negative meanings and highlighting the positive qualities of this menstrual body. Along this line, authors such as Miranda Gray (2010), Clarissa Pinkola (2001), Anna Salvia Rivera (2003) and Casilda Rodrigañez (2015), who could be seen as ecofeminists despite not using that term themselves, are key references. These authors celebrate femininity, perceive menstrual blood as sacred and see the menstrual cycle even as an empowering experience in women's lives. In some of the conversations with my participants, these authors were an inescapable reference, also to explain the functioning of the female body and its anatomy. Finally, in the process of the resignification of the menstrual body, many women have also come closer to the knowledge of the indigenous people of South America. To my surprise, Carmen Vicente, a medicine woman and Chief of the Sacred Fire of Itzachilatlan, with whom I have shared more than a few experiences in Ecuador, was a renowned reference among several of my interviewees. My participants spoke about specific systems of study, training and practices that they have followed for years under her leadership, which have allowed them to understand the menstrual body from a different perspective than the Western and biomedical one, and through which they have also learned more spiritual aspects of their corporeity.

### Care for the environment

Care for the environment with regard to menstrual management refers to the ways and efforts to counteract the environmental effects of the production of disposable menstrual technologies and the waste resulting from the use of these technologies. In several conversations with the producers of reusable menstrual technologies, the respondents reflected on the design of the menstrual cup and the reusable pads and their relation with the environment. Their visions take up some ideas coming from the philosophy of deep ecology in the sense that they value highly the well-being of all life forms (human and non-human) independent of the ensuing utilitarian or instrumental benefits to human beings (Devall and Sessions 2015). Berenice's reflection, for example, is very revealing. Berenice has been devoted to exploring and learning about sexuality and female anatomy since 2003, after living in Mexico. According to her, she was the first one to make reusable pads in Argentina. At first, she took inspiration from the Blood Sisters, menstrual activists located in Montreal, Canada. However, with the passage of time, she consolidated her own understanding and ways of sharing information about menstruation, women's health and the environmental impact of disposable products in a context like Argentina. Berenice has owned a reusable menstrual pads brand called Luna Roja (Red Moon) since 2003. She explained that the philosophy behind Luna Roja

> Is love, care and awareness about our bodies. That awareness is also recognising that our body is the same body as Gaia. I do not think we live in Gaia but we are Gaia. That is why Luna Roja's motto is: no precise boundary between your body and the Earth.
>
> (Berenice 2016)[4]

By not seeing a boundary between human bodies and Earth, Berenice regards humans as part of nature. As such, she sees nature not just as something external to us that we should take care of, but as something intrinsic to us, something in which we participate.

Berenice's point of view was not unique among my interviewees. Lola, a self-defined anarchist feminist, who first met the reusable pads at a punk *Do it Yourself* festival, spoke about the reusable menstrual pads that she makes and that she also teaches others to make as 'a contribution to live gracefully with our planet' (Lola 2016).[5] For Lola, *living gracefully with the planet*, is not just about not polluting; it is about doing things differently, from consuming less, to 'doing it yourself' (DIY) instead of buying products, from replacing monetary transactions with the exchange for a good or a service. Of all my interviewees who make reusable pads, Lola was the only one who works with scraps of fabric discarded by a textile company. She considers that today we live in a culture where we waste a lot and that is a big part of our environmental problems. Thus, part of her motivation to use discarded fabrics is to neutralise this habit. Another strong factor in her motivation is that using the discarded fabrics reduces the cost of the reusable pads, allowing her to sell them at a better price, which in turn allows many more women access to them.

Another of my interviewees sees care and environment from the perspective of biomimicry. Clarisa is a psychologist and has a master's degree in Teaching Special Education. She has worked on sex education projects in schools as well as with disabled children and their parents. Clarisa is the co-founder of the Argentinean menstrual cup. She explained that the menstrual cup is a *project* inspired by the Biomimicry philosophy, a topic on which she was doing her Ph.D. studies. Promoters of the Biomimicry philosophy such as the natural scientist Janine Benyus, consider that Biomimicry is 'a new way of viewing and valuing nature. It introduces an era based not on what we can extract from the natural world, but on what we can learn from it' (Benyus 2002). Other supporters of Biomimicry argue that 'humanity should not merely curb consumption, reduce population and generally adopt as far as possible a hands-off approach to nature, as earlier generations of environmentalists insisted, but rather should aim to integrate socio-economic processes with ecological processes' (Mathews 2011). Clarisa sees no separation between human and non-human actors, and it is this view of the harmony between us and other forms of life that drove her to make the menstrual cup. For Clarisa,

> The cup is harmonious with both the body of women and with nature. […] We just need to look at the genius of nature and learn from it. Nature recycles everything. Does not produce waste. That is what we are aiming with the cup.
>
> (Clarisa, 2016)[6]

In the case of Clarisa, this understanding of nature encouraged her not only to undertake the project of the menstrual cup, but also to embark on other initiatives related to the protection of the Amazonian forest. Primary forest is being logged in the Amazon to convert land into pasture for cattle grazing or to cultivate softwood, mostly pine and eucalyptus (Korol 2013). Clarisa's company established a direct alliance with an environmental organisation that works in the protection of forests, the NGO Banco de Bosques (Forest Bank), through which for each purchased menstrual cup, a donation is made to the NGO to protect one square metre of the Amazonian primary forest (Maggacup n.d.).

Some users of the cup who participated in this study, belonging mostly to the upper or middle class, were aware of the initiative of protection of the Amazonian forests and it partly motivated them to choose that brand. Valeria, a graduate in environmental sciences, was one of them:

> When I heard from her [the seller of the menstrual cup] that using the menstrual cup prevents logging, I said, *what? How are those two things connected?* At that time, I didn't know that menstrual pads were made with wood pulp, [even though] I did environmental studies. […].
>
> (Valeria 2016)[7]

Furthermore, reusable menstrual technologies are also presented as alternatives to prevent the production of disposable menstrual waste. In the *Autonomous City of Buenos Aires*, disposable menstrual waste and diapers[8] make up 5.2 per cent of the total solid waste and are thus the fourth biggest waste factor in the municipality (FIUBA and CEAMSE 2016). Just to put these numbers in perspective, in 2015 diapers and disposable menstrual technologies waste amounted to a higher volume than pruning and garden waste (4.9 per cent), construction and demolition debris (4.7 per cent) and textile materials waste (4.6 per cent) (FIUBA and CEAMSE 2016). Despite this high volume, however, waste coming from disposable menstrual technologies is not a priority component for the Ministry of Environment of the city. Therefore, this type of waste does not have a post-use or post-consumption treatment, as other components like food waste, glass or plastics do (Gaybor and Chavez forthcoming). This is particularly problematic, as this waste will remain in the landfill for years. The durability and strength of plastic from which disposable pads, the most consumed menstrual technology in Argentina (Euromonitor 2016), and tampon applicators are made can have a lifetime of hundreds of years. Even one of the largest transnational companies selling tampons claims to have stopped its production of applicators because of the quantity and quality of garbage they produce, arguing that 'plastic applicators are not easy to dispose because they have a lifespan of 500 to 1,000 years' (O.B. 2017). Despite being aware of the existence of technological alternatives that could prevent the production of this type of waste, the governmental bodies are not considering them as part of the prevention strategies to reduce waste production (Gaybor and Chavez forthcoming).

### Care for future generations

My interviewees speak about understanding the natural environment as an integral part of the lives of human beings; they see a close relationship and a dependence of the human beings on non-human others, which partially marked their motivation to do what they do. Following Martínez-Alier (2010), those who have not been indifferent to the serious environmental crisis that we are experiencing today have found multiple ways to show their disagreement, whether they opted for some forms of protest, or have tried to change the system (from within or from outside), or have (partially or fully) changed their lifestyles. The focus of what my participants do, in a certain way, has manifested mostly in the latter: a change of lifestyle, oriented to take care of the body and care of the environment. To these two, I would add the care of future generations, a cross-cutting theme between the notion of care for the body and care for the environment, as current dominant menstrual management practices affect future generations. Nonetheless, these *future generations* cannot protest or change their lifestyle, because they have not yet been born. Something similar could be said regarding non-human others, who simply cannot protest or change the system. In that sense, this dimension of care goes beyond caring for ourselves and our current environment (in the present) and contemplates those who are not yet present and those who are but do not have a voice to express themselves.

Individually or collectively, women involved in menstrual politics make efforts to change current menstrual practices and contribute socially and environmentally to the well-being of future generations. On the one hand, they are opening the discussion and problematising the large environmental impacts linked to the production and use of disposable, plastic-made menstrual technologies. This comes from the hand of creating alternatives to these burdens through the design and production of reusable menstrual technologies that have an impact on reducing waste production and logging, and on changing consumption habits with regard to menstrual management.

On the other hand, care for future generations also has to do with the new meanings and senses about menstruation. In her book *Under Wraps: A History of Menstrual Technologies*, Sharra Vostral (2008) discusses how disposable menstrual technologies are used as *tools for passing*. For Vostral, disposables help women to effectively mask their entire menstrual period and pass as non-bleeders, but at the same time, this results in promoting bodily shame and shame for being a menstruating woman, which in turn passes from one generation of women to another. Vostral argues that the ways that current menstrual practices are performed are historically connected with the menstrual hygiene industries' marketing strategies. Care for future generations in this discussion then entails passing knowledge and other understanding about the menstrual body on to the next generations. This may take the form of seeing menstruation as a natural process and not as an illness, but also understanding other dimensions connected to our current menstrual management practices, such as the connection between menstrual practices and the environment and the need to shift from consumerist habits.

Re-signifying the menstrual body has not been, according to my interviewees, an easy task, especially in the past. Many spoke of having been silenced and mocked by their friends and family and recalled having received insults on social networks. Two of my interviewees even spoke of having been expelled from a craft fair at which they sold their products (reusable pads). However, when they talk about the present time, they see that there is more respect and openness towards the subject. Despite recognising many difficulties, they find that it is already possible to talk about the topic and that many of their questions echo in the people with whom they share them.

## Conclusion

In this chapter, I have examined the perspectives of women making meanings of their caring practices around the topic of menstruation. I have explored how these meanings are part of the construction of an emerging politics of menstruation centred on caring, which, as Ana Agostino puts it, involves 'an attentive consciousness of others (and the self)' (2015: 822). The women that participated in my study spoke about how their everyday practices of care relate to individual aspirations and interests, such as good health and body self-awareness. Nevertheless, at the same time these practices of care relate to community aspirations and collective values, such as the protection of the environment and the well-being of future generations. Conceiving care from this perspective involves understanding the interconnectedness of our practices, others and the environment, and therefore transcends individual interests while seeking to reach collective goals to improve our mutual well-being. Care in this way is both a way of enabling change 'step by step' and a form of deconstruction of self-centred ways of living by challenging processes that construct individualistic subjects (Davies 2006).

Communicating these alternative meanings has not always been easy, especially when the women began this journey years ago. Many of them received insults and were mocked when they talked about the subject, even in spaces that they considered 'friendly' with the topic. Some of them recall not having the support of their families and friends and even being boycotted by them. Their perseverance despite the multiple obstacles they faced has been their first achievement, leading to a feeling of agency and empowerment. As a result, when they reflect on the present days, they have a more positive perspective: not only do they see a progressive change in the way menstruation is managed, but their voices are being heard and they are gradually becoming a stronger network. Furthermore, nowadays there is 'a wave' of entrepreneurship projects around the innovation of reusable menstrual technologies, which is expanding faster than ever in the last twenty years. Nevertheless, I must say a word on the limitations and contradictions around menstrual technologies themselves. My interviewees recognise the limitations of their efforts concerning the places where they focus their initiatives: urban areas, middle- or upper-class neighbourhoods. The prices of their products and events are often only affordable to mostly middle- and higher-class circles. Something similar can be said about the price of booklets – while some of them are free, many of them have a price, usually prohibitive for the participation of many sectors of the population. This also goes for workshops and events. However, my interviewees have also known how to be creative with alternative economic systems, based on reciprocity, voluntary contributions, exchange or gift.

Finally, women's practices around menstruation management associated with the three dimensions of care indeed show an alternative view of the body and the environment as well as of the relation between the two. From an FPE perspective, in this chapter I argued that these understandings, values and knowledge of care do not originate from the fact that they are women, but rather from their personal life experiences, trajectories, their collective learning processes and reflections, and the degrees of power they have in their context. The meanings of which they speak and the practices that arise from alternatives to the biomedical understanding of the female body make them in a certain way outsiders within their own urban, middle-class contexts. On the one hand, the process of openly speaking about menstruation and the re-signification of the menstrual body from a care perspective is transgressive, as it goes against socially stablished codes of conduct. On the other hand, they do not conceive nature as important because of the utilitarian and instrumental value it has to human beings, which is a profoundly embedded assumption in the dominant Western culture. Instead, many of them strive for environmental change through believing in the interconnectedness between human beings (not only women) with the living environment and non-human others. The exploitation of the environment is also the exploitation of our health, our future and ourselves. Thus, these approaches not only propose a significant change with respect to how we understand menstruation and its multiple economic, environmental, social, health and political dimensions. They invite us to see the well-being of life forms (human and non-human) as having its own intrinsic value regardless of any utilitarian or instrumental benefits it may offer to human beings.

## Notes

1 Focus group discussion conducted in Buenos Aires, 1 November 2016.
2 Interview conducted in Buenos Aires, 9 October 2016.
3 Interview conducted in Buenos Aires, 18 November 2016.
4 Interview conducted in Buenos Aires, 18 November 2016.
5 Interview conducted in Buenos Aires, 12 November 2016.
6 Conversation held on 3 November 2017.
7 Focus group discussion conducted in Buenos Aires, 2 November 2016.
8 In this study, diapers and disposable menstrual technologies are grouped into one single component. Unfortunately, this prevents greater precision on the exact quantity of either component.

## References

Agostino, A., 2015. Climate justice and women's agency: voicing other ways of doing things. *In*: B. Rawwida and W. Harcourt, eds., *The Oxford Handbook of Transnational Feminist Movements*. Oxford: Oxford University Press, 815–36.

Devall, B. and Sessions, G., 2015. Deep ecology. *In*: L.P. Pojman, P. Pojman and K. McShane, eds., *Environmental Ethics: Readings in Theory and Application*. Boston: Cengage Learning, 231–7.

DeVito, M. and Schecter, A., 2002. Exposure assessment to dioxins from the use of tampons and diapers. *Environmental Health Perspectives*, 110 (1), 23–8.

Economiafeminita, n.d. *Proyectos de ley: #MenstruAcción como un derecho*. Buenos Aires: Campaña #Menstruacción. [online] Available from: #http://economiafeminita.com/m enstruaccion/proyecto-de-ley/ [Accessed 17 June 2018].

Eleisegui, P., 2013. *Envenenados: Una Bomba Química Nos Extermina en Silencio*. Buenos Aires: Gárgola.

Euromonitor, 2016. *Sanitary Protection in Argentina*. Passport.

El Federal, 2015. *Encuentran glifosato en algodón, gasas y tampones*. Buenos Aires: El Federal. [online] Available from: http://www.elfederal.com.ar/encuentran-glifosato-en-algodon-gasas-y-tampones/ [Accessed 17 June 2018].

Felliti, K., 2016. El tabu de la menstruacion: Sangre azul. San Martín: Revista Anfibia.

Fisher, B. and Tronto, J.C., 1990. Toward a feminist theory of caring. *In*: E. Abel and M. Nelson, eds., *Circles of Care: Work and Identity in Women's Lives*. Albany, NY: State University of New York Press, 35–62.

FIUBA and CEAMSE, 2016. *Estudio calidad de los residuos sólidos urbanos (RSU) de la ciudad autónoma de Buenos Aires*. Buenos Aires.: Coordinación Ecológica Metropolitana (CEAMSE) y Facultad de Ingeniería de la Universidad de Buenos Aires (FIUBA).

Gray, M., 2010. *Luna Roja: Emplea los dones creativos, sexuales y espirituales*. Madrid: Gaia.

Grosz, E., 1994. *Volatile Bodies : Toward a Corporeal Feminism*. Bloomington, IN: Indiana University Press.

Harcourt, W. and Nelson, I.L., eds., 2015. *Practising Feminist Political Ecologies: Moving Beyond the 'Green Economy'*. London: Zed Books.

Harris, L., 2015. Hegemonic waters and rethinking natures otherwise. *In*: W. Harcourt and I.L. Nelson, eds., *Practising Feminist Political Ecologies: Moving Beyond the 'Green Economy'*. London: Zed Books.

Howard, C., Rose, C., Trouton, K., Stamm, H., Marentette, D., Kirkpatrick, N., Karalic, S., Fernandez, R. and Paget, J., 2011. FLOW (finding lasting options for women) Multicentre randomised controlled trial comparing tampons with menstrual cups. *Canadian Family Physician*, 57 (6), e208–15.

IARC, 2015. *Carcinogenicity of tetrachlorvinphos, parathion, malathion, diazinon, and glyphosate. The Lancet Oncology*, 16 (5), 490–1.

Infobae, 2015. Hallaron glifosato en algodón, gasas, hisopos, toallitas y tampones de La Plata. *Infobae*, 20 October.

Jackson, C., 1993. Women/nature or gender/history? A critique of ecofeminist 'development'. *The Journal of Peasant Studies*, 20 (3), 389–418.

Jarosz, L., 2011. Nourishing women: toward a feminist political ecology of community supported agriculture in the United States. *Gender, Place and Culture*, 18 (3), 307–26.

Keane, H. and Rosengarten, M., 2002. On the biology of sexed subjects. *Australian Feminist Studies*, 17 (39), 261–77.

Korol, S., 2013. *Informe nacional Argentina (2) Resistencias populares contra Alto Paraná S.A.: La experiencia de P.I.P. en la Provincia de Misiones*. Misiones: Instituto de Desarrollo Social y Promoción Humana.

LaVoz, 2015. La Plata: investigadores dicen haber hallado glifosato en algodón, gasas y tampones. *LaVoz* [online], 20 October. Available from: http://www.lavoz.com.ar/c iudadanos/la-plata-investigadores-dicen-haber-hallado-glifosato-en-algodon-gasas-y-ta mpones [Accessed 17 June 2018].

Maggacup, n.d. *Descubrí los beneficios de Maggacup!* [online] Available from: Maggacup: http://www.maggacup.com.ar/ [Accessed 17 June 2018].

Marino, D. and Peluso, L., 2015. *Residuos de Glifosato y su metabolito AMPA en muestras de algodón y derivados*. La Plata.: Presented at the III Congreso de Médicos de Pueblos Fumigados-UBA, EMISA – Universidad de La Plata.

Martínez-Alier, J., Pascual, U. and Vivien, F., 2010. Sustainable de-growth: mapping the context, criticisms and future prospects of an emergent paradigm. *Ecological Economics*, 69 (9), 1741–7.

Mathews, F., 2011. Towards a deeper philosophy of biomimicry. *Organisation and Environment*, 24 (4), 364–87.

Mazgaj, M., Yaramenka, K. and Malovana, O., 2006. *Comparative Life Cycle Assessment of Sanitary Pads and Tampons*. Stockholm: Royal Institute of Technology Stockholm.

McGaw, J.A., 2003. Why feminine technologies matter. *In*: N.E. Lerman, R. Oldenziel and A.P. Mohun, eds., *Gender and Technology*. Baltimore, MD: Johns Hopkins University Press, 13–36.

Mitchell, M., Bisch, S., Arntfield, S. and Hosseini-Moghaddam, S., 2015. A confirmed case of toxic shock syndrome associated with the use of a menstrual cup. *Canadian Journal of Infectious Diseases and Medical Microbiology*, 26 (4), 218–20.

Nightingale, A., 2006. The nature of gender: work, gender, and environment. *Environment and Planning D: Society and Space*, 24 (2), 165–85.

O.B., 2017. *Tampones Ob – Un Tampón que se adelanta su tiempo* [online]. Tampones O.B España: Available from: http://www.tamponesob.es [Accessed 17 June 2018].

Pinkola, C., 2001. *Mujeres que corren con los lobos*. Barcelona: Zeta Ediciones.

Rivera, A.S., 2003. *Viaje Al Ciclo Menstrual*. Barcelona.

Robinson, F., 1997. Globalising care: ethics, feminist theory, and international relations. *Alternatives: Global, Local, Political*, 22 (1), 113–33.

Rocheleau, D. and Nirmal, P., 2015. Feminist political ecologies grounded, networked and rooted on Earth. *In*: R. Baksh and W. Harcourt, eds, *The Oxford Handbook of Transnational Feminist Movements*. Oxford: Oxford University Press, 793–814.

Rodriganez, C., 2015. *Pariremos con placer*. Santiago, Chile: Crimental.

Rohatsch, M., 2013. ¿Estás venida? Experiencias y representaciones sobre menstruación entre niñas. *Avatares*, 6.

Sández, F., 2016. *La Argentina Fumigada*. Buenos Aires: Planeta.

Shihata, A. and Brody, S., 2014. An innovative, reusable menstrual cup that enhances the quality of women's lives during menstruation. *British Journal of Medicine and Medical Research*, 4 (19), 3581.

Shiva, V., 1988. *Staying Alive: Women, Ecology and Development*. London: Zed Books.

Telam, 2015. Investigadores de La Plata encuentran glifosato en algodon, gasas, hisopos, toallitas y tampones. *Telam*.

Tierno, P., 2005. Reemergence of staphylococcal toxic shock syndrome in the United States since 2000. *Journal Clinical Microbiology*, 43 (4), 2032–3.

Tronto, J.C., 1991. *Reflections on Gender, Morality and Power: Caring and moral problems of otherness. Gender, Care and Justice in Feminist Political Theory*. Utrecht, the Netherlands: University of Utrecht.

Tronto, J.C., 2001. An ethic of care. *In*: M.B. Holstein and P.B. Mitzen, eds., *Ethics in Community-Based Elder Care*. New York: Springer, 60–8.

Underhill-Sem, Y., 2005. Bodies in places, places in bodies. *In*: W. Harcourt and A. Escobar, eds., *Women and the Politics of Place*. Sterling, VA: Kumarian Press, 20–31.

UNOSantafe, 2015. Agroquímicos: tampones y algodones contienen glifosato. *UNOSantafe*, 26 October.

Vostral, S.L., 2008. *Under Wraps: A History of Menstrual Hygiene Technology*. Lanham, MD: Lexington Books.

Wajcman, J., 2006. The gender politics of technology. *In*: R.E. Goodin and C. Tilly, eds., *The Oxford Handbook of Contextual Political Analysis*. Oxford: Oxford University Press, 707–21.

# 13 Bodies, aspirations and the politics of place

## Learning from the women brickmakers of La Ladrillera

*Azucena Gollaz Morán*

## Introduction

In this chapter I explore the relations and tensions among people, places, labour and development through the narratives of care as practised by three generations of women from La Ladrillera, a brickmaking community. The neighbourhood is located in Tonalá, one of the municipalities with the highest levels of poverty, violence and crime of the Metropolitan Area of Guadalajara, the second largest city in Mexico. I explore the reconstruction of the intergenerational transformations of the different places the brickmaking women inhabit: body, home, environment and public arena.

My analytical framing in the chapter is to explore how embodied experiences of women expose how patriarchal and violent development practices and discourses leave deep injuries in bodies and places, and mark memories and histories. At the same time, I explore how women's political practices constitute forms of resistance to development assumptions and interventions, thus opening spaces for the revision and reformulation of care in theories about political economy and ecology.

Women's practices of difference present other ways of thinking and doing about bodies and places in transformation processes where the practices of care are essential to societies. Their practices of care illustrate how challenging it is to speak about recognition and re-signification of care as well as transformation of the gender power relations.

I start with my own story of involvement with development and how I met the women from La Ladrillera. Then I explain how the politics of place framework (Harcourt and Escobar 2002) helps me to understand women's placed-based politics as I elaborate further on the women's narratives of care and how I see the women from La Ladrillera contributing to our discussions on Feminist Political Ecology and economics of care.

## Encounters

When a storm hits La Ladrillera, freshly made bricks are destroyed. After the rain, brickmakers gather up the mud of the ruined bricks, mix it again with a shovel and step on it to make it smooth. Then, they put the mud into moulds with their hands and once more refashion the bricks with hope that this time the sun will dry them.

I first encountered La Ladrillera, in Jalisco, Mexico, five years ago when I joined the staff of an NGO that has a community centre nearby. I visited the place many times from 2011 to 2014 as part of my job. I got to know the daily routine and struggles of brickmaker families as I talked with the women and children, who were involved in the NGO's programs.

Among the diversity and particularity of their narratives, there were common stories. Rainy seasons are especially difficult because storms would destroy their job and their homes would become wet. Many of their houses were made of uncemented bricks and their roofs were made of roof tiles because their income from brickmaking is barely enough to buy food and some basic items. I saw that brickmaking is extremely physically exhausting and that sales were dropping as bricks became replaced by blocks in the construction sector. Socially, brickmaking was seen as the worst possible job in the community, so the families faced discrimination and exclusion. Additionally, women confronted further stigma because they were expected not to work but to stay at home and care for the children. But simultaneously, they shared with me many of their hopes and aspirations. These women were sure their efforts would provide a better future for their children.

Those encounters allowed me to learn about a story of the many stories of this particular history of development. I learnt about the hidden side of Guadalajara's development as the second largest and an important city in Mexico. La Ladrillera and the many places it contains has produced the bricks for the construction of the neighbourhoods, schools, hospitals, major buildings and prosperous businesses of the city.

In addition to this story of how the bricks literally make development, in La Ladrillera there are the stories of the bodies that make those bricks. At the end of 2014, I experienced an encounter-disencounter that made me see how different interventions (social policies, laws, development projects) were leaving deep injuries in women's bodies and places, in their feelings, memories and histories.

I went to the community to talk with Maria, an 11-year-old girl. Maria told me she was about to finish primary school and wanted to continue her studies. When I was leaving, the girl's mother asked me for help. She said she had been denounced for child mistreatment to the Ministry for the Integral Development of the Family (DIF). She was required to bring all her children to the psychologist and to the doctor. She was scared because she was asked to sign many papers and she didn't know how to read or write. She was worried because she was separated but not legally divorced from her husband, who was an alcoholic and who didn't want to attend the requested meetings. Her biggest fear was that her children would be taken away. She explained to me that yes, they might look dirty, and yes, they might not eat meat nor have luxurious things, but she loved them and treated them the best she could and worked extensive hours as a brickmaker to provide for them. I promised to see if the NGO could help her by providing a health certificate for the children and by giving her legal advice. I went back a week later to tell her I found some help. I was received by Maria. She informed me that her mother had become so stressed about the denouncement that she had had a heart attack and died. The last I heard was that the ministry closed the case and gave custody of the children to the father.

The episode for me was a big disencounter with the development sector. I use the metaphor encounter–disencounter inspired by Escobar's analysis of development as the encounter of two regimes of discourses and representation that dichotomised those who are 'developed' and those 'underdeveloped.' In a development encounter, identities are reconstructed which violate individual identities, histories and meanings (1995: 10). In the development process, there are many encounters every day that lead to new identities as well as to violence. I call this violence a disencounter which is the English translation of the Spanish word *desencuentro*, or non-agreement, opposition.

The disencounter experienced by Maria and her family made me reflect on the constructions and assumptions about poverty and women by development actors such as NGOs, state and civil society. I thought about the value of those brickmakers' lives; how they are invisible for the majority of people and for the state system, where they do not even count as a number in statistics. I reflected on how different social policies and development interventions are created due to this invisibility and under false constructions and assumptions of those bodies and the lives that inhabit them.

I quit the job but I kept visiting the place and working with the brickmakers in specific projects led by a friend of mine who came from the same place. In 2015, I went to The Hague in the Netherlands to study a MA in Development Studies at the International Institute of Social Studies (ISS). The decision was motived by a personal story of multiple encounters–disencounters with development interventions. But also, I had the hope to find ways to write new and different stories of development that allowed me to understand the complex relations among people, places, aspirations and policies.

During my master's studies at ISS, I thought very often about the women from La Ladrillera. When I encountered feminism within academia I thought about their particular way to live it: challenging everyday gender roles, defending their bodies and fighting with hope. When I encountered the multiple conceptualisations of poverty I thought about their own definition of it; it was so distant from academic and official development discourses. When I listened to Wendy Harcourt's lecture about bodies and places, I thought about their bodies and their multiple and complex ways of interacting with the places they live in as well as the development world.

In the summer of 2016, as part of my MA research I went back to La Ladrillera and listened to the narratives of three generations of women from three different families about their embodied experiences in relation to work, family, community and social policies intervening in those places. Encountering the place and the women again meant that I opened my ears as well as my eyes. I listened carefully to what they had to say in order to reflect at a deeper level the tensions among development, places, people and aspirations.

This chapter is informed by the field work process and my reflections on the construction of knowledges through embodiment experiences tell multiple encounters and disencounters, aspirations and hope, as a way to write new histories within development that take into account environment, care and critiques of development.

## The politics of place

The politics of place framework by Harcourt and Escobar (2002) has helped me shed light on the different political struggles that women are involved with in the different places they inhabit: body, home, surrounding environment and the public arena. Women are the protagonists of place-based political activities in and from those sites.

The body constitutes 'the first place where women are engaged in political struggle. These include struggles for autonomy, for reproductive and sexual integrity and rights, for safe motherhood, for freedom from violence and sexual oppression' (Harcourt and Escobar 2002: 8).

Home is the second place. It is

> where many women still derive their most important social and political roles and identities. The home serves paradoxically as both a safe space where women have considerable power as well as a site where they experience a great degree of violence and oppression.
>
> (Harcourt and Escobar 2002: 9)

Environment or the community, as it is called in this research, constitutes the third place. "People's environments include the meanings, values and general ways of being that characterise and distinguish between different communities" (Harcourt and Escobar 2002: 10–11).

And the public arena, the fourth place, puts on stage culture as political, 'because meaning, and the power to produce or determine meaning, is constitutive of our lived experiences as well as our analysis of them.' In this way women politically contest the dominant culture (Harcourt and Escobar 2002: 11).

This framework of analysis helps us see how women's daily embodied political experiences are situated in place within a context of globalisation. The framework recognises the strategic relation between the local and the global through the concept of glocalities which explains how globalisation does not happen 'from above' or 'from below' but always in 'between' (Harcourt and Escobar 2002: 13).

The framework allows us to question the development regime's discourses and interventions that exercise a body politics that is patriarchal, economic and managerial in every opportunity that it has (Escobar and Harcourt 2005). This deployment of the power of development is done within a globalised capitalist system.

To make visible the concreteness of places and the politics of the differences carried by women within them, we need to see the creative women's involvement with globalisation, and their questioning of the development regime over women's bodies, as a response to the effects of neoliberal forces of the capitalist system (Escobar and Harcourt 2005). If we understand that politics 'is largely made up of contests over meaning: the interplay between culture and power,' this opens spaces for the creation of different and 'potentially transformative solutions' (Harcourt and Escobar 2002: 11–12).

## La Ladrillera

I understand La Ladrillera as a place in constant transformation that contains many places that are intrinsically interconnected and that have been co-constructing each other over a long time: community space, home, women's bodies. Community space or women's surrounding environment is a fundamental part of who they are; it has constructed their bodies and families in many ways. Simultaneously, women and their families have constructed the place according to their needs and aspirations. This co-construction has been done generation by generation and it also entails the public arena for development processes.

In La Ladrillera, the different spaces revolve around brickmaking. During the 1950s–1980s, the area was transformed from abandoned land into a brickmaking community by migrants from rural areas during a massive rural–urban migration in Mexico. Families became brickmakers on arrival. The land offered them a place to live, work and raise a family.

Brickmaking became an intrinsic component of the identity of the community and families, marking the women's bodies. That labour plays a major role in the relations, tensions and intersections inside every place and among them.

My research looks at La Ladrillera as a place of community defined by the complex interaction of its geography, connections with other places, history, livelihood system, inhabitants and social relations. It constitutes women's environment (Harcourt and Escobar 2002).

This environment entails multiple interconnected layers at the levels of the economy, politics and social relations. 'As such it is inextricably connected to all aspects of survival: to issues of livelihood, justice and quality of life' (Harcourt and Escobar 2002: 9).

The environment in La Ladrillera has been constructed through time. Therefore, this research entails its history as part of that complex, multi-layered web in order to understand the community in constant transformation, not fixed in time.

La Ladrillera is a small neighbourhood located in Santa Paula, one of the biggest brickmaking and pottery areas in Tonalá, *Municipio Alfarero* (Pottery

Municipality) next to Guadalajara, Jalisco, Mexico (Basulto and Garcidueñas 2015). Within Santa Paula, La Ladrillera is one the neighbourhoods with the highest number of brickmaking ovens. The municipality map includes the Pajaritos zone as part of La Ladrillera (IIEG 2014) but for the women that participated in the research, Pajaritos is a different neighbourhood.

La Ladrillera was part of Arroyo de Enmedio's farm, one of the most important in Guadalajara during colonial times. After the Mexican Revolution, the land was expropriated and became federal property (Basulto and Garcidueñas 2015). When migrants arrived, the place became exclusively a brickmaking community for nearly 30 years. Now there are brickmakers, ex-brickmakers and people with different occupations.

In La Ladrillera, some houses are made out of bricks but are not cemented. Others are not even made of bricks and cement, and are too small for the inhabitants. Some others are built with non-durable materials like plastic, wood or cloth. There are a few big houses that are fully made out of cemented bricks; these are mainly owned by non-brickmaker families.

Public services are limited. There is no formal connection to electricity. Getting clean water is a struggle. Sanitation is a problem. Only the houses located on the principal street and near the square have drainage and running water. The majority of the other houses get water from wells and use latrines. There are water pollution problems due to latrine waste. Roads get flooded. There is one public kindergarten and one primary school. In order to attend secondary education, teenagers compete for a place in schools located in nearby communities.

Brickmakers from La Ladrillera face challenging conditions. Their average daily income is about 100 Mexican pesos (approximately $US 7.00). For many families this is not enough to eat three times a day, let alone to buy other very necessary items (cleaning products, clothes, etc.).

Brickmaking requires brickmakers to get up early in the morning, prepare the brick mix (dust, water, sawdust and cow dung) and step on it to make it smooth. They make the bricks by pouring the mix on moulds and putting them on a yard's floor under the sun. When the bricks are dry on top, they are accommodated in different positions to dry them all around. They then put the dried bricks in an oven and burn them for a day until the colour turns orange-red. After they are cooled they are sold to intermediaries who own trucks that will carry them to construction stores.

Women usually work close to home in yards owned by them, their husbands, relatives or landlords. Some women take part in the complete brickmaking process while others only in certain activities. Children also participate in different brickmaking activities.

Artisanal brickmaking in Mexico is an important sector that brings employment to more than 35,000 people. It has an annual production of 30–50 per cent of the total annual production of bricks, making a huge contribution to the construction sector (Cárdenas *et al.* 2012), fundamental for the country's development.

Since the 1980s and within a context of increasing neoliberal policies in Mexico, the construction sector has been replacing artisanal bricks with blocks because the latter are produced by industrialised processes at a lower cost. This situation has diminished the sales of artisanal bricks. Current environmental laws put some brickmaking communities at risk of being banned or relocated because the level of pollutants emitted is higher than allowed (Ortiz 2012). Certainly, brickmaking is a highly polluting activity due to the materials and fuels used, but changing them increases the production cost.

Brickmakers face many challenges: high production costs, low product prices and a shortage of trading schemes (Romo *et al.* 2004). Brickmaking can be seen as leading to multiple oppressions: poverty, inequality, exclusion and marginalisation.

The state gives little support to brickmakers. They are invisible to the state in ways that negate their bodies and lives as the 'Other.'

## The brickmaker women and their families

Brickmakers carry in their bodies the historical marginalisation of the poor and the non-white as a result of the colonisation of Mexico. But given the prevalence of a colonial gender system in which gender and race play a major role in defining social positions (Lugonés 2008), female brickmaker bodies are valued differently than male brickmakers' bodies, even if they experience life in the same place and perform the same job. Bodies are the first place we inhabit and the first place of political struggle (Harcourt and Mumtaz, 2002; Underhill-Sem, 2002). Brickmakers' bodies are determined by the surrounding context, their work and histories which determine their experience of social, economic and power relations (Lugonés 2008).

Women's brickmaker bodies in La Ladrillera are less valued and less visible than the men's. Sometimes they are not even recognised as workers. Their bodies contain their life stories and the stories of their mothers, grandmothers and families, including the community history and national history that has systematically exercised violence against women's bodies. Their bodies carry imprints of race/class/gender and occupation (Petchesky 2015).

The body is a metaphor but also a materiality (Butler 1999, Grosz 1999). Women's bodies from La Ladrillera are constructed through multiple discourses and practices: development and its repressive interventions in the form of laws, regulations and social policies; societal ideals about heteronormativity, gender and sexuality; community practices around women's behaviour; and women's own discourses and practices. Therefore, their bodies, private and public at the same time (Butler 2004), have visible and invisible marks that are product of that deployment of power over them but also of their resistance.

Among the visible marks there are injuries and scars – the product of their job and their motherhood; of illnesses that give acknowledgement of their sex/gender/age/social class. Their bodies contain painful and happy memories of situations and people they have encountered. Those marks give account of the cause and of how it was treated: by themselves?; by the community?; by the State?; efficiently?; in a negligent way? Their bodies are a map displaying all the lines that have crossed them, cut them. They may have broken bodies, incomplete bodies but in their particular way they have also repaired themselves.

Women are political actors that negotiate power relations inside home, a space encompassing contradictory forces: that of a safe space and that of a site where many forms of violence against women take place. Within those forces women perform multiple roles: grandmothers, mothers, daughters, wives, sisters etc. The activities, expected behaviour and responsibilities attached to those roles are marked by gender assumptions and are at many times delimited by oppressive and violent discourses and practices. At the same time, in those responsibilities and roles they find space for transformation and change. So, how do they negotiate their roles as women/brickmakers/wives/mothers/grandmothers/daughters? What are their experiences within home? What have they learned from their mothers and grandmothers? What do they teach to their daughters/granddaughters?

They have fought important battles over and within their bodies, families and environment. Their fights have been guided in a big part by their needs and aspirations. They politicise the multiple places they inhabit by giving them a different meaning by transforming them; but what have been those wishes? What do they want for themselves, their families and community? Which aspirations have been articulated and materialised? How do their aspirations intersect with the social policies available at the place? Which are those policies they identify as intervening in their lives and in which way? What are the futures still pending?

## A methodological note

In July and August of 2016 I dialogued with three generations of brickmaker women in La Ladrillera. This section presents the stories of the women's narratives, my reflections on those encounters and further analysis in light of the framework of the politics of place (Harcourt and Escobar 2002).

I use narratives claiming the value of subjectivity in the construction of knowledge (Joy 2000: 32–3). The method validates within the academia women's subjectivity and embodied experience through what they think and feel (physically and emotionally) about the processes they live through (Kimpson 2005). While writing these words, I recall and reflect on my dialogues with the women and the meanings they shared with me about their embodiment experiences but inevitably some meanings are lost in the translation process.

The stories expose the generational and intergenerational ways in which they have struggled and transformed over and within their bodies, families, environment and public arena. They have co-constructed the places mainly guided by their aspirations. And the places have co-constructed them.

## The places and the encounters

The women I dialogued with are:

| | | |
|---|---|---|
| Fe, Grandmother | Lu, Grandmother | Mar, Grandmother |
| Ma, Mother | Chu, Mother | Mo, Mother |
| Mari, Daughter | Ju, Daughter | Jo, Daughter |
| Pa, Daughter | | |

I am profoundly thankful to them for their trust in me, in this research and their life-changing shared knowledges.

## First generation

### *Making bricks for a living*

Migration constitutes the first tension among the women's aspirations and development processes. Their bodies marked and classified by their sex/gender/ class (Lugonés 2008) found no other space in the city than La Ladrillera, an empty and abandoned land on the edge of the city and with no other available job other than brickmaking.

In response, they appropriated the place and constructed a community to live, work and raise a family. They have given multiple meanings to the place and the job, and have fought important battles from and within those places.

Grandmothers' bodies were re-configured by brickmaking physically and metaphorically during 30–50 years of work. They became strong brickmakers who worked, built a home and a community. However, the physical impact on their bodies affected their health and now limits their mobility. In the community, they were respected as brickmakers, but for the state they were and still are invisible as economic contributors. They still struggle for an income sufficient to meet their needs.

### *The reconstruction of the community. First generation*

The women described how they constructed their homes and the community in that empty land. They got organised, divided the land and marked the streets. There were no public services, so with their means they constructed latrines and settled light connections with electricity cables.

However, that same absence of services and policies in the place caused them to be hurt so many times: to be cut while brickmaking; to have abortions or lose babies; to be denied the health services they needed and wanted; to not be allowed to materialise their aspirations of sending their children to school, so that their children would not have to continue the job of brickmaking.

I think of this community's reconstruction as a remarkable example of women's embodied resistance against the 'determined future' that the place offered to them. They resisted discursively and physically (Butler 1999, Grosz 2010) by making more bricks; by articulating more aspirations (Zipin *et al.* 2013) and transmitting those to their daughters, by advising them to act differently regarding their reproductive rights.

### Home in La Ladrillera. First generation

Raising a family in that changing context took the women through several battles in order to survive without services and to sustain their families with the brickmaking income.

Their struggles for safe motherhood, reproductive rights and their ongoing fight for health services make me think of the web of oppressions they have encountered on their way: La Ladrillera and its location are marked by exclusion; neglect of social security and health services; and the low value (monetary and symbolic) attached to its inhabitants' occupation and their classification in the social relations.

The women accepted the social role attached to them as women of the household, but at the same time their reflections about their own experience led them to advise their daughters differently, which makes me think about home as a site for intergenerational learning. Their stories of home led me to reflect on the multiples roles they performed at the same time and the gender inequality, which determined how they lived.

## Second generation

### The community. Heritage and challenges

The women's stories remind me of the complex process lived by glocalities like La Ladrillera. The women were born in the place. Their bodies have been constructed at the discursive and material level as female brickmaker bodies since they were children but have never been fixed in time (Bordo 1993, Butler 1999, Grosz 1999, Shildrick and Price 1999). They have enjoyed the transformations pursued by their mothers and they did not suffer the impact of migration, nor the complete absence of services. But they do face the increasing violence, the unsafety, the fear.

The place grew in population due to increasing migration (now urban-to-urban). The town is now divided according to people's occupation. The set of social and cultural values and practices changed, the livelihood system was diversified and is no longer exclusively brickmaking. Despite more social policy interventions, they still inhabit a place on the edge of the town where many of their needs and aspirations still have no resonance in the social policy.

## Making bricks for a living. Second generation

I reflect on how in the social stratification generated by the new community composition, female brickmaker bodies occupy the lowest position. They are discriminated against because of their sex/gender/occupation. They are seen like women out of their assigned gender roles. That has compromised their ownership, mobility and social relations more heavily. Their competencies as mothers are judged and surveyed by the community and the multiple policies that gradually started to intervene in their community, family and lives (Butler 1999, Lugones 2008, Petchesky 2015).

They face a critical situation for their livelihood system: artisanal brickmaking is threatened both by environmental regulations and neoliberal policies. They are at constant risk, but they get up every morning to make more bricks. And if the rain destroys them, they take the mud, mix it again and make more bricks. They do it without any social security; in Mo's words, the only sure thing is that they will be hurt. They do it to provide for their families and bring them a different future. They are still healing by themselves. Their bodies are not recognised as productive for the system but they are still subject to social policies that are constructed upon inaccurate assumptions of how sex, gender and occupation operate.

In response to inappropriate social policies, they perform a daily embodied resistance: generating their own discourses; attaching different meanings to their occupation according to the situation; occupying spaces that are not supposed to belong to them; 'proving' they are good mothers and defending their families; and inspiring everyone (Zipin *et al.* 2003, Butler 1999, Grosz 2010).

## Home in La Ladrillera. Second generation

Talking with the women about home, they narrated how difficult is to spend time with their children, take care for the house (for which they are mainly responsible), and work at the same time.

They learned from their mothers to work for themselves and to face life challenges the best they can. They told me, as well as their mothers, men have an easier life because usually don't do care work. But they said they could participate more.

Listening to them, I reflect on how in their homes they find safety and motivation but also violence and struggle for gender equity. At home, Mo suffered 'terrible things' (in her words) and had no justice support. She reflects on her own story and advises her daughters differently. Home becomes a site for intergenerational learning.

Social policies are constantly intervening in their bodies and families' present and future. In some ways, they are helping the women materialise their aspirations. In some others, the policies don't correspond with their priorities and even exercise violence over them. They struggle to use them according to what they think is best for them.

Health services as intervention over their bodies allows them to assert reproductive rights (important intergenerational change), but also tasks them with defending themselves from damaging or undesired treatment.

### Third generation

#### *Community, brickmaking and home. Growing up in La Ladrillera.*

The girls' narratives make me think of their exposure to violence and the community's problems but also of their politics of place: aspiring transformations. I see in their narratives that they are aware of the brickmaking situation.

Through their stories, I think of home again as a safe but violent place and as a site for intergenerational learning and aspiring. I see girls developing their own aspirations. And I reflect on their powerful discourses in resistance to the sayings that mark and discriminate against them because of their sex/gender and family occupation.

They are articulating and materialising their aspirations but also the aspirations of their mothers and grandmothers; although, as they grow up they will encounter multiple tensions with policies. I ask myself: Are they going to achieve and materialise their educational and professional aspirations?

### Three generations of brickmaker women

The three generations of women live in a moment in which their bodies, families and community live with hope but also fear because of the increasing narco-related violence. They interact every time with more social policies in a complex way that entails: the deployment of power of the discourses and interventions of the policies; its openness/rigidity and its assumptions (on gender/sex/occupation/age) about the women's lives. And at the same time, their interactions include the embodied agency of the women and the needs and aspirations of everyone (Zipin *et al.* 2003, Butler 1999, Grosz 2010).

In that sense, they appropriate openness and flexibility to use the benefits according to what they want to happen to them, to their families and community (e.g. using nutrition policy cash for education). They use them to claim their health and reproductive rights. But also, they fight back when the interventions damage their health or are not desired. They use them to articulate and materialise their educational aspirations and those of their children/grandchildren (Zipin *et al.* 2013): to transform their own body and assert ownership, autonomy, freedom, social mobility and get to know what they are interested in; to interact with their families in desired ways; to interact with the environment and be able to move within it in an independent form; to transform that environment; to interact with the social policies more efficiently, and to be connected with other people. At the same time, they struggle to materialise those aspirations within the available policies; to be part of those they want; to claim some of the promised services and entitlements; to have justice protection. They struggle to have the policies they need and desire.

## Care, the brickmaker women and their practices of the difference

In my reflections on how the practices of difference of the women from La Ladrillera are questioning the development regime, I see several insights for feminist thinking on political economy and political ecology around care.

Their daily practices demonstrate how care is essential for survival, for setting connections and better relations among humans and between humans and the environment. Their care for their families and community brought different important changes to the places they inhabit.

They played a major role in the reconstruction process of a community that was once abandoned land to a place that could offer them the possibility to realise their aspirations and to bring a different future to their children.

This is a remarkable example of how women are important political actors. But at the same time, it is an illustration of all that is required to recognise and value care work and to change power relations among genders.

The fact that social policies that are supposed to help them but instead question the way they care for their children following normative patriarchal and heteronormative sex/gender regime assumptions tells us a lot about the intrinsic link between care and gender. It is not enough to make care visible and to re-signify its value for societies, but it is also vital to profoundly shift how we think about care through a gender lens, analysing the implicit and explicit power relations.

In that sense, women from La Ladrillera demonstrate how care and hope, in the form of aspirations, can open possibilities for that change. They are continuously looking for the spaces to break patriarchal development interventions through their forms of knowledge and their lived embodied resistances, and by constructing alternative futures in the places they inhabit.

We need to be listening to their experiences as we understand how they see place, care for their families, their communities and their futures. And we should be caring for them and for other women who struggle that much for their place-based rights.

To care for other women, which could be called feminist solidarity or sorority, means a deep understanding that not all women are hurt in the same way by the patriarchal system and that not all of them tell the same experiences, but that all of them in their diversity contribute to tell louder and stronger all the transformations that need to be pursued.

Caring among ourselves opens spaces for the discussion of how there are differences among women in how we have been oppressed through hegemonic patriarchal discourses and practices around care and gender. And at the same time, it sheds light on a variety of examples of how care can be understood and practised in a different way. It means an initial way to break an individualistic understanding of well-being and leads to an understanding in which relations can be sustained in cooperation and solidarity.

In that sense, it contributes to pursuing a feminist agenda that englobes a wider range of voices, that helps to position at the top the historic battles of the women who have suffered the most from the oppressive interventions of the system, seeking liberation, social justice and equity from within.

I acknowledge this proposal can be difficult to pursue and can be painful because it entails a personal deconstructing process to liberate ourselves from internalised patriarchal practices that contribute to oppress other women. And that is the first revision to make: which of my own practices and discourses help to subjugate other women? How do the ways that I consume – products, services – contribute to enslaving other women to the system?, and so on.

To end these reflections, I state that to care and to aspire are acts of resistance and hope within development, neoliberalism and globalisation systems that constantly try to silence women's voices and desires. Caring among women demonstrates how solidarity can make stronger that resistance and bring more powerful transformations.

## References

Basulto, A. and Garcidueñas, D., 2015. *Tonalá Tradición Viva (Tonala Alive Tradition)*. Secretaría de Cultura, Mexico: Conacultura.

Bordo, S., 1993. *Unbearable Weight: Feminism, Western Culture, and the Body*. Berkeley, CA: University of California Press.

Butler, J., 1999. Bodies that matter. *In*: J. Price, and M. Shildrick, eds., *Feminist Theory and the Body: A Reader*. Edinburgh: Edinburgh University Press, 235–45.

Butler, J., 2004. *Precarious Life: The Powers of Mourning and Violence*. London: Verso Books.

Cárdenas B., Aréchiga, U., Munguía J.L., Márquez C. and Campos, A., 2012. Evaluación Preliminar Del Impacto Ambiental Por La Producción Artesanal De Ladrillo: Cambio Climático, Eficiencia Energética y Calidad Del Aire: Segunda Etapa, Informe Final Del Convenio De Colaboración INE/ADA-110071. (Preliminary Evaluation of the Environmental Impact for the Artisanal Production of Bricks: Climate Change, Energetic Efficiency and Air Quality: Second State, Final Report of the Collaboration Agreement INE/ADA-110071') No. Versión Actualizada Junio 2012. Mexico City: The Metropolitan Autonomous University and the National Institute of Ecology.

Escobar, A., 1995. Introduction: Development and the anthropology of modernity. *In*: S. Ortner, N. Dirks and G. Eley, eds., *Encountering Development: The Making and Unmaking of the Third World*. Princeton, NJ: Princeton University Press: 3–20.

Escobar, A. and Harcourt, W., 2005. Introducción: Las prácticas de la diferencia ('Introduction: The Practices of Difference'). *In*: W. Harcourt, and A. Escobar, eds., J.C. Reyes and C.O. Mansuy, trans., *Las Mujeres y las Políticas del Lugar (Women and The Politics of Place)*. Mexico City: Gender Studies Program, National Autonomous University of Mexico, 11–25.

Grosz, E., 1999. Bodies-Cities. *In*: J. Price and M. Shildrick, eds., *Feminist Theory and the Body: A Reader*. Edinburgh: Edinburgh University Press: 381–7.

Grosz, E., 2010. Feminism, materialism, and freedom. *In*: D.H. Coole and S. Frost, eds., *New Materialisms: Ontology, Agency, and Politics*. Durham: Duke University Press, 139–57.

Harcourt, W. and Escobar A., 2002. Women and the politics of place. *Development*, 45 (1), 7–14.

Harcourt, W. and Mumtaz, K., 2002. Fleshly politics: women's bodies, politics and globalisation. *Development*, 45 (1), 36–42.

IIEG Instituto de Información Estadística y Geográfica, 2014. La Ladrillera. (Extract of the map Tonala neighborhoods) [online]. Available from: http://www.iieg.gob.mx/simeg/datos/geografia/MapaColoniasTonala.pdf [Accessed 23 October].

Joy, M., 2000. Beyond a God's eyeview: alternative perspectives in the study of religion. *In*: S., Marcos, ed., *Gender/bodies/religions: Adjunct Proceedings of the XVIIth Congress for the History of Religions*. Cuernavaca, Mexico: ALER, 19–42.

Kimpson, S., 2005. Stepping off the road: A narrative (of) inquiry. *In*: L.A. Brown and S. Strega, eds., *Research as Resistance: Critical, Indigenous and Anti-Oppressive Approaches*. Toronto, ON: Canadian Scholars' Press, 73–96.

Lugonés, M., 2008. The coloniality of gender. *Worlds and Knowledges Otherwise*, 2 (2), 1–17.

Ortiz, H., 2012. Diagnóstico Nacional Del Sector Ladrillero Artesanal De México: Informe Final ('National Diagnostic of the Artisanal Brick-Making Sector in Mexico: Final Report'). México: Servicios Profesionales para el Desarrollo Económico S.C.

Petchesky, R., 2015. Owning and disowning the body: A reflection. *In*: R. Baksh and W. Harcourt, eds., *The Oxford Handbook of Transnational Feminist Movements*. Oxford: Oxford University Press, 252–70.

Romo, M., Córdova G. and Cervera, L., 2004. Estudio Urbano-Ambiental De Las Ladrilleras En El Municipio De Juárez ('Urban-Environmental Study of Brickmaking in the Municipality of Juarez'), *Estudios Fronterizos*, 5 (9), 9–34.

Shildrick, M. and Price, J., 1999. Openings on the body: a critical introduction. *In*: J. Price, and M. Shildrick, eds., *Feminist Theory and the Body: A Reader*. Edinburgh: Edinburgh University Press, 1–14.

Underhill-Sem, Y., 2002. Embodying post-development: bodies in places, places in bodies. *Development*, 45 (1), 54–9.

Zipin, L., Sellar, S., Brennan, M. and Gale T., 2013. Educating for futures in marginalised regions: a sociological framework for rethinking and researching aspirations. *Educational Philosophy and Theory*, 47 (3): 227–46.

# 14 Towards an urban agenda from a Feminist Political Ecology and care perspective

*Ana Agostino*

## Introduction

This chapter is informed by my experience as the ombudswoman of Montevideo, the capital of Uruguay, a position I have held for the last three years. Heading an institution with the mandate to promote respect for human rights, the best performance of departmental and/or municipal services and the achievement of greater transparency and efficiency of governmental administration has given me the chance to deepen the knowledge of the daily experiences of citizens in a variety of spheres and to make inputs for the improvement of their life conditions. The processes of understanding and contributing to the transformation of these experiences have been guided by three broad analytical frameworks which have guided my work on the ground and my research: a multicultural approach to human rights, experiences and analysis from transnational feminist movements, and the critical views of post-development. It is within these three frameworks that I will share experiences, analyses and suggestions aiming to contribute to a sustainable, caring and equitable urban agenda.

My engagement with Latin American social movements, working with rural women in South Africa in the mid-90s, coordinating the Feminist Task Force of the Global Call to Action Against Poverty (GCAP) for five years, writing my PhD thesis on post-development, publishing together with transnational feminist academics papers on women and climate justice, contributed to a synergy of these frameworks which has informed my professional and personal experience. Key concepts emerged in that journey that have informed the work that I am currently doing: hospitality, care, a deep questioning of the centrality of economics, gender mainstreaming, diversity and politics of place. These concepts will emerge throughout this chapter, helping in the understanding of the challenges we face at the urban level but also as facilitators of other ways to look at and construct a new agenda.

## *Defensoria de Vecinas y Vecinos de Montevideo*[1]

The Ombudsinstitution of Montevideo (*Defensoria de Vecinas y Vecinos*, DVVM) was created by the departmental legislative body in line with the Paris Principles,[2] a set of international standards related to the National Human

Rights Institutions (NHRIs) adopted by the United Nations General Assembly resolution 48/134 on 20 December 1993. They are created by the states but are independent and autonomous, and have the mandate to promote and defend human rights, as well as to control the administration. Although the Paris Principles talk about the national institutions, with time their jurisdictions expanded to include institutions with provincial, departmental, municipal and local mandates. Carlos Constenla, president of the Latin American Institute of the Ombudsman (ILO), argues that in fact, this is an institution that emerged at the municipal level and it is there that it justifies more than at any other scale its nature, its efficacy and its reason for existence, in close proximity with the citizens (Constenla 2016: 82).

In the case of the DVVM, it implements its mandate by responding to and acting upon the complaints and demands from the residents of Montevideo associated to the acts of the municipal and departmental government, doing research in order to suggest and recommend solutions to the specific problems presented to the institution as well as to issues of general concern for the population of the department (this includes specific recommendations to the government, public positioning and publications), and training and implementing community mediation as a response to conflicts and/or as a means to promote dialogue among citizens and between citizens and the departmental authorities. All of this is guided by a human rights perspective and a gender mainstreaming policy. It is important to say that both are contested concepts, particularly in the last few years when we are witnessing a growing attack on human rights.[3] In the next lines, I will expand on the particular views of these concepts that guide our work.

### Human rights: A multicultural concept

As a human rights institution the Ombudsinstitution needs to take a stance on the meaning and implementation of human rights, as it not only informs its work but the DVVM has a mandate to promote and educate in this perspective. Paraphrasing Andrea Galaverna, ombudswoman for the city of Bariloche in Argentina from 2013 to 2017, for human rights institutions this perspective means to monitor the state conduct, prevent human rights violations by the state, provide protection when there have been violations, pressure the state to investigate, sanction and repair the violations, and promote people's participation and the state's accountability. She also argues that there are fundamental premises linked to this perspective including that human rights are enforceable, they aim at changing the relations of power and the resulting inequalities, require the active participation of the holders of the rights and imply a differential approach in terms of gender and ethnic-cultural perspectives so as to promote equal opportunities and prevent discrimination (Galaverna 2016: 153–4). As Luis Perez Aguirre argued, all human groups have deep sentiments, beliefs and essential characters that define their culture, they have an ethos that informs their assumptions, their behaviours, their *Weltanschauungen* (worldview). This ethos is part of the foundation for choosing a human rights perspective, which is not merely rational, but on the contrary is the response to 'a cry heard and felt in one's own flesh [...] the cry of one who has become a victim, who has been stripped of their dignity or of their rights.' He further argues that the Universal Declaration of Human Rights is the product of a long and complex process in response to innumerable cries throughout the world and throughout history (Perez Aguire 1998: 51–2). This ethos can be linked to what James Taylor called 'a pre-existing horizon of significance,' that gives meaning to our existence 'against the background of things that matter [...] the demands of nature, or the needs of my fellow human beings, or the duties of citizenship, or the call of God, or something else of this order [that] *matters* crucially' (Taylor 1991: 38–41, emphasis in original).

The reality of this ethos, of this pre-existing horizon of significance, by its mere enunciation, shows that there cannot be only one, universally valid, view of human rights. This though, has been the mainstream vision as argued by Boaventura de Sousa Santos:

> The concept of human rights rests on a well-known set of presuppositions, all of which are distinctly Western: a universal human nature that can be known by rational means that is essentially different from and higher than the rest of reality; and a concept of the individual as possessing an absolute and irreducible dignity that must be protected from society, the state or other forms of hierarchy.
>
> (2002: 44–5)

Three elements can be identified in this concept: (i) rights are associated to the individual; (ii) they are the same for all individuals; (iii) it is through a rational approach that we understand, define and promote human rights. It can be argued though that this approach can only explain the legal category of human rights (including the Universal Declaration and its binding treaties) but does not pay attention to the fact that a natural right reflecting the intrinsic dignity of human beings and of peoples, existed before the positive right of the law. It can also be argued that it is not primarily through reason that we understand the meaning of these intrinsic rights, but by something much deeper and fundamental, which is the capacity to feel with others, be transformed by their feelings and experiences and transform them in turn. These feelings and experiences are culturally determined. And, contrary to a universal view, as Santos further argues, 'to elevate to the maximum possible the level of consciousness of cultural incompleteness is one of the most crucial tasks in the construction of a multicultural emancipatory concept of Human Rights' (Santos 2002: 44–5).

Furthermore, as I argue later in the section on care, ontologically, being human is caring (for ourselves, for others, for nature), which puts at the centre the need to see rights not only as individual but transcending the person. In this respect, it is important to remember that already the Universal Declaration of Human Rights – a document from the 1940s and therefore not yet gendered or including an environmental perspective – emphasised the mutual responsibility towards one another and the general well-being in Article 29:

(1) Everyone has duties to the community in which alone the free and full development of his personality is possible. (2) In the exercise of his rights and freedoms, everyone shall be subject only to such limitations as are determined by law solely for the purpose of securing due recognition and respect for the rights and freedoms of others and of meeting the just requirements of morality, public order and the general welfare in a democratic society.

(UN General Assembly 1948)

As argued before, the various peoples and cultures of the Earth have their own visions of human dignity, with different emphases on reciprocity, articulation with others, respect to other cultures and to nature, among other aspects. It is on this basis that Santos argues for the need to reconceptualise human rights as multicultural (Santos 2002: 44). And beyond that, there would not be a construction known as human rights without the capacity to feel, to listen, to have pain with those whose dignity in one way or another has been affected.

## *Hospitality*

As a result of a process of critical engagement with these concepts and in the framework of exchanging ideas and analysis with other human rights institutions, I presented the notion of the Defensorias as 'places of hospitality,' a view around which I have built the work of the DVVM.

The term hospitality refers to 'friendly and liberal reception of guests and strangers.'[4] This definition refers clearly to one who opens his/her house to someone not known, someone who is different. In his analysis of the concept, Jacques Derrida even says that maybe we cannot talk of hospitality if the person we receive already talks our language, shares with us all that is associated to a common tongue. He therefore says that

absolute hospitality requires that I open up my house and that I give not only to the foreigner (provided with a family name, with the social status of being a foreigner, etc.) but to the absolute, unknown, anonymous other, and that I *give place* to them, that I let them come, that I let them arrive, and take in the place I offer them, without asking of them either reciprocity (entering into a pact) or even their names.

(Dufourmantelle and Derrida 1997: 25, emphasis in the original)

In this light, hospitality is a type of encounter that necessarily will transform the guest and the host, without understanding each other, with no need for that understanding in order to make place, that is, to recognise the person and its particular way of being in the world (Agostino 2007: 207–8). This mutual transformation is possible when moving away from a traditional view of hospitality rooted in mistrust of strangers to which our house is open while at the same time it is transformed into a fortress. In this configuration each part keeps its role: the guest must adjust and the host keeps the power granted by the possession of the offered resources. In relation to this view, and engaging with the work of Derrida on hospitality, Maurice Hamington sees a role for feminist hospitality that can 'subvert hospitality-infused hierarchies and minimize the inferred power relations grounded in property to facilitate connections among people. In this manner, sharing is less instilled with hidden agendas and more directed toward the well-being of the guest.' He further argues that 'feminist hospitality explores the antimony between disruption and connection: The guest and host disrupt each other's lives sufficiently to allow for meaningful exchanges that foster interpersonal connections of understanding.' This connection breaks the view that the 'host gives and the guest receives.' The concept of feminist hospitality as he describes it 'resists this directionality, instead valuing the exchanges between host and guest as reciprocal [...]; the distinction between guest and host is blurred as both learn and grow together' (Hamington 2010: 24–8).

It is in this light that I argue that the Defensoria is a place of hospitality. The choice of the word *place* is not random: while being a place of hospitality, it gives place to a diversity of voices. In feminist analysis, place is an important category, based on the political, material and symbolic appropriation, that activates rights and duties and allows for the manifestation of diverse identities, capacities, interactions and initiatives. As argued by Wendy Harcourt and Arturo Escobar in 'Women and the Politics of Place,' 'even in a globalized world, place is still the way people know and experience life' (Harcourt and Escobar 2002: 8). It is where resistances and realities unfold, where events take place, where we are able to see (and to not see depending as well on place) and understand and propose and transform. In their analysis they talk of a *global sense of place* that includes the body, the home, the environment and the social public space.

> Politics based around these four areas question the presumption that knowledge is only 'important' if it is detached, objective and rational, and instead points to the importance of material, subjective and personal vantage points. Women's place-based politics is embedded in, rather than removed from, the material lives they are trying to change.
>
> (Harcourt and Escobar 2002: 11)

This is particularly true for a place like the Defensoria, as its essence is to receive the views, complaints, concerns and expectations of the citizens of Montevideo, and to act upon them. It is a place to feel with others, transform and be transformed. It is a place to care.

### Gender mainstreaming

The Defensoria was created in 2006. Very early in its operation it joined the Network of Women Defenders[5] of the Ibero-American Federation of

Ombudsmen, with the aim of incorporating a gender perspective in its institutional management. In 2009, the institution installed a human rights and gender programme as a specialised area, which aimed at strengthening the incorporation of a gender perspective in its strategic lines and institutional policy, to contribute with the Equality Plan from the departmental government and to promote actions in defence of the rights of women in articulation with other public and private organisations. All these steps are in line with the global efforts for gender mainstreaming incorporated in the Beijing Platform for Action agreed upon at the fourth United Nations World Conference on Women and resulted from decades of struggle to achieve gender equality by women around the world. Gender mainstreaming has evolved throughout these decades, keeping the essential threads as defined by the United Nations Economic and Social Council (ECOSOC) in 1997:

> the process of assessing the implications for women and men of any planned action, including legislation, policies or programmes, in all areas and at all levels. It is a strategy for making women's as well as men's concerns and experiences an integral dimension of the design, implementation, monitoring and evaluation of policies and programmes in all political, economic and societal spheres so that women and men benefit equally and inequality is not perpetuated. The ultimate goal is to achieve gender equality.
>
> (OSAGI 2002: 1)

The programme installed at the Defensoria led to an inclusive language in the tools of internal systemisation (annual and/or thematic reports) and in the data system to permeate the communication policy and the general vision of institutional management. Since 2014, when I took office, and in coordination with the Network of Women Defenders, we took on the challenge of implementing an Institutional Gender Policy. The incorporation of the gender perspective as a cross-cutting view implies the possibility and opportunity to move from an apparent neutrality in relation to the reproduction of gender inequalities, towards the analysis and implementation of internal policies and methodological strategies which effectively and explicitly act upon the stereotypes that reproduce these inequalities. The principle of equality of results is a guideline for the fulfilment of the right to equality and non-discrimination. The policy has the following objectives:

1 To promote the incorporation of values, principles and attitudes with a gender perspective in the organisational culture, in order to reduce and/or eradicate discriminatory attitudes both in the interpersonal relations of the staff and in the quality of care provided;
2 To deepen the integration of the gender perspective in the internal strategies of the institutional management, improving the tools of planning, management and evaluation;

3　To coordinate with relevant national institutions for the implementation of the policy, promoting good practices and the best use of resources available for their implementation.

These three years have been very far-reaching in the implementation of this policy with clear results and broad recognition at the local, national and international level.[6] All the work done at the Defensoria is informed by our gender policy, including the core work of responding to citizens' demands.

### Demands from citizens and the urban challenges

Since its establishment in December 2006, the DVVM has received almost 15,000 complaints and consultations relating to all areas under the responsibility of the departmental and municipal governments. The main topics presented to the institution in this period have been noise pollution, sanitation, cleaning of the city and waste management, public trees, taxes, housing, transit and public transport, open space markets, street lighting, road-pavement, building control, permits for commercial and industrial establishments, health, animal ownership, accumulation syndrome, public spaces, environmental protection, guarantees for equality and non-discrimination, among others. There has also been a very high presence in the consultations in relation to the coexistence (*convivencia*) between neighbours. All these topics are presented from the material, quotidian experience of those who individually or collectively take the time to first present a formal claim to the relevant authorities, and then to follow it up with the DVVM when no satisfactory solution has been implemented. As a trend, almost two-thirds of cases have been presented by women.

All these issues that affect the lives of human beings relate to local policies, which implies that human well-being greatly depends on municipal governments managing soundly their duties. When this does not happen, the Defensorias become the institutions that protect and promote the fulfilment of rights at the closest level to the citizens. And the presentation of their cases to these institutions becomes, in turn, a mechanism for citizen participation. There is a high possibility that their complaint, demand or proposal, once taken, analysed and presented by the institution as recommendation to the authorities, will become new public policy (Constenla 2016: 87).

Although the list of areas in which citizens present their complaints seems to reflect a variety of unconnected topics, when working with them and making policy proposals, it becomes clear that they fit into the challenges relating to a sustainable view of urban management, including social, ecological and economic aspects of people's and communities' lives. In my role as head of the institution I have responded to these challenges, incorporating a gender analysis that links these dimensions and allows for culture and knowledge influences into the building of alternatives that relate to Feminist Political Ecology (FPE) as it will be described in later sections.

Going back to the *global sense of space*, it is possible to say that the experience that leads to presentation of the complaint encompasses four dimensions: the body, the home, the environment and the social public space. On a daily basis, the Defensoria sees examples of individuals, mostly women and on many occasions women's groups, who 'in their daily lives are qualifying global processes' (Harcourt and Escobar 2002: 8). From their body experience of what is missing, or what is not functioning properly and impacts on their home, they develop a sense of what should be taking place in that localised sphere which, by definition, will affect others in their surroundings and eventually in the neighbourhood or city at large. They will then engage in active mobilisation, first demanding that the local authority fulfils its duty and then presenting their case to the human rights institution with the mandate to control and propose actions that will lead to the generation of knowledge and proposals to transform reality. It is not necessarily a conscious path from the home to the social public space; rather, it is a collective process in which the Defensoria plays the role of enabling exchanges and critical engagements which eventually, and as a result of the participation of several role-players, lead to a new reality. Many of the complaints start from the demand of 'my right' to a clean sidewalk, to a quiet street, to sanitation and so on. Placing these demands within the framework of an urban agenda that is based on a sustainable, just and equitable perspective, is one of the challenges of our institution.

## Sustainability and sustainable development: A post-development and gender perspective

Sustainability has been key to the formulation of the current development framework, including the Agenda for Sustainable Development approved by the UN General Assembly in 2015 that contains the 17 Sustainable Development Goals (SDGs) as well as the New Urban Agenda resulting from the United Nations Conference on Housing and Urban Sustainable Development, Habitat III, which took place in October 2016 in Quito, Ecuador.[7] The mainstream concept of sustainability that informs these documents and their implementation programmes does not allow for a fundamental shift in the dominant economic model which is at the heart of the current ecological crisis. Placing myself in a post-development and gender perspective, I would argue that, unless economic growth is fundamentally questioned as the key for development, even if calling for resilient, environmentally friendly, inclusive and sustainable growth (UN-Habitat 2016: point 43) and women's views on sustainable livelihoods are not taken into account, there is no possibility of moving into a true sustainable future.

### Post-development

Since the first UN Development Decade was launched in 1961 various concepts and programmes have been advanced to improve the living conditions for millions of human beings around the world. Development was the key word that summarised those efforts. Throughout the decades, the lack of improvements and the persistence of inequalities led to the formulation of new approaches and emphasis. All of these initiatives remained tied to development. The challenge was to strengthen, to improve, to transform and to enhance the methods under the development discourse in order to achieve better results. The prospect that the expected results might not be possible under development was never part of the scenario. This changed with the emergence of what became known as post-development. Two major books can be identified as the collective expression of this particular way of thinking and that made it known in academic and other circles: *The Development Dictionary*, edited by Wolfgang Sachs and published in 1992, and *The Post-Development Reader*, compiled by Majid Rahnema with Victoria Bawtree and published in 1997. The key argument of this school of thought can be summarised as the conviction that reformulating development is not possible or desirable and that what is needed instead is to formulate and implement alternatives *to* it. To arrive at this conclusion, post-development writers deconstructed the concept of development, affirming that it is a historically produced discourse consisting of a field of control of knowledge, a sphere of intervention of power and forms of subjectivity which mould individuals and societies (Escobar 1987: 13–14); an effort to Westernise the world arrogating itself the right – and the duty – to determine how the lives of other peoples and cultures ought to look; and the setting of universal standards and methods of reaching pre-determined goals which might have varied over time but have without exception remained attached to economic growth. Some of the key elements of the development discourse formulated by post-development writers refer to how (i) it defines and leads more than half of humanity to perceive themselves as underdeveloped; (ii) legitimises intervention; (iii) aims at the elimination of diversity; (iv) postulates economic growth as a synonym of development. In the formulation of these criticisms post-development offers clues for identifying other practices that constitute, by their own formulation and implementation, alternatives to the mainstream. Post-development has helped to generate debate and

> contribute to the construction of an ethos beyond development. As part of this debate, central ideas have been put forward that do not aim to replace development but to generate ecologies [...] that oppose the monocultures resulting from the hegemonic criteria of rationality and efficiency that dominate development. These ecologies (as part of a narrative that promotes the recovery of people's own language of desire and culture) contribute to the unveiling of other ways of doing things and restore their ability to constitute themselves in valid alternatives.
>
> (Agostino 2007: 210)

It is within this framework that I will analyse sustainability in the coming paragraphs.

*Sustainability*

The concept of sustainability refers to mankind's ability to live within the boundaries of the physical environment, now and indefinitely into the future (Martine and Villarreal 1997). Debates about sustainability and its association with development discourse came up as a result of concerns that in the 1970s were beginning to become increasingly evident about the impacts that the predominant model of development, closely linked to that of economic growth, were having on the environment.

The first United Nations conference on the 'human environment' was held in Sweden in 1972 and led to the creation of the United Nations Environment Program (UNEP). In the same decade, a number of papers were published which revealed concerns about the viability of the prevailing production and consumption model. One of them was 'The Limits to Growth' of the Club of Rome (Meadows *et al.* 1974: 185), which analysed the planetary limits against the constant growth of population, land occupation, production, consumption, waste etc. In this work, the close relationship between development and the environment was clearly raised, and a series of economic and ecological standards involving a state of 'non-growth' was called for. In 1973 E. F. Schumacher published *Small is Beautiful: Economy as if People Mattered* in which he raised the challenge of moving to a new way of life, with new methods of production and consumption, a way of life designed for permanence. In line with these works and also with the need to address environmental issues with a global approach, the International Union for Conservation of Nature (IUCN) and the World Wildlife Fund (WWF), with the support of UNEP, developed in the early 1980s a World Conservation Strategy where a conceptualisation of sustainable development appears. In 1983, UNEP convened the creation of a Global Commission on Environment and Development with the objective of reviewing and making proposals on critical environmental issues, proposing new forms of international cooperation that could guide the necessary changes and increase the levels of understanding and individual commitment of social organisations, companies, institutions and governments in this area (World Commission on Environment and Development 1987: 356–7). The outcome of this commission's work was the famous report 'Our Common Future' that includes the best known definition of sustainable development: development that meets the needs of the present without compromising the ability of future generations to meet their own needs.

This definition includes, on the one hand, the concept of needs that must be fulfilled – in particular those of the great majorities that have been postponed – in the attainment of a better quality of life, and at the same time the recognition of the existence of natural limits that must be taken into account in order not to affect the future possibilities of continuing to satisfy them. This double dimension was taken up again at the Earth Summit in Rio in 1992, in Agenda 21, one of the final documents of the conference, which called for the implementation of production and consumption modalities that address both challenges. 'The Future We Want,' the final document of the Rio+20 Summit that took place in June 2012 emphasised that 'it is necessary to further incorporate sustainable development at all levels, integrating its economic, social and environmental aspects and recognizing the links between them, in order to achieve it in all its dimensions' (UN General Assembly 2012: 2, par. 3).

One of the consequences of the recognition of existing limits and the continuous call to articulate the three dimensions should have been the implementation of transformations in the dominant production and consumption models associated with the continuous exploitation of nature and the permanent growth of production and consumption. It is possible to affirm, however, that sustainable development in many cases was replaced by sustainable growth legitimising in the process the continuity of the same practices. As Richard Douthwaite argued, 'sustainable development is economic growth that has somehow been made more equitable and environmentally careful. However, since growth itself is not sustainable, the concept is a dangerous contradiction in terms' (Douthwaite 1992: 286). Part of the problem has been that debates on sustainability within the United Nations have always taken place linked to the development discourse. That is to say, the need for development and its positive character were never put into question.

It has been perhaps that lack of clarity of the concept of sustainability, which admits diverse and even opposing readings, that has made it immensely popular, so much that to speak of development today is to speak of sustainable development without necessarily having any reflection on what the sustainable adjective implies. Since 1987, when 'Our Common Future' was presented for the first time, the analysis of its meaning has not ceased, without this impacting either on the continuity of dominant models or the implementation of large projects with negative environmental and social impacts, all in the name of sustainable development.

According to the United Nations Secretary-General's High-level Panel on Global Sustainability (2012: 11–12), two key reasons explain the fact that, despite the enormous popularity of the concept, its practical implementation is still very limited. The first is the lack of political will, given that the times of sustainable development are not the times of the political processes aimed at short-term benefits. And the second is the continuity of economic dominance in the visions of development, so that economic decisions related to policies continue to be taken without considering environmental sustainability as one of its factors. That is, the necessary transdisciplinarity and the equal consideration of social, environmental and economic dimensions, is still absent in the discourse – and in the implementation – of sustainable development.

The concept of sustainability in turn varies according to the prevailing perception about nature and about the role of science and technology. Based on these perceptions, we distinguish between weak, strong and super strong sustainability. The first raises the possibility of substituting all forms of capital. Nature, therefore, seen as natural capital, can also be replaced by the application of scientific methods. Strong sustainability, however, while recognising the importance of technological efficiency, understands that certain elements of natural capital cannot be substituted. The super-strong, in turn, does not see nature as capital but assigns intrinsic values to it independently of its usefulness to humans. Each of these visions implies a different relationship with nature (Pearce and Atkinson 1998: 5, UNDP 2012: 12–13). This is one of the elements of analysis of political ecology that engages with how power relations impact on the use, access and control of nature. The pre-eminence of science and of market forces are not neutral and are underpinned by a world vision in line with mainstream development views which focus on efficiency and rationality to extract and add value to nature. As we will see later, feminist scholars have also engaged in this debate, adding a gender dimension to the analysis. The next section will highlight some of this analysis, including women's contributions towards the formulation and implementation of sustainable practices (Agostino 2015: 823–6).

What is clear is that sustainability is a concept in dispute, which explains the diversity of approaches that coexist and reflect very different notions about the relation of human beings to nature but also of human beings to each other and to their material and immaterial environment. As we saw previously, the articulation between social, economic and environmental dimensions is the determining factor of sustainability. This means that decisions made regarding ways to satisfy needs or to seek welfare should be informed by the impact that the different options will have in each of those dimensions. Observing what happens in practice, it is possible to affirm that the prevailing view of sustainability privileges economic growth by presenting it as a necessary condition in order to respond to the needs of the population and incorporates some social and environmental considerations to legitimise the use of the term sustainable. This form of continuity with the dominant models of production and consumption legitimised by a language oriented to give an image of sustainability without implementing substantive transformations could be called 'green hypocrisy' (Robinson 2004: 374). In this sense, it is necessary to enable processes that help a collective and gender sensitive elaboration of sustainability and the identification of strategies to achieve it. Without opening it for debate, the dominant view imposes itself with the consequence that numerically significant sectors of the population feel excluded, but also their knowledge and experiences are wasted when choosing the course or courses of action that may be more favourable. This is substantial since, as John Robinson puts it, 'sustainability is fundamentally a matter of human behaviour, and of negotiation about preferred futures under conditions of deep contingency and uncertainty' (2004: 379–80).

### *Looking at sustainability from a gender and post-development perspective*

Women's organisations and women in academia have contributed at length to shaping the understanding of sustainability throughout various decades. This long involvement in relation to sustainability and sustainable development has been analysed by Irene Dankelman in 'Women advocating for sustainable livelihoods and gender equality on the global stage' (Dankelman 2012: 21–41) as well as by other feminist scholars (Dankelman and Davidson 1988, Shiva 1988, Wichterich 2012). It can be argued that after the intense mobilisation of women during the preparatory process for UN Conferences held in Rio and Beijing, women's voices have not ceased to be present and with articulated and clear visions on sustainable development in all the UN gatherings that followed. They have been active at the global level but also, and most importantly, in their countries and regions, mobilising locally, linking daily and concrete struggles with the language of conventions and treaties, providing local data, presenting alternative reports, putting forward testimonies and narratives to feed into the global negotiations. Women's organisations have succeeded in securing their presence and the spaces for critical and propositional engagement. Academic women, and in particular feminist scholars, have produced fundamental works.

In spite of these achievements, it has been difficult to materialise one of women's fundamental demands calling for a change in the dominant economic mode of production and consumption and the centrality of it. The recent Habitat III conference offers yet another example of the resistance towards this necessary shift that might be summarised in the idea of moving from '*sustainable development* to *sustainable livelihoods.*' As Sumi Krishna wrote, sustainable livelihoods refers to 'a framework of analysis and a strategy that focuses on human lives and the structures that shape people's well-being' (2012: 12). The focus on economic growth in development has even been recognised by the UN itself: 'The objective of Development is that people can enjoy long, healthy and productive lives – a simple truth but one often forgotten in the rush to accumulate more possessions and greater wealth' (UNDP 1992: 12). This rush has continued to permeate the development discourse and it has motivated women's organisations around the world to challenge it. Some of the UN documents from the period – as part of the long walk redefining sustainability – have, with different emphasis, included the concept of livelihoods. One example is Agenda 21, stating that 'The long-term objective of enabling all people to achieve sustainable livelihoods should provide an integrating factor that allows policies to address issues of development, sustainable resource management and poverty eradication simultaneously' (Krishna 2012: 13). The formulation is very clear: sustainable livelihoods is the horizon for which policies in various areas have to be defined and implemented. The content and shape of sustainable livelihoods have been defined by women through various processes at local, national and international levels, in grassroots, in policy and in academic spaces (Harcourt 2012).

The Women's Tribunals on Gender and Climate Justice (Agostino and Lizarde 2012) are an example of the full participation of women in the definition of policies in response to climate change, including a series of recommendations on women's rights to land, training, inputs and credit; recognition of traditional knowledge and traditional agricultural practices; ceasing to be owners and to become carers of the planet; moving towards production and consumption modes in harmony with the planet's capacities. Molly Scott Cato (2012) argues that in order to create sustainable livelihoods we must begin by reversing the process of separation from the land, and to start perceiving ourselves connected by social relationships and with our environment rather than by the markets. She further argues that a sustainable economy must be a cooperative economy and analyses why women tend to be more responsive to it. These are other examples that show how women have contributed at length towards a concept of sustainability that challenges the mainstream views analysed above and that continues to inform UN main spaces and development frameworks.

As argued at the beginning of this section, the New Urban Agenda resulting from the Habitat III Conference and the 2030 Development Agenda that includes the 17 SDGs are key documents in the mainstream response to the challenges posed by climate change. Although a new language that puts sustainability at the centre has been incorporated, the necessary move from development to livelihoods has not been achieved. Economic growth continues to be at the very centre of the Development Goals. Goal 8 calls to promote sustained, inclusive and sustainable growth, and throughout the document there are various references to growth as a condition for achieving the whole framework. The New Urban Agenda – a comprehensive document that mentions livelihoods, incorporates gender and cultural diversity as elements to be taken into account in the formulation of policy and calls for local governments to have an important role in the implementation – continues, nonetheless, to put economic growth at the centre. As stated in the section related to the Implementation Plan, and in particular around 'Sustainable and inclusive urban prosperity and opportunities for all,' the document says in point 43:

> We recognize that sustained, inclusive and sustainable economic growth, with full and productive employment and decent work for all, is a key element of sustainable urban and territorial development, and that cities and human settlements should be places of equal opportunities allowing people to live healthy, productive, prosperous and fulfilling lives.
>
> (UN-Habitat 2016)

It is clear that the move from development (informed by accumulation and wealth) to livelihoods (informed by well-being and the harmonic relationship with nature) is still pending.

## Human rights institutions and the new urban agenda

Several members of Ibero-American Federation of Ombudsmen (FIO), including the *Defensoria de Vecinas y Vecinos de Montevideo*, under the coordination of the ombudsman from Ecuador, participated actively during the preparatory process and at the Habitat Conference with the understanding that our institutions can contribute towards the definition and implementation of an urban agenda. The objectives of this participation were to visualise the role of the human rights institutions in the promotion, protection and defence of human rights within the framework of the New Urban Agenda and to highlight the importance of having mechanisms of enforceability and observance for the full exercise of all rights in the urban context. A document was collectively prepared to this effect (FIO 2016).

The challenges the Habitat Conference had to respond to were not new; they were those that have informed the existing international human rights frameworks and other spaces related to sustainable development. These frameworks have developed in response to persistent and growing inequalities, in particular in urban environments. The participating institutions identified as key challenges the increasing population in the urban space and the limits of the physical environment with respect to the growing demands imposed on it, not only associated to the number of the population but mainly to the prevailing modes of production and consumption and its associated consequences.

As human rights institutions, the participation was informed by the need to work towards solutions beyond business as usual; to contribute to the recognition that the strategies carried out for decades failed, and will continue to fail even if they are formulated in a language in accordance with the dominant international discourses; to advocate for the inclusion of a multicultural human rights perspective that could allow for other existential ontologies, other cosmovisions, other knowledges (which as a result of the epistemic violence that has characterised the Western world, have been denied their capacity of contributing to the solution of the challenges we face as individuals, as collectives and as humanity) and to make inputs into the agenda. There was also a motivation to take on the epistemological challenge to imagine the cities in which we want to live and in which future generations can live full and satisfying lives. This relates to what Jordi Borja points out, saying that cities are the ideas about the cities, since the city is, above all, a construction that

> is born of the thought, of the capacity to imagine a habitat, it is not only a construction under which to find shelter, not only a temple or a fortress as a manifestation of power [...] To make the city is to order a space of relationship, is to build significant places of life in common.
>
> (Borja 2013: 26)

### Right to the city

A key point for the FIO human rights institutions was the idea that the New Urban Agenda must be based on a human rights approach, taking the Right to the City as the encompassing right. As part of the process, I was in charge of contributing with a gender perspective to the position document of FIO, and my contribution was informed by an FPE view.

According to the World Charter of the Right to the City,[8] this right is interdependent with all internationally recognised human rights, including all civil, political, economic, social, cultural and environmental rights already regulated in international human rights treaties. The charter also states that it is a collective right of all people living in cities, without discrimination on the basis of gender, age, health conditions, income, nationality, ethnicity, migratory status, political, religious or sexual orientation. It further says that the right to the city protects in particular vulnerable and disadvantaged groups, giving them legitimacy of action and organisation, respect to their uses and customs, with the aim of achieving the full exercise of the right to self-determination and an adequate standard of living. The formulation of the charter was the result of the active and articulated participation of various civil society movements and organisations over several years.

From an inclusion and gender perspective I highlighted two elements to bring into the debate: (i) the collective and democratic process of drawing up the Right to the City and (ii) the recognition of the particularities and differentiated needs of the population living in the cities. For an equitable use of cities within the principles of sustainability, democracy, equity and social justice as called upon by the charter, differentiated policies and affirmative programmes are needed that are constructed democratically and that guarantee the access of women – and other groups historically absent from decision-making processes over resources and policies – to all the rights that make up the right to the city[9] (Huairou Commission 2016). These key elements were part of the conceptualisation and definition of human rights standards and a gender perspective in the urban context for which the following categories were suggested and included in the FIO document:

- Habitable city (including the rights to adequate housing, water and sanitation, energy, information and communication, mobility, public spaces and services, infrastructure, human security, convivial city, cultural diversity);
- Inclusive city (rights to equality and non-discrimination, to work, to public spaces and services, and infrastructure for all);
- Sustainable city (right to a healthy environment, sustainable and responsible management of public goods and services, care and protection of natural, cultural and historical heritage);
- Democratic city (right to participation, democratic management of the city, transparency, democratic and equitable enjoyment of the city);
- Educating city (right to collective construction of city and citizenship).

Beyond proposing these categories each associated to a series of rights, the document argued that the problems of urban development are issues related to the lack of standards that ensure the full exercise of human rights. It called, therefore, for the observance and enforceability of human rights in the areas of work established for Habitat III, in a context of equality and non-discrimination. Specifically, it talked about the need for human rights institutions to propose, follow-up and monitor policies that ensure the inclusion of a diversity of perspectives; to work towards the fulfilment of the right to the city and all its components according to cultural, historical, ethnic, gender, age and social particularities. In this sense, it argued that one of the roles of the Defensorias is to cooperate with making visible other ways of doing, of interpreting and of being in the world. Relating this role to the construction of the New Urban Agenda, it called for the inclusion of these other ways as valid and relevant alternatives to be considered in order to move towards fair, equitable and sustainable ways of life.

## Feminist Political Ecology and care: Challenging the agenda

From an FPE standpoint, building a New Urban Agenda that is based on human rights and a gender perspective means much more than to mainstream these concepts into the agenda. It requires critically engaging with it and questioning it on the basis of these perspectives as well as challenging the continuity of the dominant views associated with production and growth. This includes, as mentioned in the previous sections, incorporating the concrete contributions from women present in the United Nations conferences cycle in the 1990s, in particular at the Earth Summit from 1992, based on concepts linked to FPE and women and sustainability. As argued by Christa Wichterich:

> Ecology and sustainability are not gender neutral; the analysis of gender relations is vital for understanding the relationships between nature and society and for overcoming the environmental crisis; without gender justice there will be no environmental justice, no sustainability nor a good life for all.
> (2012: 9)

It is from this perspective that an FPE view is key for a true transformation of the agenda.

A Feminist Political Ecology view places gender as 'a crucial variable – in relation to class, race and other relevant dimensions of political life – in constituting access to, control over, and knowledge of natural resources' (Sundberg 2017: 1).[10] It incorporates a gender analysis into the relationship, management and use of nature; the decision-making processes and socio-political forces that influence development and environmental policies; the links between ecology, economy and society; the culture- and knowledge-specific influences into sustainable practices; knowledge production related to nature (and processes by which some of these are made irrelevant by the dominant perspective in what constitutes epistemic violence); the relations between humans and non-humans; the symmetries of different forms of oppression and the domination of nature; among other dimensions. FPE highlights the engagement of women as political actors with the capacity to produce relevant knowledge, implement creative and sustainable ways to relate to nature and question power relations that reproduce gender inequalities in decisions about environmental policies. Furthermore, it calls for a holistic approach in the relationship between human beings and nature, incorporating objectives of subsistence and sufficiency.

A key element in this approach is *care*. The word care only appears in the New Urban Agenda in relation to healthcare but not as a category in itself. Care is an intrinsic function of 'the social' that has been historically associated to the feminine and that on occasions may become a burden linked to gender mandates, be devalued and made invisible in its contribution and relevance. It is important to incorporate a new view linked to the ethics of care, which opens the possibility to have hope for a better world, a world in which the community dimensions become central, where care is the basis for connections, not only among humans but also at the community level and with nature, contributing to more sustainable livelihoods, in as far as fulfilling needs is not exclusively linked to the markets (and to economic growth) but – and mainly – to reciprocity, to what we can do for each other, to solidarity. Carol Gilligan, as a cultural feminist, analysed the importance of the ethics of care as central to being human – moving away from the stereotypical presentation of it as a female trait – calling for society to 'recognize for both sexes the central importance in adult life of the connection between self and other, the universality of the need for compassion and care' (Gilligan 1985: 28). Deepening into the understanding of care, the philosopher Martin Heidegger has argued that care is an ontological phenomenon that is at the base of any interpretation of what it means to be human (Agostino 2015: 821–2).

These two concepts provide the ground to look at relations of differentiation and domination based on gender and at the essential aspects of caring and their impact on environmental policies. As mentioned earlier, including a gender perspective in a new urban agenda also implies the need to question those dimensions of the agenda that give continuity to historically dominant views associated with productivity and growth, and to anchor the analysis on the political struggles of women in terms of rights, responsibilities and knowledge. Feminist thinking and practice have allowed us to challenge conventional wisdom regarding a variety of categories such as gender, sexuality, identity, the centrality of the monetary economy *vis-à-vis* the centrality of care; they have also promoted the incorporation of these dimensions into an intersectional approach from which new perspectives on possible worlds are articulated, including a non-Eurocentric human rights perspective anchored in interculturality.

From this point of view, also the categories presented by the FIO human rights institutions (habitable, inclusive, sustainable, democratic and educative city) can be redefined and enhanced under the perspective of FPE. The challenge is to think of these categories holistically, in terms of individual physical characteristics, gender, age, place and location, communities and livelihoods, policies and environment. The following are examples of possibilities that open up as a result of incorporating this perspective: we move from talking about transport to talking about mobility and plan the city not on the basis of the rhythm of cars and the centrality of trade but on the ability of human beings (and their particular needs and aspirations) to access and enjoy public spaces; water and sanitation become a category based on a guaranteed right which is at risk due to the dominant economic model. From this point of view, the access to water and sanitation for quotidian life is intertwined with the need to question extractivist modes of production that externalise costs (contamination of water and soil, impacts on health and environment), with clear differentiated impacts on women and men; women's particular concerns in relation to access to sanitation associated to their responsibilities towards the household are recognised and drawn into the planning of the service provision. While governments tend to deliver only technical solutions, it is possible to promote ecological and other sanitation alternatives as part of citizen-state cooperation with which women tend to be more involved; the right to a healthy diet within an urban environment implies various considerations related not only to what we eat but to where and how this food is produced and transported, how the generated waste is treated and recycled, whether industrial or ecological food production is prioritised; the role of women in this whole chain is central, and considering their participation and views contributes to questioning the centrality of the economy and the utilitarian view of nature.

From these few examples, the conclusion can be drawn that there is a major challenge to incorporate all dimensions of sustainability in the analysis of public policies, municipal programmes and services. This implies considering the externalities of economic activities or infrastructure projects that impact on nature, on the living conditions of women – who are often the most affected – and on future generations. The approach involves moving to new forms of sustainable management with greater citizen participation. In Uruguay, for example, it is possible to generate energy at the private level and connect to the grid. Similarly, people or groups could generate their own services, which require a new (or existing but invisible) citizen culture of cooperation, use of public spaces to facilitate the response to certain demands from various practices – more space for organic production, popular kitchens, shops for free exchange of goods and services, eco-shops, bicycle stations, shared cars, trips in common etc. It also involves regulatory changes that make space for these practices. This requires as a condition the recognition that climate change and other problems associated with sustainability in cities do not find their resolution exclusively in science and technology and in the deployment of economic resources, but, fundamentally, in daily life accompanied by public policies that enable and favour other ways of doing, of interpreting and of being in the world. The practices of women who have engaged themselves with a critical gender analysis of the relationship between dominant economic models and nature[11] are a fundamental contribution in this regard.

### Implementing other views at the local level

In this section I will share some examples of concrete actions, proposals for public policies and other measures taken by the Defensoria as a result of trying to translate into concrete actions the ideas, views and commitments shared above. The proposals have been organised following the categories proposed by the FIO Institutions at Habitat III.[12]

*Habitable city*

- For the last eight years, the Defensoria has been coordinating an inter-institutional group on '**abandoned houses.**' The aim is to promote the possession of these houses by the authorities to secure social housing for those in need of it, with a perspective of inclusion and sustainability guaranteeing the right to the centrality of the city, as opposed to the tendency to expand into areas without services.

- Following a demand from a group of neighbours in an area of the city without sewer systems, in 2015 the Defensoria presented a recommendation to the departmental government for the implementation of **ecological sanitation systems**. The grounding for this recommendation was the right to water and sanitation combined with the recognition of other knowledges and the importance of people's participation in the carrying out of alternatives. Although it was not implemented, it generated extensive debate, articulation with other policymakers at departmental and national level as well as academic researchers, and a commitment by various stake holders to continue working on the basis of the recommendation.

- The Defensoria is a member of the Consultative Council on **Public Transport**, representing the interest of users. Our participation has the aim of promoting public transport *vis-à-vis* the growing usage of private cars, and to include a gender perspective in transport policies.

*Inclusive city*

- **Acoustic contamination** is one of the major complaints presented at the Defensoria. We have made several recommendations, in particular associated to places of night entertainment and their impact on the environment, which were taken and included into proposals for new legislation. Also as a result of recommendations from our institution, this legislation includes clauses on **non-discrimination and prohibition of sexist content or images** in relation to the right of access and permanence in various types of establishments.

*Sustainable city*

- We worked together with the departmental government on endemic waste dumps in public spaces. With community participation from neighbourhood residents (mainly women and youth) and social organisations, we used art projects and interventions to recover these spaces for public use. We are also working in the long term on the issue of waste management, promoting classification at source, composting and moving towards the concept of **zero waste**.

- In collaboration with the departmental and municipal governments and agroecology networks, we have created a **Healthy Montevideo Space** (conceived as a place where healthy and communal ways of life are presented and opportunities for exchanging and interacting are created, including organic production, natural nutrients and products, sensitisation on gender and diversity etc.).

- We propose, through annual and other reports, alliances, coordination and presentations, to incorporate the dimension of **sustainability in the analysis of all departmental policies**, municipal permits and services. This implies considering the externalities of economic activities or infrastructure projects that impact on nature, on the living conditions of citizens and on future generations.

### Democratic city

- The Defensoria promotes debate and has become a reference in the city with respect to the protection of the **public space as a privileged scenario for democracy**.

### Educating city

- Since 2013, more than 500 people have been trained by the Defensoria in **community mediation**, promoting a culture of peaceful resolution of conflicts incorporating a gender perspective. Those trained included inspectors from the departmental government, community policemen and policewomen, departmental and municipal officials, community leaders, educators and neighbourhood councillors, among others.

In all the examples shared, women have been at the centre of the processes. First of all, as was already stated, they represent over 60 per cent of all the cases we receive at the Defensoria. Secondly, when we analyse how the various issues that we deal with impact on the population, the role of women in the care economy makes them the ones mostly affected by the implementation of urban policies. And thirdly, women tend to be the ones mostly involved in community groups and local initiatives. Looking at those examples it can be seen that all of them refer, in one way or another, to relations of power in the use, access and control of nature. The analysis of those relations, combined with the concern for a balance between environmental, social and economic dimensions, and the permanent awareness of the differentiated impact on women and men, informs all the decisions we take in terms of the areas we prioritise, the courses of action we decide upon, the alliances and collaboration we build and work on. We aim at implementing the proposals and recommendations together with the women and men that come to our institution, recognising in them political actors with the capacity to produce relevant knowledge and implement creative and sustainable alternatives.

## Final reflections

In this paper I have tried to analyse how to contribute towards the construction of a new urban agenda from a FPE and care perspective. I have done this on the basis of my concrete experience as the head of the Ombudsinstitution from Montevideo, the Defensoria de Vecinas y Vecinos, an institution that I presented and described as *a place of hospitality*. Throughout the chapter, I brought in what I believe are the essential characteristics of such a place, aiming to contribute to the fulfilment of citizens' human rights. I emphasised the need for a multicultural approach of human rights which values diversity and overcomes the imposition of mainstream views on policies and programmes influenced by the centrality of economics and technical solutions. I highlighted as well how care is an intrinsic function of the social and the basis for interactions and connections among human beings at the community level and with nature, impacting on the long-term responses that we can provide to social, economic and ecological challenges. I also brought up the particular readings of the urban demands put forward by citizens and the responses that incorporating a gender policy and a sustainability approach into our work allowed for. Efforts were made throughout the article to highlight that the gender and sustainability concepts that guide our work result from embracing the views put forward by post-development and FPE. It is as a result of this engagement that the tasks entrusted to an institution like the Defensoria (and other human rights institutions with which we have worked towards Habitat III) have been redefined allowing for the implementation – or recommendation for the implementation – of policies and programmes that aim at the well-being of citizens on the basis of their diversity. This is an ongoing task for which FPE provides an ideal framework to read – and promote – quotidian practices aimed at building sustainable, caring and equitable cities.

## Notes

1  In the days that I was writing this article, the name of the institution was changed in a session of the Legislative Body of Montevideo. The proposal was presented by our institution on the grounds of inclusive language. The Spanish language uses the masculine as such and also as generic, leading to the feminine to be invisible on many occasions. The institution was called Defensoria del Vecino, which refers in singular to the masculine of neighbour. The new name, voted by 19 in 30 of the departmental legislators, is 'Defensoria de Vecinas y Vecinos de Montevideo,' making the feminine explicit.

2  See more at: http://www.ohchr.org/EN/ProfessionalInterest/Pages/StatusOfNation alInstitutions.aspx

3  As a reaction to the enjoyment by growing sectors of society, particularly of rights related to gender and diversity, conservative movements are increasingly engaged locally and internationally with the aim 'to undercut the objectives and operation of human rights systems, transform the human rights framework, and transmit new rights norms infused with their values and messaging' (OURs Working Group, AWID 2017, p. 12).

4  The Concise Oxford Dictionary.

5  Red de Defensorias de Mujeres de la Federacion Iberoamericana de Ombudsman.

6   As part of this recognition, during the last assembly of the Ibero-American Federation of Ombudsmen in November 2016, the Defensoria was elected global coordinator of the Women Defenders.

7   Other international instruments adopted in this period are in line, in their formulations, with the centrality of a sustainable development approach, such as the process of Financing for Development (FfD) and the United Nations Framework Convention on Climate Change (UNFCCC).

8   Carta Mundial por el Derecho a la Ciudad, http://www.hic-al.org/documentos/cartade rechociudad.pdf

9   See in particular Red Hábitat (2010), Taller de Proyectos e Investigación del Hábitat Urbano-Rural. *Género, Vivienda y Hábitat: Estado de Situación en Bolivia y Propuesta de índice de cumplimiento del Derecho a un Hábitat y a una Vivienda Adecuados con Perspectiva de Género*. Bolivia: La Paz. From page 58, Conclusiones, discusiones sobre la construcción del índice.

10   See also Rocheleau *et al.* 2013, Harcourt and Nelson 2015.

11   Examples of these could be found in the experiences shared by the Women's Tribunals on Gender and Climate Justice, as well as from the analysis of women's contributions on sustainability cited throughout this text. It is important to say, though, that further research on concrete practices by women in different contexts within a variety of social, economic, ethnic and other dimensions can contribute to a deeper understanding of Feminist Political Ecology's contribution to the building of a new urban agenda. In this respect, research in relation to the work done by the Defensoria with respect to the provision of municipal services and women's engagement is planned for 2019.

12   See page 24.

## References

Agostino, A., 2007. Post-development: Unveiling clues for a possible future. *In*: A. Ziai, ed., *Exploring Post-Development: Theory and Practice, Problems and Perspectives*. London: Routledge, 197–211.

Agostino, A. and Lizarde, R., 2012. Gender and climate justice. *In*: W. Harcourt, ed., *Women Reclaiming Sustainable Livelihoods: Spaces Lost, Spaces Gained*. New York: Palgrave Macmillan, 257–65.

Agostino, A., 2015. Climate justice and women's agency: voicing other ways of doing things. *In*: R. Bakash and W. Harcourt, eds., *The Oxford Handbook of Transnational Feminist Movements*. Oxford: Oxford University Press, 815–36.

Borja, J., 2003. *La Ciudad Conquistada*. Madrid: Alianza Editorial.

Constenla, C.R., 2016. La naturaleza municipal del Defensor del Pueblo. *In*: *Defensorias Locales: Su Aporte a la Gestion Municipal y Departamental*. DVVM, DPBA, ILO, 82–99. Available from: http://www.defensordelvecino.com.uy/wp-content/uploads/2016/12/INFORME_defensorias-locales_v3.pdf [Accessed 16 June 2018].

Cato, M.S., 2012. Your sharing co-op. *In*: W. Harcourt, ed., *Women Reclaiming Sustainable Livelihoods. Spaces Lost, Spaces Gained*. New York: Palgrave Macmillan, 109–24.

Dankelman, I. and Davidson, J., 1988. *Women and Environment in the Third World: Alliance for the Future*. London: Earthscan.

Dankelman, I., 2012. Women advocating for sustainable livelihoods and gender equality on the global stage. *In*: W.Harcourt, ed., *Women Reclaiming Sustainable Livelihoods: Spaces Lost, Spaces Gained*. New York: Palgrave Macmillan, 29–41.

Douthwaite, R., 1992. *The Growth Illusion: How Economic Growth Has Enriched the Few, Impoversihed the Many, and Endangered the Planet*. Dublin: Green Books.

Dufourmantelle, A. and Derrida, J., 1997. *Of Hospitality*. Stanford, CA: Stanford University Press.

Escobar, A., 1987. *Power and Visibility: The Invention and Management of Development in the Third World*. Berkeley, CA: University of California.

FIO, 2016. *Las Instituciones de Derechos Humanos y la Nueva Agenda Urbana*. Quito, Ecuador: FIO.

Galaverna, A., 2016. Defensoria del Pueblo de Bariloche, Argentina. *In: Defensorias Locales: Suaporte a la Gestion Municipal y Departamental*. DVVM, DPBA, ILO., 153–61. Available from: http://www.defensordelvecino.com.uy/wp-content/uploads/2016/12/INFORME_defensorias-locales_v3.pdf [Accessed 16 June 2018].

Gilligan, C., 1985. In a different voice: women's conceptions of self and morality. *In:* H. Eisenstein and A. Jardine, eds., *The Future of Difference* [online]. New Brunswick, NJ: Rutgers University Press. Available from: http://sfonline.barnard.edu/sfxxx/documents/gilligan.pdf [Accessed 5 February 2013].

Hamington, M., 2010. Towards a theory of feminist hospitality. *Feminist Formations*, 22 (1), 21–38.

Harcourt, W. and Escobar, A., 2002. Women and the politics of place. *Development*, 45 (1), 7–14.

Harcourt, W., ed., 2012. *Women Reclaiming Sustainable Livelihoods. Spaces Lost, Spaces Gained*. New York: Palgrave Macmillan.

Harcourt, W. and Nelson, I.L., eds., 2015. *Practising Feminist Political Ecologies: Moving beyond the 'Green Economy'*. London: Zed Books.

Krishna, S., 2012. Redefining sustainable livelihoods. *In:* W. Harcourt, ed., *Women Reclaiming Sustainable Livelihoods. Spaces Lost, Spaces Gained*. New York: Palgrave Macmillan, 125–41.

Martine, G. and Villarreal, M., 1997. *Gender and Sustainability: Re-assessing Linkages and Issues*. Rome: FAO.

Meadows, D.H., Meadows, D.L., Randers, J. and William, W.W., 1972. *The Limits to Growth. A Report for The Club of Rome's Project on the Predicament of Mankind*. New York: Universe Books.

OSAGI, 2002. *Gender Mainstreaming: An Overview* [online]. New York: UN. Available from: http://www.un.org/womenwatch/osagi/pdf/e65237.pdf [Accessed 18 November 2017].

OURs Working Group, AWID, 2017. *Rights at Risk: The Observatory of the University of Rights Trends Report 2017*. Toronto, ON: AWID.

Pearce, D. and Atkinson, G., 1998. *Development: An Evaluation of its Usefulness Ten Years After Brundtland*. CSERGE Working Paper PA 98-02, Norwich, UK: CSERGE.

Perez Aguirre, L., 1998. *Si Digo Educar para Los Derechos Humanos*. *Dehuidela* 15, 50–6. Available from: https://es.slideshare.net/mariaeugeniarodaoroman/perez-aquirre [Accessed 18 November 2017].

Rahnema, M. and Bawtree, V., 1997. *The Post-Development Reader*. London: Zed Books.

Robinson, J., 2004. Squaring the circle? Some thoughts on the idea of sustainable development. *Ecological Economics*, 48, 369–84. Available from: http://ipidumn.pbworks.com/f/SquaringtheCircleSustainableDevelopment.pdf [Accessed 5 June 2017].

Rocheleau, D., Thomas-Slayter, B. and Wangari, E., 2013. Gender and environment. A feminist political ecology perspective. *In:* D. Rocheleau, B. Thomas-Slayter and E. Wangari, eds., *Feminist Political Ecology: Global Issues and Local Experience*. London: Routledge, 3–23.

Sachs, W., 1992. *The Development Dictionary: A Guide to Knowledge as Power*. London: Zed Books.

Santos, B.S., 2002. Toward a multicultural conception of human rights [online]. *In*: B. Hernández-Truyol, ed., *Material Imperialism: A Critical Anthology*. New York: New York University Press, 39–60. Available from: http://www.ces.uc.pt/bss/documentos/toward_multicultural_conception_human_rights.pdf [Accessed 5 June 2017].

Schumacher, E.F., 1973. *Small is Beautiful. Economics as if People Mattered*. New York: Harper and Row.

Shiva, V., 1988. *Staying Alive: Women, Ecology and Development*. London: Zed Books.

Sundberg, J., 2017. *Feminist Political Ecology* [online]. Available from: https://onlinelibrary.wiley.com/doi/pdf/10.1002/9781118786352.wbieg0804 [Accessed 18 November 2017].

Taylor, C., 1997. *The Ethics of Authenticity*. Cambridge, MA: Harvard University Press.

UN General Assembly, 1948. *Universal Declaration of Human Rights*. New York: UN General Assembly. Available from: http://www.un.org/en/universal-declaration-human-rights/ [Accessed 9 June 2018].

UN General Assembly, 2012. *The Future We Want*. Resolution 66/288. New York: UN General Assembly.

UNDP, 1992. *Human Development Report 1992*. Oxford: Oxford University Press.

UNDP, 2012. *Uruguay: Sustentabilidad y Equidad: Material Complementario del Informe Sobre Desarrollo Humano 2011*. Uruguay: UNDP.

UN Conference on Housing and Sustainable Development, Habitat III, 2016. *Draft outcome document*. Available from: http://habitat3.org/wp-content/uploads/Habitat-III-New-Urban-Agenda-10-September-2016_95815.pdf [Accessed 22 February 2017].

UN Secretary-General's High-level Panel on Global Sustainability, 2012. *Resilient People, Resilient Planet: A Future Worth Choosing*. New York: UN. Available from: http://www.acp.int/sites/acpsec.waw.be/files/GSP_Report_web_final.pdf [Accessed 22 February 2017].

Wichterich, C., 2012. *The Future We Want: A Feminist Perspective. Publication Series on Ecology*, 21. Berlin: Heinrich Boell Stiftung.

Women, homes and communities, Huairou Commission, 2016. *Engendering the New Urban Agenda' Report of the Expert Group Meeting*. Brooklyn, NY: Huairou Commission.

World Commission on Environment and Development, 1987. *Our Common Future*. Oxford: Oxford University Press.

# Index

Note: Page numbers in italics indicate figures. Page numbers in bold indicate tables.

Printed in the United States
by Baker & Taylor Publisher Services